CONTENTS

Contents

THE ARDEN SHAKESPEARE

THIRD EDITION
General Editors: Richard Proudfoot, Ann Thompson
and David Scott Kastan

THE TWO NOBLE
KINSMEN

THE ARDEN SHAKESPEARE

* Third Edition

THE ARDEN SHAKESPEARE

THE TWO NOBLE KINSMEN

John Fletcher and William Shakespeare

Edited by
LOIS POTTER

The general editors of the Arden Shakespeare have been
W. J. Craig and R. H. Case (first edition 1899–1944)
Una Ellis-Fermor, Harold F. Brooks, Harold Jenkins
and Brian Morris (second edition 1946–82)

Present general editors (third edition)
Richard Proudfoot, Ann Thompson and David Scott Kastan

This edition of *The Two Noble Kinsmen* by Lois Potter
first published 1997 by Thomas Nelson and Sons Ltd

Thomas Nelson and Sons Ltd
Nelson House   Mayfield Road
Walton-on Thames   Surrey

Nelson Australia
12 Dodds Street   South Melbourne
Victoria 3205   Australia

Nelson Canada
1120 Birchmont Road   Scarborough
Ontario   1K 5G4   Canada

I⒯P ® Thomas Nelson is an International
Thomson Publishing Company
I⒯P ® is used under licence

Editorial material © 1997 Lois Potter

Typeset in Ehrhardt by
RefineCatch Limited, Bungay, Suffolk
Printed in Croatia

British Library Cataloguing in Publication Data
A catalogue record for this book is available from the British Library
Library of Congress Cataloguing in Publication Data
A catalogue record has been applied for

ISBN 0–17–443463–4 (hbk)
ISBN 0–17–443462–6 (pbk)

LIST OF
ILLUSTRATIONS

GENERAL EDITORS' PREFACE

The Arden Shakespeare is now nearly one hundred years old. The earliest volume in the first edition, Edward Dowden's *Hamlet*, was published in 1899. Since then the Arden Shakespeare has become internationally recognized and respected. It is now widely acknowledged as the pre-eminent Shakespeare series, valued by scholars, students, actors, and 'the great variety of readers' alike for its readable and reliable texts, its full annotation and its richly informative introductions.

We have aimed in the third Arden edition to maintain the quality and general character of its predecessors, preserving the commitment to presenting the play as it has been shaped in history. While each individual volume will necessarily have its own emphasis in the light of the unique possibilities and problems posed by the play, the edition as a whole, like the earlier Ardens, insists upon the highest standards of scholarship and upon attractive and accessible presentation.

Newly edited from the orginal quarto and folio editions, the texts are presented in fully modernized form, with a textual apparatus that records all substantial divergences from those early printings. The notes and introductions focus on the conditions and possibilities of meaning that editors, critics and performers (on stage and screen) have discovered in the play. While building upon the rich history of scholarly and theatrical activity that has long shaped our understanding of the texts of Shakespeare's plays, this third edition of the Arden Shakespeare is made necessary and possible by a new generation's encounter with Shakespeare, engaging with the plays and their complex relation to the culture in which they were – and continue to be – produced.

THE TEXT

On each page of the play itself, readers will find a passage of text followed by commentary and, finally, textual notes. Act and scene divisions (seldom present in the early editions and often the product of eighteenth-century or later scholarship) have been retained for ease of reference, but have been given less prominence than in the previous series. Editorial indications of location of the action have been removed to the textual notes or commentary.

In the text itself, unfamiliar typographic conventions have been avoided in order to minimize obstacles to the reader. Elided forms in the early texts are spelt out in full in verse lines wherever they indicate a usual late-twentieth-century pronunciation that requires no special indication and wherever they occur in prose (except when they indicate non-standard pronunciation). In verse speeches, marks of elision are retained where they are necessary guides to the scansion and pronunciation of the line. Final -ed in past tense and participial forms of verbs is always printed as -ed, without accent, never as -'d, but wherever the required pronunciation diverges from modern usage a note in the commentary draws attention to the fact. Where the final -ed should be given syllabic value contrary to modern usage, e.g.

> Doth Silvia know that I am banished?
> (*TGV* 3.1.221)

the note will take the form

221 banished banishèd

Conventional lineation of divided verse lines shared by two or more speakers has been reconsidered and sometimes rearranged. Except for the familiar *Exit* and *Exeunt*, Latin forms in stage directions and speech prefixes have been translated into English and the original Latin forms recorded in the textual notes.

COMMENTARY AND TEXTUAL NOTES

Notes in the commentary, for which a major source will be the *Oxford English Dictionary*, offer glossarial and other explication of verbal difficulties; they may also include discussion of points of theatrical interpretation and, in relevant cases, substantial extracts from Shakespeare's source material. Editors will not usually offer glossarial notes for words adequately defined in the *Concise Oxford Dictionary* or *Webster's Ninth New Collegiate Dictionary*, but in cases of doubt they will include notes. Attention, however, will be drawn to places where more than one likely interpretation can be proposed and to significant verbal and syntactic complexity. Notes preceded by * involve readings altered from the early edition(s) on which the text is based.

Headnotes to acts or scenes discuss, where appropriate, questions of scene location, Shakespeare's handling of his source materials, and major difficulties of staging. The list of roles (so headed to emphasize the play's status as a text for performance) is also considered in commentary notes. These may include comment on plausible patterns of casting with the resources of an Elizabethan or Jacobean acting company, and also on any variation in the description of roles in their speech prefixes in the early editions.

The textual notes are designed to let readers know when the edited text diverges from the early edition(s) on which it is based. Wherever this happens the note will record the rejected reading of the early edition(s), in original spelling, and the source of the reading adopted in this edition. Other forms from the early edition(s) recorded in these notes will include some spellings of particular interest or significance and original forms of translated stage directions. Where two early editions are involved, for instance with *Othello*, the notes will also record all important differences between them. The textual notes take a form that has been in use since the nineteenth century. This comprises, first: line reference, reading adopted in the text and closing square bracket; then: abbreviated reference, in italic, to the earliest edition to adopt the accepted reading, italic semi-colon and noteworthy alternative reading(s), each with abbreviated italic reference to its source.

Conventions used in these textual notes include the following. The solidus / is used, in notes quoting verse or discussing verse lining, to indicate line endings. Distinctive spellings of the basic text (Q or F) follow the square bracket without indication of source and are enclosed in italic brackets. Names enclosed in brackets indicate originators of conjectural emendations when these did not originate in an edition of the text, or when this edition records a conjecture not accepted into its text. Stage directions (SDs) are referred to by the number of the line within or immediately after which they are placed. Line numbers with a decimal point relate to centred SDs not falling within a verse line and to SDs more than one line long, with the number after the point indicating the line within the SD: e.g. 78.4 refers to the fourth line of the SD following line 78. Lines of SDs at the start of a scene are numbered 0.1, 0.2, etc. Where only a line number precedes the square bracket, e.g. 128], the note relates to the whole line; where SD is added to the number, it relates to the whole of a SD within or immediately following the line. Speech prefixes (SPs) follow similar conventions, 203 SP] referring to the speaker's name for line 203. Where a SP reference takes the form e.g. 38 + SP, it relates to all subsequent speeches assigned to that speaker in the scene in question.

Where, as with *King Henry V*, one of the early editions is a so-called 'bad quarto' (that is, a text either heavily adapted, or reconstructed from memory, or both), the divergences from the present edition are too great to be recorded in full in the notes. In these cases the editions will include a reduced photographic facsimile of the 'bad quarto' in an appendix.

INTRODUCTION

Both the introduction and the commentary are designed to present the plays as texts for performance, and make appropriate reference to stage, film and television versions, as well as introducing the reader to the range of critical approaches to the plays. They discuss the history of the reception of the texts within the theatre and scholarship and beyond, investigating the interdependency of the literary text and the surrounding 'cultural text' both at the time of the original production of Shakespeare's works and during their long and rich afterlife.

PREFACE

There are advantages to editing a non-canonical work by a canonical author. Directors and critics of *The Two Noble Kinsmen*, like those who edit it, tend to be enthusiasts: not only do they produce work of generally high quality, they are eager to discuss it and generous in communicating their ideas. So I have been indebted to many people during my preparation of this edition, probably even more than those whose names appear below.

When I first began to edit this play, I assumed, with some regret, that it would have almost no performance history. In fact, it turned out to have more than I had imagined and it had even more by the time I had finished. I have benefited enormously from talking to those who have been involved with the play in the theatre: Henk Gras sent me a video of the Utrecht production and supplemented it with his explanatory notes; Hugh Richmond let me see the video of his UC Berkeley production and has been consistently helpful in many ways. Julian Lopez-Morillas supplied me with much useful information about his 1985 production of the play for the Berkeley Shakespeare Festival and helped me get photographs of it. I am especially grateful to Nagle Jackson for permission to attend rehearsals of his Oregon Shakespeare Festival production in the summer of 1994, to those members of his cast who talked with me about their experience of acting in the play, to Hilary Tate and the offices of the Oregon Shakespeare Festival for facilitating my work there, and to Daniel Stephens, the production's choreographer, for some interesting material on the morris dance. For information on other productions, I am indebted to Edward Burns (who directed the play at the University of Liverpool), François Laroque (who told me about the one at Courneuve), Peter Meredith (who sent me a programme of one at Oxford), William Taylor and Masako Maekawa (who supplied me with information about a Japanese production of the play).

Though I have tried to make this a theatrically orientated edition, I also wanted it to be an old-fashioned scholarly one, erring on the side of completeness, even pedantry, rather than omission. For making it possible for me to give this kind of treatment to a play normally seen as almost two-dimensional, I am grateful to the Folger and Huntington Libraries, especially to Georgianna Ziegler and Jean Miller at the Folger Shakespeare Library, to Niky Rathbone at the Birmingham Shakespeare Library, and to all those institutions and individuals who have given me permission to reproduce illustrations. Others who have kindly shown me published and unpublished material, or just talked or written to me about the play and its context, are Noel Blincoe, Roy T. Erickson, Barbara Everett, Jay Halio, Jonathan Hope, James Knowles, Gordon McMullan, Barbara Mowat, Jeanne A. Roberts, Eric Sams, Grant Smith, Eugene Waith and Paul Werstine.

Some have done even more: Richard Abrams and T. W. Craik have commented extensively on parts of the typescript (the occasional appearance of their initials in the commentary can indicate only part of my indebtedness to them). Professor Naseeb Shaheen sent me the invaluable list of biblical references in *The Two Noble Kinsmen* that will appear in his forthcoming volume on biblical references in Shakespeare's final plays, to be published by the University of Delaware Press.

Little of the introduction, in its final form, is based on previous lectures or publications, but I have been fortunate in having many opportunities to talk about the play: at conferences on 'The Politics of Tragicomedy' (Jonathan Hope and Gordon McMullan, Wadham College, Oxford, in 1989); 'The Show Within' (François Laroque, Montpellier, 1990); and 'Shakespeare's Last Plays' (Hugh Richmond and Alan Armstrong, University of Southern Oregon, 1994); and in other talks at the Stratford Summer School (1986); the Folger Shakespeare Library (1990); the Graduate Renaissance Seminar (Oxford, 1991); Charles University, Prague (1994); and the Harvard Seminar in Literary and Cultural Studies (1994). Teaching a seminar on 'Drama in Context: 1613 as a Test Case' at the Folger Shakespeare Library (1990) provided the opportunity to explore and discuss the play's background with an excellent group. An exchange visit to Paris III/Sorbonne Nouvelle in 1995 gave me not only the time to finish work on this edition but the opportunity to participate in ongoing research projects on courtesy (Dominique Goy-Blanquet and Jacques d'Arras, of the University of Amiens and Paris VII) and friendship (Richard Marienstras of Paris VII).

I owe particular thanks to my excellent research assistants at the University of Delaware, Pamela Vasile, Mark Netzloff and Rebecca Jaroff, who saw the project through from the earliest stages (Ms Vasile) to the checking of references (Mr – now Dr – Netzloff did much to improve its accuracy and clarity of detail) and the proof-reading and indexing (in which Ms Jaroff's meticulous and intelligent work was beyond praise).

The suggestions of the two Arden general editors most concerned with this project have been unfailingly excellent. Richard Proudfoot very kindly made available his own extensive materials collected for a projected edition of Shakespeare Apocrypha, a category to which the play is no longer considered to belong. Their value will be apparent from the frequent occurrence of his initials in my notes. Ann Thompson's initials should occur more often than they do, since many of my notes were written in response to her penetrating questions, which ensured that no idea or phrase went unexamined.

Alison Kelly's copy-editing was exemplary. The Routledge proofreader, Roger Fallon, saved me from several errors. Like all Arden editors, I owe a great debt to Jane Armstrong. I am also grateful to Penny Wheeler and Belinda Dearbergh of Routledge and to Jessica Hodge of Nelson. Since authors rarely see the jackets of their books in time to comment on them, I would like to say how well I think Newell & Sorrell have captured the play's haunting and disturbing beauty.

I should like to dedicate this edition to my own noble kinsmen: my brother, G. R. Potter, and his daughters Lauren and Alayne.

Lois Potter
Newark, Delaware

INTRODUCTION

The Two Noble Kinsmen is a Jacobean dramatization of a medieval English tale based on an Italian romance version of a Latin epic about one of the oldest and most tragic Greek lègends; it has two authors and two heroes. It first appeared in 1634, without preface or dedication, the only extraneous information being supplied by the title page: 'Presented at the Blackfriers by the Kings Maiesties servants, with great applause: Written by the memorable Worthies of their time; Mr John Fletcher, and Mr William Shakspeare. Gent.' 'Gent.', or 'Gentleman', applied to both Fletcher and Shakespeare, whose names were bracketed together. Neither collaborator could confirm or deny the attribution: Shakespeare had died in 1616, Fletcher in 1625. Despite this explicit title page, most discussions of the play have centred on the question of its authorship – a topic, of course, closely bound up with its evaluation. The one other piece of contemporary evidence is an entry, dated 8 April 1634, in the Stationers' Register, where the publisher, by paying a small fee to the Stationers' Company, established his ownership of the book he was about to publish. Here, the play is described as a tragicomedy – the first play to be so listed since 1615.

This introduction will begin with the implications of the contemporary statements just mentioned. After considering the play's mixed messages about its genre, I shall look at the numerous elements of the collaboration: not only the authors themselves but their historical, theatrical and literary contexts. Complex as the collaboration process was, the end product can be discussed as a coherent work – not in spite of, but because of, the circumstances of its production.

THE GENRE: TRAGICOMEDY

Because, until recently, it was so little known and performed, *The Two Noble Kinsmen* can still be genuinely suspenseful even for readers and spectators who know its main source, Chaucer's *Knight's Tale*. Until the final scene of the play, it is not at all clear whether the ending will be comic or tragic. Whoever made the Stationers' Register entry (probably the publisher, John Waterson) clearly thought that it was both; he needed only to look at the final speech of Theseus (5.4.112–37) which makes plans for both a funeral and a marriage and stresses the paradox that 'The conquered triumphs; / The victor has the loss'. But tragicomedy is not really quite the right word. Giambattista Guarini, the theorist of the genre, stressed in his *Compendio della Poesia Tragicomica* (1602) that its object was not to alternate tragic and comic scenes but to create a genuinely mixed genre with a unified mood and atmosphere, lacking both the horrific elements of classical tragedy and the grotesque elements of classical comedy. Fletcher attempted something like this at the beginning of his career, with *The Faithful Shepherdess* (1608–9), but its theatrical failure suggests that audiences were not yet ready to lose the variety to which they had been accustomed in drama. *The Two Noble Kinsmen* works quite differently. Throughout, the play offers contradictory indications about the direction it intends to take.

The first act is largely static, almost a closet drama. The interruption of the opening wedding procession, by three queens in mourning, establishes a pattern of disrupted rituals that continues through the play. Whereas much of the play condenses its source, 1.1 actually expands it. Chaucer's Theseus immediately agrees to the queens' request that he make war on Creon and enable them to bury their dead husbands' bodies. In the play, by contrast, Theseus devotes considerable time to the decision as to whether to sacrifice his wedding day – and night – to the call of duty. The characters are extremely self-conscious about living up to the occasion; it is as if they knew that they were taking part in a tragedy. Some of the language is grotesque, as when one of the queens urges Hippolyta to imagine how she would feel if Theseus were lying dead on the battlefield, 'Showing the sun his teeth, grinning at the moon'

(1.1.100). Palamon and Arcite, introduced in the second scene, are equally self-conscious about their conversation, which keeps drifting away from its apparent subject into generalized and irrelevant social satire. Their situation, when they hear that Theseus is marching on Thebes and realize that they will have to fight on behalf of a ruler they despise, is more ironic than tragic. Scene 3, another conversation, reveals that Hippolyta respects the close friendship of Theseus and Pirithous and that Emilia's closest relationship, also with a friend of her own sex, was ended by death when both girls were 11. Emilia does not think that she will ever care as much for a man as she did for her friend. Normally in drama any young person who talks like this can be expected to undergo a rapid conversion, and this is what Hippolyta herself thinks will happen. Act 1 concludes with the victory of Theseus and the formal mourning of the queens. Though the evil Creon never appears, these scenes make a strong moral point: the gods are just and, sooner or later, will punish evil. With the departure of the queens, the plot seems resolved. Only the discovery of the half-dead Palamon and Arcite in 1.4, and Theseus' insistence that his doctors should try to save their lives, point to the future.

From the start of Act 2, on the other hand, we are in the world of romantic comedy, with the ordinariness of the Jailer, his Daughter and her Wooer set against the Daughter's idealization of the two kinsmen (whose miraculous recovery from their supposedly fatal wounds is taken for granted). The men's enthusiastic praise of their friendship is exaggerated to the point where (like Emilia's rejection of love) it is bound to collapse, and it does so almost as soon as Emilia appears. After Arcite has been freed from prison, two events seem to prepare the way for a happy ending: his introduction to Emilia in disguise and the love of the Jailer's Daughter for Palamon, which inspires her decision to free him. An audience might well look forward to a double wedding at this point, with the discrepancy of rank between Palamon and the Daughter no doubt resolved by the revelation that she is really of noble birth. With hindsight, one can see that the authors are also trying to prepare for the tragic ending by stressing Arcite's horsemanship as early as 2.5, but no one unfamiliar with the play could guess what use would be made of these hints.

3

Act 3, which takes place entirely in the woods, draws on a pun that is never made in the play itself: the double meaning of *wood* as 'insane'. Palamon's appearance, '*as out of a bush*', suggests a wild man, and the play suddenly veers in the direction rejected in the Prologue: the tale of Robin Hood. Arcite's story – attracting the ruler's attention at a sporting competition, being welcomed at court, then taking advantage of his position to steal the ruler's venison, wine, and armour – corresponds to one told of Little John in fytte 3 of the early-sixteenth-century *Litel Gest of Robin Hood* (reprinted several times before 1600) and, in later ballads, of Robin Hood himself. The Daughter, no longer comic in her obsession with Palamon, goes mad. The Schoolmaster, who is 'excellent i'th' woods' (2.3.55), directs a performance of a country dance in which everyone takes it for granted that the Daughter's madness will be a positive asset. The act ends with the combat between the two men that was promised in 3.1. Like the wedding in 1.1, it is interrupted. Theseus, facing another set of kneeling women (joined, this time, by Pirithous), has yet again to change his mind in public. He creates conditions that are meant to formalize and contain the combat by making it an all-or-nothing affair: the winner will marry Emilia but the loser and all his party must die.

Neither Palamon nor Arcite appears in Act 4. Instead, they are present in the fantasies of the Jailer's Daughter and in Emilia's attempt to choose between them on the basis of their pictures. Most of the act is taken up with the madness of the Jailer's Daughter, whose offstage attempt to create a tragic ending for herself has also been interrupted, in this case by her devoted fiancé. Her family and friends try to cure her by means of various sorts of play-acting, aided by a doctor who may be either a quack or a sage. On her next appearance in 4.3 she is lost in visions of the afterlife and it seems likely that she will die in despair if she cannot have Palamon.

The spectacular opening of Act 5 seems like a return to the static mode of Act 1, and corresponds to the scenes of oracles and prophecies that characterize tragicomedy. In tragedy, typically, the hero receives an evil omen which comes true in a sense he does not expect; in tragicomedy, the omen may be conditional (like the 'if' in 'if that which is lost be not found' in *The Winter's Tale*, 3.2.136) or it may come true in a beneficent rather than an evil sense. In *The*

Two Noble Kinsmen, though Emilia is left puzzled, both men receive good omens. Both also get what they asked for, but with tragic results. Tragicomedy specializes in bringing happiness out of near-disaster, which is why Guarini considered it the only kind of drama that truly reflected Christian belief (Guarini, 245). Shakespeare and Fletcher, however, seem to have been more struck by Chaucer's pagan gods, who, like the 'juggling fiends' of *Macbeth*, 'keep the word of promise to our ear / And break it to our hope' (*Mac* 5.8.21–2). The play that began with a wedding procession, interrupted by mourning queens, ends with an interrupted triumph, an interrupted execution, and the promise of mourning followed by a wedding. Sandwiched between the scenes that resolve the main plot comes the 'cure' of the Daughter's madness. Her final scene (5.2) leaves it unclear whether she recognizes the supposed Palamon and whether such a recognition will cure or perpetuate her insanity – though the Jailer in 5.4 offers an optimistic interpretation of events.

The Knight's Tale also ends with the attempt to reconcile conflicting emotions. Theseus stresses the need to accept human mortality and ordains the marriage of Palamon and Emily in order to make two sorrows into one perfect joy; we have the Knight's word for it that the ending is blissfully happy for the two surviving lovers. But Chaucer's Palamon and Emily have earned their happiness by many years of grief. The speed with which the Jacobean dramatists rush to their conclusion makes their juxtaposition of tragic and comic events, and Theseus' attempts to justify them, seem increasingly forced. Having first consigned Palamon and his friends to death and gone to celebrate Arcite's victory, 'Right joyful, with some sorrow' (5.3.135), Theseus later welcomes the unexpected reversal of events by planning to mourn 'A day or two' for Arcite before attending Palamon's wedding (5.4.124). Audiences would probably have recognized the biblical allusion (see the note on this line), which makes his words much less casual than they sound to modern ears. Nevertheless, the Epilogue which follows is rather startling in its attempts to make the audience follow Theseus' advice and cheer up.

Many other Jacobean plays have the same abrupt shifts of tone and open endings as *The Two Noble Kinsmen*; an obvious example is

Webster's *The Duchess of Malfi*, which was probably being re-hearsed at the same time. Whether we see such plays as confused or subtle depends on our perception of the authors' intention, which in turn depends on our faith in their talent. When a play is known to be the work of two authors, it is tempting to attribute in-consistencies and uncertainties of tone either to disagreements be-tween them or to breakdowns in the collaborative process. It there-fore seems important to understand this process as fully as possible.

THE COLLABORATORS

John Fletcher

The play's date is generally agreed to be 1613–14, for reasons that will be discussed below (p. 34). At that time John Fletcher was 33 and Shakespeare 47. That Fletcher's name is the first to appear on the title page may mean only that the publisher believed in alpha-betical order, but it seems likely that the play belongs slightly more to him than to Shakespeare. Although a fair amount is known about his life, there are also some substantial gaps in the record, making him in many ways as mysterious a figure as his co-author. What follows is summarized from the pioneering research of his nineteenth-century editor Alexander Dyce, and from subsequent work by Philip Finkelpearl and Gordon McMullan.

Fletcher was the odd man out in a family consisting largely of distinguished and literary churchmen. His grandfather had been a militant Protestant; his father Richard, living in easier times, ap-parently owed his distinguished career to personal charm and the favour of Elizabeth I, whose chaplain he had been before becoming Bishop of London. In 1594, the Bishop, a widower since 1591, married a beautiful woman, very recently widowed. Whether be-cause of her reputation or because the marriage seemed too obvi-ously inspired by feelings unsuitable to a clergyman, it gave rise to a number of scurrilous poems; the satirist Sir John Davies treated his Inns of Court friends to a series of epigrams, widely circulated in manuscript, punning on Fletcher and lecher (Davies, 177–9; Beal, 1:1.217–18). Abruptly denied the Queen's favour, the Bishop, 'seeking to lose his sorrow in a mist of smoke' (Fuller, 275), died ·

suddenly while taking tobacco in 1596. It turned out that he was heavily in debt. John (then 16 years old) is generally thought to have been at Cambridge at the time, but there is no record of his activities until the early seventeenth century. If he was unable to remain at the University, he obviously had strong incentives to begin supporting himself. With a scandal and financial ruin in his background (not unlike what seems to have happened, on a smaller scale, to Shakespeare's father), he probably did not have much to lose when he turned to playwriting in the early years of James I's reign.

He was possibly helped in the intervening years by patronage. Finkelpearl and McMullan emphasize the importance of Fletcher's connection with the Earl of Huntingdon's circle based at Ashby de la Zouche. Francis Beaumont, Fletcher's first collaborator, was probably acquainted with the Earl 'almost from birth', since his family came from the same part of the country (McMullan, 15). Fletcher may have met Beaumont through his patron, or it may have been the other way round. He seems to have remained on friendly terms with the family for the rest of his life. Through them he would have known the other writers they patronized, such as Michael Drayton. Both he and Beaumont had met Ben Jonson by 1607, when they contributed commendatory verses to the first edition of *Volpone*. He probably benefited not only from these acquaintances themselves but also from their libraries (Jonson had a fine one); playwrights depended on access to all kinds of source material. Beaumont had further advantages as a member of the Inner Temple and could have introduced Fletcher to Inns of Court writers such as the pastoral poet William Browne. It has been suggested (Gayley, 140–4) that Beaumont and Fletcher are portrayed as the shepherds Remond and Doridon, two close friends, in Browne's *Britannia's Pastorals*, which began to appear in 1613. If this were true, the poem would be valuable evidence that the legendary friendship, of which so much was made by later writers, had a basis in fact.

Beaumont and Fletcher wrote their first collaborative plays for the fashionable children's companies of St Paul's and Blackfriars. Especially for a gentleman like Beaumont, who may have come to playwriting via amateur theatricals at university, the Inns of Court, and Ashby, these small theatres with their elite audiences probably seemed preferable to the commercial playhouses. The boys' companies deferred more to their authors than the star-dominated adult companies, a fact that initially attracted playwrights with intellectual pretensions. Dates and authorship of the early plays are hard to fix because many of them were revised for later revivals (McMullan gives a useful canon and chronology, 267–9). At the most conservative estimate, Fletcher by 1612 had collaborated on two tragedies, two romantic–satiric comedies, and a tragicomedy, while his solo works included a pastoral tragicomedy, *The Faithful Shepherdess* (1608–9), two sex-war comedies, *The Woman's Prize* (1611) and *Monsieur Thomas* (1610–13), and a tragedy, *Valentinian* (1610–12). At least some of these plays had been highly successful.

In 1613 Beaumont withdrew from playwriting, and from their jointly shared lodgings, on his marriage with an heiress. If Finkelpearl is right, he suffered a stroke shortly after this date and died three years later. By 1613 the boy actors had lost much of their prestige and some companies had merged with adult groups. Fletcher continued writing for one such group (see p. 65), perhaps because he was now collaborating with Nathan Field, a former child star now in his twenties. However, the King's Men were the leading company in London, playing far more frequently than the children and always looking for talented writers to supply the consequent demand for new plays. Fletcher may have come to the notice of their leading dramatist, Shakespeare, as a result of *The Woman's Prize, or the Tamer Tamed*, which offers itself as (or was perhaps adapted to become) a continuation of *The Taming of the Shrew*, with incidental parodies of other Shakespeare plays. He and Shakespeare were probably involved in three collaborations, though *The Two Noble Kinsmen* is the only surviving one to bear both their names (see p. 12, below). A few years later Fletcher took over as the company's leading dramatist (Field's own move to the King's Men may have been an incentive) and continued to write both alone and in collaboration until he died of the plague in 1625. He was buried in St Mary Overy (now Southwark Cathedral). Philip Massinger, his last important collaborator, was buried in the same grave in 1640; Fletcher wrote twice as many plays with him as with Beaumont (McMullan, 144), but no one ever developed a legend about the Fletcher–Massinger friendship.

The tributes to Fletcher's character in the prologues and epi-
logues written for posthumous productions of his plays may have
been motivated by the need to 'sell' a now out–of–date author. Still,
Richard Brome, who knew him, pointed out in his verses to the
1647 Beaumont and Fletcher Folio that many could witness to the
truth of his claim:

> You, that have known him, know
> The common talk that from his lips did flow,
> And run at waste, did savour more of wit
> Than any of his time, or since, have writ.

Unfortunately, little of this wit has survived outside the plays themselves. Fletcher shared Shakespeare's lack of concern about publishing his works and only one brief example of his handwriting is
extant. His few personal comments, if they *are* personal, occur in
verses to other playwrights and the preface to the published text of
The Faithful Shepherdess, which he clearly wanted to defend after
its theatrical failure. These tend to speak contemptuously of audiences' inability to judge serious work. Fletcher may have been
snobbish or he may simply have been adopting the tone of his
friend Ben Jonson, notoriously high-handed in addressing audiences and readers.

Finkelpearl suggests that Fletcher's verses on *The Honest Man's
Fortune*, which are assumed to be contemporary with that play, may
show Fletcher's mood at the time of Beaumont's marriage in 1613
(Finkelpearl, 212). The verses are printed in full in Appendix 1.
Since their title specifically ties them to the play, a collaboration by
Field, Fletcher and Massinger which depicts a good man's un-
deserved sufferings and final reward, it may be wrong to interpret
them as a personal statement, but they are more like one than anything else that Fletcher wrote. The authorial persona expresses
cynicism about astrologers, though not about divine providence,
and finally advocates a stoic self-sufficiency like that to which Palamon and Arcite aspire in 2.2. A few lines have sometimes been
anthologized:

> Man is his own star, and the soul that can
> Render an honest and a perfect man

> Commands all light, all influence, all fate;
> Nothing to him falls early or too late.
> Our acts our angels are, or good or ill,
> Our fatal shadows that walk by us still. . . .
>
> (33–8)

Near the end of the poem, the speaker appears to reject love ('an exhalation', or meteor, which is soon 'spent'). Though the hero of *The Honest Man's Fortune* is saved from poverty by his marriage, Fletcher's poem declares that, even if love could bring 'Increase to wealth, honour, and every thing' (76), he would still prefer another mistress, 'knowledge and fair truth' (79). His couplet on friendship says simply,

> Friends' promises may lead me to believe,
> But he that is his own friend knows to live.
>
> (83–4)

This might reflect disillusionment with Beaumont, but betrayed friendship and the desire for self-sufficiency are omnipresent themes in Renaissance literature. 'If Fletcher felt abandoned and bereft,' Finkelpearl adds (212), 'it certainly did not affect his productivity'.

There is no evidence that Fletcher ever married. The best-known account of his relationship with Beaumont, on the authority of men who were remembering events of fifty years ago, occurs, characteristically garbled, in Aubrey's *Brief Lives*: 'They lived together on the Banke side, not far from the Play-house, both batchelors; lay together – from Sir James Hales etc.; had one wench in the house between them, which they did so admire; the same cloathes and cloake, &c., betweene them' (Aubrey, 1.96). Some twentieth-century readers, seizing on 'lay together', have taken this account as evidence of a homosexual relationship, but in the seventeenth century it seems to have been the shared mistress that captured the imaginations of the 'they' who 'did so admire' – including perhaps Jonson (see pp. 69–70, below). In Shadwell's *Bury Fair* (1689), an elderly bore named Oldwit remembers Fletcher's 'maid Joan' as someone who 'had her beer glass of sack; and we all kissed her' (quoted in Dyce, 1.xxvi).

Dryden's *Essay of Dramatic Poesy* (1667) offers the most often-quoted comment on 'Beaumont and Fletcher', which (as we shall see) usually means Fletcher: 'they understood and imitated the conversation of gentlemen much better [than Shakespeare]' (Dryden, 1.68). He was thinking primarily of *profane* gentlemen: variations between the extant manuscripts and published playtexts show that a good many oaths had to be expurgated (Bald, 68–72). *The Two Noble Kinsmen* is mostly free of profanity, except for Emilia's rather startling 'God's lid' (5.3.96). It does however illustrate another of the qualities implied by Dryden, the 'nudging', understated tone that conveys a sense of long familiarity between speakers of the same social group. Examples are the jokes of 3.3 and the *noblesse oblige* implied in the men's occasional verbal shrugs. Arcite's apparent reserve in the scenes with the countrymen and the court (2.3 and 2.5) hints at vast reservoirs of unboasted virtues and, in 3.6, when Arcite asks if Palamon's armour is too heavy, the latter replies, 'I have worn a lighter, / But I shall make it serve' (3.6.56–7). Sometimes the casualness of 'Beaumont and Fletcher' plays extends to the treatment of serious situations; heroes, however hyperbolically praised, are capable of turning into anti-heroes or are deflated by events, as are Palamon and Arcite in 2.2.

Though male friendship was something of a speciality of this drama, it is often an uneasy relationship. Amintor and Melantius in *The Maid's Tragedy* (1610) and Maximus and Aecius in Fletcher's own *Valentinian* (1610–12) end up at cross-purposes, and Maximus actually betrays Aecius. In a less-often-quoted play, Beaumont and Fletcher's *The Coxcomb* (1608–10), the subplot hero keeps congratulating himself on his beautiful friendship with a man who in fact despises and eventually cuckolds him (the plot is from Cervantes, but the exaggerated praise of friendship is the playwrights' own). A few years after *The Two Noble Kinsmen*, in *The Mad Lover*, a solo play, Fletcher returned to the theme of rivalry between friends: this time, they are brothers, and the heroine, told by her brother to 'take your choise', replies, 'I see they are so brave, and noble both, / I know not which to look on' (Bowers, 5: 5.4.338–40). The dilemma is resolved when one brother, having pretended to die, rises from his coffin, while the other, a famous soldier, renounces the lady and returns to the wars where he feels more at home. Compared to the fates of Palamon and Arcite, this ending is so much like a wish-fulfilment as to suggest that Fletcher was still haunted by the earlier play.

William Shakespeare

The traditional identification of Shakespeare with Prospero makes many readers prefer to think of *The Tempest* as his last work. Yet Shakespeare had nearly five more years to live when *The Tempest* was produced in 1611. In 1612 (Wallace, 489–510) he was a witness in a lawsuit over the financial details of a marriage that he had helped to arrange eight years earlier (some recollection of this may lie behind the Jailer's talk with the Wooer at the beginning of 2.1, though of course the discussion of dowries and settlements is common at this period). 1613 was a busy year for him. In March he bought part of the Gatehouse in Blackfriars and collaborated with Richard Burbage on an *impresa* for the shield carried by the Earl of Rutland at the Accession Day tournament on 24 March. The men are recorded as having been paid 44 shillings each for the *impresa* shield, which Shakespeare designed and Burbage painted (Chambers, *WS*, 1.87; 2.App. A, no. xxii). There may have been other, unrecorded, collaborations of this kind, since Burbage was known as a painter as well as a performer, and was in fact paid for another painted *impresa* shield in 1616 (Orgel and Strong, 180). Also in 1613, apparently, Shakespeare worked with Fletcher on two other plays: *Henry VIII* and the lost *Cardenio*. *Henry VIII* is not listed as a collaboration in the 1623 folio, but it shows definite stylistic discrepancies, however they are to be explained, and most authorship studies seem to confirm that it contains work by Fletcher. Seventeenth-century evidence for the existence of *Cardenio* consists of a record of payment to the King's Men for a court performance of '*Cardenno*' in May 1613 and the Stationers' Register entry of 9 September 1653 of '*The History of Cardenio* by Mr Fletcher and Shakespeare' (Oxf, 1341). Lewis Theobald's *Double Falsehood* (pub. 1728) may or may not be an adaptation (perhaps at one remove) of a lost manuscript of that play; if it is, it shows that, as its title suggests, *Cardenio* was based on one of the romantic subplots of *Don Quixote*, involving madness, betrayal of friendship and a woman disguised as a boy. Indeed, *Cardenio* and *The Two Noble Kinsmen* may have been left out of the First Folio simply because Fletcher, who was still alive in 1623, did not consider either play a finished product. Many of his plays underwent revision for later revivals. He may have been planning to revise *The Two Noble Kinsmen* at the time the Shakespeare folio was in production, since it appears to have been considered for viewing at court in 1619–20 (see pp. 66 and 70) and the manuscript sent to the press in 1634 had been marked up with a view to performance in 1625–6 (see pp. 26 and 71).

Those who have looked most closely at *The Two Noble Kinsmen* – that is, the translators and directors of the play – often claim to find in it an overpowering sense of melancholy which left them in no doubt that it was 'written by a man who felt old age close upon him' (Digby Day, n.p.; Hugo, 85; Leyris, 57; Constant, 30). Shakespeare, though only in his late forties, had in February 1613 lost the last of three younger brothers and might have had reason to think of mortality. Whether or not he was the 'W. S.' who published *A Funeral Elegy* in 1612 (Foster, *passim*), he had already written about the 'compulsive contest of masculine vanities resulting in senseless loss' (Abrams, 'W. S.', 449). The theme of untimely death became still more topical with the death of Prince Henry at the end of that year. Some writers have sensed a different autobiographical background. Barbara Everett notes a resemblance between the depiction of intense, self-destructive love in *All's Well That Ends Well* and the destructive force of Venus as described by Palamon (20). G. P. V. Akrigg traces the self-abnegation of the Jailer's Daughter to Shakespeare's ambivalent relationship with the Earl of Southampton.

While these suggestions may conflict with the traditional image of the serene Shakespeare writing the final romances, the play is otherwise consistent with the classicizing tendency found in his plays from *Macbeth* onward. Like the highly successful *Pericles* (probably also a collaboration), it has a classical setting and draws on an acknowledged medieval source: Gower in one case, Chaucer in the other. In devising *The Two Noble Kinsmen*, the dramatists rejected the possibility of making Chaucer, or his knight, narrate the story, as Gower had narrated *Pericles*. They also decided to dispense with certain types of of spectacle. Theseus' victory over Creon, Arcite's success in the May Day sports and the final tournament take place offstage and are followed by a triumphal entry. Other events are replaced by descriptions. Their rhetoric is sometimes presented with self-conscious formality, as when Pirithous and the Messenger in 4.2 are told to 'Speak' – that is, deliver a formal set-piece – about the newly arrived knights. Even when the speaker of such lines is not a 'Messenger', his character is often lost in his role (for example, Hotspur in *1 Henry IV* 1.3.94–111), and in this respect the two dramatists largely agree. The Wooer in Fletcher's 4.1 and Pirithous in Shakespeare's 5.4 enter in haste, with news that must be told at once, then deliver a long speech that draws attention to itself. Pirithous' speech even contains a half-line ('On end he stands') of the kind that has been associated with Virgil's own descriptive technique; it can be paralleled in the Prologue to *Troilus and Cressida* (line 11) and in the Player's 'Pyrrhus' speech in *Hamlet* 2.2 (Maxwell, 'Virgilian', 100). There is nothing for the other actors to do but listen in frozen horror. The less formal kind of messenger is represented by the Jailer's two friends in 4.1, strongly reminiscent of the anonymous Gentlemen in *The Winter's Tale* (5.3) and in *Henry VIII* (2.1 and 4.1), who are characterized by their ability to share in, even gush over, the private lives of the royal family. It is not clear whether it was Shakespeare (in *Cymbeline* and *The Winter's Tale*) or Beaumont and Fletcher (in *Philaster*) who first hit on the idea of combining various choric roles in characters whose social status gives them some inside knowledge of public events but whose responses to it are divided or inadequate. The dramatists may owe something to Jonson's handling of such figures in *Sejanus*.

Even the sense of anticlimax at the end of 5.4 can be paralleled in other late Shakespeare plays. Many supposedly Fletcherian qualities can be found in Shakespeare himself near the end of his career: for instance, the tendency to deflate the hero. Antony, Coriolanus, Posthumus, even Leontes at times, express intense emotion in a style that is presented as rant. In the opening scene of *The Winter's Tale*, praise of the young Prince Mamillius is undercut by a joke about the motives of those who say they want to live until he grows up; even in the moving final scene, the grief-stricken

Leontes cannot help noticing the wrinkles on the face of the supposed statue who is about to be revealed as his living wife. In *Coriolanus*, the Volscian lords can be seen trying bathetically to 'make the best of it' (5.6.146) after the murder of the hero, just as Theseus in the *Kinsmen* urges his court to 'be thankful / For that which is' (5.4.134–5). It is possible that Shakespeare was thinking of the Euripidean tragic ending, where a similar descent into platitudes by the Chorus seems intended to bring the audience back into the real world.

Probably because of the nature of its source, *The Two Noble Kinsmen* lacks many of the qualities associated with Shakespeare's late romances. The notion of forgiveness surfaces in Arcite's last speech and Theseus' comment on it, but it is hard to feel that Arcite has wronged his cousin in the way that Iachimo has wronged Posthumus or Antonio has wronged Prospero. The play lacks even the characteristic late-Shakespearean division of the characters into the very old and the very young, and the strong sense of what it feels like to be a particular age, except perhaps in Emilia's judicious summary of the difference between her youthful friendship with Flavina and the mature one of Theseus and Pirithous (1.3.55–9). Though the kinsmen are conscious of their youth, there are no obviously old characters with whom to contrast them; Egeus, who provides this perspective in *The Knight's Tale* (Burrow, '*KT*'), is not present in the play. Old age, always corrupt, appears to exist only at the court of Creon, in Palamon's address to Venus, and in his speech from the scaffold, where he rejoices that he shall escape it. There are no reunions of long-lost children with parents; indeed, no one, apart from the Jailer's Daughter, *has* a parent. Intense relationships occur only between people of the same age-group; Theseus is primarily the husband of Hippolyta and the friend of Pirithous, not a potential father-figure for Palamon and Arcite. The audience is presumably not expected to recall that he will eventually have a son by Hippolyta – the Hippolytus who is dragged to death by his own horses and may have given Boccaccio his inspiration for the death of Arcite.

At times (for instance, at the beginning of Act 3) the play can be seen as a return to such early romantic comedies as *Love's Labour's Lost*, *A Midsummer Night's Dream*, and *The Two Gentlemen of*

Verona (the title of which it perhaps echoes), with their lovers and hunters escaping into the forest, their rivalry of two men for one woman, their depiction of spectacularly incompetent performances and the comic figures (often pedants like Gerald) who attempt to stage them. The unruly horse of 5.4 recalls the ones described at length in *Venus and Adonis* and *The Lover's Complaint*. The Jailer's Daughter has reminded readers of many Shakespearean heroines, as we shall see. At times, the epic subject-matter results in all-purpose epic language that might have been written twenty or thirty years earlier. For example, Theseus, calling Palamon 'as brave a knight as e'er / Did spur a noble steed' (5.3.115–16), echoes the formulaic lines from *3 Henry VI*, also found in the 1595 octavo called *The True Tragedy of Richard Duke of York*: 'two braver men / Ne'er spurr'd their coursers at the trumpet's sound' (5.7.8–9). The most striking resemblance between *The Two Noble Kinsmen* and Shakespeare's other late works is, of course, the language of the parts generally ascribed to him, but this topic deserves separate attention (see pp. 97–9).

THE AUTHORSHIP QUESTION

When John Dryden claimed that 'Shakespeare writ better betwixt man and man; Fletcher, betwixt man and woman' (Dryden, 1.260), he initiated a much-used critical distinction. William Collins in 1743 contrasts Fletcher, who could depict 'Each glowing Thought, that warms the Female Mind', with 'stronger *Shakespear*' who 'felt for *Man* alone' (quoted in Spencer, 'Shakespeare', 78). This gendered language can be traced to the longstanding belief in the friendship of Beaumont and Fletcher, and in the nature of Fletcher's role in it, a belief largely created by the 1647 folio of their works. Called *Comedies and Tragedies written by Francis Beaumont and John Fletcher*, it contained, among its thirty plays, some by Beaumont alone, some by Fletcher alone, and some by Fletcher in collaboration with writers other than Beaumont. The publisher, Humphrey Moseley, defended his title on the grounds that the two authors belonged together: 'since never parted while they lived, I conceived it not equitable to separate their ashes'. The poets who contributed commendatory verses accepted the poetic fiction; even

Aston Cockain, who protested against the injustice to Massinger, agreed that 'Fletcher was *Beaumont*'s Heir': 'His Plays were printed therefore, as they were / Of *Beaumont* too, because his [Beaumont's] Spirit's there' (Langbaine, 218). Unable to find a portrait of Beaumont, the publisher commissioned a frontispiece showing Fletcher alone, but the engraver depicted his bust rising, somewhat incongruously, from the twin peaks of Parnassus, thus reminding readers of the friendship (see Fig. 17, p. 338).

This presentation has to be understood in the context of 1647. The London playhouses had been closed since the outbreak of the English Civil War in 1642. In the hope that Parliament might be persuaded to reopen them, royalist writers joined with the now-unemployed actors of the King's Men to present the English theatre as a morally and socially civilizing institution. At the same time, they used the occasion for political purposes. The caption over Fletcher's portrait recalls (five years after Parliament's abolition of episcopacy) that the dramatist was a bishop's son. The friendship and wit so strongly emphasized in the commendatory verses to the volume must have had a basis in fact, but they also contributed to the establishment of a 'cavalier' ideal.

Later editors not only accept the myth but take it still further. Jacob Tonson's introduction to the 1711 edition declares that Beaumont and Fletcher were 'Men as Remarkable for their Friendship to each other, as for the Writings with which they have Obliged the World' (1711, 1.viii). For Thomas Seward in 1750, they were attractive as members of a literary community. 'Jonson, Beaumont and Fletcher's Club-Room at the Mer-maid' sounds, as he describes it, rather like Samuel Johnson's club. He actually adapts lines from *The Two Noble Kinsmen* (2.2.79–81) to describe their relationship: 'They were an endless Mine to one another; They were each other's Wife, ever begetting New Births of Wit' (1.xiii). He was probably influenced by the commendatory verses to the 1647 folio by Sir John Berkenhead:

> What strange Production is at last display'd
> (Got by two Fathers without Female aid)
> Behold, two *Masculines* espous'd each other,
> Wit and the *World* were born without a Mother.

Not knowing how widespread the practice of collaboration was among professional dramatists of the Elizabethan–Jacobean period, the editor of the 1812 edition, Henry Weber, imagined 'a degree of literary intimacy, which has, probably, never before, or since, endured for so long a period'. To wonder, as he did, at their 'entire renunciation of individual fame' (Weber, 1.xxxiii) is to attribute too high a degree of altruism to them; nevertheless, he was right about their fate. In particular, Fletcher often appears in indexes, bibliographies and library catalogues only with the cross-reference, 'See Beaumont, Francis'.

Collaboration is 'like marriage', as someone told Moss Hart when he was about to start work with George Kaufmann (Hart, *Act One*, 274), and those who use this comparison are irresistibly drawn to distinguish the male and female halves of the partnership. Nineteenth-century scholars could write about the Beaumont and Fletcher relationship without any apparent unease. After quoting Aubrey's account of the shared cloak and wench (p. 10, above), Alexander Dyce, who was responsible for the best nineteenth-century edition of the dramatists, displayed only urbane scepticism: 'this community of goods was not during the whole period of their friendship; for Beaumont did not die a bachelor, and his marriage must have left Fletcher in undisturbed possession both of the lady and the wardrobe' (1.xxvi). But the century's obsession with metrical tests and the fact that the most easily recognizable feature of Fletcher's style is his use of 'feminine endings' (unstressed final syllables) eventually led to an extraordinary conflation of aesthetic and moral judgements on his work. Thus, the writer of a generally good book on Beaumont could call his author, in comparison to Fletcher, a 'dramatist, poet, man of far sounder fibre, and more virile marrow' (Gayley, 411). Discussions of the Shakespeare–Fletcher collaboration have been similarly gendered.

Many readers have approached *The Two Noble Kinsmen* with only one aim: to identify the specifically Shakespearean passages. Anthony Trollope annotated his copy (now in the Folger Shakespeare Library): 'Fletcher, surely', 'Shakespeare *all over*', and so on. H. N. Hudson's edition of the play (1881) distinguished the Fletcher passages by placing an asterisk before each line. Interestingly, two French translators arrived at opposite conclusions about its authorship: François-Victor Hugo felt that only a translator could appreciate how different the two authors actually were (73–4), while Pierre Leyris often found Shakespearean 'resonances' in scenes generally attributed to Fletcher (52).

The few arguments based on external evidence (that is, the play's publication history) do not amount to much. The fact that the play did not appear in the First Folio of 1623 or the second one of 1632 is not conclusive; the same is true of *Pericles* and the other 'lost' Shakespeare plays, *Love's Labour's Won* and *Cardenio*. W. J. Lawrence rests his case against Shakespeare's authorship mainly on the use of the word *writer* in the singular at line 19 of the play's Prologue; Paul Bertram, arguing that the play is wholly by Shakespeare, claims that Fletcher was too busy writing and collaborating on other plays in 1613 to have been involved in this one. The appearance of Shakespeare's name on the 1634 title page was attributed by George Steevens to the greed of the 'canting bookseller' (2.169) on the mistaken assumption that Shakespeare's name would have been a better advertisement for a play than Fletcher's on its own. It is true that, two years after the 1632 Shakespeare Folio, Waterson might perhaps have had a motive for claiming that his new publication was a still-unprinted Shakespeare play. But Fletcher's prestige also stood high in 1634, only a year after the highly successful court revival of his *Faithful Shepherdess*. Moreover, it may be significant that *The Two Noble Kinsmen* shared the same printer (Thomas Cotes) with another Waterson publication, *Pericles* (1635); the latter was finally accepted into a supplement to the Shakespeare Third Folio of 1664.

Because the external evidence is so scanty, most authorship studies of *The Two Noble Kinsmen*, including those just cited, have been largely based on internal evidence. Paul Bertram and Samuel Schoenbaum give useful histories of the authorship controversy up to the 1960s, and these can be supplemented with the good discussion in Eugene Waith's 1989 edition and the bibliography by Harold Metz. A sense that there were two distinct styles in the play goes back at least to Charles Lamb (1808), although Steevens, who assembled an impressive collection of parallels between Shakespeare's other plays and *The Two Noble Kinsmen*, argued that these actually disproved his authorship, as such a genius would never

19

have imitated himself (2.174). Systematic attempts to distinguish the shares of the authors began as early as William Spalding's still-valuable *Letter on Shakespeare's Authorship of The Two Noble Kinsmen* (1833). He and his immediate successors focused mainly on metre, predictably contrasting 'the flowing style of Fletcher' with 'the more manly one of Shakespeare' (Spalding, 45). Fletcher did seem easy to identify: by about 1610 he had developed a very distinctive rhythm, characterized by complex patterns of rhythmic repetition and frequent extra syllables (Hoy, 'Language'). However, as Bertram points out (22), nineteenth-century attempts to compare the frequency with which dramatists used feminine endings and run-on lines were often vitiated by their use of texts in which editors had already tampered with the metre.

Later studies have become more sophisticated in their use of linguistic, metrical and thematic parallels. Alfred Hart, analysing the play's vocabulary in 1934, found in the so-called non-Fletcherian scenes far more newly coined hyphenated compounds, new 'main-words' (that is, not compounds), and unusual grammatical constructions (for example, nouns used as verbs, like *chapel* in 1.1.50). Fletcher, by contrast, used little new vocabulary and his compounds were of a more predictable type, like the four ending in '-eyed' (e.g. 2.2.37). The main flaw in such approaches is their failure to allow for conscious and unconscious imitation of one author by another. Some dramatists, like Shakespeare and Thomas Heywood, were also actors who had to memorize each other's lines; some, like Fletcher, may occasionally have transcribed their collaborators' lines while preparing a final version or revising an earlier play. In addition, the role of memory in the educational process and the habit of frequent theatre-going made it easy for writers to pick up each other's stylistic mannerisms. Fletcher, like most writers, had more styles than one; he quotes and imitates other playwrights, including Shakespeare. Other playwrights also imitate him – at least, this seems the most likely reason why 'Fletcherian' lines have been found in plays in which, other evidence indicates, Fletcher had no hand (Hoy, 91). If we can recognize Fletcher's style, his contemporaries certainly could, in which case they could also parody it.

In the twentieth century imagery has been one of the commonest ways of trying to identify authorship, but it is becoming increasingly obvious that imitation and common sources (including proverbs) make it hard to be sure of the uniqueness of even the most apparently idiosyncratic images. E. A. Armstrong's image clusters – the recurrence of combinations of apparently unrelated words – at one time seemed to promise something like genetic fingerprinting, on the assumption that the clusters were unconscious associations derived from events in the real world such as no one but the author had experienced (Whiter, *passim*). Armstrong himself, when *Shakespeare's Imagination* was first published in 1946, argued that clusters virtually disappear after *The Tempest* and that *The Two Noble Kinsmen* shows 'his influence rather than his handiwork' (188). After reading the discussion of the play's clusters in Kenneth Muir's *Shakespeare as Collaborator* (112–22), Armstrong recanted in an appendix to his second edition (1963), though he continued to feel that the examples in the play were the product of a mind past its prime (216–17). At the same time, he noted that the osprey–sovereignty–death cluster, which Muir pointed out as a link between *Coriolanus* and *The Two Noble Kinsmen* (Muir, 117–18), could also be found in Peele's *Battle of Alcazar* (1588–9) and might be part of some still-unidentified literary tradition (Armstrong, 204). As other critics have applied the cluster approach, it has been less and less easy to be sure of its usefulness. Richard Harrier suggested in 1967 that the famous Shakespearean cluster involving various combinations of flattery, dogs, sweets and kneeling, first pointed out by Walter Whiter in the eighteenth century and further analysed by Caroline Spurgeon and C. H. Hobday (3–18; see note to 1.1.107), might derive from the showers of sweets that fell in the pageants for royal receptions – occasions, he points out, marked by flattery. 'Therefore,' he concluded, 'what may seem to us an oddly personal operation of Shakespeare's associative powers could have been a common experience to which he gave verbal definition' (Harrier, 67).

For this reason, scholars are now trying to break down possible stylistic evidence into micro-elements (vocabulary, grammar, spelling, punctuation) that can be statistically quantified and are unlikely to be used or imitated consciously: for instance, 'function words' (such as *but*, *no*, *and*, *for*) and contractions. Although

21

Shakespeare's use of contractions greatly increased during his career, Fletcher's is consistently even greater. A useful summary of the research is given in the Oxford *Textual Companion* to Shakespeare, complete with statistical tables summarizing various uses and contractions of function words (Taylor, 87–8, 102–5). Cyrus Hoy's series of articles in the journal *Studies in Bibliography* (1956–62) has been largely corroborated by the research of the individual editors of the plays in Fredson Bowers' edition of *The Dramatic Works in the Beaumont and Fletcher Canon* (1966–96). One difficulty with their method is that, as has been pointed out, Shakespeare's hand is usually deduced through the absence of Fletcherian features rather than the presence of specifically Shakespearean ones (Hope, 204; Masten makes the same point about Beaumont (341–2)). While the statistical evidence needs to be used with caution, however (see Smith, 'Statistical'), all of it points to divided authorship – more so in the case of *The Two Noble Kinsmen* than in that of *Henry VIII* (Taylor, 87).

While an author's rhythm is one of the things most easily imitated, it is often the result (or the cause) of certain consistent grammatical choices. Fletcher's frequent use of *ye*, especially as an object, is one of these. In the Epilogue, at lines 9–10 and 13–14, it is a plural form, since the speaker is addressing the audience, but Fletcher also employs it in the singular, as in Arcite's 'If that will lose ye, farewell, Palamon' (2.2.179). The spelling does not necessarily show anything about its pronunciation; rather, it indicates that the actor was to stress the verb rather than the following pronoun, thus creating a feminine ending and a light colloquial effect. Scribal transcripts and compositorial practice may account for the fact that this usage is much commoner in some works than in others, disappearing from some plays altogether. It has been suggested that the copyists of Fletcher's plays sometimes normalized his 'ye's to 'you's. It may equally well be true that he wrote neither 'ye' nor 'you' but 'yᵉ', which scribes could expand as they pleased.

The same problem arises with other variants which are syllabically identical. For instance, by contrast with Shakespeare's relatively old-fashioned 'hath' and 'doth', Fletcher nearly always writes 'has' and 'does'; however, this type of change could be made by a copyist, consciously or unconsciously, without affecting the metre. Other linguistic variations may be used for other purposes. Palamon and Arcite use 'ye' 4 and 6 times respectively (Spevack), but they differ considerably in their use of the second-person pronouns: Palamon says 'thee' 26 times, 'thou' 46 times and 'you' 38 times; Arcite says 'thee' 6 times, 'thou' 14 times and 'you' 83 times, a difference greater than can be explained by the fact that Palamon's part is about sixty lines longer than Arcite's. In this case, the choice of pronouns appears to be a characterization device, consciously used by both authors.

Hence, Jonathan Hope argues (*Authorship*, 64), the grammatical distinction between 'you' and 'thou' is too heavily conditioned by other factors (genre, stylistic register, and character) to be a useful test of authorship. He has recently recommended a type of authorship test based on another kind of grammatical preference which, because it affects the metre of verse passages, is not easily susceptible to scribal alteration. The use of verb forms with 'do' or 'did' (for example 'I do take' or 'I did think so' when the 'do' is not emphatic) was becoming considerably less common in the last years of the sixteenth century and is thus more likely to be found in an older, middle-class dramatist with a rural background (Shakespeare) than a younger one with an urban and upper-class background (Fletcher). When applied to *The Two Noble Kinsmen*, this test reinforces the traditional division of authorship, though many scenes, like the Daughter's soliloquies, are too short to provide evidence for a decision. The only use of the construction in a Fletcher scene comes in the Schoolmaster's doggerel speech ('I . . . Do here present' (3.5.112)), where it is probably meant to be redundant and pompous (Pope was later to ridicule verses where '*Expletives* their feeble Aid *do* join' (*Essay on Criticism*, line 346)). Shakespeare himself may have associated the construction with solemnity: the five examples in 5.1 occur in the prayers addressed to Mars and Venus. It has an important effect on his metre, since *hath* and *doth*, with monosyllabic verbs, always create an iambic foot. But one example ('I did think so too') also occurs in 4.3.66, a prose scene and one whose attribution is uncertain. Here, the motive may be characterization: the Wooer, though a young man, is usually stiff and old-fashioned in speech.

COLLABORATION AND CENSORSHIP

Though collaboration was the commonest way of supplying the heavy demand for new plays at a time when a week was a long run, we know very little about how it was done: whether dramatists worked on their own, submitting their scenes to a 'plotter' who supplied consistency where it was lacking, or whether they worked so closely together that, as Moss Hart says of his work with Kaufmann, 'it would be impossible to tell who suggested which or what, or how one line sprang full-blown from another' (*Act One*, 305). Since Shakespeare's hand has been identified chiefly in the first and last acts, it used to be assumed that these were his prerogative as the senior dramatist. However, most scholars who accept *Henry VIII* as a collaboration think that Shakespeare wrote the first scenes and Fletcher the last ones, which suggests a high degree of equality. Studies in the authorship of the Beaumont and Fletcher canon show that Fletcher worked in virtually every possible combination and that even when he himself was the chief writer for the King's Men he frequently wrote the middle acts, with Massinger taking the opening and closing scenes (Hoy, *passim*).

A story about the Beaumont and Fletcher collaboration, probably too good to be true, describes them planning their next play in a tavern and being turned in by an informer when 'Fletcher undertook to kill the king therein' (Fuller, 439; see also McMullan, 86). This obviously suggests a very close and amiable working relationship. No one seems to imagine anything comparable for *The Two Noble Kinsmen*. Dyce, who edited the play in 1846, was so convinced that Shakespeare would never have allowed Fletcher to degrade Ophelia by creating the Jailer's Daughter that he could explain the play only as the result of two independent efforts: Shakespeare had initially begun a revision of a lost *Palamon and Arcite* play of 1595, but left it unfinished, after which Fletcher took it up, 'retained all those additions which had been made to it by Shakespeare, but tampering with them here and there' (1.lxxxvi). Dyce is unlikely to be right about *Palamon and Arcite*, since this old play (to which Shakespeare *added* while Fletcher *tampered*!) did not belong to the King's Men. Still, his view of the composition process was once widely accepted. A.C. Swinburne's imaginary prologue to *The Two Noble Kinsmen* implies that Fletcher was completing a work left unfinished at Shakespeare's death:

> Stark silence fell, at turn of fate's high tide,
> Upon his broken song when Shakespeare died,
> Till Fletcher's light sweet speech took heart to say
> What evening, should it speak for morning, may.

Another attempt to imagine the two writers at work, Horace Howard Furness's short play, *The Gloss of Youth* (1920), shows them at cross-purposes. Shakespeare, depressed by the theatre public's inability to appreciate anything but comedy, does not really care about the story. When Fletcher politely points out that his lines are hard to understand, Shakespeare contemptuously tears up the page. Fletcher urges him on to the next scene, promising that 'thou shalt have all the *serious* parts'. In his amusing '*Tempest* in a Teapot', Anthony Dawson, following a conjecture made by Theodore Spencer in 1939, imagines Shakespeare's fellow actors so appalled by the style of *Henry VIII* that they insist on Fletcher's participation in the next play.

Collaboration (not necessarily unhappy) strikes me as somewhat closer to the truth than Dyce's theory of consecutive composition. The play's structure, with its almost complete separation of main plot and subplot and its large number of soliloquies, seems designed to facilitate collaboration between two people who did not expect to have much opportunity to talk about the work in progress. Hoy's division of the play (89) gives Acts 1 and 5 (except 5.1.1–33 and 5.2) wholly to Shakespeare, as well as 2.1 and 3.1–2. Other scholars are doubtful about the authorship of 1.4–5, and 3.2, but Hope (86) claims both as Shakespeare's. Thomas Horton's work on function words, which otherwise confirms most of the traditional divisions, adds 2.3 and 4.3 to the scenes that Shakespeare might have written (Horton, 329–30). Most of these distinctions are made on a linguistic basis and (because the textual samples are so small) cannot easily take account of minor adjustments and revisions that one writer may have made to another's work. A close study of the play from the dramaturgical point of view, however, suggests that a number of such adjustments were in fact made.

Because of the state of the 1634 Quarto, we have unusually interesting evidence of the play in process – not only during the collaboration, but also in later revivals. For example, the first stage direction of 1.1, in the quarto, begins '*Enter* Hymen', but then adds, between colons, '*:a Boy, in a white Robe before singing, and strewing Flowres:*', which surely means that someone decided that it would be more effective to bring on the boy singer, rather than Hymen, at the head of the wedding procession. Perhaps it even means that the song itself was a late addition to the plans for the opening scene. While the insertion might have been made by the author himself in the process of composition, the quarto punctuation, with colons separating the different characters, corresponds to the manner of Edward Knight, the book-keeper for the King's Men from 1625 to 1633. Not only is it unusual to begin a play with a song, but the elaborate procession, interrupted before anyone has spoken, must inevitably be mystifying to spectators unfamiliar with the Chaucerian source. The identity of the characters has to be deduced from references to Thebes, Creon and Hercules, until the Second Queen finally addresses Hippolyta by name at 1.1.77. There is similar evidence of the book-keeper's hand at the beginning of 1.4 (see p. 124), another scene which looks as if it had been slightly revised. Though the speech in which Theseus urges everyone to try to save Palamon and Arcite (1.4.28–47) is difficult in a characteristically 'Shakespearean' way, it also contains five examples of a 'Fletcherian' contraction, '*em* for *them*. Perhaps these resulted from Fletcher's having transcribed Shakespeare's writing at this point.

It is in discrepancies between the first two scenes of Act 2 that the change from one writer to the other shows most clearly. Scene 2 begins with the entrance of Palamon and Arcite, yet 2.1 gives them no exit from the upper level where they are first seen. In 2.1 the Jailer's Daughter talks about what the kinsmen have been saying to each other; in 2.2 they seem to be meeting for the first time since the battle. These problems are easily solved, or not noticed, in the theatre. They are interesting because they indicate that Fletcher wrote at least some scenes before he saw what Shakespeare had written. Later in 2.2 Fletcher refers to the 'Keeper' of the prison, both in stage directions and in dialogue. In the rest of the play, he calls him 'Jailer' – presumably because he discovered that this was what Shakespeare had already called him in 2.1. Another example of possible Fletcherian revision occurs in 2.5, when the disguised Arcite has just been taken into service at court. Pirithous offers to supply him with a horse, but 'a rough one', for the afternoon; then Theseus invites Arcite to join the court in the next day's May celebrations and hints that Emilia ought to provide a horse for her servant. Two examples of foreshadowing seem excessive. I suspect that Pirithous' line was meant for deletion: Fletcher, having read the beginning of Act 3 where Arcite says that Emilia has given him two horses (and perhaps also the speech in Act 5 which shows that one of these horses was to kill Arcite), decided to alter the earlier scene. The two dramatists may, indeed, have had different ideas about the disguised Arcite's relationship with Emilia, a subject ignored by Chaucer but slightly developed in his main source, Boccaccio's *Teseida*. At the beginning of Shakespeare's 3.1 Arcite is exulting in Emilia's favour, but in Fletcher's 2.5 she is much more detached and in 3.5 (where his presence is admittedly problematic – see the note on 3.5.93 SD) she pays no attention to him at all.

All of Act 2 after the first scene is attributed to Fletcher. Between 2.4 and 3.5 the scenes written for the subplot heroine, the Jailer's Daughter, are too short to allow for successful tests of authorship. The sheer number of her soliloquies suggests that they were needed to separate scenes in the main plot which were expected to involve a large number of actors. Kristian Smidt has suggested of *Hamlet* that Shakespeare may have written the soliloquies 'without committing himself at first to their exact positioning' (83). Something similar may explain the misnumbering of scenes in the 1634 edition of *The Two Noble Kinsmen*; Act 2 has two scenes numbered 4, while in Act 3 scenes 5 and 6 are numbered 6 and 7. Perhaps the soliloquies existed on separate sheets and were added or transposed to suit the technical demands of a story which, as F. W. Brownlow points out (208–9), has a beginning and end but not much in the middle. Still, the dramatists have linked the action of this part of the play with references forward and backward in time which give an illusion of consistency (Palamon even anticipates objections when he comments in 3.6 on the surprising rapidity with which he has recovered from his half-starved state in 3.1).

Closer examination shows some confusion. Giorgio Melchiori,

who gives a chronology of the play's action, points out that the Jailer's Daughter takes several days to go through the same experiences that the kinsmen are having in one (6.975–6). Inconsistency with regard to the time-scheme is not unusual in drama, but it reinforces my suspicion that some of the writing may have been done without much sense of context. Both Shakespeare and Fletcher, in their unaided plays, use abrupt scene openings that imply a previous thought or discussion on the part of their characters, as in Brutus' 'It must be by his death' (*JC* 2.1.1) or Fletcher's 'And as I told your worship' (*The Woman's Prize*, Bowers, 4: 4.2.1) or 'We dare not hazard it' (*Bonduca*, Bowers, 4: 3.2.1). In several scenes of *The Two Noble Kinsmen*, by contrast, the characters speak out of a dramatic vacuum, as if the writer was making a new beginning. As N. W. Bawcutt says (33), the author of the end of 3.6 seems deliberately to be following the pattern of repeated kneelings in Shakespeare's 1.1. Yet he does not seem to have known what was going to happen in 3.5. Palamon's words at the beginning of 3.6 recapitulate what was stated at the end of 3.3 and could have been taken for granted. Such vagueness would be surprising if this part of the scene were by Fletcher, the supposed author of the two previous ones. Perhaps he was uncertain about the length and nature of the morris-dance sequence that was going to occur in 3.5. Or perhaps he did not write 3.5 at all; some have wondered whether Beaumont, the author of the masque that was being alluded to in this scene, might have been invited to connect it himself to the play. Yet, though at first sight the morris-dance scene seems irrelevant (some modern productions have cut it altogether), Fletcher has taken trouble to integrate it into the rest of the play. The discussion of plans for the dance in 2.3 is closely linked with the villagers' encounter with the newly released Arcite. The pursuit of the tanner's daughter by Gerald, the schoolmaster organizer of the dance, is hinted at in both 2.5 and 3.5. Palamon threatens to shake his gyves and make a 'new morris' (2.2.276), while the Daughter in her madness talks of dancing 'an antic' in front of Theseus in order to beg Palamon's life (4.1.75).

Though both 3.6 and 4.1 are thought to be by Fletcher, there is some overlap and inconsistency between them. At the beginning of 4.1 the Jailer's friends recapitulate some events from 3.6 but also mention others that did not happen there; these have to do with the Daughter's part in the plot, and attempt to tie it more closely to the main one. The reference at 4.1.21–4 to Palamon's giving money for the Daughter's dowry seems inconsistent with his similar gift in 5.4, a Shakespearean scene, when Palamon appears to hear of her marriage for the first time. A possible explanation is that the author of 4.1 was still expecting someone else (Shakespeare?) to write 3.6 and ended up having to write it himself, possibly on the basis of Shakespearean material.

Scenes 2 and 3 of Act 4 most clearly indicate some confusion in the text. Scene 2 marks an entry for Emilia who has not previously exited; 4.3 gives an exit to the Jailer's Daughter, but it is followed almost at once by a speech for her, with no direction for her re-entry. Such errors are not in themselves unusual in dramatic texts (see p. 125, below), but 4.2 has other peculiar features. It opens with Emilia's soliloquy over the portraits of Palamon and Arcite, and is at once followed by a direction for her entrance with an anonymous Gentleman. Both the Gentleman and Theseus (who enters ten lines later saying, 'Bring 'em in') seem to expect the immediate entrance of Palamon, Arcite and their knights. Instead, two messengers enter, though only one of them speaks. The idea of bringing in the knights is now forgotten, but, in answer to Theseus' abrupt questions, the messenger and Pirithous describe three of the knights at length and Theseus, inspired by their speeches, rushes off to see them. The descriptions might perhaps have been appreciated as an act of homage to Chaucer (though Chaucer describes only two knights, this is otherwise the passage most obviously derived from *The Knight's Tale*), but in the scene as a whole they seem a clumsy insertion. Emilia's soliloquy, as Waith notes (Oxf[1], 21–2), is very similar to the one Shakespeare gives her in 5.3. The latter is clearly essential, given the decision to place the tournament off stage, and the resemblance between the two speeches is not altogether surprising, since most of Emilia's lines in the second half of the play are about her inability to choose between the two men and her grief at being the cause of so much bloodshed. The confusion over her entrance suggests that the first soliloquy was either cut or added at a late stage. Montgomery and Taylor, in the *Textual Companion*, consider the latter possibility slightly more likely. I agree; it seems to me that at some point 4.2 was meant to depict the return of Palamon and Arcite, entering in procession with their knights. This procession was later moved to the beginning of 5.1, and Emilia's soliloquy was either moved from a position later in the play or written to help fill the gap between the men's departure and return.

The authorship of 4.3 has been debated; some scholars argue that the Jailer's Daughter, after 3.2, is entirely Fletcher's creation, others that Fletcher would never have written an entire scene, even a mad scene, in prose. A change of author at the start of 4.3 may explain why the Daughter knows something about a schoolmaster but calls him Giraldo rather than Gerald, his name in 3.5. If so, this might be the one point in the play to show Shakespeare accommodating to his colleague, rather than vice versa. However, there may be other reasons for the name change, including simple playfulness (see pp. 354–5). Moreover, the author of 5.2 clearly knew the end of 4.3, to which the opening lines refer – but, again, with an air of recapitulation that suggests someone writing out of context. While a case may be for either dramatist's authorship of these scenes, it seems to me that both were probably written at a time when 5.1 was still not fully worked out.

The series of addresses to the gods in 5.1 is probably the most obviously Shakespearean scene of the play, but it looks as if Shakespeare, when writing it, was unclear how it would be staged. The impressive exchange between Palamon and Arcite that starts at line 18 conveys no obvious sense of location. On the other hand, the lines given to Theseus at the beginning of the scene –

> Now let 'em enter . . .
> > Let the temples
> Burn bright with sacred fires and the altars
> In hallowed clouds commend their swelling incense
> To those above us.

> > > (5.1.1, 2–5)

– prescribe a spectacular processional entry, with candles, incense and an altar. I agree with those who think that these lines are by Fletcher; replacing whatever he had originally planned for

4.2, they provide a transition to and a setting for the speeches that follow.

By contrast with the pageantry of 5.1 the rest of the play is visually rather disappointing. After stressing, in 4.2, 5.2 and 5.3, everyone's breathless eagerness to see the fight, the dramatists deliberately deprive their audience of it, conveying the tournament through offstage sounds and Arcite's accident through the messenger speech of Pirithous. There is neither funeral procession nor funeral pyre. Though the sense of anticlimax may be deliberate, something more elaborate may originally have been planned. The transition between scenes 3 and 4 is remarkably awkward. Theseus orders the execution of Palamon and his knights, adding 'Let it here be done. / The scene's not for our seeing; go we hence' (5.3.133–4). As a way of dealing with the death of a major character, these lines are so perfunctory as to be an insult to the audience as well as to Palamon, though their very casualness may be a clue that no such death will occur. Their main purpose seems to be to maintain continuous action from scene 3 to scene 4. I suspect that they were interpolated; they contradict what seems to have been the original intention (presumably Shakespeare's) of making a break between the two scenes. Why did he want the break? Perhaps in order to suggest a sufficient lapse of time to account for all the offstage events that precede Pirithous' entrance in 5.4. Perhaps, also, he wanted an actual scene change. In 5.4 Theseus comments, 'In this place first you fought' (5.4.99), and at 3.6.291–2, supposedly located in that very place, he had declared his intention to 'plant a pyramid' (or pillar) at the tournament site – a locational pattern that derives from Chaucer (see p. 44 below). It seems likely that at some point Shakespeare envisaged the final scene taking place on the same spot as 3.6, possibly marked by the presence of the pyramid itself, but that he or someone else finally decided to avoid a scene change so late in the play.

Such minor inconsistencies bear out the suggestion that there may have been a change of plan in the course of writing (Proudfoot, 'New', 260). The parallel wedding and victory processions in 1.1 and 1.4 and parallel songs of wedding and funeral in 1.1 and 1.5 (probably composed specially for the play) make Act 1 look, as Waith says (Oxf[1], 63), like a prologue. The triumphal procession for

Theseus in 1.4 and the 'funeral solemnity' of 1.5 (paralleling the marriage song at the beginning) create a strong sense of closure, particularly as the queens, who dominate the symmetrical opening and closing scenes, never appear again. Proudfoot suggests that Shakespeare had completed Act 1 at the time of the Globe fire and that the need for a new Blackfriars play for the autumn led to the co-opting of Fletcher and perhaps a third dramatist, who finished the play hurriedly ('New', 220).

My own hypothesis is that the two dramatists began writing concurrently, but that Fletcher constructed the final draft. In 1.4, 2.2, possibly 2.5, and 5.1, he seems to have been working on, or in the light of, Shakespearean material; nothing suggests that Shakespeare was ever working on Fletcher's. Whereas it is claimed that in *Henry VIII* the dramatists' influence on each other's style was reciprocal (Tarlinskaja, 217), in *The Two Noble Kinsmen* the influence appears to have been one-way. The most likely explanation is that Shakespeare was no longer in London when the play was put into its final form. Irwin Smith has suggested that Shakespeare's purchase of property at the Blackfriars in March 1613 put him in a difficult financial situation when the Globe burned down in June and he, as a sharer, became liable for a substantial sum towards the rebuilding. Since he did not sell the Gatehouse, which is mentioned in his will, Smith argues that he must instead have sold his shares in the King's Men, which are not mentioned there (*Blackfriars*, 252). This might have led to his finishing his part of the collaboration quickly – perhaps even before it was clear how soon the company would be able to replace any costumes and properties lost in the fire – leaving the play for Fletcher to put together once it had become clear how elaborately it could be staged. If a third hand was involved, as Richard Proudfoot suggests, the most likely candidate would be either Beaumont himself or Nathan Field, the actor-dramatist with whom both Beaumont and Fletcher had already collaborated. Though I do not agree with Donald Hedrick's suggestion that Field was the author of the entire non-Fletcherian portion of the play, I am struck by a curious resemblance between Act 1 of *The Two Noble Kinsmen* and the first of the *Four Plays in One* that Fletcher wrote with Field, probably for the Lady Elizabeth's Men, some time between 1612 and 1615. This sequence of short plays (the triumphs of honour, love, death and time respectively) is based loosely on the famous *Triumphs* of Petrarch, where processions in honour of love, chastity, death, fame and time succeed each other, each accompanied by historical and literary examples of the abstraction they commemorate. The first of the *Four Plays*, 'The Triumph of Honour', is ascribed to Field and based on the same story as Chaucer's *Franklin's Tale*. Like it, Act 1 of *The Two Noble Kinsmen* represents the triumph of continence over lust in a ruler. Theseus' entry as 'victor' in 1.4 could have involved the same triumphal car as at the end of each of the *Four Plays*. The latter (at least, in the part written by Field) are also plays within a play, presented before a fictitious newly married king and queen of Portugal – a fact that, as Suzanne Gossett notes (103), makes it possible, though not provable, that they belong to the period following the royal wedding of 1613. Since Field had in any case worked with Fletcher on *The Honest Man's Fortune* in that year, he would probably have known something about his colleague's other project, and of course the resemblances just noted might result simply from the influence of *The Two Noble Kinsmen* on the *Four Plays*. But it seems to me likely that Field had something to do with the *Kinsmen*. Even if he was only one of the original actors, he would probably have had an important effect on its writing (see p. 65, below).

One should also consider an alternative explanation for some of the play's inconsistencies, particularly in Act 4. Gary Taylor and McDonald P. Jackson suggest that the anomalous stage direction in 4.3.39, which tells the Daughter to exit without marking a re-entry for her, might result from the cutting in the theatre of the lines which follow, since they are directed against lecherous courtiers, a subject on which the Master of the Revels was 'particularly sensitive' at this period (*TxC*, 559). A further possibility is that the relationship of Theseus and Pirithous, which seems an important part of the play in Act 1 but is never developed after this point, was sacrificed when it was perceived as a potential reference to James I and his favourite Robert Carr, who became Earl of Somerset in 1613. Favourites were a touchy subject in general. In 1608 the child actors of the Blackfriars had provoked the King to a short-lived ban on all theatrical performances in London by depicting him

'with all his favourites' (Clare, 139–40). The 1609 quarto of
Pericles, another work in which censorship has been suspected
(*TxC*, 559), is at its most garbled at the points where it deals with
Helicanus, whom Pericles deputizes to act for him in his absence,
and his confidant Escanes, who arouses the jealousy of the other
courtiers (*Per* 2.4.17–20). Cuts in the role of Pirithous might have
been made, if not in 1613, then at a later date – either for a 1619–20
revival or for one in 1625 – given the unpopularity of Carr's
successor, the Duke of Buckingham. It has been suggested (by
W. Griffin, quoted in Clare, 200) that this unpopularity explains
the disappearance in the 1623 Shakespeare folio of an exchange,
found in all the earlier quartos, where Richard III tells an earlier
Duke of Buckingham, 'I am not in the giving vein today'
(*R3* 4.2.116).

This stress on the contingent element in the collaborative process may give the impression that I see *The Two Noble Kinsmen* as a
confused and contradictory work. But anyone with experience of
the theatre will know that contingency is an inevitable part of the
process by which a script becomes a play. The actors and audience
of a television series perceive it as a coherent whole despite the
inconsistencies that result from its being written over a long period
of time and by several different authors. Actors and audiences of
this play, similarly, have little difficulty in ignoring its apparent
contradictions. To take only one of the examples mentioned above
(p. 27), actors who wish to make Emilia's relationship with the
disguised Arcite more consistent can either play her more warmly
in 2.5 or suggest that he is deluded in 3.1. That is why, having
'deconstructed' the play in this section, I have chosen not to do so
in the text or the notes, which, as far as possible, will refrain from
identifying the assumed author of each scene.

THE DATE

The combination of a number of facts, none of them absolutely
conclusive on its own, makes it possible to arrive at a fairly precise
dating of *The Two Noble Kinsmen*. One is the relationship (first
pointed out by Littledale) between the morris dance in 3.5 and the
second antimasque dance from Beaumont's *Masque of the Inner*

Temple and Gray's Inn (Appendix 3), which has the same mixture of characters described in the Schoolmaster's speech in 3.5.121–32. Performed as part of the celebrations of the wedding of James I's daughter Elizabeth and Frederick, Prince Palatine, on 20 February 1613, this dance was encored by its distinguished audience. Beaumont's published description of the masque says that its novelty was one reason for its success, so it cannot have been seen already on the public stage. The other limiting factor is the reference to the name of Palamon 'out of the play' in Jonson's *Bartholomew Fair* (6:4.3.70), the first performance of which took place on 31 October 1614. Between these two dates came another event that would certainly have affected any production by the King's Men: the burning of the Globe Theatre on 29 June 1613. The reference to 'our losses' in the last line of the play's Prologue is generally taken – rightly, I think – to mean this fire. It is true that, as has often been pointed out, the Prologue need not date from the first performances of the play, and the King's Men suffered other 'losses' throughout the period (Shakespeare died in 1616, Burbage in 1619, Fletcher in 1625). But the light tone of the Prologue is more appropriate to a discussion of money worries, which by convention are comic to everyone except the person who has them; the Epilogue goes on to claim that a hiss will 'kill our market'.

It may be possible to narrow the period still further. John Webster's preface to *The White Devil* (1612) complains that his play was presented 'in so dull a time of Winter' that it lacked 'a full and vnderstanding Auditory'. The Prologue of *The Two Noble Kinsmen* also refers to 'dull time' (31); perhaps, like *The White Devil*, it was premiered in winter.

CONTEXTS: PUBLIC

Nuptials and funerals

The winter of 1612–13 had been a period in which, as at the end of *The Two Noble Kinsmen*, a funeral was quickly followed by a marriage. The wedding of James I's daughter Elizabeth had originally been planned for Epiphany, the end of the Christmas season, in 1613. Her bridegroom, Prince Frederick of Heidelberg, arrived from Germany in October 1612 and made his triumphal entry into the English court on 18 October. The popular Prince of Wales, Henry, became seriously ill shortly thereafter and his death on 6 November plunged the court into mourning. James I's initial reaction was to announce that the marriage would be deferred until May (*CSPV*, 452, 458). But he was soon being urged to hasten it. Frederick wanted to return to his own country and its pressing political affairs; James's own followers were conscious of the expense of entertaining their large retinue of visitors. Despite all these pleas, James publicly insisted (perhaps actually recalling *Hamlet*) that 'mourning should be mourning, and marriage rejoicings rejoicings' (*CSPV*, 474). In private, however, he himself had written to his ambassador in France as early as 14 December, proposing to replace Henry with his younger brother Charles in the ongoing negotiations for a marriage between the prince and a French princess (Akrigg, *Letters*, 328–30). At the end of January the Venetian ambassador reported that the king had agreed to Frederick's request for a wedding on the last Sunday before Lent, St Valentine's Day. Elizabeth was still wearing black on the day of her betrothal (Nichols, 513) and, though the court went out of mourning for the wedding itself, a portrait now in the National Portrait Gallery in London shows her with knots of black ribbon on her dress in memory of her brother. The numerous epithalamia made for the occasion rarely failed to rhyme *nuptials* with *funerals*.

It is likely that in their official capacity as King's Men, the shareholders not only marched in the funeral procession of the Prince of Wales in 1612 but attended the ceremonies surrounding the wedding of his sister in 1613. After both Richard Proudfoot (1970) and Muriel Bradbrook (1971) had suggested a connection between the end of the play and the events of 1612-13, books on Prince Henry by Henry Williamson (1978) and Roy Strong (1986) aroused considerable interest in his possible role as inspiration for *The Two Noble Kinsmen*. Glynne Wickham's controversial attempt to identify Emilia with Princess Elizabeth, torn between her love for her dead brother Henry Frederick (Arcite) and her fiancé Frederick Henry (Palamon), is far too schematic, but many scholars have felt that there must be some relation between the play and these public events. J. R. Mulryne suggests that the play's subject-matter and imagery reflect the prince's known interests in horses, armour and sailing. Others have queried whether Fletcher and Shakespeare would necessarily have admired the young man's military ambitions. It has been argued that the dramatists were depicting the tension between the pacifist policy advocated by James I and the militant Protestantism represented by Prince Henry (Carney, 106–8), or even offering a critique of the military values espoused by the prince (Hadorn, 55). There may be some significance in their choice of title, since the two earlier plays based on Chaucer's poem had been called *Palamon and Arcite*; the choice of the unusual title *The Two Noble Kinsmen* may have been intended to recall the short-lived friendship and brotherhood of the young English and German princes. 'How like a golden dream you met and parted,' wrote Campion in his *Songs of Mourning* for the prince (124).

If the royal funeral helps to account for the dark tone of the play's ending, the royal wedding might seem an appropriate context for its first scene. But the jaunty opening of the Prologue – 'New plays and maidenheads are near akin' – and its comparison of a good play, which can be enjoyed more than once and still seem new, with a wife who still looks like a virgin even after her wedding night, would have been more appropriate to another wedding that took place later in 1613. On 25 September of that year, Frances Howard, Countess of Essex, was granted an annulment after a panel of two midwives and four matrons examined her and pronounced her still a virgin. When, on 26 December, she married James's favourite, the Earl of Somerset, she wore her hair flowing as a sign of virginity. The widespread derision that greeted the annulment decision (see Lindley, 109–15) may explain the sceptical tone of the Doctor's admission that, at 18, the Jailer's Daughter 'may be' a virgin; Frances Howard was 19 at this time.

Militant Protestantism

The image of the three queens who interrupt the wedding procession is theatrically striking; it may also have had a political resonance. Suffering countries are often depicted as women and countries with no lawful ruler as widows, as, for instance, in John Bale's *King Johan*, where England is 'a widow'. A common image for the United Provinces of the Spanish Netherlands was that of Belgia and her daughters: a famous and much-imitated engraving, first published in 1569 and reworked well into the seventeenth century, showed these allegorical figures kneeling and pleading with an enthroned Duke of Alva, the figurehead of oppressive Spanish Catholicism (Tanis & Horst, 51). The widowed Belgia reappears in Book 5 of Spenser's *Faerie Queene* (10.7), and Heywood's poem on the marriage of Princess Elizabeth in 1613 revived this image when he praised Frederick for his efforts on behalf of 'Faire *Belgia*, and her seventeene daughters', each of whom 'in former times hath beene / A beauteous Lady, and a flourishing Queene' (Heywood, C4').

If militant Protestantism of this kind found expression even in celebratory verses on the 1613 wedding, this was partly because of the sense that the reformed religion was under threat. The assassination of Henry IV of France in 1610 at the hands of a Catholic fanatic had been much lamented by Protestants; the death in 1612 of his namesake, Henry Prince of Wales, was a second blow to the cause. It is significant that John Donne, himself a convert from Catholicism, responded to the Prince's death with a poem beginning, 'Look to me, *Faith*; and look to my *Faith*, GOD'. Similarly, in 1.2 of the play, there may be a deeper meaning in Palamon and Arcite's fear of losing their faith and Palamon's insistence that they can be saved by faith (see note on 1.2.46) even in the corrupt court of Creon.

Jokes inspired by the semi-forbidden subject of religious controversy, like Sir Toby's drunken 'Give me faith say I' (*TN* 1.5.129), are not unusual in Shakespeare. Behind the apparently gratuitous references in *The Two Noble Kinsmen* may be the recent resurgence of that controversy, this time in the light of the new challenge from Arminianism – a Protestant movement considered by some to be as threatening as Catholicism itself. The views of Jacob Arminius had been known to, and even accepted by, some Cambridge scholars as early as the late 1590s (Tyacke, 29–38), but his books first became widely available in 1610, the year of the Remonstrance and Counter-Remonstrance in the Netherlands. They attempt to modify some of the harsher tenets of Calvinism, particularly its insistence that God had predestined the salvation and damnation of human beings before their birth and that they themselves were powerless to alter their fate. James I took a stand against the new doctrine as early as 1611, when he intervened to prevent the appointment of an Arminian as professor of theology at Leiden. In 1613 the visit to England of a well-known Arminian scholar, Hugo Grotius, had some success in modifying English attitudes (Harrison, 167–203). However, Nicholas Tyacke has shown that official belief, as reflected in sermons preached at Paul's Cross, 'the most public pulpit in the land', was consistently Calvinist until 1628, with twenty-seven sermons of James's reign giving the Calvinist view of predestination (253). Both the Huntingdon circle and their most admired literary model, Spenser, were associated with militant, though non-Puritan, Protestantism. Fletcher was clearly not as intransigent as his father, who had tried to convert the Catholic Mary Queen of Scots just before her execution, but he would later collaborate with Massinger in two topical plays dealing with the Netherlands: *The Jeweller of Amsterdam, or, the Hague* (*c.*1616–19) and *Sir John van Olden Barnevelt* (1619). The first of these (which also involved Nathan Field) is lost, but the second is definitely anti-Arminian, though it appears to have become even more so as the result of official censorship. Since the authors of *The Two Noble Kinsmen* are generally careful to avoid obvious religious anachronisms (Naseeb Shaheen finds fewer biblical references than in any other play of the Shakespeare canon), the influence of this period of religious questioning can only be indirect. In any case, such concerns are already present in the source. Chaucer himself is claimed by the Protestant martyrologist John Foxe as an early sympathizer (2.639) and Thomas Speght's 1602 edition, in the headnote to *Troilus and Criseyde*, draws attention to the fact that 'Chaucer liberally treateth of the divine purveiaunce' (Speght, 143$^\mathrm{v}$).

If *The Two Noble Kinsmen* was revived in 1619–20 the call to arms in 1.1 might well have resonated still more than in 1613, since there now seemed a strong possibility that the country might go to war on behalf of Elizabeth and Frederick, whose acceptance of the crown of Bohemia had precipitated what would later be called the Thirty Years' War. Though thwarted by James I's non-interventionist policies, the prospect of a European war was still very much in the air early in Charles I's reign when the play was next being considered for performance. The opening marriage procession would have been as appropriate for 1625–6 as for 1613, since 1625 was the year of James I's death and Charles I's marriage with Henrietta Maria of France. By the time of the play's publication in 1634 Elizabeth was herself a widowed queen, Frederick having died in 1631.

CONTEXTS: LITERARY

The Theban story before Chaucer

The history of Thebes is mythical. Its walls rose to the sound of music; its people sprang up from the ground when its founder Cadmus sowed the teeth of a dragon. The dragon–offspring immediately began killing each other, and fratricide and incest continued to dominate Theban history to the point where it became an archetype of the evil city. The story of Oedipus, which combines virtually all the great tragic themes, was the gods' revenge on the whole house of Cadmus. When Oedipus went into exile, his sons Eteocles and Polynices agreed to share the rule of the kingdom by turns. At the end of the first year, seized by the lust for power, Eteocles refused to give up the throne. Polynices made war on him, at the head of an army from Argos. At the siege of Thebes, he and all his allies were killed, as was Eteocles. Oedipus' brother Creon succeeded.

All three of the great Greek dramatists wrote plays on the Theban story, usually in order to contrast Creon's tyranny with the enlightened Athenian civilization embodied, as often in Greek drama, in the figure of Theseus. The structure of Euripides' *Suppliants*, in particular, is remarkably close to Act 1 of *The Two Noble Kinsmen*. A chorus of women, supported by Theseus' mother Aethra, plead with Theseus to intercede for them with Creon. He at first refuses, then gives in to his mother's persuasions. A debate between Theseus and Creon's herald follows, corresponding to the defiance that has apparently taken place between the first and second scenes of *The Two Noble Kinsmen*, and after the Chorus has called on the gods for help a messenger enters to relate the victory over Thebes. In the final scene, the women lament their husbands;

then their sons enter in procession carrying the urns with their fathers' ashes.

Euripides' *Phoenissae*, which deals with the mutual defiance of the brothers before the attack on Thebes, was, as Emrys Jones points out, one of his most popular plays in the Renaissance (Jones, *Origins*, 92). Seneca adapted it and *The Suppliants*, with other Greek plays, to make an even better known Latin tragedy, adding an episode which, although apparently unfinished, had a powerful influence on the Renaissance imagination: Jocasta, mother of the warring brothers, kneels to them and begs them to spare their country. *Coriolanus* is the most striking development of this motif. The most influential classical retelling of the legend was Statius' epic, the *Thebaid*, which develops both the rivalry between the brothers and the relationship between the exiled Polynices and the exiled Tydeus, who fight at their first meeting and then become sworn friends. (This friendship becomes still more important in the medieval version called the *Roman de Thèbes*.) Statius' gruesome depiction of war, and his evident compassion for the sufferings of the weak, gave rise to a belief (expressed by Dante in *Purgatorio* 22.90) that he had been a secret Christian. Chaucer mentions him in the same breath as Virgil, Ovid, Homer and Lucan (*Troilus and Criseyde*, 5.1792).

Boccaccio's *Teseida*, probably completed in the late 1340s, turned the *Thebaid* into romance by transforming the war of two brothers over a city into the fight of two cousins over a woman. The great war epics of the past had made cities and women interchangeable – Helen causes the fall of Troy; Lavinia will eventually give her name to the first city built by Aeneas. Just as Statius had imitated Virgil, so (it has been argued) Boccaccio followed his example in an episode-by-episode imitation of Statius (Anderson, 50). Both Palemone and Arcita recognize that they are reliving the story of Eteocles and Polynices (see, for instance, *Teseida*, 5.13). Arcita's exile and wanderings, which follow his release from prison, make him a counterpart of the exiled Polynices. When Polynices is thrown from his chariot during a competition halfway through the poem, Statius exclaims that if Polynices had indeed died at this point he would have been remembered as a hero, not a traitor to his country (108–12). As David Anderson points out, this 'alternate ending' may have suggested the fate of Arcita in Boccaccio's poem (72, 107).

Chaucer and Boccaccio

Chaucer may have read the *Teseida* on one of his journeys to Italy in the 1370s. He must have known it well, as he made extensive use of it in other works before finally retelling its central story. In particular, he returned several times to the descriptions of the temples of Mars and Venus, and his unfinished *Anelida and Arcite* (before 1380) makes Creon's Thebes the setting for a story of a forsaken woman. R. A. Pratt (604–5) may be right in saying that Chaucer would never have given the name Arcite to a character who wins and then abandons a woman if he had intended at that stage to write a poem with a hero of the same name, but, once Chaucer's works had been collected into a single volume, readers might have been influenced by the existence of what Speght's 1602 text calls the tale 'Of Queene Annelida, and false Arcite'. In *The Two Noble Kinsmen*, Palamon insists on the word 'false' in connection with Arcite, and Arcite acknowledges his falseness in his final speech.

Chaucer's most extended tribute to Boccaccio's poem survives as *The Knight's Tale*, usually thought to date from the mid-1380s (Fig. 1). It is about one-third the length of the *Teseida*. By contrast with Boccaccio, Chaucer seems to have wanted to remove the links with classical literature. Theseus' defeat of Hippolyta, which occupies the first book of Boccaccio's poem, is dealt with in one line. There is no mention of Oedipus, Eteocles or Polynices, and the mourning women exist simply to inspire Theseus' campaign. Neither Palamon nor Arcite is concerned with Juno's wrath. Emilia is much less interesting, .much more purely symbolic, than in Boccaccio.

Moreover, Chaucer alters the balance between the two heroes. Boccaccio, who is thought to have portrayed himself as Arcita, not only makes him the first to see Emilia but gives him three times as many lines as Palemone and an extremely protracted and moving death (Pratt, 603). Chaucer makes Palamon the first to see Emilia, and has him insist on a prior commitment of sworn brotherhood that Arcite is betraying. Whereas both young men in Boccaccio are full of reverence towards the childlike Emilia, Chaucer

1 The opening of *The Knight's Tale* in the edition of Chaucer's *Works* by Thomas Speght, 1602

discriminates between them: Palamon takes her for a goddess, whereas Arcite desires her as a woman.

The reduction of scale extends to the handling of space, though not of time (in both versions, the events take about ten years). Boccaccio's *Teseo* makes the site of Arcita's funeral pyre the grove in which he had sung his love songs to Emilia, and Palemone commemorates him by building a temple to Juno on the same site; Chaucer locates the tournament lists there as well and places the oratories to Mars, Venus and Diana in the tournament amphitheatre itself. The sense of crowding parallels the construction of the plot, which seems designed to create as many dilemmas as possible: which young man 'hath the worse' – Palamon, who is in prison but able to see Emilia, or Arcite, who is free but banished? Who deserves Emilia more – the man who prays for victory or the one who prays to have her? Much criticism of the *Tale*, like subsequent criticism and performance of the play, has done little more than take sides in these debates.

The main plot and its sources

Like *Pericles*, but unlike any other Shakespeare play, *The Two Noble Kinsmen* openly acknowledges its chief source at the start. Its debt to *The Knight's Tale* is made clear both in the Prologue and in the Epilogue's reference to the play as a 'tale'. Though the Prologue gives no indication that Chaucer was indebted to others for his story, the dramatists would certainly have known the *Thebaid*, if only because of John Lydgate's *Siege of Thebes*, a retelling of Statius, which was first added to Chaucer's *Works* in Stowe's edition of 1561 and reprinted by Speght in his 1598 edition (revised in 1602).

They might also have known Boccaccio's poem, though it had been forgotten in England by the end of the seventeenth century, when Dryden could only speculate on the possibility of an Italian source for *The Knight's Tale*. Francis Thynne's *Animadversions* on Speght's Chaucer (1599) states correctly that *The Knight's Tale* was taken 'out of the Thesayde of Bocas' (Kinsley, 4.2061). There were two sixteenth-century French translations of the *Teseida*, both of which attributed it correctly. At least one of these, a condensed prose version of 1597 by someone known on the title page only as le Sieur D.C.C., might have been known to one or both of the dramatists. Though Melchiori thinks that Shakespeare knew only Chaucer's version (6.xlviii), there are times when the dramatists seem closer to the *Teseida* than to *The Knight's Tale*. The opening scene, where the request of the three queens creates a conflict of love and duty not present in Chaucer, could have been inspired by *Teseida* 2.2–5, where Teseo, on his honeymoon, sees a vision of his friend Peritoo, who urges him to return to his duties in Athens. Palamon's brief *ubi sunt* passage in the play's prison scene (2.2.6–8) echoes both Arcita's three-stanza lament over the ruins of Thebes (*Teseida*, 4.14–16) and the death speech in which he lists the worldly pleasures that he leaves behind him: '*Omè, dove lascio io i cari amici? / Dove le feste e il sommo diletto? / Ove i cavalli, omai fatti mendici / del lor signore?*' [Ah me, where do I leave my dear friends? Where the feastings and the supreme delight? Where the horses, impoverished now, without their lord?] (10.108). The three prayers to the gods in 5.1 occur in the sequence of the *Teseida*, whereas in the *Tale* it is Palamon who speaks first, followed by Emilia, then Arcite. (Perhaps, however, as Ann Thompson suggests (199), the order is that of Chaucer's descriptions of the three temples, which lie behind much of the language of the prayers.) Arcite's death, in *The Knight's Tale*, results from his being pitched forward when his horse stumbles; in the *Teseida*, as in *The Two Noble Kinsmen*, the horse comes over backward on top of him. The French translator, like the dramatists, omits the classical Fury sent by Boccaccio and Chaucer, making Arcite's horse go wild for no apparent reason.

If Boccaccio's portrayal of the kinsmen was weighted towards Arcite, and Chaucer's towards Palamon, the dramatists seem to have attempted to differentiate them yet retain a balance of sympathy. The character distinction does not begin until 2.2, but thereafter both Shakespeare and Fletcher seem to envisage them in terms of the conventional but effective contrast between a calm man (Arcite) and a passionate one (Palamon). This later becomes a contrast between the influences of Mars and Venus, comparable to what one finds within Othello or the Antony of *Antony and Cleopatra*. Emilia's role, inevitably, needed more extensive reworking, since Chaucer makes her speak only once, in her prayer to Diana. It may, then, be only coincidence that she sometimes sounds like Boccaccio's heroine, who also laments the effects of her beauty (8.97), fears that future ages will curse her for all the unnecessary deaths in the tournament (8.100) and says that she is incapable of choosing between the two men (8.104–5). The French translation, '*ne sçaurois-ie iamais faire de choix ny d'election*' [I could never make either choice or election] (*Theseyde*, 115') is slightly closer to Emilia's 'I / Am guiltless of election' (5.1.153–4) than Boccaccio's '*io non so qual di lor m'eleggesse*' [I do not know which one of them I would choose] (8.105). In both Boccaccio and Chaucer, she is present at the tournament; but Chaucer depicts her from the outside, presenting her affection toward the winner as typical female opportunism, whereas Boccaccio analyses her feelings in sympathetic detail. Her varied reactions to the cries of the supporters of the two contestants (8.107) may have made the dramatists decide to depict the offstage events of 5.3 through her eyes. Boccaccio's Emilia sees herself as a fatal influence because, while still a child, she was engaged to a cousin of Theseus, who died young (10.69); perhaps this is the origin of the childhood friendship with Flavina, described in 1.3 of the play.

. It is usually assumed that the most famous Chaucerian dramatization, Richard Edwards' *Palamon and Arcite*, could not have influenced the Jacobean dramatists because it was never printed: Edwards died within a month of its highly successful premiere, which he directed himself at Christ Church, Oxford, in 1566, before an audience that included Elizabeth I. The queen spoke enthusiastically of the actors and gave presents of money to the boys who played Hippolyta and Emilia. Fortunately, because of the queen's presence, several eye-witnesses left detailed accounts. These show that the play featured a very large cast, a hunting scene, a tournament, and a funeral pyre for Arcite (Durand, 511; Elliott, 221, 224). Since its one surviving fragment, a song that Emilia sings after the death of Arcite, can be found in a seventeenth-century manuscript (Rollins, 'Note', 205), it is possible that more of the play, or at least its music, was still known in 1613; some of the original cast had been in their early teens in 1566 and had every reason to remember the occasion. One of Edwards' incidents, as described by a spectator, may explain a small puzzle in the final scene of *The Two Noble*

Kinsmen. When Palamon is called down from the scaffold by Pirithous, he asks bemusedly, 'Can that be, / When Venus, I have said, is false?' (5.4.44–5). He has said nothing of the sort, unless off stage. But in Edwards's play Palamon, after his defeat, does reproach Venus, 'saying that he had served her from infancy and now she had neither desire nor power to help him' (Durand, 511). Perhaps, as R. M. Clements suggests (72), Fletcher and Shakespeare were also thinking of Edwards's one surviving play, *Damon and Pithias* (1565). As Pithias, who has remained as hostage for his friend Damon, is about to die in his place, Damon rushes in and pushes the sword aside, calling, 'Stay, stay, stay, for the kinges aduantage stay' (Edwards, *Damon*, 2028–9). The breathless entry, first of the Messenger, then of Pirithous, and their repeated cries of 'Hold' (5.4.40–1), may recall this dramatic moment.

The play's subplot may also have been influenced by the *Teseida*. In *The Knight's Tale* Palamon's escape from prison is explained by the simple statement (1467–74) that, with a friend's help, he drugged his jailer. In the *Teseida*, he pretends to be ill, sends his servant for a friendly doctor, and then, after the supposed consultation, leaves prison with the doctor, disguised as his own servant. Perhaps this combination of a doctor and changing clothes lies behind the bizarre events of *The Two Noble Kinsmen*, 5.2.

The Jailer's Daughter

The dramatists' decision to complicate the Chaucerian story with a subplot may have resulted as much from their difficulty in turning Chaucer's Emilia into a central figure of the play as from the necessity of filling in the gaps in a story that requires so many lapses of time. Though the subplot has no obvious source, the woman who falls in love with her father's prisoner is a thoroughly traditional character. Mopsa in Sidney's *Arcadia* is a comic version of the type (see Thompson, 'Jailers''). Indeed, Miranda in *The Tempest* is a Jailer's Daughter in relation to Ferdinand in 3.1; although her disobedience consists only in letting Ferdinand know her name, she has been seen as part of a line that goes back at least to Medea (Black, 30). A still closer parallel occurs in the complex legend of Theseus, which contains within it many of the motifs that are dispersed among the other characters of the play. Chaucer's *The Legend of Good Women* combines his story with material from that of Palamon and Arcite: Ariadne and Phaedra overhear Theseus complaining in prison, and not only help him overcome the Minotaur but, with the help of his jailer (a character new to this version), enable him to escape with them. The story of Theseus' subsequent abandonment of Ariadne, who had helped him find his way in and out of the labyrinth, had many literary versions. In Catullus' poem on the nuptials of Peleus and Thetis, the coverlet of the marriage bed is described (rather ominously) as woven with the story of Ariadne, whose lament is given at length. Her lament also inspired what was probably the most popular of all Ovid's *Heroides*: imaginary letters from women to their absent lovers, which became models for Renaissance poems of complaint. Like the Jailer's Daughter, Ovid's Ariadne finds herself alone, on an island, with the ship of her lover vanishing in the distance. Cold, desperate, afraid of being devoured by wolves (81–4), unable to return to the kingdom where she betrayed her father for love of Theseus, she pleads, 'turn about your ship, reverse your sail, glide swiftly back to me!' (149–51).

Although Monteverdi's opera *Arianna*, first produced in Mantua in 1608, was the most famous Renaissance interpretation of Ariadne's story, Julia, in *The Two Gentlemen of Verona*, had already described herself as having played the part of 'Ariadne passioning / For Theseus' perjury and unkind flight' (4.4.167–8) – and she is playing it even as she speaks, since her own lover has been false to her. Fletcher seems to have been equally attracted to the story. Catullus' description of the Ariadne coverlet probably inspired the famous scene in *The Maid's Tragedy*, where Aspatia, deserted by her lover, offers to be the model for an embroidery of the deserted Ariadne, attempting at the same time, as Jonathan Bate says (263–4), to rewrite the story of Theseus:

> Does not the story say, his Keele was split,
> Or his masts spent, or some kind rock or other
> Met with his vessel? . . .
>> It should have been so.
>> (Bowers, 2: 2.2.46–9)

In her madness, the Daughter imagines the rock and makes the shipwreck occur, though she imagines that Palamon's death has been caused by wolves. She also harps on the idea that her father will die as a consequence of her actions.

As Clements (193–5) and Waith (Oxf[1], 29) have pointed out, there are many resemblances between the Daughter and Viola in Beaumont and Fletcher's *The Coxcomb*, though this part of the plot is thought to be the work of Beaumont (Bowers, 1.263). Viola leaves home to elope with her lover, who misses their rendezvous because he gets drunk with friends. She is left helpless and alone, too proud to awaken her father 'to see his daughter's shame'. Her comment, 'if hee deceive mee thus, / A woman will not easily trust a man' (1.6.7–14), may echo Ariadne's words as quoted by Catullus: '*Nunc iam nulla viro iuranti femina credat*' [Henceforth let no woman believe a man's oath] (Catullus, p. 106, line 143); the Jailer's Daughter uses much the same language:

> Sure he cannot
> Be so unmanly as to leave me here;
> If he do, maids will not so easily
> Trust men again.
>
> (2.6.18–21)

Though Viola's father is a Spanish aristocrat, not a jailer, the play also contains a comic subplot about a jailer whose prisoners escape and who is briefly threatened with hanging even though the escapees are only a tinker and his wife. *The Coxcomb* was popular enough to be performed at court before Elizabeth and Frederick and would have been fresh in Fletcher's mind in 1613.

Viola does not go mad as a result of her sufferings (she is duly reunited with her chastened lover), but mad scenes, for both men and women, were to become something of a speciality of Fletcher's. The madness can be real or feigned, and how seriously it is taken seems to depend on context rather than gender. The middle-aged soldier Memnon, in *The Mad Lover* (*c*.1616), thinks himself in the Elysian fields, like the Daughter in 4.3, while the heroine of *The Wild Goose Chase* (*c*.1621), pretending to have gone

mad for the hero's love, sounds exactly like the genuinely mad
Daughter of 4.1:

> I must be up to morrow, to go to Church:
> And I must dress me, put my new Gown on,
> And be so fine to meet my Love: Heigh ho!
> Will not you tell me where my Love lies buried?
> (Bowers, 6:4.3.62–5)

The Jailer's Daughter, of course, is *not* betrayed by Palamon, only
by her own fantasies. Her ballads (see Appendix 6, pp. 361–2)
create a role for her which can end in happiness ('Child Waters',
'Young Beichan') or in disillusionment ('The Fair Flower of
Northumberland'). She thus shares with Ophelia the habit of what
Carol Neely has called 'quoted discourse' (324). Even in her final
scene she is speaking the language of proverbs, asking directions to
the end of the world (where damsels in romance go with their
lovers) and, to the Wooer's offer of a hundred kisses, adding a formulaic twenty.

Doctors and poets alike compare the disturbed human mind to a
ship tossed in a tempest (for example, in the popular medical work,
The Touchstone of Complexions (Lemnius, A3 and A8ᵛ)). Having
first observed the ship from a distance, as she goes mad (3.4), the
Daughter in 4.1 forces her family and friends to become part of its
imaginary crew. Falling in with her fantasies, they instinctively
follow the same path that the Doctor later recommends on the
grounds that 'It is a falsehood she is in, which is with falsehoods to
be combated' (4.3.93–4). Though one reviewer of the 1928 Old
Vic production found the Doctor 'a surprisingly modern forerunner of Dr. Freud' (Horsnell), his methods are essentially those
recommended in Renaissance treatises on lovesickness. For
medieval writers, *Amor Hereos* (a term of mysterious origin) was a
heroic malady that afflicted only men. Chaucer describes Arcite,
during his exile from Athens, as suffering from near-madness:
'Nat oonly lik the loveris maladye / Of Hereos, but rather lyk
manye, / Engendred of humour malencolik' (Chaucer, *Riv*, 1373–
5). This 'knights melancholie' (Laurentius, 89) was still meaningful
to sixteenth-century physicians, but in his edition of 1602 Speght

could make no sense of the Chaucerian passage; he emended *hereos* to *Eros*.

Only in the sixteenth century, Mary Wack argues, did lovesickness become a condition specifically identified with women rather than men (176). Although the Daughter's madness has been called, by comparison to male madness, '"pretty" discourse rather than a soul-ravaging disorder' (Charney, 457), she is more complex than most theatrical madwomen (including the pathetic, endlessly singing Constance of Richard Brome's *Northern Lass* (1629), who was probably inspired by her). An innocent and rather colourless presence in her first scene, she is transformed by love and madness into a singer, a dancer, a person of vivid imagination and even, like Hamlet, something of a social satirist (in 4.3 at least). Her fantasies of Palamon's death and her father's execution can easily be explained as the product not only of grief, but of an anger that she has not previously been licensed to express.

The early literature on lovesickness (some of it from Arabian physicians) states frankly that the best cure for this condition is coitus (Wack, 11–12). The danger of frustrated sexuality was a commonplace from the time of Hippocrates, who is supposed to have warned that if husbands were not provided for girls of marriageable age they might hang or drown themselves (Ferrand, 96–7). As a ballad-writer put it, in 'Dr Do-good's Directions' (*c*.1633–52),

> If a mayd be infected with the falling away,
> Which proceeds from a longing desire, some say,
> If she will be preserved and kept from decay,
> She must get her a husband without all delay.
>> (*Roxburghe Ballads*, 1.235–8,
>> quoted Wiltenburg, 120)

Andreas Laurentius (André du Laurens), after devoting several chapters to the kind of melancholy that 'commeth by the extremitie of loue', concluded that 'There are two waies to cure this amorous melancholie: the one is, the inioying of the thing beloued: the other resteth in the skill and paines of a good Phisition' (117–21). Some, however, rejected this first remedy altogether, arguing that 'vice cannot be driven out by vice' (Ferrand, 334). When the patient was a woman, the moral issue became particularly acute.

It is for this reason that the Jailer's Daughter is introduced in 2.1 as a young woman with a fiancé. Except in the astonishing lyrical speech in 4.1, the Wooer is notable chiefly for his silence. Depending on the director's interpretation, he can be either stupid or shy. The part may have been deliberately underwritten to keep him an unknown quantity until the doctor's stratagem forces him into the unfamiliar role of Palamon. Perhaps a change is suggested even before this, when the devoted but practical young man who was discussing dowries with the Jailer in 2.1 tells the Doctor in 4.3 that he would give half his estate to be on the same terms with the Daughter again – even after she has told everyone about her love for another man.

As one might expect, it is with regard to this part of the play, with its almost exclusive focus on sexual desire, that the greatest change in critical opinion has taken place. While Seward found the Daughter a 'charming Character' (10.5), and the introduction to an edition attributed to Sir Walter Scott called the progressive development of her madness 'at least as touching' as Ophelia's abrupt appearance as a madwoman (Scott, l.iii), most nineteenth-century readers saw her as a degradation of Ophelia and her final scene with the Doctor and Wooer as 'disgusting and imbecile in the extreme' (Spalding, 51). A. F. Hopkinson, who edited *The Two Noble Kinsmen* in 1894, declared that 'the marriage of the Gaoler's daughter ought to have taken place after her reason had returned, or the conclusion should have been rounded by her seeking death by her own hand' (Hopkinson, 3.xxxiv). As late as 1947, John Masefield, a sensitive critic of the play, wondered whether a staging of 5.2 would be acceptable to a modern audience. 'If you give your care to it, much of this scene of Doctor, Wooer and Jailer's Daughter can be made most touching, most tender. Still, even so???' (201).

These readers were not merely objecting to the fact that the Wooer and Daughter, still unmarried, are clearly going offstage to have sex at the end of 5.2 – an act that could be explained by reference to the ambiguous status of the betrothed woman in the Renaissance. More disturbing is the deception practised on her, which could be taken to make the Wooer's action little better than rape. It has been argued that the Doctor's use of the bed-trick is 'not intended as a means of maintaining the illusions of the jailor's daughter but of helping her to accept the realities of love and marriage by working through those illusions' (Desens, 86–7). In some productions, this therapeutic aspect has been stressed effectively. In New York (1993) and Ashland (1994), the Wooer in Palamon's clothes looked surprisingly like Palamon. Indeed, at Ashland, the Daughter's tentative 'Are not you Palamon?' and the Wooer's 'Do not you know me?' (5.2.82) showed both his reluctance to lie to her and her sense that perhaps he had been Palamon, or Palamon had been the Wooer, all along. At least one director, Julian Lopez-Morillas (Berkeley, 1985), felt that the Daughter must to some extent be aware of the real identity of her Palamon. One might compare the end of Fletcher's *Wild Goose Chase*, in which the hero, apparently tricked into marriage with the heroine while she is impersonating a rich lady, says (to save face?), 'and yet perhaps I knew ye' (5.6.81). The Daughter's final lines to the Wooer, 'But you shall not hurt me. / . . . If you do, love, I'll cry.' (5.2.110–11), touchingly suggest that her apparent eagerness for sex may have been masking fear – of sex itself, or of the betrayal that might follow it. 'This', Kenneth Tynan wrote in 1950, 'is to kill with something more than kindness – with the bitterest of compassion' (223). Audiences usually find the ending happy; it sometimes receives spontaneous applause. But some directors are reluctant to treat the deception as benign or to let the Daughter's story end so easily: in several recent productions (see pp. 86, 94, below), she has reappeared, still mad, at the end of the play.

Courtly love and friendship literature

The relation of *The Two Noble Kinsmen* to the ethos of courtly love and friendship is complicated by Chaucer's own ambivalence towards the courtly-love tradition and by the complexity of the friendship literature inherited by the Jacobean writers. Chaucer's *Parliament of Foules*, which Shakespeare clearly knew when he wrote *A Midsummer Night's Dream*, makes much of the contrast between the *gentyl* birds and the *lewd*, or lower-class ones, who are unable to see unselfish, unrequited love as anything but absurd. Reactions to *The Knight's Tale*, likewise, are often motivated by a desire to take sides with either the *gentyl* or the *lewd*. Thomas Wyatt's satire, 'Mine own John Poyns', puts the author firmly on the side of the *gentyl* when he says that he cannot 'Praise Sir Thopas for a noble tale / And scorn the story that the knighte told' (lines 50–1). He must mean not only that he regards Chaucer's story as noble but also that some of his contemporaries found it absurd. There is no indication that any Renaissance reader took the *Tale* to be a satire on chivalry, or on the knight himself, as Terry Jones (*passim*) has argued. Yet the Chaucerian tale most frequently echoed by Spenser is not *The Knight's Tale* but the one that Wyatt presents as its opposite, the burlesque *Sir Thopas* (Burrow, 146). Even before *Don Quixote* reached England (some time in the early seventeenth century, although Shelton's translation of Part 1 was published only in 1611), the literary attitude toward chivalry and courtly love was as ambivalent as that displayed in Chaucer. Beaumont and Fletcher read *Don Quixote* early; they apparently used a French translation as a source for *The Coxcomb* (1608–10) and Fletcher went on to make use of Cervantes in thirteen other plays (McMullan, 259). Yet *Don Quixote* did not destroy the courtly-love tradition. Massinger, Field and Fletcher used a *question d'amour* from Boccaccio's *Filocolo* as the basis of the plot of *The Knight of Malta* (*c*.1618). Like Seneca's *Controversiae*, which Waith has shown to be the source of several Beaumont and Fletcher plays (86–98), these *questions* pose dilemmas about love for the listeners to debate. Hardly changed, they re-emerged in French *précieux* literature, which Fletcher also read assiduously, borrowing from the highly influential *Astrée* (1610), by Honoré D'Urfé, for his comedy *Monsieur Thomas* (*c*.1610–13). Much as Counter-Reformation Catholicism responded to Protestant austerity by making the most of the miraculous and emotional aspects of religion, the romance tradition responded to Cervantes by embracing exaggeration and improbability. The perception that the most idealized sentiments are potentially the most ridiculous is vital to many plays of the period.

The mixed setting of *The Two Noble Kinsmen* – supposedly classical Greece, but based on an acknowledged medieval source – parallels its conflicting attitudes to friendship. As L. J. Mills summarizes them, such classical idealizations as Cicero's *De Amicitia* emphasize the importance of social, intellectual and moral equality between friends; by definition there can be no true friendship between dishonest people (10–14). Conflicts between friends, then, must be conflicts of generosity (as between Damon and Pithias, Orestes and Pylades in Euripides' *Iphigeneia in Tauris*, or Theseus trying to save Hercules who 'saved me from Hades' (Euripides, *The Madness of Hercules*, line 1170). On the other hand, medieval culture was hierarchical and the chivalric code emphasized relations between man and woman more than those between men (Mills, 16–17). As against idealized friendship – a product of leisure and civility – Mills cites examples of sworn brotherhood, which sometimes (as in the tale of *Amis and Amelion*) emphasize the almost identical appearance of the two men, also hinted at in the common plot device of one friend fighting in another's armour. The tale of Titus and Gysippus emphasizes interchangeability to the point where one man can marry the heroine in place of the other.

Montaigne's famous essay on his friendship with La Boétie was clearly in Shakespeare's mind at the time when he wrote *The Two Noble Kinsmen*, but, interestingly enough, he drew on it, not in the relationship of Palamon and Arcite, but in Emilia's dialogue with Hippolyta in 1.3. Waith (Oxf[1], Introduction) has pointed out the importance of this essay; I would add that Shakespeare gives Hippolyta not only the sentiments but even the rhythms of John Florio's translation of Montaigne when she speaks of Theseus and Pirithous:

> Their knot of love,
> Tied, weaved, entangled, with so true, so long,
> And with a finger of so deep a cunning,
> May be outworn, never undone.
>
> (1.3.41–4)

Montaigne had similarly described male friendship as 'the pulling of a knot so hard, so fast, and so durable' (Florio, 1.27, 200) and the way in which two people 'entermixe and confound themselves one in the other, with so universall a commixture, that they weare out, and can no more finde the seame that hath conjoyned them together' (202). (He may have been paraphrasing *De Amicitia* (xxi), which says that when friendships are broken off they should be *dissuendae magis quam discendendae* [unravelled rather than rent apart].) Emilia's account of her childhood friendship with Flavina is an implicit reply to Montaigne's contention that women's minds are not strong enough to tie such a knot as he describes. While the reference to 'fury' (1.3.79) is difficult to understand, the speech as a whole seems to recall Montaigne's adaptation of Plato's concept of same-sex love: 'the first furie, enspired by the son of Venus in the lovers hart, upon the object of tender youths-flower . . . in his infancie, and before the age of budding' (201). Indeed, the oxymoron of 'fury-innocent' may perhaps express something of the period's dual attitude: the idealization of male friendship was combined with what Alan Bray argues was 'extreme hostility' to homosexuality in the abstract but a refusal to recognise it 'in most concrete situations' (Bray, 77).

The two most highly respected English Renaissance writers, Sidney and Spenser, depicted examples of idealized male friendship, but in neither the *Arcadia* nor *The Faerie Queene* does the friendship seriously clash with love. Shakespeare, however, frequently depicts such a clash, as in *The Two Gentlemen of Verona*, and also shows in Sonnet 42 how the notion of interchangeability can allow disloyal friendship to be portrayed as extreme loyalty:

> Loving offenders, thus I will excuse thee:
> Thou dost love her because thou know'st I love her . . .
> But here's the joy, my friend and I are one;
> Sweet flattery! then she loves but me alone.
>
> (*Son* 42: 5–6, 13–14)

Arcite uses the same disingenuous arguments to justify his rivalry with Palamon:

> am not I
> Part of your blood, part of your soul? You have told me
> That I was Palamon and you were Arcite . . . .
> Am not I liable to those affections,
> Those joys, griefs, angers, fears, my friend shall suffer? . . .
> Why then would you deal so cunningly,
> So strangely, so unlike a noble kinsman,
> To love alone?
>
> (2.2.187–94)

In the light of this sophistry, it is hard to see Palamon and Arcite as ideal friends in the same sense as Sidney's Musidorus and Pyrocles in the *Arcadia*, except in so far as their friendship is based on shared excellence in sporting and military competitions. While they are still trying to console each other on their life imprisonment, Arcite makes the common claims for friendship:

> We are an endless mine to one another;
> We are one another's wife, ever begetting
> New births of love; we are father, friends, acquaintance,
> We are, in one another, families;
> I am your heir and you are mine.
>
> (2.2.79–83)

But this is after he has lamented that they will die in prison, 'And, which is heaviest, Palamon, unmarried' (2.2.29). The ideal of perfect, all-inclusive friendship is only constructed afterwards, as a replacement. Moreover, whereas Damon and Pythias or Orestes and Pylades argue over who shall die for the other (Cicero describes a now-lost Orestes play in which this scene brought the audience to its feet with cheers (7.24)), the kinsmen not only try to kill each other but, when Theseus is about to sentence them, Palamon actually asks to see his friend die first, 'That I may tell my soul, he shall not have her' (3.6.179). At such moments, one is tempted to see the play as a parody of friendship literature.

Yet other scenes seem to draw on that very literature. The depiction of the friendship is often genuinely touching, especially in the scenes where the men expect to say farewell to it forever: before the fight in 3.6 and at their parting in 5.1. The strange final scene, which is the dramatists' own conception, may be explained with reference to the philosophy of friendship. Realistically speaking, Theseus' requirement that the losers of the tournament must be beheaded, his assumption that they will want this to happen as soon as possible after their defeat, and his decision not to be present, are either absurd or sadistic. The effect of this series of decisions – apparently considered important enough to justify all the improbabilities – is to make Arcite's victory contingent on Palamon's execution and Palamon's life contingent on Arcite's death. Palamon's unexpected response, as he lifts his head from the block

– 'What / Hath waked us from our dream?' (5.4.47–8) – may simply be an allusion to the sleep of death. But it recalls an equally surprising episode in Book 4 of *The Faerie Queene*, in which Spenser literalizes the topos of *One Soul in Bodies Twain* (the title of Mills' book). Triamond, twice apparently killed in a fight, springs up again from the ground ('As one that had out of a dream been reard' (4.3.31)), because he now possesses the souls of his two dead brothers. As Theseus says to Palamon, immediately after Arcite's death, 'your day is lengthened and / The blissful dew of heaven does arrose you' (5.4.103–4). It is as if his friend's death had indeed given Palamon new life.

Literary reincarnation

Since the story of Triamond is part of Spenser's continuation of Chaucer's unfinished *Squire's Tale*, his poem not only describes but enacts reincarnation, as well as a display of friendship across the centuries. That Renaissance writers thought in these terms is clear from the often-quoted remarks of Francis Meres in 1598: 'As the soule of *Euphorbus* was thought to liue in *Pythagoras*: so the sweete wittie soule of *Ouid* liues in mellifluous and honytongued *Shakespeare*' (*Riv*, 1844). Sidney and Spenser might well have seemed to live again in the second decade of the seventeenth century: Sidney's collected works had their fourth edition in 1613; Spenser's were first published in 1611. The *Arcadia*, unfinished like both *The Squire's Tale* and *The Faerie Queene*, was imitated by Gervase Markham in continuations published in 1607 and 1613. In 1610 Fletcher's cousin, Giles Fletcher the younger, brought out *Christ's Victory and Triumph*, homage to Spenser with frequent evident borrowings from *The Faerie Queene*. Fletcher's friends Drayton and Browne were conscious followers of Spenser and he himself quotes directly from *The Faerie Queene* in *The Woman's Prize* (1.3.27–8) and possibly in *The Two Noble Kinsmen* (4.2.33). Webster's *The Duchess of Malfi*, acted 1613–14, also echoes the *Arcadia* several times.

The Prologue to *The Two Noble Kinsmen* shows that the authors saw themselves in the tradition of other adapters and continuers of earlier literature, and that they recognized the riskiness of the enterprise. The speaker hopes that their tribute to Chaucer will not result in audience hissing that will 'shake the bones' of the dead poet (17) – that is, as one might say now, make him turn in his grave – and force him to 'cry from under ground' at hearing his work so badly imitated. The reference to bones is not purely comic. In *The Duchess of Malfi* Antonio, standing in a ruined cloister, considers the ironic deception of the men buried there, who 'thought it should have canopy'd their bones / Till doomsday' (5.3.16–17) but are now exposed to the harshness of the weather; the same obsession makes the queens in 1.1 of *The Two Noble Kinsmen* harp on the dead bodies lying in the 'foul fields of Thebes'. Whoever wrote the lines carved on Shakespeare's gravestone three years later represented the poet as sharing this common view: 'Bleste be ye man y^t spares thes stones, / And curst be he y^t moves my bones' (*Riv*, 1834). In the context of the play's intense consciousness of its relationship to its source, and to Chaucer's 'bones', one might perhaps see in this epitaph a fear not only of physical exposure but also of literary desecration.

CONTEXTS: THEATRICAL

Staging at the Blackfriars

The burning of the Globe in 1613 may itself have been a source of the kind of uneasiness I have just been describing. Not much property may have been lost, if the company had stored its costumes, playbooks and properties at its other theatre, the Blackfriars, but the building itself was levelled to the ground. Though rebuilding began almost immediately, the new theatre was not ready until June 1614. In the meantime, the players relied on their smaller indoor playhouse. Thus *The Two Noble Kinsmen* must have been one of the few King's Men plays to be written specifically for Blackfriars. (The other most likely candidate is Webster's *The Duchess of Malfi*.) It is therefore the more regrettable that nothing is known about the theatre space itself. Thanks to Irwin Smith's monumental work, however, we do know a good deal about the history of the precinct and the building in which that theatre was constructed.

Blackfriars was built as a Dominican priory in 1286. Even before the dissolution of the monasteries, its buildings had been used for non-ecclesiastical purposes; later, some of the larger rooms were partitioned off to become, for example, fencing schools and private lodgings (Smith, *Blackfriars*, 12–13). Located as it was in the heart of the City of London but free of City jurisdiction because of its ecclesiastical history, Blackfriars was an obviously attractive site for entrepreneurs. A short-lived children's theatre company from 1576 to 1584 converted one of its rooms for acting purposes; the plays performed there included Lyly's comedies. In 1596 James Burbage, hoping to move from his playhouse in the north suburbs of London, acquired part of the Blackfriars property but was prohibited from using it because of a petition of neighbours who were afraid of the noise and disorder. He rented his building to a children's company, which functioned successfully from about 1600 to 1608, until the company dissolved due to a combination of bad management and a controversial repertoire. Burbage profited from its difficulties and from 1609 Blackfriars was the winter home of the King's Men, with the Globe serving as their summer playhouse.

There has been much discussion about how important the acquisition of Blackfriars actually was to writers. After all, *Henry VIII* must surely have been written with an eye to the obvious appropriateness of performing it in the Great Chamber at Blackfriars, the original setting for the divorce trial of Queen Katherine and Henry VIII, but it was almost certainly the play being presented at the Globe in June 1613, when the theatre burned down. If the same plays were given at both theatres, dramatists must have written with both in mind. However, the year that passed between the burning of the Globe and its rebuilding was an exceptional one, and one about which we need to know more. The capacity of Blackfriars has been estimated, by various scholars, at anything from 500 to 900 (Lavin, 80) – at best, only a third of the Globe's capacity. Did the smaller size of the auditorium mean that the King's Men needed to give more performances of the same play in order to accommodate the same public, or did they arrange to perform their most popular plays in another company's playhouse? Did they raise their prices in order to make up for the smaller size of their new audience or did they lower them in order to retain the less wealthy members of their old one? Did the medieval appearance of the buildings have anything to do with the choice of medieval subject-matter, or with scenes like the one in *The Duchess of Malfi* where Antonio, supposedly in the ruins of a cloister, talks about his love for 'these ancient ruins'? Did working in a theatre so strongly associated with the boy actors inspire Shakespeare, as Leah Scragg suggests (117–18), to return to the conscious artificiality of Lyly's plays of the 1580s?

All that is known for certain about the Blackfriars interior is that, unlike the Globe, it was rectangular. Richard Hosley thinks that it had a large two-storey tiring house with plenty of room to erect an inner stage setting such as would have been needed for 5.1 of *The Two Noble Kinsmen*. Its façade was elaborately decorated, and if it really did look like Richard Southern's conjectural drawing (Fig. 2), Blackfriars would have been ideal for plays with a classical setting. The theatre allowed its wealthiest spectators to sit on the stage, a fact that is much commented on and that may have encouraged an intimate atmosphere (Smith, *Blackfriars*, 236).

The traditional contrast between the outdoor playhouse with its natural light and the indoor one with its candlelight is now thought to be exaggerated: the indoor playhouses held performances in the afternoon and, to save candles, must have relied on the light from the windows as much as possible, while the outdoor stage, which seems to have been designed to remain in the shade at all times, may have achieved effective contrasts by using torches and candles for nocturnal scenes (Brown, 1–13). Still, it seems likely that the indoor playhouse made more use of lighting, some of it nocturnal, than the outdoor one. Candles needed trimming and replacing, which in turn meant breaks between the acts while music was played. As has been pointed out (Hosley, 230–1; Taylor & Jowett, 30–42), the result was to create a new emphasis on the five-act structure. *The Two Noble Kinsmen*, as noted earlier, links its various scenes in a way that suggests continuous action, but it also seems to assume a time-lapse between acts. Taylor gives some examples (Taylor & Jowett, 42) and one might add others: for instance, Palamon and Arcite's supposedly terminal wounds heal between Acts 1 and 2; at the start of Act 3, both have been out of

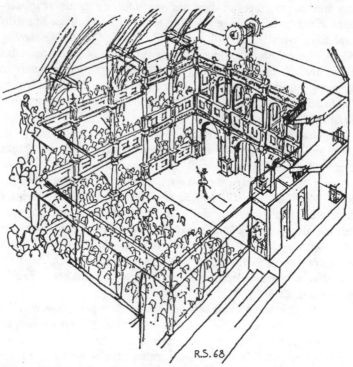

2 The Blackfriars: a conjectural drawing by Richard Southern

prison for some time, Arcite as a member of the court and Palamon
as a starving, manacled fugitive; they journey to Thebes and come
back with their knights in Act 4 while the Jailer's Daughter remains seriously deranged, and Act 5 is taken up with the resolution
of both plots. The Jailer's Daughter has several nocturnal scenes
and it is possible that some of the other scenes in the middle of the
play are meant to be nocturnal, though *The Two Noble Kinsmen*
does not exploit the darkness as much as Webster does in *The
Duchess of Malfi*.

Other features of the Blackfriars might have affected the staging
of *The Two Noble Kinsmen*. The three stage doors which Hosley
hypothesizes (228) would have facilitated the end of Act 1, where

each of the three queens departs with the hearse bearing her husband's body, and perhaps the opening of Act 5: Theseus and his court apparently enter from one door while Palamon and Arcite, each with his knights, presumably come from opposite sides of the stage (though they might also, perhaps, have entered from the auditorium). The central door could have concealed an elaborate altar, or (with the curtains opening and closing between visits) a series of altars to the different gods addressed in 5.1. Alternatively, three different altars might have been used, since that of Diana requires a trap door, more likely to have been positioned in front of the tiring house than within it. This scene also calls for atmospheric, supernatural music, probably from above, in the music room. It does not, apparently, require the descent of any of the three gods addressed in it.

Knowing more about Blackfriars would make it easier to understand the intended staging of the prison scene. Although the quarto stage direction calls for Palamon and Arcite to enter at the start of 2.2, no separate exit is marked for them in 2.1, where they are perceived *above*; some editors cut the entry direction, assuming the action to be continuous. But this would mean the playing of a long scene on a platform which, if Hosley is right, would have been either a curtained music room or a 'shallow area some 6 or 7 feet wide at the foot of one of the boxes of the tiring-house gallery over the stage' (Hosley, 232). Lines 2.1.39–40 indicate that the men are only partly visible from below; if the audience can see them no better than the Jailer can, it will be hard to sustain interest in 2.2, but of course the dialogue between the Jailer and his daughter may be intended to create an illusion of distance between the downstage characters and the prisoners: 2.2 depends on the assumption that the men cannot hear the women talking and that the two women neither see nor hear the men. If the actors did descend to the floor level, they were given very little time in which to do it, even if the Daughter's last line in 2.1 is spoken as a soliloquy to cover their descent. Irwin Smith, noting the plural in the Jailer's 'The windows are too open' (2.2.265), suggests that Palamon and Arcite appeared at two windows above the stage. Alternatively, the 'windows' may simply have meant the curtained space above. The garden where Emilia walks may have required a change of scene, but it would be equally possible (as Richard Proudfoot suggests) for her to enter with her flowers, already gathered, in a basket, as does Marina in *Pericles* (4.1.12 SD).

Casting and repertory

We have no evidence about the original casting of *The Two Noble Kinsmen*. Arguing that the King's Men operated on a strictly hierarchical principle, T. W. Baldwin assigned the roles of Palamon and Arcite to the company's leading actors, John Lowin and Richard Burbage (Baldwin, 201–4). However, at 47 and 40 respectively, they were surely too old for characters whose youth is so often stressed in the text. If *The Two Noble Kinsmen* was being rehearsed at the same time as *The Duchess of Malfi*, in which we know that Burbage and Lowin had the major roles of Ferdinand and Bosola, it would have made sense to cast them in smaller parts (perhaps Theseus and the Jailer, respectively) and take the opportunity to bring on a couple of younger actors. For such a comparatively long play, *The Two Noble Kinsmen* is unusual in its lack of large roles: Palamon's part, the longest in the play, is about half the length of Richard III's.

Also unusual is the large number of female characters. If all were played by boys, as T. J. King assumes in *Casting Shakespeare's Plays* (King 252), *The Two Noble Kinsmen* had more speaking roles for boys than any Shakespeare play since *Richard III*. Even if (as I think) the three queens were acted by men, a large number of boys is still needed for the small non-speaking roles of the nymphs in 1.1, the morris dancers in 3.5, the 'maids' who accompany Emilia at the altar of Diana and the other maid who comes on stage with the Jailer's Daughter in her final scene. Fletcher's plays usually contain a number of good parts for boy actors – the result of his experience with the boys' companies, for which he was still writing at this period. It is clear that the role of the Jailer's Daughter was written for a boy with a real following, perhaps (since he also had to sing) the one who had played Ariel in *The Tempest*. Famous boy actors of women's roles were Richard Robinson, who played the unnamed Lady in *The Second Maiden's Tragedy* in 1611 and Richard Sharpe, the Duchess of Malfi in 1613; either might have played the Daughter or Emilia, in many ways a more difficult role.

The part of the Daughter may even have been written (or expanded) for a talented visitor. Heywood's *Rape of Lucrece* (1608) has a large singing role for a character called Valerius, and the published text refers to songs added by 'the stranger that lately acted Valerius his part'; subsequent editions of this play include still more songs (see Greg, 1.273–4).

All this is assuming that the play always belonged exclusively to Blackfriars and to the King's Men, as the title page states. Perhaps we should also consider other possibilities. The period 1613–14 appears to have been one of fluctuation for theatre companies. The Lady Elizabeth's Men, an adult company, amalgamated in 1613 with the Children of the Queen's Revels, formerly the boy company that had played at Blackfriars, intending to play at both Whitefriars and the Swan (Foakes, 'Playhouses', 31). The alliance seems to have lasted only until the lease on the Swan Theatre ran out in 1614, but this is precisely the period in which *The Two Noble Kinsmen* was probably performed (Middleton's *Chaste Maid in Cheapside*, which requires nine female characters on stage at once, was performed by the amalgamated company during the same year (Richard Proudfoot)). A similar amalgamation – that of the King's Men and the Queen's Men, who normally played at the Red Bull – took place at about the same time. According to Heywood, the two final plays in his epic dramatization of Greek legend, *The Iron Age*, were 'Publickely Acted by two Companies, vppon one Stage at once, and haue at sundry times thronged three seuerall Theaters, with numerous and mighty Auditories' (Greg, 3. 1219). The occasional merging of two companies, or the borrowing of a particularly talented actor by another company, might enable a more spectacular production and help with the sharing of expenses in a slack period.

Both the Queen's Revels and Lady Elizabeth's Men were companies for which Fletcher had previously written. Nathan Field, who has already been mentioned as one of his main collaborators, was a star performer in both, successively; he joined the King's Men in 1616 (*JCS*, 2.434–6), apparently succeeding to Shakespeare's share in the company. Joseph Taylor was also a member of Lady Elizabeth's Men from 1611 until 1616. He joined the King's Men in 1619 and inherited many of the roles formerly played by Richard Burbage, who had died early that year (*JCS*, 2. 590–8), eventually becoming, along with Lowin, the leader of the company. Field and Taylor, both still in their twenties in 1613, sound like the ideal Palamon and Arcite, and must surely have played the parts once they had moved to the King's Men. In *Bartholomew Fair*, where Jonson parodies the *Kinsmen* (see p. 69, below), he makes someone ask which of the puppets is 'Your best Actor. Your *Field*?' (5.3.88). This is a characteristic Jonsonian in-joke, since *Bartholomew Fair* was written for Lady Elizabeth's Men, Field's company. If Field played Winwife, the character who at one point chooses the name Palamon (see p. 70, below), we might guess that he had also played the latter role in the *Kinsmen*. He had been a central figure in the theatre even as a child. Jonson patronized and to some extent helped to educate him; he had acted leading roles in Jonson's early satiric plays for the Children of the Chapel at the age of about 13 and was long remembered for his playing of the romantic and heroic role of Chapman's Bussy d'Ambois. The contemporary portrait (Fig. 3) may be as close as we can get to the kind of actor that Fletcher, at any rate, had in mind for one of his heroes. If Field played Palamon, the prayer to Venus must have taken on an even more cynical tone than has sometimes been suspected, since he had something of a reputation as a cuckold-maker (*JCS*, 3.301). Plans for the play's revival in 1619–20 may have been linked to Taylor's arrival in the company, and may have been affected by Field's early death, which took place some time before August 1620.

The repertory of the King's Men at this period indicates an interest in large-cast classical or medieval plays with music – as is evident from the company's participation in Heywood's mythical extravaganzas. *Pericles* had already shown the effectiveness of ro-mantic and chivalric material presented with a mixture of narrative and pageantry. The author of its source tale, Gower, had acted as chorus for *Pericles*, while Heywood used Homer as his chorus in *The Golden Age*, *The Silver Age* and *The Brazen Age*. The stories of the Olympian gods would have been fresh in the minds of regular theatre-goers even if the wedding masques of 1613 had not made them the focus of attention. *The Knight's Tale* had been the basis both for the famous Oxford production of 1566 and for a version,

3 Nathan Field

also called *Palamon and Arcite*, listed in Henslowe's diary as having four performances at the Rose Theatre between 17 September and 9 November 1594 (Henslowe, 24–5). In all, as Ann Thompson has pointed out, at least thirteen plays, excluding Shakespeare's, were adapted from Chaucerian plots between 1558 and 1625 (Thompson, 17). I have already mentioned Field's use of *The Franklin's Tale* for one of the *Four Plays in One*, and Fletcher himself turned *The Wife of Bath's Tale* into *Women Pleased* (1618).

More specifically, it is interesting to think of the play being rehearsed and performed not long after the court masques of 1613 and more or less alongside Webster's *Duchess of Malfi*. The three masques offered to Frederick and Elizabeth (by George Chapman, Thomas Campion and Beaumont) have so many resemblances that Jerzy Limon has suggested some kind of collusion among the authors (125). For instance, Beaumont had he- and she- baboons in his antimasque; Campion included an entire baboon antimasque, danced by small boys. Campion's main masquers represented stars who turned back into mortal men, while Beaumont's Knight masquers had stars on their armour. Some of these resemblances can be explained by the predictable nature of ceremonial flattery and the predilection of designers for subjects involving metamorphosis. It is hardly surprising that two of the three masques should use the conceit of the marriage of the Thames and the Rhine and depict statues coming to life. The fact that Inigo Jones designed at least two of the masques (we do not know who was responsible for Beaumont's) may also explain their similarities. In any case, the plays produced in the aftermath of these spectacular events show the influence of all three of them, not merely the Beaumont masque of which Fletcher is likely to have heard a good deal. For instance, the emphasis on the pyramid/pillar at the end of *The Two Noble Kinsmen* may recall the obelisk in the final tableau of Campion's 'Lords Masque', where it represented immortal fame. As I have already suggested, the decision to produce Webster's *Duchess of Malfi* may have had casting implications for *Two Noble Kinsmen*. One or both of the co-authors must already have been impressed by Webster's earlier tragedy, *The White Devil* (pub. 1612), with its frequent allusions to Shakespeare and its praise, in the preface, of both Shakespeare and Fletcher. Webster's handling of Vittoria's trial scene was a clear influence on the dramatization of the divorce trial of Katherine of Aragon in *Henry VIII*. Both *The Duchess* and *The Kinsmen* include spectacular religious rites at exotic altars and mad dances; while one reason may be reciprocal influence, both kinds of spectacle had figured largely at court in 1614 (see Appendix 4).

THE PLAY'S AFTERLIFE

Pre-publication allusions

If allusion and parody are a sign of success, the 1613–14 production of *The Two Noble Kinsmen* probably qualifies as one. The
earliest likely allusion occurs in Henry Parrot's *Laquei ridiculosi*, a
collection of epigrams published in 1613 (which, under the Julian
calendar, could be as late as 24th March, 1614):

> Two wooers for a wench were each at strife,
> Which should enjoy her to his wedded wife:
> Quoth th'one, shee's mine, because I first her saw,
> Shee's mine, quoth th'other, by *Pye-corner* law;
>   Where, sticking once a *Prick* on what you buy
>   It's then your owne, which no man must deny.
>
>   (no. 3, B1ᵛ)

Parrot alludes to *Hamlet* in his subtitle, *Springes to Catch Wood-
cocks*, and in a previous book, *The Mouse Trap* (1606), so it is probably not just coincidence that this epigram recalls part of another
play, the confrontation in 2.2 between Palamon, who 'saw her first'
and Arcite, who wants to 'enjoy her'. This scene has always been
successful in modern productions; the epigram may be evidence
that it was equally memorable to its first audiences.

Ben Jonson's reaction seems to have been similar to Parrot's. He
had been on the Continent, as tutor to Sir Walter Raleigh's son,
during the events of 1612 and early 1613, but seems to have begun
writing *Bartholomew Fair* shortly after his return in June 1613;
some friends heard him read aloud from the scene of the puppets
in June or July that year, at which time it was taken primarily as a
satire on Inigo Jones (Riggs, 193). In its present, probably revised, form, the play's final scene may well parody *The Two Noble
Kinsmen* in its ridiculous puppets, Damon and Pythias, who share a
single 'drab' between them and constantly fight and make up.
Jonson may have been interested in the play because of its Chaucerian source: he owned and annotated a copy of the 1602 Chaucer
(now at the Folger Shakespeare Library). It has been suggested
(Chambers, 3.314) that the 'two faithful friends o' the Bankside'

(6:5.3.9–10) parody not only Palamon and Arcite but also Beaumont and Fletcher and their shared 'wench' (see p. 10, above). However, the satire could equally apply to a Shakespeare and Fletcher collaboration, or indeed to the triangulated situation depicted in Shakespeare's sonnets, first published in 1609. As Clements points out (4–5), the parody extends to the main plot of Jonson's play: Grace Welborn, stopping the fight between Winwife and Quarlous, points out to them the absurdity of their situation. Echoing Theseus' words to Emilia, 'They cannot both enjoy you' (3.6.274), she declares, 'If you both love me, as you pretend, your own reason will tell you but one can enjoy me' (6:4.3.7–8). Refusing to choose between two men about whom she knows nothing, she devises a comic variation on fate: each of them is to write a name on a piece of paper and she will then ask the next passer-by to choose between them. The successful lover, Winwife, chooses the name Palemon (*sic*), which he says he is taking 'out of the play'. There is no doubt that he means *The Two Noble Kinsmen*; the only other dramatic character proposed is the Palaemon of Daniel's Oxford play, *The Queen's Arcadia* (1610), meaningless in the context of a public performance in 1614. Since Jonson was professedly fond of Fletcher (Jonson, 1.137), the parody need not be taken as anything more than further evidence that the play had aroused interest and, perhaps, controversy.

Jonson also seems to refer to the play's Prologue in an epithalamion sent to the Earl of Somerset on his wedding morning in December 1613. In 1614 he contributed commendatory verses to an anonymous poem called *The Husband*, a sequel and companion-piece to Thomas Overbury's *The Wife*. Punning on the two titles, he concluded by assuring *The Wife* that her *Husband* was 'such, as (if my word will waigh) / Shee need not blush vpon the *Mariage-Day*' (Jonson, 8.386). The apparent echo of the Prologue's line 4 may be mere coincidence, but it is possible that, like Parrot, Jonson was particularly struck by the play's emphasis on sexuality.

Evidence for the play's stage history before the closing of the theatres in 1642 is literally fragmentary. A scrap of paper in the Revels Office (reprinted in Bentley, 1) indicates that it was one of a number of plays being considered for performance at court in 1619–20. A Red Bull play dated 1619–23 is called *The Two Noble*

Ladies and the Converted Conjuror. Since the two noble ladies are not its main subject, it is possible that its title was chosen in response to the revival of the Blackfriars play. The occurrence of the names of two hired men (Tucke and Curtis) in stage directions at 4.2.70 and 5.3.0 of the quarto suggests that it had a further revival in 1625–6, the only period at which both these actors belonged to the King's Men.

The main influence of these revivals seems to have been felt (as Proudfoot has noted) by Fletcher's friend and collaborator, Philip Massinger. For instance, one speech of his *Believe as You List* (1631) closely imitates two passages from Shakespearean scenes (1.3.6–8 and 1.2.7–12):

> though I knowe
> the Ocean of your apprehensions needes not
> the rivelet of my poore cautions . . .
> > wee with ease
> swimme downe the streame, but to oppose the torrent
> is dangerous, and to goe more or lesse
> then wee ar warranted fatall.
>
> > > (5.1.161–3, 171–4)

Massinger became the leading dramatist for the King's Men after Fletcher's death in 1625. Since *Believe as You List* was licensed in 1631, before the printing of *The Two Noble Kinsmen*, he must either have had access to a manuscript of the play or have remembered the lines from performance. Richard Brome's *The Lovesick Count* (not printed until 1659) might derive from the printed text; as Charles Forker has pointed out (161–4), it offers an idealized version of the conflict and provides a happy ending.

Publication history

In publishing *The Two Noble Kinsmen* in 1634, with the title page's curious stress on the gentility of both authors, John Waterson may have hoped to profit from the growing prestige and popularity of Shakespeare and Fletcher at the Caroline court. It was this prestige that, as I noted above (pp. 16–17), made the 1647 folio so important in a royalist context. The publisher Humphrey Moseley acquired the rights to the play in 1646, and entered it in the Stationers' Register as 'by John Flesher'. As he said later in the preface to the Beaumont and Fletcher folio, it had been his original intention to publish a volume of plays authored by Fletcher alone, and perhaps this entry was intended to prepare the way for the inclusion of *The Two Noble Kinsmen* in a 'Fletcher' volume. Instead, he brought out a folio of *Comedies and Tragedies written by Francis Beaumont and John Fletcher*, and left out all plays previously published, including the *Kinsmen*. Supposedly his motive was to keep down the price and size of the book, but he may have decided that obtaining the copyrights of published works was going to be too expensive.

It was thus only in the second Beaumont and Fletcher folio of 1679 that the play finally appeared, along with seventeen others new to the collection. Though the editors claimed to have received corrections and additions from someone who had seen the plays before the war, there is no evidence of such expert help with this play: it has merely had its spelling and punctuation slightly modernized, with the addition of a *Dramatis Personae* which omits some characters and incorrectly describes others. For instance, Hippolyta and Emilia are called 'Sisters to Theseus' and 'three [not six] valiant Knights' are listed immediately after the three queens, as if these characters had been intended to pair off. By now, the so-called 'Beaumont and Fletcher canon' included some fifty plays. The 1711 edition, a handsome set of illustrated volumes published by Tonson, used the 1679 folio as its copy text. Even the most obvious misprints (like 'Clough hee' in the opening song) remain uncorrected; the list of *Dramatis Personae*, now divided into male and female characters, is still inaccurate.

Though Beaumont and Fletcher's popularity declined after the early years of the Restoration, when they were said to be acted more often than Shakespeare or Jonson (Dryden, 1.69), their continuing importance can be seen from their subsequent editorial history. After the success of Lewis Theobald's Shakespeare edition of 1734, he advertised for co-editors of a Beaumont and Fletcher edition. Two clergymen, Thomas Seward and Thomas Sympson, responded, and, since Theobald died in 1744, they did most of the editing. Seward had special responsibility for *The Two Noble Kinsmen*, but exchanged correspondence about it with his colleagues, so all three men are credited with readings in the edition which finally appeared in 1750. Theobald had a copy of the 1634 quarto, but Seward apparently did not receive it until he had spent an inordinate amount of time with the inaccurate 1711 edition, conjecturing readings which eventually turned out to have been in the quarto all along. Instead of keeping quiet about the difficulties of the editorial process, he openly discussed it in his notes in a way that exposed him to the ridicule of later readers. Yet he and his colleagues originated most of the important corrections to the quarto. His attempts at regularizing the metre by abbreviating, eliding and even rewriting the text, though often ridiculed later, merely took up where the 1679 editors had left off (see p. 123 below). His edition is certainly preferable to that of 1778, vaguely supervised by George Colman the elder, which ridicules Seward even while quoting and borrowing from him at length.

Real scholarship begins with the nineteenth-century editors. Much of what Henry Weber did in 1812, such as his careful listing of locations for all the scenes, has been equally carefully undone by his successors. But he also provides a fair discussion of the authorship debate, scrupulously printing in full the views even of editors with whom he disagreed, such as George Steevens (see p. 19, above). Alexander Dyce provided still more material, particularly on the biographies of the authors, in his Beaumont and Fletcher edition (1843); Harold Littledale's New Shakespere Society edition (1876) offered a survey of recent and contemporary opinion on the authorship question which is unlikely to be superseded. By this time, the play was appearing in collected editions of Shakespeare. Dyce re-edited it for his complete Shakespeare in 1866 and C. F. Tucker Brooke for the *Shakespeare Apocrypha* of 1908. By 1936, the date of G. L. Kittredge's popular *Complete Works*, the play was silently accepted as part of the canon, though it still does not appear in all collections.

Seward originally wanted his 1750 edition to be an expurgated one but was dissuaded by his publisher (Seward, 1.lvi). However, Charles Knight, the first to include the play in an edition of Shakespeare (*c*.1839–41), did so only after cutting it. His footnote to 2.3, where he omitted lines 32–6, explains that Fletcher's 'grossnesses', unlike Shakespeare's, 'are the result of impure thoughts, not the accidental reflection of loose manners'. W. W. Skeat (1875), W. J. Rolfe (1883) and W. R. Thayer (1890) also expurgated their texts. Their constant stress on the difference between Shakespeare and his contemporaries can be explained by the fact that they were not so much reading Shakespeare as recalling the expurgated Shakespeare they had seen performed in interpretations that emphasized pathos and nobility.

Because of uneasiness about the indecency of Beaumont and Fletcher, they were often felt to be more fitly represented by extracts. Charles Lamb's *Specimens of the English Dramatic Poets Who Lived about the Time of Shakespeare*, first published in 1808, became the model for most later volumes of this kind. Lamb, who thought that Fletcher and Massinger were 'the only dramatic poets of that age who are entitled to be considered after Shakespeare' (Lamb, xii), chose the first scene, from the entrance of the three queens to line 219; Emilia's speech about her childhood friendship (1.3.49–82); and 2.2.1–110. A change in moral climate is at once apparent from the title page of Leigh Hunt's 1855 collection, devoted exclusively to Beaumont and Fletcher but excluding '*whatever is Morally Objectionable* in their works'. 'They were authors destined to survive only in fragments', he contended (xv). His selections (for the most part, the same as Lamb's) are captioned like poems to show how they are meant to be taken: 1.1. is called 'Affliction Must be Served Before Joy'; 1.3 is 'Girl's Friendship'; he also gives the prayers to Mars and Diana (but not, of course, the one to Venus), and 5.4 beginning from Pirithous' entrance. Exactly the same passages were selected by J. S. Fletcher for his anthology in 1887, which even borrowed most of Hunt's titles, though for 2.2 he invented his own, the unlikely 'Love's Reconciliation'. Neither of these scrupulous editors had any qualms about anthologizing passages concerning intense same-sex friendships.

Adaptation and performance before 1900

The Prologue to *The Two Noble Kinsmen* became the basis for an anonymous 'Prologue to a Reviv'd Play' printed in *Covent Garden Drollery* for 1672, which begins, 'Old Playes like Mistresses, long since enjoy'd, / Long after please, whom they before had cloy'd'

(Thorn-Drury, 83). This Prologue can be dated to the early years of the Restoration by its topical reference to the Act of Uniformity (1662). It seems likely, then, that the 'Reviv'd Play' was *The Rivals*, an adaptation of *The Two Noble Kinsmen* first performed in 1664 and published anonymously, without prologue or epilogue, in 1668. Gerard Langbaine (547) records in 1691 that he had heard it ascribed to Sir William Davenant, playwright and manager of one of the two theatres established at the Restoration, and no one has ever questioned this attribution. Davenant's theatrical career began in the late 1620s and he may well have seen the play performed. Presumably he thought of it as a success, like the others that he reworked in the same period: *Macbeth*, *The Tempest*, and a conflation of *Measure for Measure* and *Much Ado About Nothing*. The adaptation is important (and is sometimes cited in the notes to this edition) because it shows how the text was understood by someone who may have drawn on recollections of its pre-war staging.

Davenant obviously knew the classical background to Chaucer's tale (his equivalent to Pirithous is called Polynices), but he deliberately detached the play both from *The Knight's Tale* and from legend, changed the names of all the characters and set it in Arcadia. He was equally free with the plot, obviously sensing that *The Two Noble Kinsmen*, once its Chaucerian and classical sources are forgotten, has more potential for comedy than for tragedy. Cutting most of Act 1, he begins as the Arcadians return from war against the tyrant Harpacus, proud to have defeated him despite their reputation for loving only 'Pastoral delights'. The opening scene has verbal echoes of Davenant's recent adaptation of *Macbeth* (see Spencer, *SQ*), but Harpacus, like all stage tyrants of the early Restoration, is also a thinly disguised Cromwell and the Arcadians are idealized royalists. In the greatly reduced cast, Argon (Theseus) is elderly and unmarried, so his sister Heraclia (Emilia) is his only heir. The Jailer is elevated to a Provost (Davenant was probably recalling *Measure for Measure*) and his daughter acquires a name (Celania). The entertainment in the forest is very much extended; morris dancers appear – here introduced by a 'country poet' – and, in another part of the forest, there is 'a hunt in music'. Celania does not take part in the dance but sings a number of songs, though not those in the original play. Her madness is caused not by sexual frustration but by Heraclia's thoughtless decision to test her love by saying that she thinks Philander (Palamon) will be put to death – a lie that makes Celania take the decision to free him. Philander, at first afraid to place her and her father in danger by his escape, manages to talk himself into belief in the nobility of his motives, though, unlike Palamon, he shows uneasiness about hers: 'I hope 'tis pity, but I fear 'tis love' (Act 2, p. 23). By contrast with Celania, Heraclia is so thoroughly rational that she would rather let both men die than injure either of them by choosing the other. Argon is sure that 'Affection never hovers betwixt two' (Act 5, p. 49), but is unable to discover her hidden preference or to establish either man's moral superiority to the other. Since all the characters are both honourable and rational, and Celania is not an unsuitable match for Philander, a happy ending can take place as soon as all four lovers decide where honour requires them to direct their affections. Naturally, there is no Wooer and no Doctor; Celania's maid and the latter's long-suffering suitor provide comic relief instead.

Davenant's version influenced later adaptations. Richard Cumberland's *Palamon and Arcite, or The Noble Kinsmen. Alter'd from Beaumont & Fletcher* (see Dircks) may be the same as *Love and Valour, or the Two Noble Kinsmen*, described as a tragedy, which was produced at Richmond Theatre in 1779, or it may date from later in his career; I incline to think it an early play, as Cumberland wrote two Massinger adaptations at the same period. The surviving MS (British Library Add MS 25,990) looks like a hastily written draft submitted for consideration by a theatre manager. Cumberland, a humanitarian and sentimental dramatist, removed both anti-feminist passages and those (like 1.3.18–25) that made Hippolyta and Emilia seem too 'Amazonian'. Like Davenant, he raises the social status of the Daughter (here called Celia), but he does not use the change to create a happy ending: Celia's madness is not cured, and she dies offstage. Despite their grief over Arcite's death, Emilia and Palamon are happy at the end, as she has had a preference for him from the start. But the play (with neither morris dance nor schoolmaster) is much more unequivocally tragic than its predecessor.

A more successful adaptation by the actor-dramatist Francis Godolphin Waldron, *Love and Madness; or, The Two Noble Kinsmen,* was performed at the Theatre Royal, Haymarket, in September 1795 (its title may allude to a play called *Love and Money*, performed at the same theatre in the previous month). Never printed, it survives in manuscript (Larpent no. 1094, in the Huntington Library). Waldron, best known for his completion of Jonson's *Sad Shepherd* (1783), reworked the play thoroughly and on the whole skilfully, adding so many songs as to make it virtually a comic opera. The songs have music by Samuel Arnold; their sources range from Davenant himself to Milton's 'On a May Morning'. A genuine liking for the play is evident in Waldron's treatment. His choice of Hermia as the name for the Jailer's Daughter is only one of several indications that his main inspiration is *A Midsummer Night's Dream*. Like Davenant, he begins with Act 2, omitting Hippolyta and Pirithous (Emilia's part benefits from the addition of some of their lines), and raises Hermia to a social level suitable for Palamon. Since he then needs to make Emilia and Arcite more obviously destined for each other, Waldron redistributes the speeches in the prison scene so that Arcite is the one who sees her first and speaks most passionately about her. He is younger than Palamon, who can thus complain with some justice that 'You play the child extremely'. It is Palamon, not Arcite, who later has the premonition that 'I never shall enjoy her', and it is he who prays to Mars, Arcite to Venus.

In the final scene an offstage fight, followed by each man gallantly insisting that he does not deserve the prize, is about to culminate in Palamon's execution when the mad Hermia rushes in. When she invokes the old custom that allows a maid to redeem a man from death on condition that he marry her, Palamon responds with refreshing common sense:

> Is it in man to spurn such proffer'd beauty,
> And rush instead, i'th' arms of griesly death?
> No! 'tis too much! . . . .
> Forgive me, bright Emilia!

For the sake of completeness, it may be worth noting that a few lines of *The Two Noble Kinsmen* appear, rather incongruously, in *Edward the Black Prince, or, She Never Told Her Love*, produced at

Drury Lane in 1828 (British Library Add MS 42,889). Frederic Reynolds adapted the plots of several Jacobean plays, particularly *Philaster* and *Bonduca*, to create this anti-French historical farrago. The hero, played by William Charles Macready, goes temporarily mad when he thinks his page and mistress are betraying him, and his soliloquy includes a few words recognizably belonging to the Jailer's Daughter. That Reynolds used no more of the play is curious; perhaps he was recalling the lines rather than transcribing them. Despite Macready and his co-star Ellen Tree, the play was unsuccessful and a reviewer in the *Examiner* (3 Feb. 1828, 67–8) objected to 'this eternal attempt to raise the irrecoverably defunct'. No further stagings are recorded during the rest of the century. The editor of *Punch*, Shirley Brookes, did however turn the plot into a story for *The Gentleman's Magazine* in 1869, carefully removing (though rather archly hinting at) the features that might make it unsuitable for family reading.

Twentieth-century productions

The Two Noble Kinsmen used to have no performance history at all. Now, however, full accounts are available in readily accessible sources: Metz ('*TNK*'), Richmond, Hamlin and Waith (Oxf[1]). I shall therefore deal briefly with productions already discussed by others, concentrating mainly on those not previously mentioned and those I myself have been able to see.

It is in production, above all, that the problem of the play's conflicting generic codes becomes most apparent. Most early revivals seem to have emphasized its pretty, fairy-tale qualities, presenting it as homage to Chaucer and a celebration of merrie England. The 1928 Old Vic production, with its medieval setting, was described (favourably on the whole) as 'an experiment in prettiness' (Birrell), or 'a fragrant, wholly unreal romance of chivalry' (S.R.L.). This revival had a strong cast – Ernest Milton and Eric Portman as Palamon and Arcite, Jean Forbes-Robertson as the Jailer's Daughter. Even so, reviewers assumed that such laughs as it got, particularly in the scenes between Palamon and Arcite, must be unintentional or the result of deliberate burlesque. Fifty years of amateur productions followed, all of them apparently in agreement with the idea of prettiness. In 1949 John Masefield, who had been asked to recommend a poetic play for amateurs who wanted to tour England with a production suitable for an all-male cast, recommended *The Two Noble Kinsmen* and wrote a letter of advice, stressing the need for visual beauty: 'Make your setting a gay flower garden . . . Use music wherever you can' (Masefield, 190).

The two earliest American productions, at least so their directors believed, were at Antioch and Harvard in 1955 (see Metz, '*TNK*', 65). In Britain, the BBC Radio production of 1956 (Tony Britton and Douglas Wilmer as the kinsmen, Marjorie Westbury as the Jailer's Daughter) may have encouraged renewed interest in the late 1950s. Two open-air productions were praised, again, for their beauty. In June 1957, Nevill Coghill and Ed Taylor, in Merton College Gardens, Oxford, directed a number of actors who, like the *Palamon and Arcite* performers of 1566, later became well known in other professions. A 1959 Reading University Drama Society production was remembered for the dance, the maypole ribbons, the torches after dark, the red rose on Diana's altar, and the swans that appeared on the river at the end (Gibbs, Regan, *The Times*). To provide even more spectacle, the tournament was staged in the distance as Emilia waited directly in front of the audience. However, most reviewers liked the comic parts best and felt that the play did not really start to work until the prison scene – a comment made of nearly every revival (see Richmond, 182). There was modest enthusiasm for the 'picturesque natural setting' of the production by the drama department at the University of Bristol (Ford), and for the brick stable of Saltram House, Plymouth, where the Interluders of Hertford achieved considerable success by making the two kinsmen look like Laurel and Hardy (Cottis). As with the 1928 production, reviewers were certain that the main plot had no *intentional* humour in it.

The 1970s interest in sexual and theatrical experimentation resulted in a new response to the play. Richard Digby Day directed it (York Theatre Royal 1973, Regent's Park 1974) in a spacious, timeless setting with visual emphasis on white and verbal emphasis on innocence. The white balloons mentioned in most reviews (the 'sign' given by Venus after Palamon's prayer) were an appropriate image for the lightness and fragility of the kinsmen's youthful idealism, which I remember as the most touching feature of the production. The morris dance was cut – it would have been hard to fit into this context – and the unrealistic setting, with its touches of orientalism, hinted at some kind of philosophy of detachment.

Dance and ritual, as Waith notes (Oxf[1], 36–7), were the dominant features of this and of several other productions of the period, such as the one at the Los Angeles Globe Playhouse (1979), which won awards for director Walter Scholz and for Suzanne Peters as the Jailer's Daughter. In the same year two other productions explored the dark side of the play's sexuality. The all-male Cherub Theatre version by Andrew Visnevski (Edinburgh Festival and Young Vic, London) was very different from John Masefield's imaginary all-male troupe. In black leather and chains, with cod-pieces for the men and the Amazons' sex designated by red and white circles painted round their nipples, the characters alternated 'spasms of fighting and kissing' (Lee). The model was not *A Midsummer Night's Dream* but *Hamlet*, both in the madness of the Jailer's Daughter and in the temple scene, where Arcite hesitated over whether to kill Palamon while the latter was praying to Venus (J.E.H.). Reviewers responded favourably to this bitter, violent production, though they tended to assume that it was offering a subversive reading of the text rather than responding to its potential: 'The actors form pictures of the brutality of passion onstage, while the bobbing pentameters tell of the idealism, the romantic folly, and the love of fair Emilia' (Hardy). Still more tragic in tone was the modern–dress French version, *Les Deux Nobles Cousins* (translated by Véronique Réaud), performed in 1979 by the Centre Dramatique de Courneuve. Heavily cut, it compressed the Daughter's madness into one scene combining 3.5 and 4.3 and turned the Wooer's speech about her attempted suicide into an account of her death (her body was carried on as he spoke). The production, as director Pierre Constant explained in the annual report of the French Shakespeare Society, treated the play as a conflict between homosexual and heterosexual love, a search for the absolute that takes place mainly in the Dionysiac woods. The ending is tragic for the Daughter and Emilia because society forces people to choose between possible kinds of love, whereas harmony might result if a triangular, bi-sexual relationship could be made to work (Constant, 30).

Probably the most successful attempt at making the play interesting to a non-specialist theatre audience was Julian Lopez-
Morillas' production for the Berkeley Shakespeare Festival in the
summer of 1985. It was performed in repertory with *A Midsummer
Night's Dream*, with significant cross-casting: the same Theseus
and Hippolyta appeared in both plays; Hermia and Lysander were
Emilia and Arcite, with Helena (Nancy Carlin) reappearing as the
Jailer's Daughter. In a particularly interesting cameo, the role of
the Doctor was taken by Dakin Matthews, who had previously
played Oberon; here, too (Fig. 4), he worked love-magic as a blind,
eccentric, but occasionally wise quack (the 'blind priest' to whom
the Daughter tauntingly refers at 5.2.78), his tattered clothes hung
with bottles and pouches containing mysterious potions. The
medieval costumes were functional rather than romantic. User-
friendly devices included cutting, ingenious but simple staging,
and the frequent enlivening of mainly verbal scenes with comple-
mentary or supplementary action. In the difficult 1.2, Palamon and
Arcite held the audience's attention by fighting as they talked;
when Emilia was comparing the portraits, each of the two men was
visible to the audience; and the tournament was staged in slow-
motion dumbshow while she spoke her agonized monologue. The
director stressed the youth of the four lovers, and the tone of the
first part of the play was mainly comic. As the chivalric code closed
its trap on the characters, it became apparent that all the conventions, however silly, were going to lead to someone's death.
Only the Daughter's story balanced the tragedy with an essentially
positive ending. Very young for her age, this Daughter confided her
soliloquies to a rag doll (Fig. 5) and her madness was part of the
trauma of growing up, from which emerged the 'ruefully humorous pathos' that Hugh Richmond considers to be the play's dis-
tinguishing tone (Richmond, 183).

The 1986 Royal Shakespeare Theatre production by Barry Kyle
attempted to recreate the sense of a warrior society (largely Japanese in its imagery) with elaborate rituals of love and war. Like all
RSC productions, it was extensively reviewed; a full range of opinions can be seen in *The London Theatre Record* for 1986 and, when
the play transferred to the Mermaid in London, for 1987. Though
some found the stylization confusing, I agree with Roger Warren

4 The Doctor (Dakin Matthews) and Wooer (Robert Sicular): Berkeley
Shakespeare Festival production, 1985

(83–4) that Kyle had thought intelligently about the play and faced
most of its issues, matching the difficult Shakespearean speeches
with highly stylized costumes and delivery, while also doing justice
to the more naturalistic subplot and the less stylized parts of the
main plot. These two plots were strongly linked through imagery
that made the most of the sexual ritual of the morris and the references to horses: in 3.5, the Jailer's Daughter rode in upon a phallic
maypole that spewed out long, white silk ribbons (referred to in
rehearsal as the 'ejaculation' (RSC, 'Promptbook')) and was later
seen in a bridle which served as her straitjacket (Fig. 6). Paul

5 The Jailer's Daughter (Nancy Carlin): Berkeley, 1985

6 The Jailer's Daughter (Imogen Stubbs), bridled like a horse, with the Doctor (John Rogan): RSC at the Mermaid Theatre, London, 1987

Barry's version at the New Jersey Shakespeare Festival was also staged in 1986; Waith (Oxf[1]) objected to the heavy cutting (the play began with 1.4), and some of the conflation of roles, but found that the Daughter's scenes and the young men's arming of each other worked admirably.

The amateur production given (in English) in April 1986 as part of the 350th anniversary celebrations of the University of Utrecht was original enough to be an exception to my general rule of discussing only professional interpretations. The director, Wijbrand Shaap, framed the play as the dream or fantasy of a twentieth-century youth who becomes Palamon – in a Renaissance Italian tunic which he finds embarrassingly short – while a tourist poster of Hercules, advertising Thebes, comes to life to become Arcite. Since the play was interpreted as a parody of Chaucer, it embraced rather than suppressed the potential comedy, sometimes going for frankly silly laughs such as the Wooer's stammering on the letter 'P' in his account of the Daughter's obsession with Palamon. Pirithous' over-enthusiastic responses to men and manliness turned 4.2 into a competition in upstaging, with Theseus almost acting out the descriptions in his effort to visualize them; the Messenger was a woman, clearly infatuated with the knights she described. In the final scene Palamon's grief at 'loss of dear love' (5.4.112) was taken seriously, but the audience was invited to laugh at the abruptness of the transition from tragedy to comedy, at the dropping of the lights as soon as Arcite died, and at Theseus' casual decision to mourn for him 'a day or two'. But there were also effective quiet moments like Emilia's 'Is this winning?' (5.3.138), and Palamon's 'What / Hath waked us from our dream?' (5.4.47–8). At the end Theseus spoke, in Dutch, the opening lines of *A Midsummer Night's Dream*; the Daughter had also babbled some of Ophelia's lines as part of her mad scene. It seemed to me that the production was suggesting a dream-like, sometimes absurd, relation between the play and its sources. I know of only one other production in a non-English-speaking country. In 1988 the play (partly rewritten by the director, the poet Gavin Bantock) was performed in English by the Lear Society of Reitaku University in Tokyo.

Of the three professional American versions in 1993–4, two were fringe productions with limited resources; nevertheless each found ways of illuminating at least part of the story. Rather than attempt to create a unified concept, Beth F. Milles directed it (for Falstaff Productions, New York, October 1993) to emphasize the sharp tonal contrasts between characters and scenes. The three queens were heavily stylized: they sometimes spoke antiphonally, sang in chorus in 1.5 and reappeared at the beginning of 5.1 with a small fire, looking like the witches in *Macbeth*. Act 2 began on a more casual note with the Jailer and Wooer fishing from one side of the upper stage level while, on the other, Arcite and Palamon were being chained to the ceiling and floor by their hands and feet; Palamon's opening 'How do you, noble cousin?' (2.2.1) was inevitably comic. When the Daughter went mad, an onstage guitarist accompanied her singing. She was present during some of the scenes involving other characters and her singing could be heard behind the combat between Palamon and Arcite in 3.6, as if to parallel her insanity with theirs. Emilia sang too, opening the second half of the performance with Sonnet 47 ('Betwixt mine eye and heart a league is took'). The Doctor, first seen as a shadow on the wall, was a mock-sinister figure, arrogant and mystifying. His powers, whatever they were, were not needed, since in 5.2 the production adopted a familiar romantic-comedy cliché: the Wooer, removing his glasses, turned from Clark Kent into Superman; he and the Daughter were already kissing by the end and needed no further encouragement from the Doctor. Heavy cutting and the lack of spectacle in 5.1 meant that the offstage events of 5.3 and 5.4 seemed even more abrupt than in the original play. The arbitrariness of the final changes of fortune seemed to be the point, but the absurdity was not, as at Utrecht, treated comically.

Eleanor Holdridge's studio production for the Red Heel Company in Philadelphia (November 1993) had so small a cast that much of the play had to be cut or reshaped, but what was left had a unified, lyrical tone, often with music in the background. A fountain dominated the stage. The cast began by dancing around it in dappled light; people washed their faces in it; and the Daughter looked into it when she imagined the shipwreck. Hippolyta and Emilia were costumed as Amazons, while Palamon and Arcite looked like figures in manuscript illuminations. The production gave Emilia and Hippolyta a close relationship (especially since it was Hippolyta who accompanied Emilia into the garden in 2.2). The Jailer's Daughter, an apologetically giggling blonde with flowers in her hair, was alarming in her madness, touching in 5.2, and mad (still) at the end. The extensive doubling, which sometimes made it difficult to know whether an actor was appearing in a new role or a new facet of a previous one, was exploited to create a sense of the play's ritualistic quality.

The 1994 Oregon Shakespeare Festival production at Ashland, directed by Nagle Jackson, looked at first sight like a return to the medieval fairy-tale tradition: there was a lot of pageantry, including a remarkably authentic morris dance complete with hobby horse, and the women's dresses had deliberately impractical long trains and long scalloped sleeves. It was impossible to imagine either Emilia or Hippolyta as an Amazon, nor was either character given the kind of feminist reading that struck reviewers of the RSC production; in fact, the actress playing Emilia (Robin Goodrin Nordli) thought of her character as a 'failed Amazon'. As in many productions, Act 1 had difficulty holding the audience, but in Act 2 the Daughter's obvious infatuation, the tongue-tied Wooer's helpless attempts at making conversation with her (Fig. 7), and the subsequent extravagances of the kinsmen's friendship evoked the romantic-comedy conventions with which the audience felt more comfortable. But these conventions were constantly undermined. The almost operatic singing of Corliss Preston as the Daughter made her songs into extra-dramatic display pieces; she became frighteningly, not prettily, mad, threatening Gerald and the countrymen with the knife she had brought in order to file off Palamon's fetters. As at the RSC, Ashland connected the Daughter's experience of the morris with her later obsession about Palamon's sexual potency, emphasizing the sexuality of the dancers (especially the suggestively costumed Bavian) and their cavortings on their way home at the beginning of 4.1. The Daughter fell asleep on stage between 3.2 and 3.4; at the end of 3.3, she awoke with a cry and Palamon, though he faintly heard it, did not go back to investigate. His reference to her as 'A right good creature' (5.4.34) was spoken aside, as if he had intuited something about 'the road not taken' in his wanderings through the woods. Spectators during the interval frequently speculated how the play would end; they never guessed right, and were never happy with the ending, which jarred with expectations created by the fairy-tale beauty of the staging.

Particularly effective in this production was the delicate balancing of the audience's sympathy between Palamon and Arcite. This

7 The Jailer's Daughter (Corliss Preston) and her Wooer (Mark Murphey): Ashland, 1994

relationship is probably what most distinguishes one production from another. At Berkeley and the RSC the two men were strongly contrasted (Figs 8 and 9). Lopez-Morillas took the view that each lover prayed to the god who represented the qualities he most needed: thus, the courtly Arcite asked Mars for help while the wiry, aggressive Palamon prayed to Venus. At the RSC the casting of a black actor as Arcite recalled the film cliché where the non-white hero dies heroically just in time to evade an awkward plot complication. In both these productions the spectators' sympathy on the whole was with Arcite; they were alienated by Palamon's paranoid suspicions in 2.2 and 3.3, as well as by his insistence that Theseus should execute Arcite first. By contrast, New York made Arcite essentially unromantic, and in Philadelphia he was a slow but formidable giant, who delivered his prayer to Mars sword in hand; when Palamon threw down his weapon at the beginning of his prayer to Venus, openly renouncing all expectation of winning by force, audience sympathy shifted to him. At Ashland, the men's youth, their naive charm, and the resemblance created by their hairstyles (Fig. 10) emphasized the problem of deciding between them. Their first scene, heavily cut, gained momentum by showing them about to escape from the corruptions of Thebes – Arcite eager to go, Palamon more inclined to discuss the issue – until news of the impending war forced them to remain. The scene in which they drink to 'the wenches we have known' (3.3) was played, effect-ively, as a comic competition in aggression, with each man trying to prove the other unworthy of Emilia. Only in the temple scene did the balance clearly shift toward Palamon, as Arcite took on the frightening qualities of the god he worshipped. His shouted prayer to Mars contrasted with Palamon's gentle appealing address to Venus (helped, admittedly, by careful cutting). Yet the playing of 5.3 restored the balance. Emilia was totally exhausted and despair-ing by the time the royal party entered from the field; Arcite, though the victor, was physically and emotionally drained, and the couple could not bring themselves to follow Theseus' urging and join hands (Fig. 11). Then Emilia realized that Arcite was indeed a 'miserable prince' (5.3.142), that the impending death of Palamon must mean to him what Flavina's death had meant to her, and she voluntarily took his hand. The fact that a loving relationship had briefly seemed a possibility made Arcite's death more touching. His "'Tis done!' (5.4.94), after she had kissed him, was an exclam-ation of triumph, reminding one that his initial ambition had been to 'love her as a woman' (2.2.165).

The modern distrust of authority figures has in some ways made Theseus more interesting, if more difficult to play, than the

8 Palamon (Louis Letorto) and Arcite (Chiron Alston): Berkeley, 1985

9 Palamon (Gerard Murphy) arming Arcite (Hugh Quarshie): RSC at the Swan Theatre, Stratford-upon-Avon, 1986

10 Arcite (Ray Chapman) and Palamon (Jay Karnes) looking at Emilia in the garden: Ashland, 1994

11 Emilia (Robin Goodrin Nordli) and Arcite (Ray Chapman) after the
combat: Ashland, 1994

authorial spokesman that he was once taken to be. In the last scene,
particularly, some productions have shown him trying, as a ruler, to
explain events which, as a human being, he finds deeply disturbing.
Some have also found interesting subtextual possibilities in his relationship with Hippolyta, whose background as a defeated and
subdued Amazon is so strongly emphasized by the queens in 1.1
and so frustratingly undeveloped in the rest of the play. Building
on textual hints of increasing strain between Emilia and her
brother-in-law, Philadelphia and Ashland suggested a triangular

relationship among the three and a sense of isolation on Emilia's part as her sister became more closely identified with Theseus. The RSC production seemed to take the view that 'the play's deepest conflict is not between the kinsmen, but between Theseus, as patriarchal ruler of Athens, and Emilia as representative of "The powers of all women"' (Abrams, 74).

It is the roles of Emilia and the Jailer's Daughter that attract the most attention in modern performances. Emilia's declared inability to choose is now more understandable than when Tucker Brooke, in 1908, quoted with approval Furnivall's famous comparison of Emilia to 'a silly lady's maid or shop girl, not knowing her own mind, up and down like a bucket in a well' (Brooke, xliii n.). At Berkeley, for instance, incredulous laughter was directed not at her but at Theseus' insistence that she should 'Make choice' between two men she did not know. Her speech with the men's portraits was played, at Ashland, as a desperate and unhappy attempt to do what everyone expected of her by talking herself into love. In many productions, her responses to the male celebration of fighting – 'Must these men die too?' (4.2.112) and 'Is this winning?' (5.3.138) – have been among the most memorable moments. Because so many of her speeches are soliloquies and she interacts so little with other characters (never speaking directly to either kinsman except briefly to the disguised Arcite in 2.5), her role is a difficult one, depending heavily on context and subtext.

By contrast, the Daughter is probably the easiest character for a twentieth-century audience to understand: a reviewer of a 1968 production thought it 'remarkable to see the seventeenth-century theatre suggesting, even in jest, that orgasm is good for you' (Cottis). Many productions now stress the relationship between the two women by similarities of costume or blocking, and they are often strongly contrasted physically, to the point of seeming archetypes of sensuality and chastity (see, for example, Figs 7 and 11). At the end of the RSC production the final image left with the audience was not that of the kinsmen but of Emilia and the Daughter, face to face for the first time in the play: both in bridal veils, both stunned and bereaved. At Ashland, the rest of the court left the stage – cued by Theseus' uneasy 'Let's go off' (5.4.136) – as they heard the Daughter's offstage singing; only Palamon and Emilia remained as she entered, still mad, in her dirty wedding dress. For a moment the two women looked at each other, touching each other's faces; then Palamon gently led Emilia away as the Daughter walked upstage, still singing the song that had begun the play.

As Sandra Clark has noted, with regard to the entire Beaumont and Fletcher corpus, 'in plays where there is no living tradition of performance the gaps where meanings are to be supplied in the theatre can never be truly filled' (Clark 154). There are many such gaps in *The Two Noble Kinsmen*. Some roles (for example the Wooer) are not so much under-written as unwritten, leaving almost everything for the actor to do. For a modern audience, more at home with the visual and subtextual than with the verbal, such a character can be genuinely effective in performance. The same is true of the other major roles – more so, I would argue, than the young lovers in *The Winter's Tale* and *The Tempest* – and even the minor parts of the Jailer, Schoolmaster, Doctor and the apparently colourless friends of the Jailer. (Ashland made a nice contrast between First Friend's unctuous tone – 'That truly noble Prince Pirithous' (4.1.13) – and Second Friend's more direct language.) Moreover, though the play's resemblance to a masque should not be exaggerated, one should also remember that, like a masque, it makes only part of its effect through words. As with the sheep-shearing feast in *The Winter's Tale* and the wedding masque in *The Tempest*, an important part of any production of *The Two Noble Kinsmen* must be the finding of visual and musical equivalents for its most spectacular effects: the opening and closing ceremonies of Act 1, the morris dance, the solemn and perhaps deliberately barbaric ritual of the temple scene, and whatever was intended to accompany Theseus' bleak closing lines.

Interpretation

Before this century much of the criticism of *The Two Noble Kinsmen* was confined to editions of the play, and earlier editors found little difficulty in accepting some elements that have bothered later ones. Seward, for instance, noted the harshness of Theseus' rule that not only the loser but his knights must die and wondered what 'gallant Idiots' would volunteer in the circumstances. But, he decided, 'Mankind were mad after Knight-Errantry; and the reader must catch a little of the Spirit himself, or he'll lose a great Part of the Beauties of this Play . . .'. Some of these 'Beauties', he felt, were moral – for instance, the fact that Palamon's comment on Creon's apparent ability to defy divine justice (1.2.79–83) is not only phrased in terms that recall the previous scene ('Widows' cries / Descend again into their throats') but immediately followed by the news that Theseus and his army are at hand. He regrets, however, that poetic justice is not more clearly followed in the fates of Palamon and Arcite: if the authors had made more of the oath of sworn brotherhood that Chaucer mentions, Arcite would have been more guilty and Palamon's success more obviously justified. Though Seward invokes historical context, his approach does not require esoteric knowledge, since romance was still a familiar convention. His main appeal is to shared moral values and he assumes that these are what give the play its abiding interest.

The dominance of the authorship question in the nineteenth century, though it led to some close analysis of the writing, had otherwise a dire effect on criticism: whether the play had any interest outside its own historical context was seen as depending only on Shakespeare's presence in it. At a time when almost no one had the opportunity to acquire familiarity with *The Two Noble Kinsmen* by editing, performing or seeing it, it inevitably seemed an abstract and shadowy work. Recent activity in all these areas has made a difference. The revival of interest in the play is due to the very qualities that once led to its disparagement: its remote and artificial story, its highly charged sexuality, and the difficult language of the non-Fletcherian scenes. The very remoteness of the story, for example, has lent itself to the approach used at both the RSC and Ashland, where the audience is invited to observe the pressure of an alien social code on the lives of individual characters. Some critics have found the play to be a critique of chivalry (Rose) or of the Jacobean court which, by selling honours like knighthood, made supposedly spiritual values available for discussion in material terms (Abrams, 'Bourgeois'). Clifford Leech suggests that 'The contradictions implicit in Shakespeare are made explicit in Fletcher' (Leech, *Plays*, 148). In an age that enjoys recognizing contradictions, this Fletcherian quality is a merit.

As for the language which, if it is Shakespeare's, must be his last surviving writing for the stage, it has consistently polarized critical opinion. De Quincey's view that the speeches in 1.1 'would have been the most gorgeous rhetoric, had they not happened to be something far better' (49 n.) is typical of the most enthusiastic tributes, but typical also in its lack of precision about what the 'something far better' might be. Contradicting De Quincey, one writer argues that the style of 1.1 is inappropriately inflated for the issues being debated in it; it serves only to create expectations that are bathetically unfulfilled (Magnusson, 384). It has also been claimed that the bathos is a deliberate subversion (by *both* dramatists) of the characters' pretensions (Lief & Radel). This dispute as to whether the play depicts or deflates heroism recalls the ongoing critical debate over *Troilus and Cressida*, a work to which it has been compared by both Edwards and Rose. A similar uneasiness has sometimes been felt about the language of the late romances in general. Russ McDonald has described the style of *The Tempest* in terms that could also be applied to *The Two Noble Kinsmen*: 'On the one hand, the repeated sounds or phrases in a brief and complicated text offer a kind of aural comfort: specifically, they create a richness of texture that seems to promise profundity. On the other, the text never fulfils the expectations of clarity which the discovery of such patterns engenders' (McDonald, 24). Similarly, the style of *Cymbeline*, with its unusual number of parentheses, has been compared to that of Henry James in his last works (Houston, 200–5). Though some of these parentheses may be the result of the play's having been transcribed by a scribe, Ralph Crane, with a particular fondness for them, the return to more 'normal' sentence structure in *The Winter's Tale* and *The Tempest* (also thought to be Crane transcripts) suggests that the complexity is the result of a conscious choice (Houston, 205).

Comparing Shakespeare to Henry James is not inappropriate. In each case there is debate about the extent to which the style is in the author's control. The parenthetical language may be seen as the self-indulgence of an ageing author; it may, however, have been created for a purpose. In Shakespeare's case, at least, it often seems to be used to express what R. A. Foakes considers the particular contribution of Beaumont and Fletcher, their sense of the 'powerful sexual drives that lie just below the surface of courtly appearances' (Foakes, 84). For instance, much of the most striking language in 1.1 is given to the queens, as in the insistent plea to Hippolyta:

> But touch the ground for us no longer time
> Than a dove's motion, when the head's plucked off.
> Tell him, if he i'th' blood-sized field lay swollen,
> Showing the sun his teeth, grinning at the moon,
> What you would do.
>
> (1.1.97–101)

The shock results from the word order (as Magnusson notes, 'the dove's flutter becomes its death throes' (378)) and from the fact that, in both parts of the sentence, the parenthetical element dominates the main subject–verb construction. The speech is also shocking because it intrudes on the private feelings of Hippolyta and Theseus, and the queens' subsequent speeches intrude still further, imagining Hippolyta on her wedding night, when 'her twinning cherries shall their sweetness fall / Upon thy tasteful lips' (1.1.178–9).

Hippolyta's reply, addressed to Theseus, is equally difficult, but for different reasons:

> Though much unlike
> You should be so transported, as much sorry
> I should be such a suitor, yet I think,
> Did I not by th'abstaining of my joy,
> Which breeds a deeper longing, cure their surfeit
> That craves a present medicine, I should pluck
> All ladies' scandal on me. Therefore . . .
>
> (1.1.186–92)

The final word (along with the earlier 'Though', 'as', and 'yet') gives the illusion of clarity. By contrast, the omission of the pronouns that go with 'unlike' and 'sorry', and the vague referents of 'so' and 'such', make the actual meaning difficult to arrive at. The difficulty may result from a clash between the speaker's need to make a suitable public statement and her private embarrassment both about the subject-matter and about the queens' behaviour.

One might compare 1.2 of *The Winter's Tale*, where Leontes and

Hermione are equally over-insistent as they urge Polixenes to prolong what already seems to have been too long a visit at the court of
Sicily. In each case, the language is *embarrassing*, and it dramatizes
embarrassment. In the earlier play, the language eventually finds its
outlet in the plot, since Hermione's overcharged, laboriously flirta-
tious appeal leads directly to her husband's suspicion that she is
committing adultery with his friend. In *The Two Noble Kinsmen* the
sensual language used by the queens about both Hippolyta and
Emilia has consequences only in Hippolyta's later reminder to
Theseus of 'all the chaste nights I have ever pleased you' (3.6.200),
to which he replies – whether embarassed or amused – 'These are
strange conjurings.' By contrast, Palamon's prayer to Venus dwells
on his ability to keep quiet about sexual secrets, an important virtue in courtly love. Apart from a few expressions of desire in
2.2, and perhaps in Arcite's soliloquy at the start of Act 3, the play
differentiates the naive sensuality of the Jailer's Daughter and the
men's recollection of their previous sexual exploits from the self-
conscious purity of their rivalry for Emilia. The best moments, in
both authors, are those in which what is being said is clearly not the
whole of the meaning – as when Fletcher depicts the kinsmen
attempting to behave with artificial jollity (3.3) or, in the arming
scene (3.6), to suppress the affection that is awakened in them by
old memories. Indeed, the abrupt end of 3.3 results from Palamon's angry interpretation (right or wrong, we never know) of some
lines of Arcite which, in themselves, mean almost nothing:

> There was a time
> When young men went a-hunting, and a wood,
> And a broad beech; and thereby hangs a tale –
> Hey ho.
>
> (3.3.39–42)

It has been suggested that the subplot acts as an outlet for the
reticence shown in the main plot. For instance, Emilia's quiet
refusal of Theseus' urging her towards Arcite at the end of 2.5 is
immediately followed by the Daughter's exuberant 'Let all the
dukes and all the devils roar ...!' (2.6.1) – 'as though she
has become the secret voice of Emilia's resentment' (Abrams,
'Bourgeois', 159).

The notion of the play as offering a 'secret' subtext has inspired many recent readings. Bruce Smith describes Palamon's and Arcite's desire to escape Thebes as 'a flight from sexual experience' (70); Abrams sees Arcite's love for Emilia in 2.2 as arising out of the desire 'to spite Palamon' (74) and the end of Emilia's conversation with her woman in 2.2 as a 'flirtation which ends in the women going to bed together' (70). Drawing on Ovid's *Metamorphoses*, Bate describes Emilia's relation with Flavina, so strongly associated with flowers, as a variation of the Adonis story: 'In Emilia's image, the paired flowers become two phoenixes – a wonderful contradiction of the bird's defining uniqueness – and thus proclaim the perfection of same-sex love' (Bate, 265). A reviewer of a modern-dress revival in 1970 saw Emilia in 1.3 as 'going through a mild lesbian phase' – one, however, which soon gives way to 'the virile attractions of the captives' (Curtis). Edwards and Waith ('Sh and F'), while not going this far, do find that the play not only makes single-sex friendship more attractive than love but represents it nostalgically, as an edenic state that is never adequately replaced by married love.

Some accounts are more critical of the young people, pointing out their immature and narcissistic behaviour (Abrams, Rose) or accusing Emilia of choosing the roles of child and victim in order to evade responsibility (Hillman). Certainly, the kinsmen's conversation in prison, as they sigh for the sons they will never have – sons whose chief function will be to admire and imitate their glorious fathers – recalls one definition of narcissism: 'What we love is the young and beautiful image of ourselves: the love object that actually is an object' (MacCary, 29). Without being psychologists, the audience at Ashland at once got the joke when Palamon's and Arcite's complacent comments on their friendship were followed by Emilia's 'What flower is this?' and the reply, ' 'Tis called Narcissus, madam.' (2.2.119). Audience expectation at this point is that their immature and self-satisfied friendship – and Emilia's equally trivial concerns – are about to be replaced by something better.

It is, however, questionable whether what follows *is* in fact better. Catherine Belsey recognizes this problem, even while rejecting the homoerotic interpretation: 'The men's explicit preferences are heterosexual. The whole plot depends on this . . . they admire each other greatly for their former heterosexual conquests.' At the same time, she notes that their attempt to distinguish between 'love' and 'desire', in 2.2.159, has collapsed by the time Palamon speaks his anguished lines to the dead Arcite (5.4.109–12), in which the words 'desire' and 'love' are applied both to heterosexual love and to homosocial friendship (Belsey, 52–3). Theseus and Hippolyta may be meant to represent the ideal – a close marital relationship that is not incompatible with close single-sex friendship (on the husband's part at least). But they, and Pirithous still more, are kept too far in the background to provide a true alternative. Perhaps the impossibility of resolution is built into the structure: 'the audience, like Emilia, is in an impossible position and cannot choose' (Hickman, 145).

Still, no reading of the play can be satisfactory that does not also take account of its remarkable imaginative unity. Though Paul Bertram has found few to agree with him that *The Two Noble Kinsmen* is entirely the work of Shakespeare, his account of the play is still one of the best ever written, and one of his main arguments for his view – that the same themes and images can be found in scenes traditionally ascribed to two different authors – is borne out by much subsequent work. Abrams ('Bourgeois') and Katrina Bachinger trace the elaborate metaphor of the ship at sea from the play's Prologue (where the play itself is the ship), to the Daughter's fantasies of shipwreck, to the point at which Arcite himself, 'a vessel . . . that floats but for / The surge that next approaches' (5.4.83–4), becomes the wreck. Jeanne Roberts, among others, notes how the two plots are linked by the gift-horses (those given by Emilia to Arcite and the one which the Daughter imagines Palamon has given her); she also points to the implicit pun on *bridle* and *bridal* (142).

There are obvious reasons why both horses and the sea recur so often in the language of the play; they are metaphorically interchangeable (Palamon calls their horses 'proud seas under us' at 2.2.20) and Neptune was the god of both. The sea, according to Ralph Berry, is always symbolically present in any theatre with a platform stage, where the actor looks out over the heads of the audience as over so many bobbing waves (Berry, 16). Perhaps the actor is also like a charioteer trying to control a team of horses. The association of restless horses with sexual desire and betrayal is often considered specifically Shakespearean: obvious examples occur in *Venus and Adonis* and *The Lover's Complaint*. However, the horse is essential to the plot of *The Knight's Tale*, and present also in the imagery of Chaucer's *Anelida and Arcite*, where Arcite behaves like a restive horse with Anelida, then is bridled by his new love (Gillam, 394). Like the sea, the horse cannot easily be depicted on stage, though Barry Kyle's 1986 RSC production made the horse symbolism vividly present in his treatment of the Daughter (see Fig. 6, p. 84) and in the final scene where, to accompany Pirithous' narrative, a giant banner depicting a wild horse gradually rose and unfurled behind him.

Given the importance of the horse for the play's conclusion, it is hardly surprising that both Shakespeare and Fletcher filled the play with anticipatory references. Horses, however, have such powerful symbolic connotations as to leave the way open for infinite interpretations. If the Prologue in *Henry V* makes the horse stand for everything the stage cannot show ('Think, when we talk of horses, that you see them'), the wild horse in 5.4 of *The Two Noble Kinsmen* may embody everything it *must not* show. Certainly, bridled and unbridled horses conventionally represent (as in Alciati's well-known emblem collection) passion controlled or uncontrolled. Boccaccio's treatment of Arcite owes something to the story of Hippolytus, son of Theseus, who refused to worship Aphrodite and was dragged to his death by his own horses. The allegorical implications of the myth were obvious to the Renaissance and rearing horses (that is, horses standing on their hind legs alone) are frequently depicted in art of the period. The painter Lomazzo recorded two examples of vivid verbal description of horses which he recommended to his readers. One was Ariosto's account of a horse trying to shake off its rider (*Orlando Furioso* Book 2 stanza 7), which Ariosto's translator, Sir John Harington, glossed by explaining that the horse represented 'unbridled desire' (Harington, 15). Lomazzo's other example is a messenger speech from the Greek romance *Clitophon and Leucippe*, by Tatius Achilles, describing how a young man is killed by a horse his lover had given him. The romance might have been known to Shakespeare through William Burton's translation of 1597, dedicated to the

Earl of Southampton. A small Holbein painting once belonging to Prince Henry's collection shows a man being carried away by a wildly galloping horse, with the motto '*E cosi desio me mena*' [Thus desire leads me] (Strong, 194). There is, then, evidence for an erotic, even a homoerotic, reading of Arcite's accident. Most critics of the play offer an interpretation of Pirithous' narrative in 5.4, often without noting that the narrative is itself an interpretation: Pirithous makes it clear that Arcite's death results from his superb control of the horse, which can destroy him only by destroying itself.

The horse is only one of many visual and verbal images in the play. As was suggested above (p. 68), one possible explanation for its imaginative unity is that both dramatists were influenced both by Beaumont's masque and by the emblem books which Inigo Jones and others are known to have used as sources for set and costume designs. For instance, the climax of the masque (see Appendices 3 and 4) was the revelation of the knight masquers in a setting dominated by Jupiter's altar. Waith has made the interesting suggestion that the hind that Emilia offers to Diana (which is not in Chaucer's tale) is meant to recall the hind that Diana substitutes for Iphigenia when she is about to be sacrificed (Oxf[1], 191n.). The audience looking at Emilia in performance (Fig. 12) might not think of the Iphigenia story or of an image from Ovid's *Metamorphoses* such as is reproduced here (Fig. 13), but – especially in view of Arcite's reference to his knights as 'my sacrifices' (5.1.34) – it would surely sense that Emilia is taking part in a sacrifice, perhaps being sacrificed herself. Richard Proudfoot has suggested that the altar of 5.1 might become the scaffold of 5.4, thus emphasizing a conflation of religious and secular motives similar to that in Beaumont's masque, where the knights appear as 'consecrated persons'. Roberto Calasso's fascinating synthesis of classical myths, *The Marriage of Cadmus and Harmony*, points out that the earliest legends make the god 'copulate and kill himself at the same time' (106); Calasso finds vestiges of this practice in the story of Iphigenia, who is told that she is to be married, when in fact she is to be sacrificed: 'the flavor of marriage lingers on in the sacrifice, just as the flavor of the sacrifice lingers on in marriage. A tangible object unites the two events: the crown. One is crowned whether going to the altar as a

12 Emilia (Amanda Harris) at the altar of Diana: RSC at the Swan Theatre, Stratford-upon-Avon, 1986

victim or as a bride' (107). Perhaps because of the Renaissance interest in recreating classical triumphs and weddings, the drama-

13 The hind replacing Iphigenia on the altar of Diana, by Crispijn van de Pas, from Ovid's *Metamorphoses* (1602)

tists had evidently perceived the importance of crowns and wreaths in the classical world, for the play is full of them, from the wheaten garlands worn by the women in the first scene to the 'victor's wreath' which falls from Arcite's head just before he is crushed by his horse.

Garlands are made by intertwining branches of leaves or flowers. The curious twinning/twining pun which twice produces an interpretative crux in *The Two Noble Kinsmen* has a possible origin both in emblem books and in the weddings of 1613. The classic emblem of friendship, as Peggy Simonds has pointed out (248–68), is also an emblem of marriage: the intertwining vine and elm described by Catullus in an epithalamion, later used by Alciati and many successive emblematists (Fig. 14), and drawn on by Jonson in *Hymenaii* (1606); many poets must have re-read some of these works as they prepared their own tributes for the 1613 wedding. The two words become as intertwined in the play as the phenomenon they purport to describe; both 'twining' and 'twinning' are

*Amicitia etiam post mor-
tem durans.*

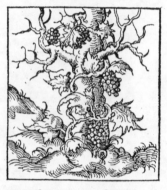

*Arentum senio,nudum quoq; frondibus ulmum,
Complexa est uiridi uitis opaca coma.
Agnoscitq;-uices naturæ,& grata parenti
Officij reddit mutua iura suo.
Exemploq; monet,tales nos quærere amicos,
Quos neque disiungat fœdere summa dies.*

14 Emblem of friendship from Andreas Alciati, *Emblemata*, no. 16

appropriate for the *twinning* cherries of Hippolyta's lips in 1.1.178
(presumably Shakespeare's) and, equally, for the reference in 2.2.64
(presumably Fletcher's) to the fortunes of Palamon and Arcite
being *twined* together; Emilia compares the objects of Pirithous'
divided attention to twins (1.3.32–3). The Theban legend and Statius' *Thebaid* are themselves full of twins and twin-like figures –
figures, that is, who (like the children/siblings of Oedipus) threat-
en the concept of difference. The importance of twins and doubles
for Shakespeare's work has often been noted, sometimes with reference to his having been the father of twins. Joel Fineman recognizes the Theban story as one possible source for the Shakespearean theme of fratricidal rivalry between interchangeable, often parallel, male figures (Hal and Hotspur, Brutus and Cassius, Hamlet
and Laertes). For some reason, twins seem to have been theatrically
popular in the period of *The Two Noble Kinsmen*. In January 1612

the King's Men performed a play by (Richard?) Niccolls, now lost, called *The Twins' Tragedy*. In *The Duchess of Malfi*, a play dominated by images of shadows, mirrors and echoes, the Duchess's twin brother, Ferdinand, both loves and murders her.

If a friend is a second self, then all friends are in a sense twins. They are also intertwined in what Hippolyta calls the 'knot of love' between Theseus and Pirithous (1.3.41). Emilia speaks of its 'intertangled roots' (1.3.59), while the Daughter later hopes that her love for Palamon, which she rightly suspects of being unreciprocated, 'Will take more root within him' (2.6.28). These images of binding were made visual in the RSC production through the repeated act of tying strings into knots and the ceremonial binding of women, particularly the queens, in long sashes resembling the Japanese obi. In 4.2 the ceremonial bonds were held by Pirithous and the Messenger, who bound them around Emilia's wrists as they spoke of the knights who were coming to fight for her love; the effect was to externalize her sense that the tournament was above all a threat to her.

Such staging provides a twentieth-century equivalent of something that is undoubtedly present in the play, an elaborate patterning of visual and verbal effects. Emrys Jones's important study of *Scenic Form in Shakespeare* draws attention to the shapes created by constantly changing stage groupings. The dominant scenic pattern of *The Two Noble Kinsmen*, established in 1.1, is the interrupted procession, which becomes part of a sequence of interrupted events (see Edwards) and is repeated, verbally, in the frequent parentheses by which speakers interrupt their own words. The interrupted procession in 5.3 is also reminiscent of the shape which Jones (22) analyses in 1.2 of *Julius Caesar*: a procession arrives and departs, leaving behind someone who, having refused to go and watch an offstage spectacle, now tries to interpret the offstage sounds. Another important scenic pattern can be related to the morris dance, which has been described (Bachinger) as the unifying symbol for the whole play. It is impossible to tell simply from the text why the absence of a single female dancer should threaten to wreck all the plans Gerald and his pupils have made. If their show had featured some complicated group manoeuvre, such as the mock-beheading and resurrection of the fool which sometimes features in this dance, it would have had an obvious thematic link with the near-beheading of Palamon in the final scene and the sacrificial role of the victor/victim Arcite, a Summer Lord to Emilia's Queen of the May. But the main dance formation appears to be what Gerald calls 'trace and turn' – or the 'hey', as Julian Pilling (28) translates it – movement in a circle, with the dancers weaving in and out, perhaps criss-crossing ribbons round a maypole, in the shape of a wreath. This criss-crossing is also the scenic pattern in Act 3, where the kinsmen and the Daughter, in alternating scenes, keep missing each other. Cicely's failure to turn up for the dance is probably nothing but a way of justifying the Daughter's inclusion. But the substitution is part of a pattern that runs throughout the play: Pirithous takes Theseus' place in the first scene; the Daughter takes Cicely's place in the dance; the Wooer takes Palamon's place (or his own rightful place) in the Daughter's bed; and Palamon finally takes Arcite's place as Emilia's husband.

Linguistic and visual patterns can be decoded in the various ways I have been indicating, but it is possible that they exist for their own sake. Marco Mincoff has suggested that by 1613 there were two currents in English literary style. One, which he associates primarily with Jonson, but of which he also claims Fletcher as an example, is based on a 'classical ideal of lucidity and correctness, a style that scarcely ever startles or reveals by flashes, and whose effects, when it seeks for brilliance, are made by more oratorical means'. The other, which he identifies with Donne, the later Shakespeare, and Webster's tragedies, is difficult and 'metaphysical' (Mincoff, 104). *The Two Noble Kinsmen* is unusual in having several images that seem to derive from Donne: in particular, that of the 'dove's motion, when the head's plucked off' (1.1.98) may, Proudfoot thinks, have been inspired by his *Second Anniversary*, which opens with some striking lines on the twitching of a severed head and body. The two *Anniversaries* (1611 and 1612) were the first of Donne's poems to be published. Webster's borrowings from them in *The Duchess of Malfi*, and perhaps Fletcher's in his verses on *The Honest Man's Fortune* (see Appendix 1), may have brought them to Shakespeare's attention, though of course he may already have known other Donne poems in manuscript. It is possible that the essence of the difficult style was, as in Donne, the pleasure of difficulty itself. Stephen Orgel has argued that one need not necessarily explain the obscurity of Renaissance language: 'the age often found in incomprehensibility a positive virtue' (436). The linguistic labyrinth may be one from which no exit is possible.

Thus there need be no explanation for the play's abrupt reversals, both comic and tragic: for instance, the kinsmen's confident prophecy, just before they see Emilia, that nothing will ever destroy their friendship, or the literal reversal that freezes Arcite with his legs 'higher than his head' (5.4.78), like a grotesque baroque statue, just before his horse falls backward on him. At the equally unlikely end of Tourneur's *The Atheist's Tragedy* (1611–12), the villain D'Amville accidently strikes himself with the executioner's axe while attempting to behead someone else. He sees the hand of providence in his fate and is at once converted from his atheism. Arcite learns no such lesson – in a play with a non-Christian setting, he probably could not – yet the length and grotesqueness of Pirithous' description of Arcite's accident draws attention to its freakish, arbitrary nature, and, for Theseus at least, to the helplessness of human beings in the face of divine power.

It is probably a coincidence that Pirithous' first line in 1.3 – 'No further' – should be the equivalent of the motto *Non plus ultra* that Hercules is supposed to have set up alongside his famous pillars at the Straits of Gibraltar, with the message that human beings should not exceed their limits. If the god Hercules leaves Antony (*AC*, 4.3), he has long since left the world of *The Two Noble Kinsmen*, as Theseus, his former comrade, frequently recognizes. But the later play, almost equally full of reminiscences of Hercules, is also full of images of boundaries: the Second Queen's initial reminder to Hippolyta that Theseus has saved her from 'o'erflowing' her proper 'bound', Palamon's reflection that fate 'hath bounded our last minute' (1.2.103), Arcite's reference to 'the heavenly limiter' (5.1.30), and the Daughter's question, 'How far is't now to th'end o'th' world, my masters?' (5.2.72). One of the first creators of boundaries, according to Plutarch, was Theseus himself, who set up a pillar marking the founding of Athens as a city-state (see Gillies, 8, 190 n. 12).

No less conscious of boundaries, the authors and actors themselves, through the Prologue, express anxiety about the 'deep water' (25) in which they are trying to swim. As Theseus and the others feel towards Hercules, so they represent themselves as feeling towards Chaucer: 'it were an endless thing / And too ambitious to aspire to him' (22–3). But they are quoting him even at that moment: Chaucer, saying farewell to his *Troilus and Criseyde*, told his 'litel myn tragedye' to avoid competing with its predecessors and only 'kis the steppes where as thou seest pace / Virgile, Ovide, Omer, Lucan, and Stace' (Chaucer, *Riv*, 5.1786, 1791–2). The mention of Stace (Statius) recalls that the *Thebaid* itself ends by disclaiming any intention of rivalling the divine *Aeneid*, wishing only to '*longe sequere et vestigia semper adora*' [follow afar and ever venerate its footsteps] (Statius, 12.817).

Indeed, the allusions to and near-quotations of earlier works may, as in Webster's *The Duchess of Malfi*, remind one of the survival of voices from the past. The authors of *The Two Noble Kinsmen* borrow from their own earlier works, often in contexts that question the values embodied there, and make their own characters highly self-conscious about how they will be remembered. Gerald's inflated opinion of his entertainment for Theseus is shown in his quotation from the end of Ovid's *Metamorphoses*: in Golding's translation, it reads, 'Now have I brought a woork too end which neither *Joves* feerce wrath, / Nor sword, nor fyre, nor freating age with all the force it hath / Are able too abolish quyght' (Ovid, 15.984–6). Horace made the same claim in Ode 3.30.1, '*Exegi monumentum aere perennius*' [I have erected a monument more lasting than bronze], to which Shakespeare several times alludes in the Sonnets (pub. 1609). Webster ended his preface to *The White Devil* (1612) with words that he evidently took as his motto, Martial's grand statement about books (Epigrams 10.2.12): '*non norunt, Haec monumenta mori*' [these are monuments that do not know how to die]. It says something about the mood of *The Two Noble Kinsmen* that its monument should be a pillar, symbol of limitation, and that the only reference to lasting fame should come from the pedant Gerald, wandering in from another age to quote an author not yet born. It is Theseus, the setter-up of pillars, who ends the play by warning against too much disputing with the gods, 'Who are above our question'. No wonder the Epilogue has to remind the spectators that what thay have witnessed is only 'a tale'.

TEXT

The textual notes in this edition explain, in abbreviated form, the difference between the edited text and the one on which it is based (the 'basic text'). In order to decide how much justification there is for emendation or addition to a basic text, an editor has to assess its reliability. What sort of manuscript lies behind it? How was it prepared for the press? How did the compositors set up the type? How thoroughly was it proofread?

As is clear from the play's publication history, the 1634 quarto of *The Two Noble Kinsmen* is the only possible basic text. Two openings from it are reproduced as Figures 15 and 16: pp. 14–15 (C3ᵛ–C4) and 46–7 (G3ᵛ–G4) respectively. (Figure 15 shows part of 1.3 and 1.4, generally thought to be Shakespeare's; 3.5 and 3.6 (here 'Scaena 7') in Figure 16 are attributed to Fletcher.) The figures in parentheses are the 'signatures' added at the printing house. For a quarto volume, each printed sheet was folded twice to make a gathering of four leaves (eight pages). This procedure allowed a number of pages to be printed simultaneously, but it was obviously essential that the type for each page should be correctly placed on the sheet – hence the 'catch-word' at the end of each page, which allowed for quick checking. The signature indicates both the gathering (usually by a letter) and the page of the gathering, numbered on one side only. Since only the first three pages of a quarto gathering were normally 'signed', neither of the openings illustrated here contains a signature.

As is apparent from the illustrations, the text has, in a sense, been edited already. That is, someone has regularized its format by indenting the speech prefixes, placing stage directions flush with the right margin, and using roman letters for scene numbers but italics for proper names and foreign words in speech prefixes and dialogue. A few play manuscripts from this period have survived, so we know that much of this standardization (particularly the typographical differentiation) was probably done in the playhouse rather than at the printer's shop. The normal playtext was written on a page folded to make three columns: one for speakers' names, two to three for the dialogue, with stage directions on the right. The compositors who set up the type at the printing house

15 Opening (pp. 14–15) from the 1634 quarto of *The Two Noble Kinsmen*, reduced in size

16 Opening (pp. 46–7) from the 1634 quarto of *The Two Noble Kinsmen*, reduced in size

followed much the same procedure except that they were generally concerned with saving paper; hence their speech prefixes are indented rather than placed in the margin. One always has to be aware that a line lacking final punctuation or using contracted word-forms may be the result of this space-saving instinct. On the two occasions where a line of dialogue was too long for the margin (Fig. 15, 1.4.4 and Fig. 16, 3.5.149), the compositors followed the standard practice of setting a 'turned-over line'. (All line references are to the edited text.)

On the other hand, some things have not been regularized. In 1.3, the name of Emilia's childhood friend is spelled one way in line 54, another in line 84. *Pirithous* of line 55 is *Pirothous* in 95. A speech prefix for the Schoolmaster has been omitted at line 3.5.135, probably because of confusion over the positioning of the stage directions; it looks as if someone at the printing house, misled by the third and fourth lines of his next speech, took it for a song with a refrain and italicized it accordingly. In some places necessary punctuation appears to have been omitted: after Emilia's 'Yes' at 1.3.54, at the end of 1.3.65, and probably after 3.5.117; a question mark also seems needed at the end of 3.5.146. Beside these comparatively minor points, what would most strike a reader accustomed to modern edited texts is the virtual absence of stage directions. In Figure 15, Theseus' 'What are those?' (1.4.13) is unexplained; in Figure 16 there is no indication as to what is meant by the Schoolmaster's references to 'this Machine' (3.5.112), what goes on after he has called for a dance, and who is addressing whom in the dialogue at the end of the scene. At the bottom of p. 47 (Fig. 16), it is obvious that the stage direction for Arcite's entrance should precede rather than follow Palamon's greeting of him (this may be a case of a compositor saving space by not breaking up a line of dialogue).

In attempting to deal with the sorts of peculiarities I have just described, the editor has to draw on knowledge of the period in which the text was written and published. What follows will look first at some ways in which editors try to find out more about the kind of text they are dealing with. Then it will examine aspects of the text in more detail, taking examples mainly from the pages reproduced here, and summarize current opinion as to the nature of the manuscript given to the printer.

114

Compositorial analysis

In twentieth-century editing, the role of the compositor who set
the type from which a page was printed has become a subject of
great interest, because it is important to know whether differences
(say, in spelling) in different parts of the basic text might be due to
different hands in the original manuscript or only to the practice of
different compositors. Compositor analysis has become less confident, and more complex, since it was first introduced in 1920
(Taylor, 41–7). The earliest work was done on the 1623 Shakespeare Folio, and distinctions were made chiefly on the basis of
preferred spellings, but it is now recognized that even these
preferences are not consistent: they can be affected by printing-
house conventions, the nature of the manuscript copy, and the
need to fit the right number of lines to a page. As with the authorship tests described on pp. 19–23, it is now recognized that only the
coincidence of many separate defining factors can really identify an
individual compositor. A large project like the Folio would have
involved a good many compositors, since it took longer to set up a
sheet of copy than to print off a series of sheets. A small quarto like
The Two Noble Kinsmen could have been set by only one compositor, but shared typesetting and shared printing were common
practices even with small publications.

In fact, despite the apparent similarity between the two openings
illustrated here, Frederick Waller (*TNK* and 'Printer's') and Paul
Werstine arrived independently at the conclusion that the quarto
was the work of two different compositors. Both scholars looked
for small details of presentation which might result from automatic
habits. For instance, on pp. 14 and 15, punctuation marks within
the line are not normally preceded or followed by spaces, but there
are exceptions at 1.3.73, 1.4.5 and 1.4.9. On pp. 46–7, on the
other hand, it is easy to see that many of the colons are set off with
spaces before and after them, while the commas are squeezed in
without spacing except in one line (3.5.149) where the compositor
must have realized that he was going to have to run over anyway
and therefore needed to create a neat break. Waller found that one
compositor used white spacing in this position 80 per cent of the
time, the other only 30 per cent. There may be dispute as to what

does and does not constitute a space in early printing technology; nevertheless, this difference is large enough to be significant.

The Flavia/Flavina error mentioned above is almost certainly the compositor's; the Pirithous confusion, on the other hand, recurs throughout the text (see notes to the List of Roles, p. 133) and clearly derives from the manuscript.

Press correction

Page 15 (Fig. 15) contains one of the relatively few press corrections in the quarto, the substitution of *smeard* for *succard* in 1.4.18. Press correction at the seventeenth-century printing house went on while sheets were still being run off the press, with the result that different copies of the same book will show different mixtures of corrected and uncorrected sheets. Of the forty-five copies of *The Two Noble Kinsmen* known to exist, Waller examined thirty-one, Bowers sixteen. They found only two corrections on sheet C, two on E, and one each on K and M. Only one forme of each of these sheets was proofread – in other words, only four out of the twenty-six formes that would have been used to set up the entire play. These figures may give a misleading impression of printing-house sloppiness. We can tell that a page was corrected only if we find an uncorrected page with which to compare it, but the number of corrected formes would normally have been much greater than the number of uncorrected ones. Thus in many cases we probably have no evidence that correction took place at all. The significant corrections so far discovered are:

	Uncorrected	*Corrected*
C1ᵛ (1.2.70)	on;	on
C4 (1.4.18)	succard	smeard
E2ᵛ (2.3.6)	fins	sins
E3 (2.3.24 SD)	*Garlon*	*garlond*
K2ᵛ (4.3.54)	behold	behind
K2ᵛ (5.1.76)	his	her
M4 (5.4.79)	victoros	victors

A small number of copies also contain what Richard Proudfoot describes as an intermediate state of correction on sheet C, with *succard* uncorrected but with *on* (the dramatist's spelling of *one*) at line 70 instead of *on;*. The probable explanation is that someone realized the need for punctuation in line 70, but put the semicolon in the wrong place, after instead of before *on*. The absence of authorial proofreading is obvious. No author, for instance, would have missed the *Flauia–Flauina* confusion; the compositor did not make a connection between the word set at line 84 and the one already set in line 54. These corrections are interesting not only because they sometimes (as on sheet C) supply readings that would be hard to arrive at otherwise. The initial misreading can also show something about the handwriting that was misread (for instance, *her* in 5.1.76 may have been misread as *his* because it was spelled *hir*) and hence about the provenance of the manuscript; the extent of correction can also give some indication of the general reliability of the printed text.

Punctuation

By 1634, nouns were beginning to be capitalized more heavily than in earlier years; commas still tended to appear between subject and verb and before conjunctions; full stops, or periods, occurred more rarely than in modern texts, and '?' was sometimes used where one would expect '!' (for instance, Emilia's speech in 4.2 contains 'what an eye? / Of what a fyry sparkle, and quick sweetnes, / Has this young Prince?' (4.2.12–14)). As Bowers points out ('Readability', 214–15), not all Elizabethan compositors even had exclamation marks in their cases of type; many questions are rhetorical – halfway between exclamations and questions – like Palamon's 'Oh you heavens, dares any / So nobly bear a guilty business?' (3.1.89–90). Conversely, the absence of a question mark after 'How does my sweetheart' (3.5.146), though it may be an error, may also be a clue to Theseus' delivery of the line, as the author imagined it. In manuscripts, writers often do not bother to punctuate at the end of a line. They may have felt that the edge of the page itself constituted a break.

Pages 14–15 (Fig. 15) contain a remarkable number of parentheses. These have a variety of functions. Some are used where modern convention might prefer commas. Sometimes, as in modern punctuation, they indicate an aside, not quite important enough to be part of the sentence; in both Emilia's and Hippolyta's speeches, seen here, they also indicate a change of tone. Sometimes they indicate a change in the person addressed. For instance, Theseus in 2.5.48–9 obviously begins by speaking to Hippolyta, but then goes on, 'Sweet, you must be readie, / And you *Emilia*, and you (Friend) and all'; the 'Friend', clearly, is addressed to Pirithous. For some reason, there are many more parentheses in the first part of the play, and in scenes attributed to Shakespeare. One reason may be that they represent additions to the original manuscript. But, as noted above (p. 107), a parenthetical structure is important in the play, whether or not it is designated by the punctuation marks known as parentheses or brackets.

There has been debate for some time about the value of following seventeenth-century punctuation. As is often said, it is rhetorical; that is, a comma is likely to come at a point where a speaker might be expected to pause (even if this is between a subject and a verb) rather than where it is logically needed. The punctuation of *The Two Noble Kinsmen* is very heavy, in the mid-seventeenth-century mode rather than the lighter one of the late sixteenth century. I suspect that at times it may convey something of the original tone, as in the nudge-nudge pauses of the Prologue:

> New Playes, and Maydenheads, are neare akin,
> Much follow'd both, for both much mony g'yn,
> If they stand sound, and well . . .
>
> (1–3)

One can imagine an actor making the most of all these short pauses, looking around for a laugh on *Maydenheads* and the double meaning of *sound*. While it may look as though *Playes* and *Maidenheads* were meant to be extra-emphatic, Figs. 15 and 16 show no clear pattern of capitalization. Most modern editors use lower case even for nouns that are used as personifications (like Peace, 1.2.23; see p. 129). I have capitalized the latter even where the quarto did not (see list on p. 129), to alert the modern reader to the special usage. Conversely, the complete lack of full stops or periods in the whole of Emilia's long speech on p. 14 (Fig. 15) helps to suggest the 'high-speeded pace' on which her sister comments. But in most cases the punctuation was probably the work of the printer. Adding punctuation (especially in the form of exclamation marks) often has much the same effect as adding stage directions. Thus it is important to find a way of making the meaning as clear as possible without preventing the reader or actor from recognizing *intentional* ambiguity.

Lineation and scansion

Many Renaissance plays are written in a mixture of verse and prose. *The Two Noble Kinsmen* is largely in verse, with two prose scenes (2.1 and 4.3), and two scenes (2.3 and 3.5) in which the verse is so loose that it is hard to tell it from prose. The distinction was not always any clearer to Renaissance compositors than it is to us. In the 1634 quarto, for instance, the prose of 2.1 and much of 4.3 is printed, like verse, with unjustified right margins, while in 2.3 the compositor seems to have a change of mind as to whether to set verse or prose. The reason may have been that, as Hans Gabler (Bowers, 6.6) has noted, dramatists after about 1620 used quarto- rather than folio-sized paper for writing playscripts. As a result, verse lines often extended to the right margin and became indistinguishable from prose. Whereas the dramatic blank verse of Shakespeare's earlier plays was generally regular, his later writing relaxes the rhythm by allowing extra unstressed syllables and running on from one line to the next. Fletcher's writing carries the first practice still further.

The result is that at times, for instance in Gerald's first speech (3.5.1–22), the rhythms of blank verse are so loose that it is difficult to know where lines begin and end. At lines 15 and 18, for example, several possible lineations will result in a good blank verse line:

> And unto him I utter learned things

or

> I utter learned things and many figures

> At length, I fling my cap up – mark there! – then

or

> I fling my cap up – mark there! – then do you

The problem becomes even more acute when a verse line is divided among two or more speakers. Seventeenth-century printers were not concerned to preserve the shape of a blank verse line in these circumstances, and editors at present are divided as to whether such lines should be treated as 'short lines' (which means printing them like prose) or as 'shared lines' (which means deciding where they begin and end). Both Shakespeare and Fletcher were so used to writing blank verse that they almost automatically produced sets of speeches that added up to complete lines. But often there is a spare half line which can join itself to either the preceding or the following line of text. A good example is the exchange at 1.3.85–6. I have divided the lines as follows:

> [HIPPOLYTA]
> Love any that's called man.
> EMILIA
>   I am sure I shall not.
> HIPPOLYTA
>   Now, alack, weak sister,

But there is an equally possible alternative (which Waith adopts in his edition for the Oxford Shakespeare):

> [HIPPOLYTA]
> Love any that's called man.
> EMILIA
> I am sure I shall not.
> HIPPOLYTA
>   Now, alack, weak sister,

My scansion might result (depending on elision and stress) in either a masculine or a feminine ending; Waith's is definitely feminine. This is one reason why metrical tests based on line endings are difficult to use effectively (see Bertram, 21–34). The editorial decision makes a difference to the actors who speak the lines, since the speaker who ends a line of verse can seem both to enter into the rhythm of the previous speaker and to cap what has just been said. For instance, in the quarrel between Palamon and Arcite at 2.2.166–70, this exchange occurs:

[ARCITE]
    So both may love.
PALAMON
    You shall not love at all.
ARCITE
    Not love at all,
    Who shall deny me?
PALAMON
    I that first saw her . . .

Here, the decision between two kinds of lineation is also, to some extent, an interpretative one. Leigh Hunt, in 1855, suggested:

[ARCITE]
    So both may love.
PALAMON
                  You shall not love at all.
ARCITE
    Not love at all! Who shall deny me?
PALAMON
                        I.

By contrast, this is my version:

[ARCITE]
    So both may love.
PALAMON
    You shall not love at all.
ARCITE
                  Not love at all!
    Who shall deny me?
PALAMON
    I that first saw her . . .

Hunt's reading gives Palamon literally the last word. In mine, the metre breaks down after Arcite's rebuttal; the rhythm, originally showing the almost instinctive rapport of the two men, comes to reflect the breach between them. I preferred this effect, but readers and actors, who study the notes will be aware that it is the result of a choice which could have been made differently.

A possible solution to lineation difficulties is to abandon the attempt at differentiating verse which can only be scanned with effort. Waith (Oxf[1]) prints Gerald's first speech as prose, while acknowledging that many of its lines have blank-verse rhythms. With regard to divided lines and short lines, it can be argued (as it has been by Bertram (29)) that, since the question is so insoluble, it is better not to force a series of short lines into a blank-verse unit (see also Bevington, 266–70). Nevertheless I decided to retain a basic blank-verse shape, because this edition is intended for readers as well as actors. Both Shakespeare and Fletcher, at this stage of their careers, were blank-verse virtuosos who seem to have enjoyed creating smooth lines out of apparently disparate elements. For instance, at 3.5.91, if the Countryman's 'Do, do!' is lost in the general response to the Daughter's dancing, the result is a line that scans, even though there is no particular need for it to do so. I should add that my textual notes do *not* include details of the line endings of passages printed as verse in the quarto and as prose in this edition, or vice-versa.

Both Shakespeare and Fletcher also have a trick, possibly learned from Donne, of letting the stress of the verse line dictate its meaning. In Palamon's speech to Venus, the metre forces the reading 'I / Believed it *was* his, for she swore it was' (5.1.116–17; my emphasis). Fletcher may have been doing the same thing at 3.5.77, where Gerald's exchange with the Daughter is lineated like this in the quarto:

SCHOOLMASTER
 And are you mad good woman?
DAUGHTER
 I would be sorry else.
 Give me your hand.

With a different lineation –

SCHOOLMASTER
       And are
 You mad, good woman?
DAUGHTER
       I would be sorry else.

– the speaker would be forced to stress *are*. I suspect that this is how

Fletcher actually heard the lines, but I have not felt sure enough to alter them.

Seward's 1750 edition was based on the belief that all the scenes printed as verse really were meant to be verse, and he did his best to make them so. He also attempted to regularize the metre of other scenes by a process of expansion, elision and contraction. For instance, this is his reading of the Wooer's first speech in 5.2:

> Oh, very much: The maids that kept her company
> Have half persuaded her that I'm Palamon;
> Within this half-hour she came smiling to me,
> And ask'd me what I'd eat, and when I'd kiss her:
> I told her presently, and kiss'd her twice.

He has been ridiculed for it ever since, though, as Bertram points out (27), his eighteenth- and early-nineteenth-century successors kept many of his changes and the lineation that resulted from them. Seward had a tin ear, but he was essentially following the practice of the 1679 and 1711 editors, who likewise modernized the contractions into a form familiar to them. Seventeenth-century texts frequently elide adjacent vowels, as in modern French and Italian. The speed of Fletcher's dialogue suggests that many words were meant to be shortened (for example 'I'd' for 'I would'), even where they have not been so indicated in the text. Modern British pronunciation elides many vowel sounds in words like 'every' and 'flower'; in this edition such words are written in full, on the assumption that the reader does not need to be told that they are pronounced 'ev'ry' and 'flow'r'. It is harder to be sure about pronunciations that add extra syllables to a line. For instance, 'r' is often rolled and treated like an extra syllable (*bonefier* is sometimes found as a spelling of *bonfire*); Fletcher apparently pronounces 'sire' with two syllables. Reaching a consensus on scansion, and hence on lineation, is important mainly because notes and concordances are keyed to line numbers. With computer analysis becoming increasingly important, the line will probably become less significant as a measurement; for instance, the most exhaustive Shakespeare concordances, those of Marvin Spevack, give not only the number of lines each character speaks but also the number of words and the number of speeches.

Stage directions

The Two Noble Kinsmen is unique among printed texts of Shakespeare in that it includes some 'anticipatory directions' (examples can be seen in the left margin on pp. 14 (Fig. 15) and 46 (Fig. 16)) of a type that are often found in theatre promptbooks. They are obviously directed to people backstage at the playhouse, not to a hypothetical reader. The one on p. 46 is in fact the last such direction to appear in the quarto, though it is unlikely to have been the last one to appear in the manuscript. This fact suggests that the compositors (perhaps inexperienced at setting playtexts) discovered that these directions were not meant for printing and discontinued the practice.

The marginal directions are set in roman type rather than italics; the one opposite Emilia's speech in 1.3 also makes use, rather oddly, of colons. Several scholars (Greg, 39 n.; Waller, 'Printer's', 64–5) have noticed the resemblance of this punctuation to that of other manuscript promptbooks known to be in the handwriting of Edward Knight, the book-keeper for the King's Men *c.*1625–33. The unusual typeface is probably the compositors' attempt to re-create the large print which characterizes such directions in play manuscripts. The distinctive colons also occur in non-marginal stage directions, like the one on p. 15 at the beginning of 1.4, which suggests that some of them may have been added by Knight (Werstine, 21). 'Enter Theseus', with its capital 'E', looks like the original beginning of this direction; the prompter would then have inserted specific directions for offstage sounds.

From the direction on p. 14, we learn that while Emilia and Hippolyta were playing their intimate scene, six major characters and at least six minor ones were preparing for a carefully synchronized entrance – Theseus, in a triumphal procession, meeting the three queens. I have assumed that the marginal directions represent the point at which the stage manager began to assemble his actors and musicians (in this case, allowing some thirty-five lines, plus the time taken by the offstage sound effects, before their entrance). But it is also possible (as Richard Proudfoot suggests) that the word 'ready' means that by that point in the text the performers (and, as at 1.4.26–7 and 3.5.65–6, the hearses, chairs and stools) should actually be in position and ready to enter. The distinction is important for anyone trying to visualize the conditions of performance. An early line-up in 1.3 might have been necessary if, as Masefield suggested (193), the offstage actors were expected to join the company's musicians in creating the sounds of the battle that is supposed to take place between 1.3 and 1.4. The direction for 'Cornets' at the end of 1.3 obviously belongs with the beginning of 1.4 and shows how the sound of the enemy's retreat was to be created.

Waller has argued that some features of the stage directions, like the absence of an entrance for Palamon and Arcite at the beginning of 1.4 and the vagueness about the number of 'wenches' at the opening of 3.5, indicate that the play was printed from an authorial manuscript, since a promptbook necessarily had to be more exact. But he himself notes that in one other play manuscript annotated by Knight, Massinger's *Believe as You List*, the author's original stage direction is deleted and replaced with a larger one in the margin six lines earlier (Waller, 'Printer's', 64). It is possible that the same thing happened with the original direction for the entry of Palamon and Arcite (whether they were brought on at the beginning of 1.4 or just before Theseus notices their presence). The prompter's point of view is a backstage one; he can get everyone on stage, but has to trust them to get themselves off again, which is one reason why exit directions are so often missing from printed plays of this period.

Waller's most convincing example of an authorial type of stage direction is the one at the beginning of 3.5, which asks for '2 *or* 3 *wenches*'. Certainly, no prompter would allow this kind of vagueness. But, as has been shown above (pp. 34–5), the dance was probably a special case: it was borrowed or adapted from Beaumont's Masque of the Inner Temple and Gray's Inn and may have been rehearsed separately. If the 'wenches' were engaged only for the dance, Fletcher may not have known what number would be involved.

The odd wording of the marginal stage direction in Figure 16, 3.5.135 (the cue for the dance), must represent a misreading of whatever was crowded into the margin. The compositors omit a speech prefix for Gerald, giving the whole speech, improbably, to

Pirithous. They seem not even to have realized that the first and second lines of Gerald's speech would have been separated by a good deal of stage activity. Montgomery (Oxf) suggests that *School*, an abbreviated speech-prefix, got mixed up with the rest of the marginal note, which ought to read 'Knock for the Dance' (*TxC*, 632). But the direction remains puzzling: did knocking replace, or supplement, Gerald's throwing up of his cap as an entrance cue? Leech suggests (179) that the prompter had forgotten the visual cue mentioned in the text and inserted a sound cue instead and Leslie Thomson has found evidence of 'Knock Act' being used in this way (188). From Beaumont's descriptive pamphlet, we know that the original effect depended on synchronized spontaneity, 'the Men issuing out of one side of the Boscage, and the Woemen from the other'. Perhaps the dancers (supposedly hidden in the bushes but really behind the doors at the back of the stage) were unable to see Gerald and had to be cued for their entrance by someone backstage. Or perhaps the knock was the cue for the musicians, who were *dispersed* (see 3.5.33) and might have had difficulty coordinating their first note. Some modern productions have created business to explain why Gerald is finally reduced to calling for his dancers to enter: either he discovers that he has lost his cap – stolen by the Bavian (Berkeley) or thrown away in a fit of exasperation (Ashland), or else the dancers are struck with stage-fright and need extra cajoling to bring them on. The 'Enter' which occurs in the marginal direction may refer to the entry of the dancers or to Gerald's re-entry after the dance.

I have already noted (p. 114) the difficulty of clarifying the direction of the dialogue at the end of this scene. Playtexts from this period rarely indicate the person to whom a line is addressed, and *The Two Noble Kinsmen* never does so, though a change in the addressee is sometimes indicated by parentheses. All stage directions of this type can thus be assumed to be editorial and I have not credited them in the notes.

This example shows how editing a text can also involve imagining it in performance. One then has to decide whether to add stage directions to help the reader imagine it too. Editorial practice in this respect has changed over the years and at present the tendency is to be generous with such directions. The difficulty is that there

126

are many points at which any one of *several* things might be happening. To choose only one possibility, and dignify it with the status of a stage direction, is to risk closing off interpretation for both readers and performers. I have therefore chosen the more cumbersome method of adding as few directions as possible in the text itself, using the notes instead for discussion of the most likely alternatives.

Emendations of difficult passages

Emendation was common in the earliest editions; editors with no knowledge of Renaissance handwriting or printing conventions recklessly suggested alternatives to anything they found at all difficult to understand. The reaction against this attitude was a conservative approach that has itself only recently been challenged, particularly in the new Oxford Complete Works of Shakespeare. On the whole, the practice of most editors is still to make their text look as much as possible like a modern one in everything but the actual words. But many critics are distinctly suspicious of the Shakespeare 'not of an age but for all time' who emerges from this treatment, especially when he is contrasted with his contemporaries, often available only in old-spelling texts that firmly anchor them in a particular historical period. The compromise made in the otherwise excellent *Riverside Shakespeare*, which retains a few archaic spellings with no special justification, has not been generally accepted. Now that modern technology makes the reproduction of original texts relatively easy, it is possible to show something of the process (as here) and thus avoid presenting an emendation as if it were self-evidently the correct reading.

Both the openings reproduced here contain, along with the minor technical problems already mentioned, substantial textual ones. It is regrettable that Emilia's speech in 1.3 about her friendship with Flavina, the most frequently anthologized in the play, is also one of the most difficult. Lines 72–3 (*her affections ... were*); the hyphenated *fury-innocent* of line 79; the meaning of *old importments bastard* (80) and the question of whether to emend *sex individual* (82), do not spoil the effect as much as one might expect, since, as often in the play, the general sense is clearer than the precise grammatical construction. In attempting to clarify such a passage, the editor needs to decide whether its confusion results from misreading by the compositors or confused writing by the author. The various alternatives suggested in the textual notes mostly depend on the first assumption, while my very conservative reading of the text depends on the second. The various emendations normally ignore the hyphen in *fury-innocent*, yet this is not a feature likely to be misread; Bowers points out (8.270) that 'the hyphen suggests some compound in the manuscript'. In looking again at Montaigne, an obvious influence on this scene (see pp. 55–6), I became convinced that *fury* was not a misreading, however difficult it might be to make sense of its use in the construction as a whole. An eighteenth-century commentator on Seward's edition, Benjamin Heath, decided, after analysing this passage in some detail, to leave it as it was: 'Patching up a text, so as to give it the glimmering of a meaning, is so far from being of service, that it tends only, by removing all suspicion of a Mistake, to perpetuate the corruption' (Heath, 88). I have followed his example.

The difficulties with pp. 46–7 (Fig. 16) are of another kind. Without more information, it is impossible to know what is meant by the Schoolmaster's references to *Morr* and *Is* and how these were *glewd together* at line 118. Bibliographical knowledge is valuable here chiefly in showing that the dash that follows both nouns is often used to indicate some kind of stage business. The nature of this business, the equally mysterious direction following line 135, and what exactly happens at the end when Theseus and Pirithous give presents to the Schoolmaster, are matters for the director rather than the bibliographer, and can benefit from research into the context of performance such as I have outlined in Appendices 4 and 5.

The manuscript copy

The Oxford editors in 1987 (*TxC*, 625–9) believed that the manuscript behind the quarto of *The Two Noble Kinsmen* was either 'a revised holograph' or 'a scribal transcript to which revisions were made'; in either case, it 'was annotated by a book-keeper, *c*.1613', and 'further annotated, probably by Edward Knight, in preparation for a revival, *c*.1625–6' (629). In subsequent work (Taylor & Jowett, 241) they have endorsed the second alternative, which also seems to me the more likely of the two. More work on the output of the printer, Thomas Cotes – how much did he normally revise his authors and impose a house style? – will perhaps settle the question for good.

The quarto is a well-printed text by the standards of the period, but with one or two anomalies, which may be evidence of revision. Other errors were probably the result of difficulty in reading the original manuscript. The fact that there is only one authoritative edition limits editorial disagreement to relatively minor emendations and the addition of stage directions, with the further debate as to whether to treat the prison scene in Act 2 as continuous with 2.1. Clearly, the task for a modern editor is to regularize the presentation of the text, so that variations of format are not mistaken for significant symbols; to correct obvious errors, identify others that may not be immediately apparent, and suggest alternative possibilities where there is no clear solution; and to supplement incomplete information. The resulting text must be as clear as possible, but should retain original features even where these are confusing. Each editor has been able to make some contribution to the play, but there is still much to do. In particular, the increasing availability of computer databases should make it possible to write with much more certainty about the authorship question.

Note on personifications

The folowing have been silently capitalized because they are clearly envisaged as personifications in the text: Prologue 7 Modesty; 1.1.13 Nature; 1.2.19, 23 Peace, 67 Chance; 1.3.40 Death; 1.5.8. Pleasure; 2.1.28 Fame; 2.2.38, 57 Fortune, 104 Time; 2.5.29 Honour; 2.6.8 Love; 3.1.15 Lady Fortune; 4.2.7 Nature, 14, 42 Love, 21 Fame, 21 Honour, 52 Fancy, 108 Victory; 5.4.20, 112 Fortune.

For a note on the editions cited, see page 364.

THE TWO
NOBLE KINSMEN

LIST OF ROLES

Speaker of the PROLOGUE

BOY	*singer in the wedding procession*
HYMEN	*figures in the wedding procession*
Nymphs	

ATHENIANS

THESEUS	*Duke of Athens*
PIRITHOUS	*friend of Theseus*
HIPPOLYTA	*bride of Theseus, an Amazon*
EMILIA	*sister of Hippolyta*
OFFICER (Artesius)	*officer of Theseus*
HERALD	
WAITING WOMAN	*to Emilia*
JAILER	
DAUGHTER	*to Jailer*
WOOER	*to Jailer's Daughter*
BROTHER	*to Jailer*
TWO FRIENDS	*of Jailer*
DOCTOR	
MAID	*companion to Jailer's Daughter*
SCHOOLMASTER (Gerald)	
FIVE COUNTRYMEN	(*among them* Arcas, Rycas, Sennois)
TABORER (Timothy)	
Actor playing BAVIAN	
FIVE COUNTRYWOMEN	Barbary, Friz, Luce, Maudlin, Nell
GENTLEMEN	
EXECUTIONER	
TWO MESSENGERS	

THEBANS

THREE QUEENS	*widows of besiegers of Thebes*
ARCITE	*Cousins, nephews to Creon,*
PALAMON	*King of Thebes*
VALERIUS	
THREE KNIGHTS	*supporters of Arcite*
THREE KNIGHTS	*supporters of Palamon*

Speaker of the EPILOGUE

Servants, Guards, Attendants, etc.

LIST OF ROLES Not in Q. A perfunctory and inaccurate list is supplied in F and a different, equally inaccurate, one in the 1711 edition. For suggestions as to the original casting, see pp. 64–6. Doubling (though impossible to identify precisely) would have been easy. Many of the main-plot characters never meet those in the subplot; many, such as the Three Queens, the Schoolmaster and the Doctor, make only cameo appearances; and others may have been used only as dancers.

1 Speaker of the PROLOGUE Although the Prologue is immediately followed by a procession that probably required the entire cast, the speaker could have been any one of the actors, with his Act 1 costume concealed beneath the long black cloak which was traditionally worn by the 'Prologue' (see Induction to Jonson, *Cynthia's Revels*). He is uncharacterized, except as an actor. The audience was apparently expected to recognize him as a spokesman for the company. The reference to weakness (24) might indicate a boy actor; on the other hand, if Gerald spoke the lines there would be an interesting play-within-a-play effect at his reappearance as Prologue in 3.5.99 (RA). He may carry a book, representing the works of Chaucer.

2 BOY This might have been a professional singer or a member of the cast, perhaps the same boy who played the Jailer's Daughter.

3 HYMEN not the god of marriage himself, but (as in *AYL* 5.4.107) an actor; he wears a yellow robe and carries a torch with which to light the nuptial fire.

4 Nymphs young women dressed like the local deities of woods and streams, with flowing robes, long hair and flower garlands or wheaten wreaths

5 THESEUS The earliest and most legendary of the heroes in Plutarch's *Lives*, which is the main source for his character. His legend often overlaps with that of his supposed kinsman Hercules. Plutarch's explanation is that Theseus admired and imitated

Hercules (Plutarch, 34–5) and the dramatists retain this characteristic (see p. 109 above). The play omits the less savoury aspects of his legend, but his adventures in the Cretan labyrinth, his abandonment of Ariadne, his promiscuity and his descent to the underworld are referred to indirectly. He has the fourth-largest part, 326 lines.

6 PIRITHOUS Best known as a famous classical example of friendship. As Proudfoot has pointed out, the variant spellings of his name are one of the clearest indicators of dual authorship. In 1.1 he is *Pirithous* in the SP and addressed twice as *Pyrithous*; in 1.3 he is referred to in dialogue as *Pirithous* and *Pirothous* (possibly a misprint, but possibly a recollection of the Chaucerian spelling *Perotheus*). His name evidently has three syllables, stressed on the first (see 1.1.219). In 2.2, though the name continues to be spelled *Pirithous*, scansion requires it to be a four-syllable word, stressed on the second syllable. In 2.4 the SPs give his name in both forms and it continues to have four syllables; in 3.5 he is abbreviated in SPs as both *Pir.* (once) and *Per.* (four times); in 3.6, 4.1, 4.2 and 5.1 he is consistently *Perithous* (or abbreviated to *Per.*); in 5.3 he is *Perithous* in two SDs (probably added by the book-keeper) and in the first SP, but the spelling in the rest of the play reverts to *Pirithous* (since his name is not spoken in these scenes, there is no evidence of its pronunciation). In other ways too, he seems to have given the dramatists trouble. His thematic importance, as an example of friendship that reinforces rather than conflicts with married love, is not reflected in the size of his part, though he is entrusted with two very difficult speeches (4.2.91–116 and 5.4.48–85). The roles of Helicanus and Escanes in *Pericles* are similarly undeveloped (see pp. 33–4 above).

7 HIPPOLYTA The Amazonian queen whom Theseus married after conquering her in battle, also called Anti-

133

ope (though the latter is named as a separate person in *MND* 2.1.80). See duBois (32–3) for other versions of her legend. Amazons are traditionally associated with lust (Shepherd, 271); hence, the name is sometimes given to lascivious women, as in Fletcher's *The Custom of the Country* (*c.*1620) and Ford's *'Tis Pity She's a Whore* (*c.*1629); the Hippolita who appears in Fletcher and Massinger's *Sea Voyage* (1622) tells her fellow Amazons that she 'was not made / For this single life' (Bowers, 9:2.2.34–5). Nothing in the play indicates whether Hippolyta and Emilia are dressed like Amazons, with buskins, skirts looped up and bows and arrows. Amazons were said to cut off one breast to make it easier to shoot their arrows; boy actors could have achieved this effect, but it is unlikely that they did.

8 EMILIA A character invented by Boccaccio. Chaucer anglicized her name to Emily but the play uses both forms, depending on the needs of the metre. Spelled both 'Emilia' and 'Aemilia', the name occurs elsewhere in Shakespeare (*CE*, *Oth*, *WT*). Hers is the third-largest part in the play, 368 lines.

9 OFFICER (Artesius) A non-speaking character, not listed in the initial Q SD for 1.1, who comes into existence only when Theseus addresses him at 1.1.159 (as 'Artesuis', presumably a transposition or misreading of the MS). There are many possible sources for his name; its female form, Artesia, occurs in Sidney's *Arcadia*. He is addressed by it only because Theseus at this point is trying unsuccessfully to convince the three queens that he is deputizing a trusted officer on their service. He may have been played by one of the two small-part actors named in the SD at the beginning of 5.1; they were probably present whenever the play calls for officers or attendants.

11 WAITING WOMAN Her appearance is called for only in 2.2, but in most productions she is present in all court scenes and becomes the 'servant' in 5.3.

12 JAILER He is called *Jailer* in 2.1 (spelled both *Jayler* and *Jaylor*) but in Q he becomes *Keeper* in 2.2, both in the dialogue and in SPs. His daughter also refers to him as 'the mean keeper of [Palamon's] prison' (2.4.3), though this is less significant, as the words were interchangeable. When he reappears in 4.1 he is *Jailer*, and so to the end of the play. He may be 'mean' only in comparison to a prince, since the keeper of a state prison like the Tower of London would normally be a knight.

13 DAUGHTER The absence of proper names for this character, her father, her suitor and the other characters in this part of the plot is not unusual. Webster's *Duchess of Malfi*, for instance, has no other name and the names of many Shakespeare characters are known through their speech prefixes rather than from the dialogue. The Daughter *is* named in all later adaptations (see pp. 75–7 above). She has 324 lines, nearly as many as Theseus.

14 WOOER If this part was taken by a young actor, as 4.3.76 indicates, he might have doubled one of the female roles, or any of the court party, since he never appears in scenes with them. In some productions, he becomes one of the countrymen in 2.3 and 2.5, though his presence, with the Daughter, in the morris of 3.5 would be incompatible with his account in 4.1. The fact that he has no lines in 4.1 after the entrance of the Daughter, though some intervention from him could be very affecting, suggests that he may have needed to exit to play one of the messengers in 4.2.

16 TWO FRIENDS of the Jailer. Like the Jailer's BROTHER, they speak only in 4.1. To judge from 4.1.1–31, they are attendants on Theseus and should be present in 3.6 to hear the debate they describe later.

17 DOCTOR A change in authorship has sometimes been detected in the transi-

tion from the pompous but sympathetic, prose-speaking Doctor of 4.3 to the cynical, even misogynistic, verse-speaker of 5.2. However, many actors have used the discrepancies to create an effectively varied portrait. Moreover, the mainly sympathetic Scottish doctor in *Macbeth* is also surprisingly cynical in his final lines (5.3.61–2).

18 MAID It has been argued that this is a 'ghost' character, but see n. to 5.2.39 SD.

19 SCHOOLMASTER (Gerald) a typical stage pedant who owes something to Rhombus in Sidney's *Lady of May* (1578–9) and Holofernes in *LLL* (*c*.1595). It is not clear whether he is meant to be identical with Giraldo, Emilia's Schoolmaster, mentioned by the Daughter in 4.3.13. See Appendix 4, pp. 354–5.

20 FIVE COUNTRYMEN Four countrymen appear in 2.3; three others (Arcas, Sennois and Rycas) are said to be planning to join the maying, and Rycas at least is present in 3.5. There may, then, be as many as seven countrymen in all, though one may be identical with Timothy the Taborer and another with the Bavian. It is also possible that the countrymen in 2.3 are not speaking about offstage friends, but referring explicitly to one another. In any case, there are clearly meant to be six male dancers in 3.5, since the absence of a sixth woman creates a gap in the planned performance. I am assuming that the Bavian would pair off with a woman dancer but that the Taborer would not. Arcas, in Statius's *Thebaid*, is a contender in the funeral games; the name (also spelled Archas) occurs frequently in works with a classical setting and even in Fletcher's *Loyal Subject* (1618), which is set in Russia. Arcas is also another name for Mercury; Thompson (*Chaucer*, 185) points out that Mercury appears to Arcite at the same point in *The Knight's Tale* (*KT*) where Fletcher introduces the countrymen. The

names Rycas and Sennois have no obvious origins. Rycas looks like a coinage formed on the same principle as Arcas; Sennois (the current form for 'Sienese' – see *AW* 1.2.1) may be a misreading of Sennius (as with Artesius, above) or of one of the other classical names that the authors could have found in Plutarch: Simois, the river flowing by Troy; Sinnis, a murderer killed by the young Theseus (Plutarch, 36); or Solois, who loved the Amazon Antiope and committed suicide for her sake (Plutarch, 55–6).

21 TABORER (Timothy) Perhaps a generic name for someone who played the pipe and drum in popular entertainments; the piper who appears with the morris dancers in the anonymous *Jack Drum's Entertainment* (1600) is called Timothy Tweedle (RP). The part may have been taken by a theatre musician; Ingram (80) points out that Fletcher sometimes incorporates them into his plays. As Laroque (132) notes, the fife and drum are sexual symbols and the player may have made obscene gestures with these instruments. See Figure 20, second from left.

22 BAVIAN a baboon, an animal thought to be a cross between a dog and an ape; here, an actor impersonating one. Cotgrave's French–English dictionary defines Babion, the alternative form, as both baboon and 'crafty knave'. They seem to have been something of a craze in this period: the name is a synonym for fools in *The Gull's Hornbook* (1608) and *The Roaring Girl* (1611); Lording Barry's *Ram Alley* (1611) refers to a woman trying to imitate their contortions; and the leading comic of the Red Bull, Thomas Greene, specialized in dancing in a baboon costume (see Baskervill, 117 (RP)).

23 FIVE COUNTRYWOMEN Their names are given in 3.5.26–8. A sixth, Cicely, is named at 3.5.45 but fails to appear. These would have been boys, like all the antimasquers.

27 THREE QUEENS Perhaps played by men rather than boys, given the

unusually large number of boy players required in 1.1. The First Queen, in *KT*, is described only as 'the oldest lady of them all' (912); in the classical sources she is called Evadne, a name which Beaumont and Fletcher gave to the heroine of *The Maid's Tragedy* (1610–11).

28 ARCITE probably derived, as Skeat suggests, from the Greek Archytes. He is Arcita in Boccaccio, with three syllables and the 'c' pronounced like 'ch' in 'church'. In *KT* he is usually Arcite (two syllables, stressed on the second, rhyming with 'quite', 'lite' and 'smyte'). The verse sometimes requires three syllables ('"Alas," quod he, "Arcita, cosyn mine"' (1281)) and a shift of stress, as in 'The pryere stint of Arcita the stronge' (2421). In the play, both authors stress the first syllable. The occasional Chaucerian spelling *Arsett* and the variant spellings in Henslowe's references to the 1595 *Palamon and Arcite* (arset, harset, a'sett) (Henslowe, 24–5) indicate that the 'c' in his name was soft, but in some modern productions it is pronounced like 'k'. He has 514 lines, the second-largest role in the play.

29 PALAMON anglicized from the Italian *Palemone* and stressed on the first syllable. Palaemon (stressed on the second syllable) is a very common name in classical literature (occurring several times in Statius) and in pastoral literature in the vernacular:

Guarini's *Pastor Fido*, Spenser's *Shepherd's Calendar*, Brooke's *Melanthe*, Daniel's *Queen's Arcadia*. With 589 lines, he has the largest part in the play, well behind some contemporary dramatic heroes (Coriolanus has 886 lines, Leontes 682) but more than Posthumus and Iachimo in *Cym* (441 and 432 respectively).

30 VALERIUS a common name in plays with a classical setting, e.g. Thomas Heywood's *Rape of Lucrece* (and cf. Valeria in *Cor*); also used for one of the outlaws in *TGV* (5.3.8)

31–2 KNIGHTS In the *Teseida* and *KT* the tournament that decides the lovers' fate involves 100 knights on each side. None of the knights in *TNK* is seen fighting. Only Palamon's knights speak, and they have very few lines. Their roles seem largely decorative and may have been taken by dancers. See Appendix 4 (pp. 352–3).

33 **Speaker of the** EPILOGUE The speech seems to have been written for a popular boy actor, who is invited to emphasize his youth and the tension between stage persona and 'real' self. The most likely candidate is the actor who played the Jailer's Daughter, especially as he is not on stage in the final scene. But the speaker's (feigned) timidity, his insistence that he 'cannot say' what he should, and his asking the audience to admit having been in love with 'a young handsome wench' might also be an effective way of completing Emilia's role.

THE TWO
NOBLE KINSMEN

[PROLOGUE]

Flourish. [Enter Speaker of the Prologue.]

New plays and maidenheads are near akin:
Much followed both, for both much money gi'en,
If they stand sound and well. And a good play,
Whose modest scenes blush on his marriage day
And shake to lose his honour, is like her   5
That after holy tie and first night's stir
Yet still is Modesty and still retains
More of the maid, to sight, than husband's pains.
We pray our play may be so, for I am sure
It has a noble breeder and a pure,   10
A learned, and a poet never went

PROLOGUE 1 SD **Flourish** Fanfare of trumpets or cornets, usually accompanying entrance or exit
2 **followed** sought after
3 **stand, sound, well** sexual puns, referring to male potency and to freedom (male or female) from venereal disease
4 **scenes** the entire content of the play. Taylor suggests (*TxC*, 630) that *his*, in 4 and 5, is a misreading of *hir* (her). But 'his' was still the standard neutral possessive: it seems in keeping with the sexual imagery just noted, which is both male and female, that the play should be imagined as male but compared to a bride about to lose her virginity (*honour*).

5 **shake to lose** tremble at the prospect of losing
6 **holy tie** wedding
  stir activity, especially sexual
7 **Modesty** the personification of modesty. A good play retains its freshness, as a good wife still looks like a virgin after the first night.
8 **pains** endeavours
9 **I am** probably pronounced *I'm*, as printed in F. For elisions, see p. 123 above.
10 **breeder** father. Chaucer's own purity is a guarantee of the purity of his offspring.
11 **went** existed; 'literally, "walked"' (Oxf[1])

PROLOGUE 0.1 *Enter* . . . Prologue] *Oxf subst.; not in Q*   9 I am] *Q;* I'm *F*

137

More famous yet 'twixt Po and silver Trent.
Chaucer, of all admired, the story gives;
There, constant to eternity, it lives.
If we let fall the nobleness of this   15
And the first sound this child hear be a hiss,
How will it shake the bones of that good man
And make him cry from under ground, 'Oh, fan
From me the witless chaff of such a writer
That blasts my bays and my famed works makes
     lighter   20
Than Robin Hood!' This is the fear we bring;
For, to say truth, it were an endless thing
And too ambitious to aspire to him,
Weak as we are, and, almost breathless, swim

---

12 **Po ... Trent** rivers in northern Italy
   and northern England, used as a
   shorthand for the civilized world. The
   Po is mentioned because of the
   famous Latin and Italian poets who
   were Chaucer's sources.
13 **gives** Perhaps, continuing the opening image, he gives it in marriage, as
   the father gives the bride.
14 **There** i.e., in his works (Craik)
   constant to eternity married to
   eternity; i.e., immortal
15 **let fall** fail to live up to
   the nobleness of this the tale's noble
   ancestry
18–19 **fan ... chaff** Chaff was removed
   from corn with a winnowing fan;
   metaphorically, it is worthless rubbish.
19 **writer** Though *wrighter*, the Q spelling, is common (and found in Fletcher's part-holograph verse letter to the
   Countess of Huntingdon), it may
   imply that such a figure is, like the
   'playwright, cartwright' Webster (see
   Bradbrook, *Webster*, 169), only a hack.
   The singular form has been taken as
   evidence against collaborative authorship (Lawrence, 450) but, given the

needs of rhyme, it should not be
pushed too far. Montgomery suggests
that *such a wrighter* means 'any writer
who' (*TxC*, 626). For a similiar confusion of 'parents' and 'Author' in
early editions of *KBP*, see Masten,
346–8.
20 **blasts my bays** 'destroys my laurel
   wreath', the symbol of poetic fame,
   which was supposed to protect one
   from being 'blasted' by lightning
21 **Robin Hood** 'a Tale of Robin Hood',
   proverbially, an unbelievable and trivial story. Waith (Oxf[1]) cites 'Tales of
   Robin Hood are good for fools' (Dent,
   T53).
22 **endless** both never-ending and useless (without an end or purpose)
24 **Weak as we are** Some editors begin a
   new sentence at this point. While *we*
   refers mainly to the actors, the sense
   of inadequacy refers mainly to their
   play and thus perhaps to the writer(s).
   I take *swim* to be an infinitive, parallel
   to *aspire*, and repunctuate accordingly.
   swim i.e., sail (used metaphorically of
   the boat). It may also refer literally to
   the actors' sense of themselves as out
   of their depth (see 26n., below).

24 and,] *this edn*; and Q   breathless,] *this edn*; breathless Q

In this deep water. Do but you hold out   25
Your helping hands and we shall tack about
And something do to save us. You shall hear
Scenes, though below his art, may yet appear
Worth two hours' travel. To his bones sweet sleep;
Content to you. If this play do not keep   30
A little dull time from us, we perceive
Our losses fall so thick, we must needs leave.

Flourish. [*Exit.*]

[1.1]   [*Music.*] *Enter Hymen with a torch burning; a* Boy, *in a*

25–6 **Do . . . hands** a conventional request for applause; cf. 'Lend us but half a hand' (Dekker and Webster, *Westward Ho!* (1604), 5.4.309–18) and 'With the help of your good hands' in the *Tempest* Epilogue. For other examples of the play as a sea voyage, see Berry (16). Masten (339–40) compares the many 'hands' involved in a work of theatrical collaboration. RA notes how many helping hands appear in the play from 1.1 (where they assist the queens to rise) to Arcite's 'Reach thy hand' (5.4.91).

25 **Do but you please**

26 ˙**tack about** change the direction of the sails to keep a straight course. 'The wind is here imagined as being produced by applause' (Proudfoot). Q reads *take about*; as Bowers notes, F's *tack* is an alternative spelling, also found in 3.4.10 and 4.1.152. Littledale notes a parallel with Fletcher's *The Loyal Subject*: 'tack about for honour' (3.2.53). The shift from swimming to sailing in the speaker's language may be simple inconsistency. Or *swim* and *sail* may be used interchangeably, each as a figure for the other; thus, *take/tack* might refer to the change of direction which will bring the breathless actors towards their helpers, either on shore or in the theatre audience. The image of swimming recurs in 1.2.7–

12; that of sailing in difficult waters in the Daughter's fantasies, 3.4.5–11 and 4.1.141–52.

28 **may** that may

29 **two hours' travel** metaphorical: the journey through the play. Some editors emend to *travail*; the word clearly means both journey and labour. Littledale cites other references to two (or three) hours as the normal duration of a performance; the best-known is the Prologue to *RJ*.

29–30 **To . . . you** The implied verb is 'we wish'.

31 **dull time** 'period of slack trade' (Proudfoot). See also p. 35 above.

32 **Our losses** primarily, financial disasters; but see p. 35 above
leave cease, 'give up acting' (Leech)

1.1 In Boccaccio and *KT* this episode occurs just outside Athens, near the temple of Clemency, and the suppliant women speak only to Theseus. He and Hippolyta have already been married for some time.

0.1 HYMEN His costume (see List of Roles) would have made him recognizable as the classical god of marriage and thus clarified the purpose of the opening procession. Waith (Oxf[1]) compares the elaborate reconstruction of a classical wedding in Jonson's *Hymenaei* (1606).

26 tack] *1711;* take *Q*   29 travel] *Q;* travail *Dyce*   30 keep] *1778;* keep, *Q*   32 SD *Exit.*] *Oxf; not in Q*   1.1] *Actus Primus. Q*   0.1 *Music.*] *after* The Song. 1 SD *Q*

white robe, before, singing and strewing flowers; after Hymen, a Nymph encompassed in her tresses, bearing a wheaten garland. Then THESEUS *between two other nymphs with wheaten chaplets on their heads. Then* HIPPOLYTA *the bride, led by* PIRITHOUS *and another holding a garland over her head (her tresses likewise hanging). After her,* EMILIA, *holding up her train; [Artesius; attendants; musicians].*

BOY [*Sings.*]

> Roses, their sharp spines being gone,
> Not royal in their smells alone
> But in their hue;

0.2 *before* in front of Hymen. SDs at the beginning of a scene usually list characters in order of entrance. Perhaps the song was a late addition to the scene. See p. 26 above.

0.3 *Nymph* strictly, a nature spirit, but often used, as here, to mean any young woman in generalized fancy dress (see List of Roles)
encompassed ... tresses with her hair hanging loose as a token of virginity
wheaten garland associated with peace in *Ham* 5.2.41. Here, it is a symbol of 'fertility, but also virginity' (Proudfoot compares 64–5, below, and 5.1.160).

0.4 *chaplets* garlands

0.5 *the bride* i.e., dressed as a bride

0.6 *another* vague, because the details of the procession would have been worked out in rehearsal rather than in the writing process. Since the bridegroom enters between two women, the bride is probably led between two men. At the royal wedding in February 1613 Princess Elizabeth was led between her brother and her uncle. The likeliest supporter for Hippolyta is Artesius, named only at 159.
her tresses Hippolyta's

0.7 EMILIA ... *train* Princess Elizabeth's train was carried by at least fourteen ladies (Nichols, 2.543); that only Emilia is available for this task shows the demand for boy actors in this production.

1 SD *Sings* Q prints the direction for music in the margin opposite the song, and the opening SD seems to indicate that the boy enters singing these words.

1–12 The flowers mentioned in the song belong to different times of the year. For Littledale's edition of the play the New Shakspere Society's editor, F. J. Furnivall, invited the comments of two botanists. One (R. C. A. Prior) felt that 'the writer did not know much about plants'; the other (W. Whale) noted that 'The flowers named may be all called Spring-flowers, but of course some blowing rather later than others.'

1 *spines* thorns. The thornless rose symbolizes perfection; compare later images of roses at 2.2.135–43 and 5.1.163–71.

2–3 *royal ... hue* scarlet or 'purple' (which, as Waith, Oxf[1], points out, is red), colours traditionally reserved for royalty

---

0.5 PIRITHOUS] *Seward (Theobald);* Theseus *Q*   0.7–8 *Artesius ... musicians*] *Weber; not in Q*   1 SD] *Bawcutt;* The Song. Musike. *Q*

Maiden pinks of odour faint,
Daisies smell-less yet most quaint,   5
  And sweet thyme true;

Primrose, first-born child of Ver,
Merry springtime's harbinger,
  With harebells dim,
Oxlips in their cradles growing,   10
Marigolds on deathbeds blowing,
Lark's-heels trim: *Strews flowers.*

All dear Nature's children sweet

---

4 **Maiden pinks** 'i.e., fresh pinks, also used for strewing upon the grave of a maiden or a faithful wife' (Skeat, who quotes Queen Katherine's request that her corpse be strewed with 'maiden flowers' (*H8* 4.2.168))

5 **Daisies . . . quaint** Furnivall (Spalding, p. v) could not believe that Shakespeare would have nothing better than this to say about Chaucer's favourite flower (see Prologue to *Legend of Good Women*, 40–3). The qualified phrasing may recall 'violets, dim, / But sweeter than the lids of Juno's eyes' (*WT* 4.4.120–1), especially in conjunction with *dim* in 9, below.
quaint trim, neat

6 **thyme** Q's spelling, *Time*, brings out the pun: time, proverbially, is the test of truth (see Dent, T324, T329a, T338, T580). Littledale quotes 'Time is to trie me' from 'A Nosegaie always sweet' in *A Handful of Pleasant Delights* (1584), which gives symbolic meanings to a number of flowers.

7 **Ver** spring

8 **harbinger** forerunner, herald

9 *****harebells** wild hyacinth, or *scilla nutens* (bluebells). Skeat's emendation has been generally accepted, because

primroses do not resemble bells, though Littledale argues that *bells* has the general sense of 'blossoms'.
dim dusky (because they grow in shady places)

10 **Oxlips** related to the primrose; Gerard's *Herbal* (635–8) groups them together.
in . . . growing 'The growth of the leaves would certainly give one an idea of the stem and Oxlip flowers being lodged in a cradle [?saucer]' (Prior (see 1n., above)).

11 Gerard's *Herbal* says nothing about this characteristic, but Rolfe suggests that *death beds* could mean graves: Skeat compares 'marigolds / Shall as a carpet hang upon thy grave / While summer-days do last' (*Per* 4.1.16). RP quotes the anon. *How a Man May Choose a Good Wife from a Bad* (1602), where a man who wishes his wife dead calls his second choice a marigold that would grow 'From out her grave' (sig. E1). The contrast between 10 and 11 creates a cycle of birth and death, like the more extended passage in *WT* 4.4.73ff.

12 **Lark's-heels** *flos regius*, or larkspur
trim neat

6 thyme] *(Time)* Q   7 Primrose, first-born] *Seward; Prim-rose first borne, Q*   9 harebells] *Skeat; her bels Q*   12 SD] *Strew / Flowers. / after 14–15 Q*   13–14 sweet / Lie] *sweete-/ Ly Q*

Lie 'fore bride and bridegroom's feet,
   Blessing their sense.   15
Not an angel of the air,
Bird melodious, or bird fair,
   Is absent hence.

The crow, the sland'rous cuckoo, nor
The boding raven, nor chough hoar,   20
   Nor chatt'ring 'pie,
May on our bride-house perch or sing,
Or with them any discord bring,
   But from it fly.

---

14 *Lie 'This verb [lie] is the first that
has yet occurred, and agrees with all
the preceding nominatives' (Skeat).
Whether it is a subjunctive, inviting
the flowers to lie before the couple, or
a present indicative (Bawcutt takes it
in conjunction with *is* in 18), or an
imperative (Oxf¹), can be clarified
in performance only by choosing
whether the boy should enter strewing flowers or begin strewing them
now, as Q's SD indicates.

15 pleasing all their senses

16 *angel Q has *angle* (according to
Bowers, a 'rare spelling' of *angel*, to
which it was changed in the 1679
Folio). Chaucer uses *waryangles*
(*Friar's Tale*, 1408) and Speght's 1602
edition glosses it as 'birds full of
noise'. Lists of birds, as of flowers, are
traditional in wedding poems. Spenser's *Epithalamion* urges his bride to
awake to the sweet singing of the birds
(78–85) and wishes the birds of ill-
omen far away from the bridal bed
(345–8). The wedding of Elizabeth
and Frederick took place on Valentine's Day 1613, and several poems
written for the occasion, Donne's and
Heywood's among them, refer to St
Valentine's marrying the birds on that

day (see also *MND* 4.1.139–40).

19–24 'Is the epithalamium broken off by
the entrance of the Queens?' (Walker,
3.340). Masefield (191) suggests that
the last stanza is a 'defence or exor-
cism to be sung in a very different
mood and key, to avert the evil omen
of the three approaching figures in
black'.

19 sland'rous cuckoo because its cry
told every man that he was a cuckold
(see *LLL* 5.2.910 and *MND* 3.1.136).

20 boding prophesying evil fortune. Cf.
'I would croak like a raven, I would
bode, I would bode' (*TC* 5.2.181–2).
   *chough hoar a jackdaw, which has a
grey (or hoary) head; see Harting
115–19

21 'pie magpie

22 The line would make better metrical
and grammatical sense without the
first word. But the verbs in this song
appear to be stating, not merely wishing for, the absence of evil-omened
birds – which lends still greater irony
to the sudden arrival of the queens
and to 40–2, below.
   bride-house 'The house where a
wedding is held' (*OED*), now used
only in dialect

---

16 angel] *F; angle Q; augel (Theobald)*   18 Is] *Q; Be Seward*   20 chough hoar] *Seward; Clough
hee Q*

Enter three Queens *in black, with veils stained, with imperial crowns. The* First Queen *falls down at the foot of* THESEUS; *the* Second *falls down at the foot of* HIPPOLYTA; *the* Third *before* EMILIA.

1 QUEEN [*to Theseus*]
　For pity's sake and true gentility's,   25
　Hear and respect me.

2 QUEEN [*to Hippolyta*]   For your mother's sake
　And as you wish your womb may thrive with fair
　　ones,
　Hear and respect me.

3 QUEEN [*to Emilia*]
　Now, for the love of him whom Jove hath marked
　The honour of your bed and for the sake   30
　Of clear virginity, be advocate
　For us and our distresses. This good deed
　Shall raze you out o'th' book of trespasses
　All you are set down there.

THESEUS
　Sad lady, rise.

HIPPOLYTA　　　Stand up.

EMILIA　　　　　　No knees to me!   35
　What woman I may stead that is distressed
　Does bind me to her.

24.1 *stained* dyed (Proudfoot); black
24.1–2 *imperial crowns* In *KT* the speaker says only that each of them 'hath be a duchesse or a queene' (923). Waith (Oxf¹) cites *OED* ('Of or pertaining to a sovereign state') to show that the adjective need not refer to empire.
25 **pity's . . . gentility's** 'pity' and 'gentilesse' are key words in Chaucer. Cf. the Queen's words in *KT*: 'Some drop of pitie, through thy gentilnesse / Upon us wretched women let thou fall' (920–1).
26 **respect** pay attention to

29–30 **him . . . bed** your future husband, as yet unknown but already destined by Jove for that honour (cf. 5.3.37–40)
31 **clear** pure
33 **raze you** scrape out, erase (for you)
th' book of trespasses 'recording angel's register of sins' (Leech)
34 all trespasses listed as yours
35 **No knees to me!** Cf. 'Your knees to me, to your corrected son?' (*Cor* 5.3.57)
36 **What** whatever
stead help, be of use to
37 **bind . . . her** earn my gratitude

36 stead] *(steed) Q*

THESEUS

What's your request? [*to First Queen*]
Deliver you for all.

1 QUEEN

We are three queens whose sovereigns fell before
The wrath of cruel Creon, who endure   40
The beaks of ravens, talons of the kites
And pecks of crows, in the foul fields of Thebes.
He will not suffer us to burn their bones,
To urn their ashes, nor to take th'offence
Of mortal loathsomeness from the blest eye   45
Of holy Phoebus, but infects the winds
With stench of our slain lords. Oh pity, Duke;
Thou purger of the earth, draw thy feared sword
That does good turns to th' world; give us the bones
Of our dead kings that we may chapel them;   50
And of thy boundless goodness take some note
That for our crowned heads we have no roof,
Save this which is the lion's and the bear's
And vault to every thing.

THESEUS   Pray you, kneel not:

---

38 **Deliver** speak
39 Q, apart from '*kneel to Emilia*' at 106, gives no indication of how and when the numerous references to kneeling and rising are to be carried out. Many editors assume that the queens kneel throughout the scene, joined by Hippolyta at 192 and Emilia at 200. Leech directs them to rise at 77; Waith (Oxf[1]) has the Second and Third Queens rise when they are first invited to do so (37), while the First Queen remains kneeling until 76, and the Third Queen, after kneeling to Emilia at 106, rises at 119. I have largely followed Montgomery's stage directions, which seem theatrically effective, though they require emending Q's SD at 106 to '*[kneeling still] to Emilia*'.

40 **Creon** the first connection of the play to the Theban legend; see p. 40 above
41–2 Waith (Oxf[1]) compares 'Where dwell'st thou? – Under the canopy . . . I' th' city of kites and crows' (*Cor* 4.5.38–43).
44 **urn** place in an urn
45–6 **eye . . . Phoebus** the sun
48 **purger of the earth** Theseus, whose banner, in *KT*, bears 'the red statue of Mars' on a white background (975–7), here seems identified with the god himself. Bawcutt compares 5.1.62–6.
50 **chapel** place in a chapel; see *urn*, 44, above, another example of a noun used as a verb
51 **of** out of
52 **crowned** crownèd
52–4 another apparent reminiscence of *Cor* 4.5 (see 41–2n., above)

---

40 endure] *(Mason);* endured *Q*   41 talons] *1711 (subst.);* Tallents *Q*   42 fields] *Q;* field *F*

I was transported with your speech and suffered   55
Your knees to wrong themselves. I have heard the
   fortunes
Of your dead lords, which gives me such lamenting
As wakes my vengeance and revenge for 'em.
[*to First Queen*]
King Capaneus was your lord. The day
That he should marry you, at such a season   60
As now it is with me, I met your groom.
By Mars's altar, you were that time fair!
Not Juno's mantle fairer than your tresses
Nor in more bounty spread her. Your wheaten wreath
Was then nor threshed nor blasted; Fortune at you   65
Dimpled her cheek with smiles. Hercules our
   kinsman,
Then weaker than your eyes, laid by his club;

55 **transported** 'carried away by my thoughts' (Skeat compares *Tem* 1.2.76)

58 **vengeance and revenge** This apparent redundancy also occurs in *R2* 4.1.67 (Littledale).

59 **King . . . lord** In *KT* the queen herself tells Theseus this. The name is spelled Campaneus in the 1602 edition of Speght's Chaucer, and pronounced with stress on the second and fourth syllables. Here it is stressed on the first and third. In Greek, it has three syllables, as in Jonson, *Catiline*, 5: 4.5.755 (RP). 'Probably Fletcher would not have committed this false quantity' (Spalding, 30n.).

60 **should marry** was about to marry

61–2 **I met . . . fair** The punctuation is ambiguous: *by Mars's altar* is either the place where Theseus (as a participant in the wedding procession) met Capaneus or a mild oath. The latter is more likely, since Theseus elsewhere swears by Mars (see 1.4.17).

63 **Juno's mantle** Jonson, in *Hymenaei*, describes her mantle as covered with lilies and roses (Jonson, 7: lines 219–20). Leech suggests that the lines evoke the spread tail of the peacock, traditionally associated with Juno. Bawcutt refers to the mantle worn by Juno when she wants to seduce Zeus (*Iliad*, 14), an episode which also seems to be in the dramatist's mind at 175 below.

64 **spread her** Apparently used reflexively, the verb refers to the abundance of the Queen's hair which, like Hippolyta's, would have been worn loose for the wedding.

64–5 **wreath . . . threshed . . . blasted** 'Here Theseus may be supposed to point to one of the "wheaten chaplets"' (Skeat). But Theseus may have a more abstract meaning: the queen, when·he last saw her, was a virgin, unharvested by her husband, unblasted by fortune.

66 **Hercules** probably pronounced with two syllables: 'Ercles' (Skeat cites 'Ercles' vein' in *MND* 1.2.29). See List of Roles for Theseus' relationship with Hercules.

59 lord. The] *1711 subst.;* Lord the *Q*   61 groom.] *Leech;* Groome, *Q*   62 Mars's] *(Marsis)*

He tumbled down upon his Nemean hide
And swore his sinews thawed. Oh, grief and time,
Fearful consumers, you will all devour!   70

1 QUEEN
Oh, I hope some god,
Some god hath put his mercy in your manhood,
Whereto he'll infuse power, and press you forth
Our undertaker.

THESEUS   Oh, no knees, none, widow.
Unto the helmeted Bellona use them,   75
And pray for me, your soldier.
Troubled I am.   *Turns away.*

2 QUEEN   Honoured Hippolyta,
Most dreaded Amazonian, that hast slain
The scythe-tusked boar; that with thy arm, as strong
As it is white, wast near to make the male   80
To thy sex captive, but that this thy lord,

---

68 ***Nemean hide** the hide which
Hercules wore after killing the
Nemean lion in one of his 'labours'.
The word is scanned the same way
(three syllables, stressed on the first)
in *LLL* 4.1.88 and *Ham* 1.4.83
(RP).

69 **his sinews thawed** His muscles
dissolved with the warmth of sexual
desire (as when he let himself become
'effeminate' for love of Omphale).

71–3 The converse of this is expressed in
Cor: 'He wants nothing of a god but
eternity, and a heaven to throne in. –
Yes, mercy, if you report him truly'
(5.4.24–6). Cf. 87 below.

73 **power** one syllable
press urge; perhaps, as in 'press
gangs': forcibly make a soldier. Mincoff (113–14) compares other images
of pressing and stamping at 108–9 and
216–17.

74 **undertaker** *OED* cites this as an example of the now obsolete meaning,

'One who aids or assists', translating
the Latin *susceptor*. If Theseus assists
the First Queen to rise during his next
speech, the stage picture embodies
her words.

75 **Bellona** the Roman goddess of war.
Theseus insists on his own humanity.

77 SD *Turns away* Cf. the hero standing
in silence, then turning away, in *Cor*
5.3.168. Theseus stands frozen while
the Second and Third Queens make
their petitions.

78–9 **that ... boar** Hippolyta was not
present at the famous hunt of the
Calydonian boar which included
Theseus, Hercules and the huntress
Atalanta; the reference may be in-
tended simply to emphasize her fierce-
ness as a huntress, also recalled in
MND.

80–1 **the male ... captive** Unlike
MND, *TNK* stresses the background
of war between the Amazons and
Theseus' army.

68 Nemean] *Seward;* Nenuan *Q*

Born to uphold creation in that honour
First nature styled it in, shrunk thee into
The bound thou wast o'erflowing, at once subduing
Thy force and thy affection; soldieress,   85
That equally canst poise sternness with pity,
Whom now I know hast much more power on him
Than ever he had on thee, who ow'st his strength
And his love too, who is a servant for
The tenor of thy speech; dear glass of ladies: 90
Bid him that we, whom flaming war doth scorch,
Under the shadow of his sword may cool us.
Require him he advance it o'er our heads.
Speak't in a woman's key; like such a woman
As any of us three; weep ere you fail.   95
Lend us a knee;
But touch the ground for us no longer time

82–3 Born ... in Q's *stilde* might also be *still'd*, i.e., instilled; the meaning would be the same: 'Theseus, who was born to keep created things in the same relative position of honour in which nature first appointed them' (Skeat). Craik suggests an allusion to the fact that Adam was created first, both in time and in dignity.

84 bound ... o'erflowing like water confined in a river or fountain

85 soldieress *OED* gives this as the first use of the word.

86 poise weigh

87 Whom Seward emended to *who*, but the word's immediate function as the object of *know* dominates its grammatical one as the subject of *hast*.
power on power over. Rolfe compares 'The pow'r that I have on you is to spare you' (*Cym* 5.5.418).

88 ever one syllable
ow'st ownest

89–90 who ... speech The multiplicity of relative pronouns (*that* in 78, 79, 86, *who* and *whom* in 87, 88 and 89)

makes this speech sound like a series of afterthoughts. Most of the pronouns refer to Hippolyta herself, but *who* in 89 could be either Theseus or Love (Cupid). The sense is that Hippolyta, conquered in battle, nevertheless conquers by every word she speaks or every intention (*tenor*) that Theseus intuits from her speech.

90 glass of ladies a mirror, or model, for other women. Cf. 'Let all sweet ladies break their flattering glasses, / And dress themselves in her' (Webster, *DM*, 1.1.204–5).

92 Under ... sword probably based on 'the expression "Under the shadow of thy wings", which occurs frequently in Scripture' (Shaheen)

93 require request

94 key voice, tone (as in music)

94–5 like ... three that is, *not* like an unwomanly Amazon

95 weep ... fail weep rather than give up

96 Lend ... knee kneel with us. Cf. *MM* 5.1.447.

---

83 styled] *(stilde)*   89 for] *Q;* to *Seward*   90 thy] *Seward;* the *Q*   95–6] *one line Q*

Than a dove's motion, when the head's plucked off.
Tell him, if he i'th' blood-sized field lay swollen,
Showing the sun his teeth, grinning at the moon,   100
What you would do.

HIPPOLYTA   Poor lady, say no more.
I had as lief trace this good action with you
As that whereto I am going, and never yet
Went I so willing way. My lord is taken
Heart-deep with your distress. Let him consider: 105
I'll speak anon.   [*Second Queen rises.*]

3 QUEEN   Oh, my petition was
Set down in ice, which by hot grief uncandied
Melts into drops; so sorrow, wanting form,
Is pressed with deeper matter.

EMILIA   Pray, stand up;

98 **a dove's ... off** The comma after
motion, which most editors remove,
may indicate the slight pause before
the shock effect (see pp. 98 and 108
above). Littledale compares 'Like to a
new-kill'd bird she trembling lies'
(*Luc* 457).

99 **blood-sized** soaked with blood like a
wall or paper that has been soaked
with size (a gelatinous glaze).
Littledale compares *Ham* 2.2.484:
'o'er-sized with coagulate gore'.

102 **I had ... trace** I would as gladly
follow
this good action either the attack on
Creon or the petitioning of Theseus.
Cf. 173, below.

104 **so willing way** 'so willing a journey'
(Seward). The comma after *willing* in
Q suggests that it may have been the
original ending of the sentence, or
that the compositor took it to be one.
Hippolyta may compare herself and
Theseus to Hercules at the cross-
roads, choosing between the paths of
virtue and of pleasure. The strewn
flowers would make the *way* of pleasure visible.
taken seized, enchanted. The sense is
closest to *OED v.* II ** 7.

105–6 **Let ... anon** Hippolyta now becomes part of the tableau along with
the motionless, troubled Theseus.

106–7 **my petition ... ice** 'Implying
that her earlier speech, 29–34, was
cold and formal' (Bawcutt). Cf. ' a
mockery king of snow, / Standing
before the sun of Bolingbroke, / To
melt myself away in water-drops!' (*R2*
4.1.250–2).

107 **uncandied** melted; 'candied' in the
sense of congealed occurs frequently
in Shakespeare (Littledale compares
'the cold brook / Candied with ice',
Tim 4.3.225–6, also 'discandy' in *AC*
4.12.22). Muir (112–22) points out
the relation of this 'image cluster'
to *AC* 3.13.153–66. See pp. 20–1
above.

108 **drops** her tears

108–9 **sorrow ... matter** The Third
Queen contrasts the *form* in which she
had intended to speak and the *matter*,
or subject, of her speech, too deeply
felt to be confined in any form. Form
is normally seen as pressed on matter
like the stamp on a coin, but in this
case the conjunction of form with
matter has resulted in still greater
formlessness.

104 willing way] *Seward;* willing, way *Q*   106 SD] *Oxf; kneele to Emilia. Q*

Your grief is written in your cheek.
3 QUEEN   Oh, woe,   110
You cannot read it there. [*Rises.*]
                         There, through my tears,
Like wrinkled pebbles in a glassy stream,
You may behold 'em. Lady, lady, alack,
He that will all the treasure know o'th' earth
Must know the centre too; he that will fish   115
For my least minnow, let him lead his line
To catch one at my heart. Oh, pardon me;
Extremity, that sharpens sundry wits,
Makes me a fool.
EMILIA   Pray you, say nothing, pray you:
Who cannot feel nor see the rain, being in't,   120

110 Emilia continues the Third Queen's
conceit, assuring her that her appearance expresses her feelings, in the
tears on her cheek. An unspoken pun
on 'lines' may be implied, as in *Son*
101, where the friend's beauty is
described as 'dulling my lines'; collections of elegiac poems were sometimes called 'tears'. The queen replies
that her feelings are written not on
her face but in her heart.

111 there ... There Seward changed
the second *there* to *here*, arguing that
'she evidently points at her heart'.
Mason and most later editors take the
first *there* to mean her cheeks and the
second her eyes.

*SD Since the Third Queen tells
Emilia to look into her eyes, it seems
appropriate that she should rise at this
point, if Emilia herself has not raised
her.

111–13 'there (i.e. in my cheeks and eyes)
you can behold my grief *only* in an
uncertain manner, as when you look at
pebbles which appear wrinkled
through the transparent stream above
them' (Skeat)

113 'em her grief; the comparison with
pebbles has attracted a plural object

115 the centre of the earth. *OED* cites 'I

will find / Where truth is hid, though
it were hid indeed / Within the
Center' (*Ham* 2.2.159–61). The queen
urges others to mine, or fish, the
depths of her heart to extract the feelings she is unable to utter.

116 lead his line weight his fishing line
with lead to make it sink deeper. Developing Muir's argument (see 107n.,
above), E. A. Armstrong (207) suggests that *line* is part of a cluster of
images associating fishing with
wrinkles and writing.

117 pardon me Bawcutt suggests that
the queen is afraid she might seem to
be accusing Emilia of insensitivity.

118–19 Extremity ... fool Littledale
compares *The Honest Man's Fortune* (a
Field–Fletcher–Massinger collaboration, 1613): 'Cunning Calamity /
That others' gross wits uses to refine,
/ When I most need it, dulls the edge
of mine' (Dyce, 3:3.1).

118 sundry wits some people's minds

120–1 Who cannot ... dry This sounds
proverbial, though I know no other
examples. Possibly *wet* and *dry* should
be in quotation marks: 'only someone
utterly insensitive, or lacking the most
basic vocabulary, could fail to recognize a grief so obvious as yours'.

111 SD] *Oxf subst. (after* behold 'em*); not in Q*   112 pebbles] *F; (*peobles*) Q* glassy] *Seward;*
glasse *Q;* Like pebbles in a wrinckled glassy stream *(Hopkinson MS)*

Knows neither wet nor dry. If that you were
The ground-piece of some painter, I would buy you
T'instruct me 'gainst a capital grief, indeed
Such heart-pierced demonstration; but, alas,
Being a natural sister of our sex,   125
Your sorrow beats so ardently upon me
That it shall make a counter-reflect 'gainst
My brother's heart and warm it to some pity,
Though it were made of stone. Pray, have good
   comfort.

THESEUS

Forward to th' temple! Leave not out a jot   130
O'th' sacred ceremony.

1 QUEEN   Oh, this celebration
Will longer last and be more costly than
Your suppliants' war! Remember that your fame

---

122 **ground-piece** A *piece* is a painting,
but the meaning of *ground* has to be
inferred from its context. Waith
(Oxf¹) plausibly suggests a link with
the verb 'to ground' in the sense of
'teach the rudiments' (*OED v.* 5): 'an
example to be copied as a teaching
aid'. Since *ground* can also be the
depths of the heart (*OED sb.* 1c, Bible
1611), Emilia might be developing the
Third Queen's conceit about the
centre. Real people are compared to, or
mistaken for, works of art in several
plays of this period, notably *WT* and
Webster's *WD* and *DM*. There is an
implicit allusion to the weeping
Niobe, who eventually turned to stone
and became a fountain.
123 **'gainst . . . grief** in preparation for
the time when I should wish to depict
the greatest grief (the queen, like
Hippolyta, would become a 'mirror',
or model, for women)
capital mortal
123-4 **indeed . . . demonstration** such
a demonstration of how someone
looks who has *indeed* (i.e., in reality,

not just in a painting) been pierced to
the heart by grief
125 The subject of *being* could be either
the queen ('since you are, alas, a real
suffering woman' (see 123-4n.)), or
Emilia herself ('since I am naturally
sympathetic to all members of our
sex'). The latter is consistent with 36-
7.
126 **ardently** burningly
127 **counter-reflect** the heat of your
grief will reflect off my heart and on
to Theseus', 'as from a mirror' (Oxf¹).
Reflect is stressed on the first syllable.
128 **brother's** brother-in-law's
130-1 **Forward . . . ceremony** Cf.
Caesar's 'Set on, and leave no ceremony out' (*JC* 1.2.11). Though he
does not reject the queens' request,
Theseus wants to complete the wedding ceremony before setting off for
Thebes.
133 **Your suppliants' war** the war
which they are asking him to wage.
The term recalls *The Suppliants*, tragedies by Aeschylus and Euripides;
see pp. 40-1 above.

---

123 grief, indeed] *Proudfoot;* grief indeed *Q*   132 longer] *Seward;* long *Q*

Knolls in the ear o'th' world: what you do quickly
Is not done rashly; your first thought is more   135
Than others' laboured meditance; your
     premeditating
More than their actions; but, oh Jove, your actions,
Soon as they move, as ospreys do the fish,
Subdue before they touch. Think, dear Duke, think
What beds our slain kings have!

2 QUEEN   What griefs our beds,   140
That our dear lords have none!

3 QUEEN   None fit for th' dead.
Those that with cords, knives, drams' precipitance,

---

134 **Knolls** tolls, like a bell. *OED* quotes
this as an example of usage without
the meaning of a death knell. But the
ominous connotations may be intended: cf. 'Theseus, / Who, where he
threats, appals' (1.2.90).

134–9 **what ... touch** For other examples of this type of hyperbole see
Edgar's Dover cliff speech (*KL*
4.5.13) and Florizel's praise of Perdita
(*WT* 4.4.135ff.). The queen claims
both that Theseus' wisdom enables
him to do on the spur of the moment
what others can do only after long
consideration *and* that his very
thoughts have the power of actions.

136 **meditance** meditating; the only example of this usage in *OED*

138 **as ospreys ... fish** The osprey, or
fish-hawk, was a bird to which fish
were thought to yield by turning on
their backs: hence, it became a symbol
of natural authority (see *Cor* 4.7.33–
5). Brockbank (pp. 273–4n.) cites examples from Peele and Drayton, and
quotes Case, who points out that the
word is spelled *asprey* in the Q of
TNK, as in the F text of *Cor*.

140 **What beds** by contrast with the
marriage bed that awaits Theseus and
Hippolyta

What griefs our beds 'Have' is
understood from the previous line:
'our beds are full of grief because our
lords have no resting place'.

141 **fit ... dead** perhaps playing on the
phrase 'fit for the living'

142–5 'The whole speech implies that
human favour allows a decent burial
even to suicides' (Skeat).

142 *****drams' precipitance** precipitating
one's death by taking poison. Other
readings have been suggested (see
t.n.). Seward took the queen to be listing four separate means of suicide,
one of which was *precipitance* (throwing oneself off a precipice). The latter
(a recognized Roman punishment
with which Coriolanus is threatened)
is surprisingly common in Renaissance literature: the hero of Tasso's
Aminta (acted 1582) attempts it, as
does Gloucester in *KL*. Colman
(1778) takes the phrase to mean the
act of precipitating one's death by one
of these three means, all of them in
the possessive. Bowers, who is followed here, thinks it marginally more
likely that *precipitance* refers only to
drams; the queen distinguishes poison
from medicine and a quick from a
slow poison.

---

138 move] *F;* mooves *Q*   ospreys] *(Aspreyes)*   142 drams' precipitance] *Leech;* drams precipitance *Q;* drams, precipitance *Seward*

Weary of this world's light, have to themselves
Been death's most horrid agents, human grace
Affords them dust and shadow –

1 QUEEN   But our lords   145
Lie blistering 'fore the visitating sun,
And were good kings when living.

THESEUS   It is true.
And I will give you comfort,
To give your dead lords graves – the which to do,
Must make some work with Creon.

1 QUEEN   And that work   150
Presents itself to th' doing.
Now 'twill take form; the heats are gone tomorrow.
Then, bootless toil must recompense itself
With its own sweat; now, he's secure,
Nor dreams we stand before your puissance   155
Rinsing our holy begging in our eyes
To make petition clear.

2 QUEEN   Now you may take him,

---

145 **dust and shadow** their graves
146 **visitating** a variant of visiting, meaning surveying (Skeat cites Cotgrave, '*visiter*' (French)). *OED* cites this as the only example of this sense in English. Cf. the 'visiting moon' (*AC* 4.14.68). Leech suggests a further sense of 'inflicting harm'; households suffering from the plague were said to be visited. .
149 **To give** 'by giving' (Brooke). RP compares Fletcher's *Double Marriage*, Bowers, 9: 3.3.283. The lineation is confusing (see t.n.); Seward wanted to regularize it by reading, after *comfort*, '[And engage / Myself and powers] to give your dead lords graves'. Craik suggests, more concisely, 'and take order / To'.
151 'needs to be done immediately' (Bawcutt). *Presents*, like 'presently', carries a strong sense of 'in the present'.

152 fuses the ideas and images associated with acting 'i'th' heat' (compare *KL* 1.2.11), striking while the iron is hot, and perhaps the Third Queen's sense of her own intended words dissolving into formlessness
153–4 **bootless . . . sweat** Their useless labour will have to be its own reward. Cf. 1.2.31–4.
154 **secure** self-confident (generally, as here, with the implication of over-confident)
155 **puissance** power (three syllables)
156–7 **Rinsing . . . clear** washing their prayers with their tears to make them both purer and more intelligible (continuing the image of the 'glassy stream' in line 112). Q's spelling, *wrinching* (probably phonetic, as Littledale suggests), also occurs in *H8* 1.1.167 (a scene generally considered Shakespearean).

---

144 human] *(humaine)*   147–8 It . . . comfort] *one line Q*   149–51] *Q lines* graves: / Creon; / doing: /   155 Nor] *Seward;* Not *Q*   156 Rinsing] *(Wrinching)*

Drunk with his victory –
3 QUEEN   And his army full
Of bread and sloth.
THESEUS [*to Officer*]   Artesius, that best knowest
How to draw out fit to this enterprise   160
The prim'st for this proceeding and the number
To carry such a business – forth and levy
Our worthiest instruments, whilst we dispatch
This grand act of our life, this daring deed
Of fate in wedlock.
1 QUEEN [*to Second and Third Queens*]
                                   Dowagers, take hands.   165
Let us be widows to our woes; delay
Commends us to a famishing hope.
THE QUEENS   Farewell!
2 QUEEN

We come unseasonably; but when could grief
Cull forth, as unpanged judgement can, fitt'st time
For best solicitation?
THESEUS   Why, good ladies,   170
This is a service, whereto I am going,

158–9 **full / Of bread** Cf. 'He took my
father grossly, full of bread' (*Ham*
3.3.80). In Ezekiel, 16.49, it means a
surfeit of food (Skeat) and refers to
Sodom, which resembles the Thebes
of 1.2. Shaheen points out that,
among sixteenth-century translations,
bread is the reading only of the
Geneva Bible; it also occurs in the Au-
thorized (King James) translation of
1611.
160–2 **How ... business** an exception-
ally tautological phrase: Artesius (see
'Officer', List of Roles) is asked to
choose the best men, the right number
of them, and those most fit to succeed
in (*carry*) this task; the over-emphatic
command fails to impress the queens,
who have confidence only in Theseus.
162 **forth** go forth
164–5 **daring ... fate** 'deed challenging

Fate' (Leech)
165 **take hands** Shaking hands was a
gesture of parting rather than meeting
(see 'I hold it fit that we take hands
and part', *Ham* 1.5.128). The queens
say farewell, either to one another or
to Theseus, Hippolyta and Emilia,
and either join hands with each other
or take those of the Athenians.
166 **widows ... woes** The image suggests that their woes have died, but
the queen obviously means the opposite: they are married to grief forever
if Theseus refuses their request.
Littledale's paraphrase is perhaps the
best: 'as Creon has left our dead
lords unburied, so our woes have been
left unburied by Theseus'.
169 **Cull forth** choose with care
unpanged not distracted by suffering
171 **service** enterprise

159 Artesius] *Artesuis Q; Artesis F*   167 SP] *this edn;All Q*

153

Greater than any war; it more imports me
Than all the actions that I have foregone,
Or futurely can cope.

1 QUEEN   The more proclaiming
Our suit shall be neglected when her arms,   175
Able to lock Jove from a synod, shall
By warranting moonlight corslet thee. Oh, when
Her twinning cherries shall their sweetness fall
Upon thy taste-full lips, what wilt thou think
Of rotten kings or blubbered queens? What care   180
For what thou feel'st not, what thou feel'st being able
To make Mars spurn his drum? Oh, if thou couch
But one night with her, every hour in't will

172 **Greater than any war** Q reads
was, and Waith (Oxf¹) makes a good
case for retaining it, but Theobald's
emendation is very much in the spirit
of Theseus' previous speech and the
play's general equation of love and
war. As Bowers points out, it is also an
implicit reply to the First Queen's
claim (131–3) that the celebration was
to be longer than the war.
   more imports me matters more to
me
173 **actions** combats
   foregone undertaken before
174 **futurely** in the future
   cope come to blows with, meet in
battle (*OED v.* 3. *trans.* 7)
   The more proclaiming 'What you
have just said makes it even clearer
that . . . ' (Bawcutt)
175–6 **her arms . . . synod** alludes to
Homer's account (*Iliad*, 14) of how
Jupiter was distracted from affairs on
Olympus and the Trojan war by the
sexual blandishments of Juno, aided
by Aphrodite and Sleep. Another
common image (most famous from
Botticelli's painting) shows Mars and
Venus lying in post-coital lethargy
while cupids or satyrs play with his
armour (see 180–6, below).
176 **synod** gathering of the gods
177 **warranting** authorizing, in that

both night and the moon make it possible for her to display passion
   corslet hold tightly (like the breast-
plate which, they imply, he should be
wearing)
178 **twinning cherries** her lips, a common comparison (see also 2.2.64,
below). Q has *twyning*; Seward printed
twinning and most editors follow him,
since 'as alike as cherry to cherry' was
proverbial (Dent, C276). Skeat cites
the comparison of lips to 'two twind
cherries' in Beaumont and Fletcher's
Philaster (Bowers, 1: 2.2.75). See pp.
104–6 above.
   fall let fall
179 **taste-full** '*savoureux*, savorie, tast-
full, tart, well smacking' (Cotgrave
1611, quoted in *OED*). Theseus' lips
will be *full* (glutted) with the sweetness of Hippolyta's.
179–80 **what . . . queens?** rhetorical:
'will you think about us?'
180 **blubbered** with tear-stained faces
(not comic in this period)
183–4 **every . . . hundred** Every hour in
bed with Hippolyta will make him
want to spend a hundred more. Cf.
Bacon (81): 'He that hath a wife and
children hath given hostages to fortune' ('Of Marriage and Single Life',
first pub. in 1612 edn of *Essays*).

172 war] *Seward (Theobald)*; was *Q*   178 twinning] *Seward (Theobald)*; twyning *Q*

Take hostage of thee for a hundred and
Thou shalt remember nothing more than what   185
That banquet bids thee to.

HIPPOLYTA   Though much unlike
You should be so transported, as much sorry
I should be such a suitor, yet I think,
Did I not, by th'abstaining of my joy
Which breeds a deeper longing, cure their surfeit   190
That craves a present med'cine, I should pluck
All ladies' scandal on me. Therefore, sir, [*Kneels.*]
As I shall here make trial of my prayers,
Either presuming them to have some force,
Or sentencing for aye their vigour dumb,   195
Prorogue this business we are going about and hang
Your shield afore your heart, about that neck
Which is my fee and which I freely lend
To do these poor queens service.

THE QUEENS [*to Emilia*]   Oh, help now.

---

186 **banquet** a light first course served
before a feast to whet the appetite
bids invites

186–8 **Though ... suitor** another confusing parallelism, hinging on the
double function of *suitor*. Hippolyta
would be sorry as well as surprised if
Theseus were as irresponsibly carried
away by sexual passion as the widows
seem to imagine; would be equally
sorry to be the cause of it (i.e., *suitor*
echoes *bids* at the end of the previous
speech); and is equally sorry that she
must ask him to defer the consummation of their marriage (i.e., *suitor* looks
forward to 193ff.).

190 **surfeit** an illness brought on by
excess, often of food or drink, for
which abstinence was recommended.
There is an implied antithesis .be-
tween the queens' surfeit of grief and
Hippolyta's willing abstinence from
joy (i.e., the wedding night). See¯p. 98
above.

191 **present** immediate

191–2 **pluck ... on me** be regarded by
all women as a disgrace to our sex
(Craik)

192 *SD* Kneeling is obviously implied by
the queens' request and their words to
Emilia at 199, though precisely where
it should happen is unclear.

193–5 **As ... dumb** The response to
this, her first request to Theseus, will
show her whether she has any power
over him. While 193 sounds obedient
– she will never make any other requests if this is denied – it can also be
seen as a threat.

196 **Prorogue** postpone

196–7 **hang ... heart** both literally ('go
into battle but look after your safety
for my sake') and figuratively ('take
arms against your own love for me')

198 **fee** possession; a reward for services
offered to a feudal lord. Whiter cited
this line in 1794, pointing out the associative link between *fee*, *service* and
suit in both Shakespeare and Fletcher
(78–80).

199 SP THE] *this edn; All Q*

Our cause cries for your knee.

EMILIA [*Kneels, to Theseus*]   If you grant not   200
My sister her petition in that force,
With that celerity and nature, which
She makes it in, from henceforth I'll not dare
To ask you anything nor be so hardy
Ever to take a husband.

THESEUS   Pray, stand up.   205
I am entreating of my self to do
That which you kneel to have me. [*They rise.*]
                    Pirithous,
Lead on the bride; get you and pray the gods
For success and return; omit not anything
In the pretended celebration. – Queens,   210
Follow your soldier. [*to Officer*]
                    As before – hence, you,
And at the banks of Aulis meet us with
The forces you can raise, where we shall find
The moiety of a number for a business

202 **nature** natural feeling or affection.
OED (*sb.* 3e) cites 'compunctious vis-
itings of Nature' (*Mac* 1.5.46).
207 **to have me** (do)
   Pirithous stressed on first syllable
   here; see List of Roles
208 **get you** (to the temple), addressed
   to Pirithous, Hippolyta, or the wedding party in general. Theseus asks
   Pirithous to celebrate the marriage
   (by proxy), then hold the celebration
   in his absence.
209 **success** accented on the first syllable
   (Proudfoot). Kökeritz gives this as the
   only such example in Shakespeare.
   return the object of *pray for*: a quick
   return from the war
210 **pretended** intended
211 **your soldier** himself; cf. 76, above
   As before Q's punctuation (see t.n.)
   is ambiguous: *either* Theseus claims
   that he is, as always, their soldier –
   that is, devoted to their cause – *or*,

more likely, he is confirming his previous orders to Artesius.
212 ***Aulis** Theobald's conjecture for
   Q's *Anly* has been accepted by all subsequent editors, although with some
   uneasiness, since, as Proudfoot notes,
   it 'does not lie between Athens and
   Thebes'. The Greek fleet sailed from
   Aulis to Troy after the sacrifice of
   Iphigenia by her father Agamemnon,
   which, Waith notes (Oxf[1]), was
   another famous example of a general's
   putting the command of the gods
   before his private happiness. (See pp.
   103–5 above.)
214 **moiety** a portion (not necessarily
   half). The troops levied by Artesius
   will join those already at Aulis.
214–15 **business...bigger-looked** something which looks *bigger* (more threatening) than the *business* of the wedding (cf. 196 above) but still well
   below his army's strength.

200 SD] *Dyce subst.; not in Q*   207 SD] *Dyce subst.* after 205; *not in Q*   211 soldier. As before –
hence] *Weber subst. (Mason);* Soldier (as before) hence *Q;* soldier, as before. Hence *Leech*   212 Aulis]
Seward (Theobald); Anly *Q*

156

More bigger-looked.   [*Exit Officer.*]

[*to Hippolyta*]   Since that our theme is haste,   215
I stamp this kiss upon thy current lip;
Sweet, keep it as my token. Set you forward,
For I will see you gone.

[*Procession moves toward the temple.*]

– Farewell, my beauteous sister. – Pirithous,
Keep the feast full; bate not an hour on't.

PIRITHOUS   Sir,   220
I'll follow you at heels; the feast's solemnity
Shall want till your return.

THESEUS   Cousin, I charge you,
Budge not from Athens. We shall be returning
Ere you can end this feast, of which I pray you
Make no abatement. Once more, farewell all.   225

[*Exeunt all except Theseus and Queens.*]

215*SD Q indicates no exit for Artesius,
but it seems right that he should leave
as soon as possible after receiving his
orders. Alternatively, 217 (if addressed to him) could serve as an exit
cue, or (as Skeat suggests) he could
leave at 225.

216–17 I stamp ... token Bawcutt's
explanation of this complex image is
the clearest: '*stamp* means (1) press
and (2) make a coin by stamping a
piece of metal; *current* means (1)
moving away from him (because of his
departure) and (2) authentic (as a coin
is genuine, not counterfeit); and *token*
means (1) keepsake and (2) stamped
piece of metal used as a coin'. Cf.
Donne's 'Valediction of Weeping',
where the speaker's tears reflect the
face of his mistress: 'thy stamp they
bear, / And by this mintage they are
something worth'.

218 I will I am determined to

SD The procession probably circles
the stage on its way out, in the same
order that it entered; thus Hippolyta,
Pirithous and Emilia are the last to
leave and Pirithous can speak more
confidentially to Theseus.

220 full fully (Leech)
    bate abate, lessen

221–2 solemnity ... return Seward
corrected *want* to *wait*, assuming that
solemnity meant the wedding itself.
Colman (1778) restored *want*, taking
solemnity to mean the celebrations
appropriate to the occasion (sports,
plays, fireworks, as at the royal wedding of 1613). The latter makes more
sense in the light of Theseus' reply.

222 Cousin friend

225 abatement reduction
    farewell all spoken to the entire pro-
cession, but perhaps aimed pointedly
at Pirithous, reinforcing the command
for him to remain in Athens

218 SD] *Bawcutt subst.; Exeunt towards the Temple. Q*   225 SD] *Weber subst.; not in Q*

1 QUEEN

> Thus dost thou still make good the tongue o'th'
>   world –

2 QUEEN

> And earn'st a deity equal with Mars –

3 QUEEN

> If not above him, for
> Thou, being but mortal, mak'st affections bend
> To godlike honours; they themselves, some say,   230
> Groan under such a mast'ry.

THESEUS   As we are men,

> Thus should we do; being sensually subdued,
> We lose our human title. Good cheer, ladies:
> Now turn we towards your comforts.   *Flourish. Exeunt.*

[1.2]   *Enter* PALAMON *and* ARCITE.

---

226 **make good ... world** live up to
     your reputation
229 **affections** human feelings (in this
     case, sexual desire)
     bend bow, give way
230–1 **they ... mast'ry** The gods them-
     selves suffer under the sway of the
     powerful Eros: see, for instance,
     Faerie Queene, 3.12, and cf. 5.1.89–94,
     below.
231 **men** This word should probably be
     stressed. Theseus, as at 74, refuses
     godlike status for himself, while insist-
     ing on a lofty concept of humanity
     which makes him 'more godlike than
     the gods' (Bawcutt).
232 **being ... subdued** when we (like
     the gods of the fables) are conquered
     by sensuality
233 **We lose ... title** we become beasts
     Good cheer be cheerful
234 **your comforts** the action that will
     comfort you (see 148, above)
1.2 The opening lines indicate that the
     action has shifted to Thebes; there is
     no further localization. Although the

previous scene shows that the siege of
Thebes is a very recent event, Palamon and Arcite talk as if they were
living among all the vices usually associated with a long period of peace:
soldiers unrewarded for their courage,
debauchery and corruption endemic.
The authors may be drawing on
Chaucer's *Anelida and Arcite*, where
Creon's encouragement brings 'noble
folke' to the town (70). In any case, the
men's complaints are common ones:
see Jorgensen, ch. 5, for the preva-
lence of the view that too long a
period of peace leads to corruption.
Abrams, 'W.S.', notes that the desul-
tory, unfocused conversation imitates
the frustration of which Arcite is so
conscious (p. 451). Some productions
have tried to counteract this effect: at
York (1973) the two men were exercising as they talked; at Berkeley (1985)
they engaged in practice combat. Ashland (1994) showed them on the point
of escaping from the city when called
back by Valerius' news.

1.2] Scæna 2. *Q*

ARCITE

    Dear Palamon, dearer in love than blood
    And our prime cousin: yet unhardened in
    The crimes of nature, let us leave the city
    Thebes and the temptings in't, before we further
    Sully our gloss of youth   5
    And here to keep in abstinence we shame
    As in incontinence; for not to swim
    I'th' aid o'th' current, were almost to sink,
    At least to frustrate striving, and to follow
    The common stream, 'twould bring us to an eddy   10
    Where we should turn or drown; if labour through,
    Our gain but life and weakness.

PALAMON   Your advice
    Is cried up with example. What strange ruins,
    Since first we went to school, may we perceive
    Walking in Thebes! Scars and bare weeds   15

1 **blood** kinship
2 **prime** literally 'first', in the sense of most important, most valued; cf. 'Prospero the prime duke' (*Tem* 1.2.72)
2–3 **yet unhardened ... nature** while our 'natural' vices (perhaps such as they will recall in 3.3) are not yet unbreakable habits
5 dim the brightness of our youth – like armour that grows dusty through lack of use: see 'Perseverance ... / Keeps honour bright' (*TC* 3.3.150–1)
6 **keep** continue
   we shame we are ashamed. Both *shame* and *sully* are objects of *before*, while *keep* refers both to *abstinence* and *incontinence*: i.e., Arcite fears that Thebes will erode their moral values until they are as ashamed to abstain from sins of intemperance as to commit them. Cf. Montaigne: 'A man must imitate the vicious, or hate them: both are dangerous: for to resemble them is perilous, because they are

many, and to hate many is hazzardous, because they are dissemblable' (Florio, 1.254 (RP)).
8 **I'th' aid ... current** with the stream. The image of being carried along by a stream which will lead eventually to drowning, not difficult in itself, is so laboured in expression that it induces the frustration it describes. Cf. *Tim* 4.1.25–8: 'That 'gainst the stream of virtue they may strive, / And drown themselves in riot!' (RP).
11 **if labour through** if we should labour through it (Skeat)
13 **cried up** publicly applauded, because everything they see proves its truth
14 **Since ... school** See 'Thou know'st that we two went to school together' (*JC* 5.5.26) for this kind of bonding.
15 **Walking** either 'when we are walking' or 'walking ruins of men' (Skeat)
   bare weeds shabby (threadbare) clothing. Skeat suggests that *bare* has two syllables.

2–3 cousin: ... nature,] *this edn;* Cosen, ... nature; *Q*

The gain o'th' martialist, who did propound
To his bold ends honour and golden ingots,
Which, though he won, he had not – and now flurted
By Peace for whom he fought! Who then shall offer
To Mars's so scorned altar? I do bleed   20
When such I meet and wish great Juno would
Resume her ancient fit of jealousy
To get the soldier work, that Peace might purge
For her repletion and retain anew
Her charitable heart, now hard and harsher   25
Than strife or war could be.

ARCITE   Are you not out?

16 **martialist** follower of Mars, a soldier
    did propound held forth, set before
    himself as a goal (see *OED v.* 3)
17 **ingots** coins
18 **won** earned (by winning in battle)
    had not Skeat explains: 'Did not get
    for himself, for it went to the captain.'
    But Palamon may mean that there
    were no rewards at all, rather than
    that the rewards were misappropri-
    ated.
    flurted scorned. *OED v.* gives two
    relevant definitions of *flirt*, or *flurt*: 1
    'To give (a person) a sudden sharp
    blow or knock', and 4a *trans.* 'To sneer
    or scoff at'. Skeat cites other examples
    in Fletcher: *Rule a Wife* (Bowers, 6:
    3.5.55), *The Wild Goose Chase*
    (Bowers, 6: 2.2.162) and *The Pilgrim*
    (Bowers, 6: 3.3.91).
18–20 **and ... altar** Two ideas, and two
    separate sentences, are conflated here:
    the soldier is humiliated by the very
    peace which he has made possible;
    since he is so treated, who else will
    want to be a soldier?
21 **Juno** Her hatred for Thebes is an im-
    portant part of its legend. Chaucer
    refers to it in *Anelida and Arcite*
    ('Mars ... the old wrath of Juno to
    fulfill' (51)) and Arcite complains of it
    in *KT*, 1543–62. Provoked by Jupi-
    ter's seduction of two Theban women
    (Alcmena, the mother of Hercules,

and Semele, the mother of Bacchus),
it led to her destruction of all royal
descendants of Cadmus, the city's
founder.
23–6 **Peace ... be** Peace is envisaged as
    being made kinder, as well as physic-
    ally healthier, as a result of war – an
    image that is possible only because the
    personification has replaced the ab-
    stract idea. The cycle in which Peace
    leads to Plenty, then to Pride, Envy,
    War, Poverty and again to Peace, is
    depicted in the anonymous *Histrio-
    mastix* (pub. 1610).
23–4 **purge ... repletion** make up for
    her over-indulgence. Peace is often
    seen as a time of literal and figurative
    over-eating, which war can cure. Cf.
    'we shall ha' means to vent / Our
    musty superfluity' (*Cor* 1.1.224–5)
    and 1.1.48, above. The idea recurs in
    5.1.65–6. Rolfe notes that *repletion* is
    not used elsewhere by Shakespeare.
24 **retain** take into service. This sounds
    as if Peace has two hearts, one charit-
    able and one hard, but the meaning is
    clearly that in time of war a nation's
    heart grows kinder.
26 **out** an image from acting: to be *out* is
    to have forgotten one's lines. Both
    men seem to feel that the conversation
    is carrying them in the wrong direc-
    tion, like the stream of 9–12.

19 fought!] *Kittredge;* fought, *Q*   24 retain] *Q;* regain *Skeat;* reclaim *(Heath)*

Meet you no ruin but the soldier in
The cranks and turns of Thebes? You did begin
As if you met decays of many kinds.
Perceive you none that do arouse your pity   30
But th'unconsidered soldier?

PALAMON   Yes, I pity
Decays where'er I find them, but such most
That, sweating in an honourable toil,
Are paid with ice to cool 'em.

ARCITE   'Tis not this
I did begin to speak of. This is virtue   35
Of no respect in Thebes. I spake of Thebes –
How dangerous, if we will keep our honours,
It is for our residing, where every evil
Hath a good colour; where every seeming good's
A certain evil; where not to be e'en jump   40
As they are here were to be strangers, and,
Such things to be, mere monsters.

PALAMON   'Tis in our power,
Unless we fear that apes can tutor's, to
Be masters of our manners. What need I

---

28 **cranks and turns** the winding and crooked streets. See *OED* crank *sb.* 1a. Plutarch's *Life of Theseus* (45) refers to 'the turnings and cranckes of the Labyrinthe' (Proudfoot, xx).

29 **decays** like *ruins* (13), used of persons whose fortune (or health) is decayed

31 **unconsidered** unrespected, disregarded

34 **paid with ice** treated with cold contempt

35 **This** the neglect of soldiers

39 **colour** appearance (with the implication of falseness)

40 **jump** exactly

41–2 The difficulty of this construction results from verbal compression. The phrase *were to be* has both *strangers* and *monsters* as its object, but there is

also an antithesis between *not to be* in 40 and *to be* in 43–4. Arcite and Palamon would be strangers in their own country if they did not behave like its inhabitants, but, if they did behave like them, they would be monsters. *Here*, in 41, probably refers both to *as they are* and to *were to be strangers*.

41 **they** the other Thebans
were would be
strangers foreigners

42 **mere** absolute

43 **Unless ... tutor's** 'unless we fear that we will model our behaviour on those who themselves are imitators of fashion'. Because fashion and affectation are frequent targets of anticourt satire, apes sometimes figure in it; cf. Spenser, *Mother Hubbard's Tale*.

---

41 are here] *this edn;* are, here *Q;* are here, *Dyce¹ (Mason)*   42 be, mere] *Littledale (Nicholson);* be meere *Q*

Affect another's gait, which is not catching   45
Where there is faith, or to be fond upon
Another's way of speech when by mine own
I may be reasonably conceived, saved too,
Speaking it truly? Why am I bound
By any generous bond to follow him   50
Follows his tailor, haply so long until
The followed make pursuit? Or let me know
Why mine own barber is unblessed, with him
My poor chin too, for 'tis not scissored just
To such a favourite's glass? What canon is there   55
That does command my rapier from my hip
To dangle't in my hand, or to go tiptoe
Before the street be foul? Either I am
The fore-horse in the team or I am none
That draw i'th' sequent trace. These poor slight sores   60

45 **Affect** either 'imitate' or 'like'
   catching contagious, like an illness
46 **Where ... faith** Littledale glosses
   faith as 'self-reliance'. But the speech
   contains other religious double-
   meanings – *faith, saved* (48), *unblessed*
   (53) and *canon* (55) – ridiculing those
   who follow the fashion as if their salvation depended on it. By contrast
   with Arcite's desperate view of their
   predicament, Palamon ironically suggests that they can be saved by faith,
   not by such 'good works' as imitating
   other people's clothes. For the religious context of these lines, see pp.
   38–9 above.
   be fond upon dote upon (*fond* means
   insane)
48 **conceived** understood
49 **Speaking it** if I speak
   truly both accurately (so as to be
   conceived) and truthfully (so as to be
   saved)
   bound a common pun on the metaphorical and literal (financial) meanings (compare *MV* 5.1.135–7), partly
   based on the fact that people too concerned with the fashion often ended

up in debt to their tailors.
50–2 The fop (like Fungoso in Jonson's
   Every Man Out of His Humour (1599))
   follows his tailor's advice about fashion; the tailor later pursues him for
   payment.
50 **generous bond** *noblesse oblige* (RA)
51 **Follows** (a) importunes; (b) is guided
   by. The implied subject is 'who'.
54 **for** because
55 **To ... glass** exactly like that of some
   favourite or other. For the idea of another person as a mirror or model, cf.
   1.1.90
   canon rule; the Q spelling, *cannon*,
   brings out the intended pun
55–8 **What ... foul?** Walking on tiptoe
   with a sword in one's hand is characteristic of a *miles gloriosus* (like Captain Tipto in Jonson's *New Inn*
   (1629)); Palamon thinks one should
   tiptoe only to avoid getting one's
   boots muddy.
58–60 **Either ... trace** I will either lead
   the fashion or else be out of it
   altogether.
60 **sequent trace** following team of
   horses

55 canon] *(Cannon)*

Need not a plantain; that which rips my bosom
Almost to th' heart's –

ARCITE   Our uncle Creon.

PALAMON   He.

A most unbounded tyrant, whose successes
Makes heaven unfeared and villainy assured
Beyond its power there's nothing; almost puts   65
Faith in a fever and deifies alone
Voluble Chance; who only attributes
The faculties of other instruments
To his own nerves and act; commands men service
And what they win in't, boot and glory; one   70
That fears not to do harm; good, dares not. Let
The blood of mine that's sib to him be sucked
From me with leeches, let them break and fall

---

61 **plantain** a leaf of the herb known as the Greater Plantain, used for soothing cuts and bruises (see *LLL* 3.1.74–5). Palamon 'bleeds', figuratively, when he sees a needy soldier (20), but is only slightly hurt by fashionable foppery.

64 **Makes** Though *successes* is the subject of this verb, it probably alludes to Creon as well and hence is attracted to the singular.

65–6 **puts / Faith in a fever** makes faith ill. Cf. 46, above. The thought of Creon makes Palamon revert to the religious language which he had earlier rejected as too extreme.

66–7 **deifies . . . Chance** makes Chance the only goddess. Creon's 'successes' are still the subject.

67 **Voluble** 'capable of ready rotation' (*OED* I 2), like the wheel of Fortune; hence, changeable and inconstant. Stressed on the second syllable.
attributes stressed on the first syllable

67–9 **only . . . act** gives only to himself and his own actions the credit that should belong to those who serve him – an obvious contrast to Theseus' ref-

erence to his 'worthiest instruments' (1.1.163)

69 **nerves** strength
commands men service Seward emends to 'commands men's service', but there is a characteristic grammatical slide from 'commands them [to do] service' to 'commands what they have won in their service'.

70 **boot** booty or advantage
***glory; one** See t.n. The press corrector evidently realized that the punctuation of this line was wrong and attempted to do something about it. Littledale's suggestion, followed here, makes sense, especially since *on* was a common spelling of *one*; there might also be a case for Kittredge's emendation of *on* to *on't*: 'of it (i.e., of what has been won by men's service)'.

71 **good, dares not** dares not (do) good

72 **blood** in the literal meaning and that of relationship
sib kin, related

73 **leeches** aquatic worms, used to suck the supposedly contaminated blood of the sick, 'And when they have wel sucked & drawn til they be ful, they will fall off by themselves' (Galen, 47)

---

64 Makes] *Q;* Make *Seward*   65 power] *Seward;* power: *Q*   nothing;] *(Sympson subst.)* nothing, *Q*   70 glory; one] *Littledale (Ingram);* glory on; *Qc;* glory on *Qu;* glory on't *Kittredge*

Off me with that corruption.
ARCITE   Clear-spirited cousin,
Let's leave his court, that we may nothing share   75
Of his loud infamy; for our milk
Will relish of the pasture and we must
Be vile or disobedient: not his kinsmen
In blood unless in quality.
PALAMON   Nothing truer:
I think the echoes of his shames have deafed   80
The ears of heavenly Justice. Widows' cries
Descend again into their throats and have not
Due audience of the gods.

Enter VALERIUS.

Valerius!

VALERIUS
The king calls for you; yet be leaden-footed
Till his great rage be off him. Phoebus, when   85

74 **Clear-spirited** noble-hearted (perhaps continuing the medical metaphor, since 'spirits' were the distillation of the body's humours)
76 **loud** heard far and near
76–7 **our . . . pasture** we will be tainted by our environment (Leech). Similar to the proverbial 'Change of pasture makes fat calves' (Dent, *Prov*, C230). Cf. 'Virtue cannot so inoculate our old stock but we shall relish of it' (*Ham* 3.1.116–18).
76 **our** (two syllables)
78–9 **not . . . quality** not related to him unless like him. Cf. 'Twins? – In quality' (Webster, *DM*, 1.1.172).
80 **deafed** deafened (with their loudness). Justice was traditionally blind (impartial), but Creon's unpunished villainy makes her seem deaf as well.
81 **Widows' cries** Palamon builds on Arcite's image of *loud infamy* – ironically, after the events of 1.1. Chaucer also makes much of the loudness of the widows' cries (*KT*, 900–2). Shaheen cites a number of scriptural passages

about crying to the Lord for vengeance, particularly Exodus, 22.22–3.
83 **audience** hearing
*SD The time needed for actors to move from the upstage doors to the front of the stage usually requires entrance directions to be early. The placing of this SD in Q (see t.n.) suggests either that Valerius makes an extremely rapid entrance (as befits a messenger) or that he appears in the door at this point but (in keeping with the content of his speech) takes his time in coming downstage to address the others.
84 **be leaden-footed** do not hurry to reach him
85–7 **Phoebus . . . sun** that is, when he heard that his son Phaeton, whom he had reluctantly allowed to drive the chariot of the sun, had come so near destroying the earth that Jupiter had finally killed him with a thunderbolt (Ovid, 2.397–9). The allusion to a familiar story of presumption receiving divine punishment is obviously relevant to Creon.

83 SD] *after 83–4 Q*

He broke his whipstock and exclaimed against
The horses of the sun, but whispered to
The loudness of his fury.

PALAMON   Small winds shake him.
But what's the matter?

VALERIUS
Theseus, who, where he threats, appals, hath sent   90
Deadly defiance to him and pronounces
Ruin to Thebes, who is at hand to seal
The promise of his wrath.

ARCITE   Let him approach.
But that we fear the gods in him, he brings not
A jot of terror to us. Yet what man   95
Thirds his own worth (the case is each of ours)
When that his action's dregged with mind assured
'Tis bad he goes about?

PALAMON   Leave that unreasoned.
Our services stand now for Thebes, not Creon.
Yet to be neutral to him were dishonour,   100
Rebellious to oppose; therefore we must
With him stand to the mercy of our fate,

86 **whipstock** whip handle
87 **but** only
   to by comparison with
88 **Small ... him** Even trivial things
   put him in a rage.
89–90 **But ... sent** Lineation here is
   uncertain because of the breakdown
   of the metre; perhaps *Theseus*, drawn
   out for emphasis, is meant to complete
   Palamon's line.
92 **who** Theseus
92–3 **to seal ... wrath** to make good
   (put the seal on) what his anger has
   already promised
96 **Thirds ... worth** achieves a third of
   what he is capable of
97 **action** fighting
   dregged made cloudy, like the dregs
   of wine, by contrast with *clear-spirited*
   (74). *OED* cites Owen Feltham (1627–
   42): 'a great occasion of dregging our
   spirits'. The metaphor is based on the

medical analogy between 'vital spirits'
and the process of evaporation;
mounting from liver to heart to brain,
the spirits were supposed to become
increasingly refined, inspiring wit and
courage.
98 **Leave that unreasoned** Don't think
   about that.
100 **Yet to be** to continue to be (Oxf[1]).
   Skeat suggests that 'yet' marks a
   change of tone – 'yet, I might urge . . .'
   – as Palamon goes back on his initial
   claim that the situation needs no
   discussing.
100–1 **Yet ... oppose** *Were* (would be)
   goes with both *dishonour* and *rebelli-*
   ous; *neutral to* and *oppose* both have
   Creon as their object.
102 **stand** either 'stand with him', at
   Fate's mercy, or 'stand, with him, to
   face our Fate'

Who hath bounded our last minute.

ARCITE   So we must.

[*to Valerius*] Is't said this war's afoot, or, it shall be,
On fail of some condition?

VALERIUS   'Tis in motion.   105
The intelligence of state came in the instant
With the defier.

PALAMON   Let's to the king – who, were he
A quarter-carrier of that honour which
His enemy come in, the blood we venture
Should be as for our health, which were not spent,   110
Rather laid out for purchase; but, alas,
Our hands advanced before our hearts, what will
The fall o'th' stroke do damage?

ARCITE   Let th'event,
That never-erring arbitrator, tell us
When we know all ourselves – and let us follow   115
The becking of our chance.   *Exeunt.*

[1.3]   *Enter* PIRITHOUS, HIPPOLYTA *and* EMILIA.

103 **bounded ... minute** set the limits
of our lives
105 **On fail of** if we fail to comply with
106–7 **The intelligence ... defier**
News of war came from Creon's 'intel-
ligencer' (spy) at the same time as
Theseus' challenge. Such speed is
common in drama as a way of com-
pressing time (cf. the arrival of the
various messengers in *R3* 4.4 and *AC*
3.7); here, it also bears out the wisdom
of the queens' advice in 1.1.157–9.
107–10 **who ... health** 'for whom, if he
were a quarter as honourable as his
enemy, we would feel that shedding
our blood was as healthful as medically prescribed bleeding'. The sentence structure is confused but the
idea is a common one: for instance,
'The blood I drop is rather physical
[therapeutic] / Than dangerous to
me' (*Cor* 1.5.18–19).
109 **come** plural, because it refers not

only to Theseus but the Athenian army
110 **spent** a double meaning: their loss of
blood would purchase honour, if any
could be gained in fighting for Creon
112 **Our ... hearts** *Before* may mean
'earlier than', or, as Littledale suggests, 'further than'. Cf. 'whose hearts
have left their bodies here in England'
(*H5* 1.2.128) and *Mac* 5.4.13–14.
112–13 **what will ... damage?** What
damage will our half-hearted blows do?
113 **th'event** the outcome. Cf. 'Well,
well, th'event' (*KL* 1.4.348).
113–15 **Let ... ourselves** an ironic
comment: 'when the battle is over, let
infallible hindsight tell us what, by
that time, we will know anyway'. Cf.
'O that a man might know / The end
of this day's business ere it come! /
But it sufficeth that the day will end, /
And then the end is known' (*JC*
5.1.122–4).
116 **becking** beckoning

1.3] Scæna 3. *Q*

PIRITHOUS
    No further.
HIPPOLYTA   Sir, farewell; repeat my wishes
    To our great lord, of whose success I dare not
    Make any timorous question; yet I wish him
    Excess and overflow of power, an't might be
    To dure ill-dealing fortune. Speed to him!   5
    Store never hurts good governors.
PIRITHOUS   Though I know
    His ocean needs not my poor drops, yet they
    Must yield their tribute there. [*to Emilia*]
                            My precious maid,
    Those best affections that the heavens infuse
    In their best-tempered pieces keep enthroned   10
    In your dear heart.
EMILIA   Thanks, sir. Remember me
    To our all-royal brother, for whose speed
    The great Bellona I'll solicit; and,
    Since in our terrene state petitions are not
    Without gifts understood, I'll offer to her   15
    What I shall be advised she likes. Our hearts
    Are in his army, in his tent –
HIPPOLYTA   In's bosom.
    We have been soldiers and we cannot weep
    When our friends don their helms, or put to sea,

1.3.1 **No further** Hippolyta and Emilia
    have presumably accompanied Pirit-
    hous part way on his journey.
3 **Make ... question** have any fear or
    doubt; cf. 'make that thy question'
    (*WT* 1.2.324) (RA)
4 **an't might be** if it (such excess of
    power) were possible
5 **dure** an alternative spelling of
    endure. Hippolyta wishes Theseus
    not only enough power for success but
    also enough to deal with any conceiv-
    able ill fortune. There may be a play
    on *success* and *excess*.
    Speed success (perhaps also suggest-
    ing 'rapid success') (RP)

6 **Store ... governors** Skeat cites the
    proverb 'Store is no sore' (cf. Dent,
    Prov, S903)
7 **His ... drops** Weber compares *AC*
    3.12.8.
10 **best-tempered pieces** the pieces of
    craftsmanship tempered (like metal)
    most finely
13 **Bellona** see 1.1.75n.
14 **terrene state** earthly condition (with
    a pun on state/kingdom)
15 **gifts** (to win their favour)
19 **don their helms** put on their hel-
    mets (and depart for the wars)
    put to sea set off on a sea voyage, as
    dangerous as going to war

5 dure] *Q; cure Seward; dare (Sympson)*

Or tell of babes broached on the lance, or women 20
That have sod their infants in (and after eat them)
The brine they wept at killing 'em. Then, if
You stay to see of us such spinsters, we
Should hold you here forever.

PIRITHOUS   Peace be to you
As I pursue this war, which shall be then   25
Beyond further requiring.   *Exit.*

EMILIA   How his longing
Follows his friend! Since his depart, his sports,
Though craving seriousness and skill, passed slightly
His careless execution, where nor gain
Made him regard or loss consider, but,   30
Playing one business in his hand, another

---

20 **broached** impaled, spitted. Skeat
compares *H5* 3.3.38.
20–2 **women ... 'em** The unnatural
word order might be the result of an
insertion wrongly placed; 21–2 would
scan better as: 'That have sod their infants in the brine they wept / At killing them, and after eat them. Then, / '
etc. But perhaps the tortured style
mirrors the subject-matter. The conjunction of infant cannibalism with
the word *sod* is biblical; Shaheen cites 2
Kings, 6.28–9 and Lamentations, 4.10,
which was taken to be a prophecy of
the future sufferings of Jerusalem.
The *History of the Jewish War* by
Josephus (Joseph Ben Gorion), translated 1558, gives a detailed account
(6.3) of the mother who fed on her own
son during the siege of the city; a more
immediate source was Nashe's *Destruction of Jerusalem*, pub. 1593 (2.75,
77), and William Browne tells the same
story, to illustrate the effects of famine,
in *Britannia's Pastorals* (Browne,
2.1.705–9), pub. 1613–14. All these
sources use the word *sod*, and 'unsod'
occurs (as Littledale notes) in Fletcher's *Sea-Voyage* (Bowers, 9: 3.1.99),
again in connection with cannibalism.
21 **sod** boiled

eat still a recognized past tense in current British speech (pronounced *et*)
23 **stay** wait
of us in us. Skeat cites 'We shall find of
him / A shrewd contriver' (*JC* 2.1.157).
spinsters The word still had overtones of its original meaning, women
who stay at home and spin, unlike the
warlike Hippolyta and Emilia.
24–6 **Peace ... requiring** Peace be to
you as long as I pursue this war! when
that is ended, we shall not need to
pray for it' (Mason). Alternatively,
Pirithous says that if the two women
are granted peace equivalent to his
ardent conduct of this war, they will
have all anyone could possibly wish.
27 **his depart** Theseus' departure
29–30 **nor ... or** neither ... nor
31–3 ***Playing ... twins** Pirithous' attention has been divided, like that of a
nurse looking after twins, between his
hand (taking part in the sports connected with the marriage celebrations)
and his *head* (planning to assist Theseus in his war with Thebes). This
variation on a common idea (thoughts
are 'conceived' in the mind like children) may allude to the belief that a
woman nursing twins had enough milk
for only one of them (Paster, 237).

26 SD] *Exit Pir. Q*   31 one] *Weber (Mason);* ore *Q;* o'er *Riv*

Directing in his head, his mind nurse equal
To these so-differing twins. Have you observed him,
Since our great lord departed?

HIPPOLYTA   With much labour,
And I did love him for't. They two have cabined   35
In many as dangerous as poor a corner,
Peril and want contending; they have skiffed
Torrents whose roaring tyranny and power
I'th' least of these was dreadful; and they have
Sought out together where Death's self was lodged;   40
Yet fate hath brought them off. Their knot of love,
Tied, weaved, entangled, with so true, so long,
And with a finger of so deep a cunning,
May be outworn, never undone. I think
Theseus cannot be umpire to himself,   45

---

35 **cabined** been confined together; cf.
'cabined, cribbed, confined' (*Mac*
3.4.23)
37 **Peril ... contending** danger and
privation competing with each other
(thus making the corner 'as dangerous
as poor'). Another possible reading
would be 'contending against peril
and want' (Littledale), but the language throughout this passage seems
deliberately doubled, still playing
with the idea of twinship.
37–8 **skiffed / Torrents** travelled down
torrential rivers in a light boat (skiff).
Figurative, but possibly also a reference to the voyage of the Argonauts,
in which Theseus and Hercules took
part, dramatized by Thomas Heywood in *The Brazen Age*, pub. 1613.
Cf. also 1.2.7–12.
39 **I'th' least of these** As Seward points
out, it is not clear whether *these* refers
to *Torrents* or *tyranny and power*. In
either case, they contended with many
dangers of which even the least was
terrifying.
40 ***Sought** *Fought*, the Q reading, has
been generally accepted, but the legends of Theseus and Pirithous show

them literally seeking the lodgings of
Death. Cf. Chaucer: 'So well they
loued, as old bookes saine, / That
when that one was dead, soothly to
tell / His fellow went & sought him
downe in hell' (*KT*, 1198–200).
where ... lodged their journey to
the underworld, in an attempt to
abduct Proserpina (Ovid, 12.210–44).
In some versions of the myth,
Pirithous is killed and remains in the
underworld; in others, Theseus voluntarily stays with him and Hercules
later rescues them both.
41 **brought them off** saved them
41–4 **Their ... undone** probably a reference to the Gordian knot which was
supposed to be too intricate to untie
(cf. the reference to 'this sacred Gordian' in Webster, *DM*, 1.1.480–1). The
skilful *finger* is presumably that of
Time. *True* and *long* might refer
either to 'love' or to 'cunning'. In
saying that the knot may be *outworn*
only by death, Hippolyta does not
consider that it might be cut, as it was
by Alexander the Great. For the influence of Montaigne's essay on friendship, see p. 55 above

---

40 Sought] *this edn (Littledale);* Fought *Q*

Cleaving his conscience into twain and doing
Each side like justice, which he loves best.

EMILIA   Doubtless,

There is a best and reason has no manners
To say it is not you. I was acquainted
Once with a time when I enjoyed a play-fellow.   50
You were at wars when she the grave enriched,
Who made too proud the bed – took leave o'th' moon
(Which then looked pale at parting) when our count
Was each eleven.

HIPPOLYTA   'Twas Flavina.

EMILIA   Yes.

You talk of Pirithous' and Theseus' love.   55
Theirs has more ground, is more maturely seasoned,
More buckled with strong judgement, and their
        needs

47 **like** equal
which that is, himself or Pirithous.
This passage is often taken to mean
that Theseus cannot choose between
Pirithous and Hippolyta, but it is
more likely that Hippolyta is stating
the common Renaissance idea that a
friend is a second self.

47–9 **Doubtless ... you** Theseus' love
for Hippolyta is still greater than his
love for himself and his friend.

48 **reason ... manners** Emilia presumably means that her sister's pre-
eminence in Theseus' love should be
evident to any rational person, but
the stress on *manners* creates the possibility that she is simply paying an
expected compliment.

49–82 This speech is often compared
with Hermia's words to Helena in
MND (3.2.198–214).

49–50 **acquainted ... play-fellow** In
making *time* rather than *play-fellow*
the object of *acquainted*, Emilia may
imply that this kind of affection belongs to a particular age. Some critics
who see Emilia as a lesbian (see pp.
99–100 above) focus on the double
meaning of *enjoyed*.

52 **too proud the bed** Beds and graves
are often compared (see *RJ* passim);
for the idea of 'proud death', see *Ham*
5.2.364.
took ... moon died. The virgin
huntress Diana is also the moon goddess; Flavina was therefore, like
Emilia, her servant (cf. 5.1.140–2).

53–4 **When ... eleven** when we were
both 11 years old

53 **count** age

54 ***eleven** *A eleven*, which appears in Q, is
an alternative form, or error, for *a leven*.

56 **more ground** a firmer basis (Oxf[1])
more maturely seasoned has lasted
longer, or 'is between more mature
people' (AT)

57 **buckled** fastened. Cf. *corslet* as a verb
in 1.1.177 and Polonius' advice to
Laertes to 'Grapple [trusted friends]
... unto thy soul with hoops of steel'
(*Ham* 1.3.63).

57–8 **their ... other** i.e., in their military
roles: Emilia is aware of the importance
of shared experience in maintaining affection. Contrast Cicero's *De Amicitia*:
Laelius says that he and Scipio Africa-
nus loved each other even though neither of them *needed* the other (ix.30).

54 eleven] *F*; a eleven *Q*; aleven *Riv*; a leven *Bowers*   Flavina] *Seward*; Flauia *Q*

The one of th'other may be said to water
Their intertangled roots of love – but I
And she I sigh and spoke of were things innocent,   60
Loved for we did and like the elements
That know not what nor why, yet do effect
Rare issues by their operance; our souls
Did so to one another. What she liked
Was then of me approved; what not, condemned –   65
No more arraignment. The flower that I would pluck
And put between my breasts (then but beginning
To swell about the blossom), oh, she would long
Till she had such another, and commit it
To the like innocent cradle, where phoenix-like   70
They died in perfume. On my head no toy
But was her pattern; her affections – pretty,
Though happily her careless wear – I followed

58–64 The marginal stage direction at this point (see t.n.) is the first of several addressed to the stage manager (see Fig. 15, p. 112, pp. 124–5 above and cf. 1.4.26–7n).

60 **she . . . spoke of** condenses 'she for whom I sigh, and of whom I spoke'

61 **for** because (that is, we could not give a reason). Waith (Oxf[1], 49–50) quotes Montaigne's explanation of his love for his friend La Boétie: '*Parce que c'était lui, parce que c'était moi*' ['because it was he, because it was my selfe' (Florio, 1.202)].

61–3 **like . . . operance** Cf. Donne's 'The Relic' ('we loved well and faithfully, / Yet knew not what we loved, nor why; / Difference of sex no more we knew / Than our guardian angels do') and 'Valediction forbidding Mourning' ('Moving of th'earth brings harms and fears, / Men reckon what it did and meant, / But trepidation of the spheres / Though greater far, is innocent').

63 **operance** operation

66 **No more arraignment** It needed no further trial.

67–8 ***breasts . . . oh** Q places *O* after *breasts*; as Brooke says, 'metre and sense are both satisfied by the easy supposition that *oh* was unintentionally misplaced by the compositor'.

71 **toy** trifling decoration

72–4 **her affections . . . decking** See p. 112 above for this passage as printed in Q. The idea is clear (Emilia admired and imitated even the most casual choices of dress made by her friend) but it is hard to make grammatical sense out of the lines. In Q, the parenthesis that opens before *pretty* never closes; perhaps it was misread as a comma after *careless*.

72–3 ***her . . . wear** what she affected (that is, liked) to wear – pretty, though carelessly chosen. Though both Leech and Bowers argue for retaining Q's *careless were* at 73, most editors, following Seward, have emended to *wear*, which seems related to *decking* in 74.

73 **happily** perhaps (haply)

58–64] *marginal SD:* 2 Hearses rea-/ dy with Pala-/ mon: and Arci-/ te: the 3. / Queenes. / Theseus: and / his Lordes / ready. *Q*   67 breasts] *Brooke;* breasts, oh *Q*   68 blossom] *Q;* bosom *(Lamb)*   oh, she] *Brooke;* she *Q*   73 happily her careless, wear,] *1778 subst.;* happely, her careles, were, *Q;* happily her careles were *1711;* haply careless wear *Seward*

For my most serious decking; had mine ear
Stol'n some new air or at adventure hummed one   75
From musical coinage, why, it was a note
Whereon her spirits would sojourn – rather, dwell on,
And sing it in her slumbers. This rehearsal,
Which fury-innocent wots well, comes in
Like old importment's bastard, has this end: 80
That the true love 'tween maid and maid may be
More than in sex dividual.

HIPPOLYTA   You're out of breath!

74 **serious decking** dressing on important occasions

75 ***hummed one** Q's *on* can be a variant spelling for *one* (see 1.2.70n.), but it is also worth considering Tucker Brooke's suggestion that *on* means 'on and on'.

76 **coinage** invention, improvisation

77 **sojourn ... on** The contrast is between sojourning with the tune (visiting it) and dwelling there (living permanently with it).

78 **rehearsal** story

79 **fury-innocent** a notoriously difficult line, often emended (see t.n.). There seems some connection, not clearly worked out, between *innocent* (in the sense of baby) and *bastard* in 80. The *fury* may also relate to the rapidity and breathlessness with which Emilia evidently speaks (see 82). Blincoe suggests (337–8) that the compound is an adjective meaning 'innocent of fury' and contrasts with the rage that love inspires in Palamon and Arcite. The phrase is an oxymoron, because furies are normally sent to punish the guilty and are guilty themselves. In *KT* the tragedy at the end is caused by a malevolent fury sent from Saturn; in the play this supernatural element is eliminated, but in Florio's translation of Montaigne the word occurs in the context of same-sex love (see p. 56, above).
wots knows

80 **old importment's bastard** a false (illegitimate) version of whatever produced it: in this case, *importment*. (See *Tim* 1.2.107–9.) Hart (286–7) comments on the frequency with which Shakespeare coins words ending in 'ment'. Mason's interpretation of it as *emportement* (passion) has been adopted by several editors who assume that Emilia is apologizing for giving such a feeble rendition of the intensity of her childhood feelings. But *importment*, an obsolete word meaning 'importance' or 'significance', makes sense here. Emilia's tone is mocking as well as melancholy when she describes her seriousness over childish trifles; she may now be mocking, not the relationship with Flavina, but her own seriousness in talking about it.
end both conclusion (Emilia apologizes for having talked so much) and purpose

82 ***dividual** Seward's emendation of Q's *individuall* seems justified by the metre and by the existence of *dividual* in other contexts; RP cites 'Not to be sever'd nor dividuall' in Michael Drayton, *Endymion and Phoebe*, 517–18. However, Blincoe ('Sex') also argues plausibly for *individuall*, citing Cotgrave's definition of it as the united love of man and woman in marriage.

75 one] *1778;* on *Q*   76 musical] *F;* misicall *Q*   79 fury-innocent] *Q;* every innocent *(Lamb);* surely Innocence *Seward;* sorry innocence *(Bertram);* seely innocence *Oxf*   wots well] *Q;* wot I well *(Mason)*   80 importment's] importments *Q;* emportment's *(Mason)*   82 dividual] *Seward;* individuall *Q*

And this high-speeded pace is but to say
That you shall never, like the maid Flavina,
Love any that's called man.

EMILIA   I am sure I shall not.   85
HIPPOLYTA
Now, alack, weak sister,
I must no more believe thee in this point,
Though in't I know thou dost believe thy self,
Than I will trust a sickly appetite
That loathes even as it longs. But sure, my sister,   90
If I were ripe for your persuasion, you
Have said enough to shake me from the arm
Of the all-noble Theseus – for whose fortunes
I will now in and kneel, with great assurance
That we, more than his Pirithous, possess   95
The high throne in his heart.
EMILIA   I am not
Against your faith, yet I continue mine.   *Exeunt.*

[1.4]   *Cornets. A battle struck within; then a retreat. Flourish.*
         Then enter THESEUS *as victor,* [*with a* Herald, *other lords, and*

83 **high-speeded pace** a clue to the delivery of Emilia's speech
84–5 **you ... man** 'Like Flavina, you
shall never love any man.'
89–90 **sickly ... longs** the pregnant
woman's desire, or 'longing', for foods
she does not normally like; also the
sick person's changing appetites. In
MND Demetrius remembers his
immature love for Hermia as 'an idle
gaud / Which in my childhood I did
dote upon' (4.1.170–1) and compares
Helena to food that he loathed 'like a
sickness' but now, in his 'health', has
come to love (176–9). Compare 'I
loath it [love] now / As men in
Feavers meat they fell sick on' (Massinger and Fletcher, *A Very Woman*,
Bowers, 7: 4.2.49–50).

94 **in** go in
94–6 **with ... heart** In referring to her
sister's earlier words (47–9), Hippolyta is also suggesting a parallel: if
Emilia is sure that Theseus must, in
all reason, prefer Hippolyta to both
himself and Pirithous, the logical conclusion is that she herself will eventually prefer a husband to the memory
of her childhood friendship.
1.4.0.1 *Cornets* See note on music in
Appendix 6, p. 360.
A battle ... within Battle noises are
heard off stage. See p. 124 above.
0.2 THESEUS *as victor* Davenant's '*as
from victory*' suggests what was
meant: probably he was crowned with
a laurel wreath, with prisoners led
behind his triumphal procession.

96–7] *Q lines* heart. / faith, / mine. /   1.4] Scæna 4. *Q*   0.1 *Cornets*] *after 1.3.97 Q*

soldiers, PALAMON *and* ARCITE *on hearses*]. *The three* Queens
meet him and fall on their faces before him.

1 QUEEN
　To thee no star be dark!
2 QUEEN　　　　　　　　　　Both heaven and earth
　Friend thee forever!
3 QUEEN　　　　　　　　All the good that may
　Be wished upon thy head, I cry 'Amen' to't!
THESEUS
　Th'impartial gods, who from the mounted heavens
　View us, their mortal herd, behold who err　　　　　5
　And, in their time, chastise. Go and find out
　The bones of your dead lords and honour them
　With treble ceremony, rather than a gap
　Should be in their dear rites. We would supply't,
　But those we will depute, which shall invest　　　10
　You in your dignities and even each thing
　Our haste does leave imperfect. So adieu,
　And heaven's good eyes look on you.　　*Exeunt Queens.*
　[*Theseus notices the two hearses.*]　　What are those?
HERALD
　Men of great quality, as may be judged
　By their appointment. Some of Thebes have told's　15

0.3 PALAMON … *hearses* They may be
brought in either at the beginning of
the scene or shortly before Theseus
notices them at 13.
1 To … **dark** May nó fates be malig-
nant toward you. Cf. 'Let all the
number of the stars give light / To thy
dear way' (*AC* 3.2.65–6).
4 **mounted** high
9 **rites** spelled *rights* in Q; the word has
both meanings
　would supply't would make up
any gap (by being present myself).
Though the sentence in Q ends at
this point, 'But' in 10 suggests that

Theseus, as in 1.1, is talking about
acting both in person and by deputy:
he himself will not remain for the funeral but will return at once to
Athens.
11 **even** make even, settle (*OED v.* I 4a)
12 **imperfect** unfinished
13 **heaven's** … **you** May heaven look
on you kindly.
14 SP The Herald would be recognized
by his distinctive costume.
15 **appointment** their armour and other
trappings. Skeat cites *KT*, 1017: 'The
heraulds knew hem [Palamon and
Arcite] best in speciall.'

9 rites.] *Seward;* rights, Q　13 SD *Exeunt Queens*] *after* those Q　*Theseus … hearses*] *this edn; not
in* Q

They are sisters' children, nephews to the King.

THESEUS

By th' helm of Mars, I saw them in the war,
Like to a pair of lions, smeared with prey,
Make lanes in troops aghast. I fixed my note
Constantly on them, for they were a mark   20
Worth a god's view. What prisoner was't that told me
When I enquired their names?

HERALD   Wi' leave, they're called
Arcite and Palamon.

THESEUS   'Tis right; those, those.
They are not dead?

HERALD

Nor in a state of life. Had they been taken   25
When their last hurts were given, 'twas possible
They might have been recovered; yet they breathe
And have the name of men.

THESEUS   Then like men use 'em.
The very lees of such, millions of rates,
Exceed the wine of others. All our surgeons   30

---

16 **sisters' children** In *KT* they are described as 'of the blood riall / Of Thebes, and of sistren two yborne' (1018–19).

19 **Make lanes** cut a path. The image is used in North's translation of Plutarch's life of Coriolanus. Cf. 'Follow / The lane this sword makes for you' in *The False One*, a Fletcher–Massinger collaboration (Bowers, 8: 5.3.65) (RP).
aghast horrified (refers to the troops)
note attention

20 **mark** object of attention

21–2 **What ... leave** Both Theseus' question and the Herald's answer can be emended (see t.n.) but are clear in context: Theseus is looking for the person he interrogated earlier; the

Herald deferentially supplies the information himself.

26–7 The SD (see t.n.) which appears in the margin of Q at this point indicates preparation for the 'funeral solemnity' of 1.5.

27 **been recovered** recovered; the verb was often used transitively: cf. 'If I can recover him' (*Tem* 2.2.68)

28 **have ... men** are still alive enough to be called men

29–30 **The ... others** What little is left of their lives (perhaps with a suggestion that they have almost been drained of blood) is infinitely better than most people even in their full strength. Cf. *dregged* (1.2.97).

---

18 smeared] *(smear'd) Qc;* succard *Qu*   21 What prisoner was't] *Q;* what was't that prisoner *Dyce*   22 Wi' leave] *Dyce;* We leave *Q;* We learn *(Heath);* we 'leave *Littledale;*   26–7] *marginal SD:* 3. Hearses rea-/ dy *Q*

Convent in their behoof; our richest balms,
Rather than niggard, waste; their lives concern us
Much more than Thebes is worth. Rather than have
        'em
Freed of this plight and in their morning state,
Sound and at liberty, I would 'em dead;   35
But forty-thousandfold we had rather have 'em
Prisoners to us than death. Bear 'em speedily
From our kind air, to them unkind, and minister
What man to man may do, for our sake – more,
Since I have known frights, fury, friends' behests,   40
Love's provocations, zeal, a mistress' task,
Desire of liberty, a fever, madness,
Hath set a mark which nature could not reach to
Without some imposition, sickness in will

---

31 **Convent** assemble. Stressed on the
second syllable. Cf. 1.5.9, below.
  in their behoof for their benefit, or
on their behalf. (The two words are
often confused: see *OED* behoof.)
31–2 **our ... waste** 'Of the two extremes, be recklessly generous rather
than stingy with our most costly
medicines.' Cf. 7–9, above.
33–7 **Rather ... death** *KT* says that
Theseus 'nold hem not ransoun'
(Chaucer, *Riv*: 'nolde no ransoun'
(1024)) but does not explain why. His
behaviour is seen here as a harsh compliment to their valour,
34 **their morning state** as they were
this morning
36 **forty-thousandfold** forty thousand
times
38 **our kind air** Since the action takes
place near Thebes, *our* does not mean
Athenian (though the pure air of
Athens is praised in a Chorus to *Oedipus at Colonus*) but the 'common air'
(cf. *R2* 1.3.157) that is *kind* (natural,
as well as pleasant) to all humanity.

unkind because it was thought dangerous for wounds to 'take air'
39 **more** i.e., even more than man can do
40–5 ***Since ... reason*** This difficult
passage has been explained in a
number of ways. The two most plausible are, first, that Theseus justifies his
sympathy for the kinsmen, and ex-
cuses their fighting for Creon, on the
grounds that the various causes he
lists have been known to make men act
out of a sick will and against their
better judgment (Leech, Proudfoot,
Bowers); second, that he exhorts the
doctors to do, as people sometimes
can in the extreme situations he lists,
'even more than is humanly possible'
(Brooke). I take his speech in the
second, more positive, sense: sheer
will-power can enable the sick person
to excel (*o'er-wrestle*) the strong
person who can do only what reason
accepts as possible.
43 **mark** something at which to aim
44 **imposition** obligation (from one of
the causes just mentioned)

---

39 do,] *this edn;* doe *Q*   sake –] *this edn;* sake *Q*   40 frights,] *Q;* fights, *(Heath);* fight's *Dyce*
friends'] *Weber;* friends, *Q*   41 Love's] *Seward;* Loves, *Q*   43 Hath] *Q;* Have *(Heath)*   to]
(too)

O'er-wrestling strength in reason. For our love   45
And great Apollo's mercy, all our best
Their best skill tender. Lead into the city,
Where having bound things scattered, we will post
To Athens 'fore our army.   *Flourish. Exeunt.*

[1.5]   *Music. Enter the* Queens *with the hearses of their knights,
in a funeral solemnity.*

[*The dirge*]

Urns and odours bring away;
Vapours, sighs, darken the day;
Our dole more deadly looks than dying –
Balms and gums and heavy cheers,
Sacred vials fill'd with tears,   5
And clamours through the wild air flying.

45 **o'er wrestling** Bertram's suggestion (p. 117) that Q's *or* means 'o'er' makes sense of a difficult construction. He compares 'o'er-wrested' (*TC* 1.3.157).
46 **Apollo's mercy** Apollo was the god of healing
   our best (doctors)
48 **Where** conflates adverbs of both time ('after') and place ('there')
49 **'fore** ahead of. Q has *for*, but at least half of Theseus' army is with him at Thebes and in 2.1.48 the Jailer says that he returned to Athens 'privately in the night'. He presumably sends the two wounded men with his own small entourage.
1.5.0.1–2 Q does not specify who sings here, or even whether this is a song; the queens might have recited it antiphonally, like the dirge in *Cymbeline* (4.2.258). Most editors assume that the last line was repeated in chorus. Certainly the '*&c*' after 0.2 in Q suggests that a large number of people took part in the 'solemnity' (black mourning cloaks would have concealed the costumes of cast members).

1 **bring away** The objects of this verb are all the symbols of woe mentioned in this stanza. The queens invert the opening bridal song which gathered 'all dear Nature's children sweet' and all birds of good omen.
3 Both *dole* and *looks* are ambiguous; the line, in context, seems to make more sense if *dole* is taken in the sense of *OED sb.* 1 (portion, share or fate), rather than *sb.* 2 (grief, mourning), with *looks* as a noun rather than a verb: 'Our portion (or fate) consists of the mourners' deathly expressions – as if we were not only dying of grief but already dead of it.'
4 **cheers** outward looks (Skeat compares 'a deadly chere' (*KT*, 913))
6 **clamours ... flying** Muir (128) points out that this line is echoed in the *flying/dying* rhyme of Tennyson's lyric, 'The Splendour Falls on Castle Walls', which precedes Canto 4 of *The Princess*. Chaucer wrote of 'The great clamour' of the women at the burning of the bodies (*KT*, 995).

45 O'er-wrestling] *Leech (Bertram); (*Or wrestling*) Q* 49 'fore] *Seward; (*for*) Q* 1.5] Scæna 5. *Q* 0.1 *Music*] *after 1.4.49 Q* 0.2 *solemnity*] Solempnity *&c. Q*

Come, all sad and solemn shows
That are quick-eyed Pleasure's foes;
We convent naught else but woes.
We convent naught else but woes.   10

3 QUEEN

This funeral path brings to your household's grave:
Joy seize on you again; peace sleep with him.

2 QUEEN

And this to yours.

1 QUEEN   Yours this way. Heavens lend
A thousand differing ways to one sure end.

3 QUEEN

This world's a city full of straying streets,   15
And death's the market-place where each one meets.

Exeunt severally.

[2.1]   *Enter* Jailer *and* Wooer.

JAILER I may depart with little while I live; something I
may cast to you, not much. Alas, the prison I keep,

---

8 **quick-eyed** the first of several compound epithets with 'eyed'. Cf. 2.2.21, 2.2.37 and 2.5.29.

14 **A thousand ... ways** See Webster, *DM*, 4.2.219–20: 'I know death hath ten thousand several doors / For men to take their exits.' But the idea is common, as in Lucian's *Toxaris* (a famous dialogue on friendship): 'this god Death takes many shapes and puts at our disposal an infinite number of roads that lead to him' (165).

15–16 **This world's ... meets** Recalls *KT*: 'This world is but a throughfare ful of wo, / And we been pilgrimes, passing to and fro' (2848–9). Littledale and Masefield (194) claim to have seen gravestones with similar inscriptions. Waith (Oxf[1]) cites a close verbal parallel from Thomas Tuke, *A*

Discourse of Death (1613): 'Death meets with us a thousand ways. As into a gret Citie, or into the maine Sea, so vnto death there are many waies. It is as the center, wherein all the lines do meete; a towne of Mart, where many waies from contrarie coasts doe end' (sig. C3). See Dent, D140, for proverbial examples.

15 **straying** wandering in all directions

16 SD *severally* by different exits; see p. 62 above.

2.1.1–57 The compositor of Q set the first line as prose, the rest as verse. See pp. 118–23 above.

1 **depart** part

2 **cast** give. That is, he may part with some spare cash at the time of the marriage.

9–10] *one line Q*   10 We ... woes] *We convent, &c. Q*   12 seize] *(ceaze)*   2.1] *Actus Secundus. / Scæna I. Q*   2–57] *as verse Q*

though it be for great ones, yet they seldom come; before
one salmon, you shall take a number of minnows. I
am given out to be better lined than it can appear to   5
me report is a true speaker. I would I were really that
I am delivered to be. Marry, what I have, be it what it
will, I will assure upon my daughter at the day of my
death.

WOOER   Sir, I demand no more than your own offer and   10
  I will estate your daughter in what I have promised.

JAILER   Well, we will talk more of this when the solemnity is past. But have you a full promise of her?

Enter [the Jailer's] Daughter [carrying rushes].

When that shall be seen, I tender my consent. .

WOOER   I have, Sir. Here she comes.   15

JAILER [*to his Daughter*]   Your friend and I have chanced
  to name you here, upon the old business. But no
  more of that now; so soon as the court hurry is over,
  we will have an end of it. I'th' meantime, look ten-
  derly to the two prisoners. I can tell you, they are   20
  princes.

DAUGHTER   These strewings are for their chamber. 'Tis
  pity they are in prison and 'twere pity they should be

---

4 **salmon** large and valuable catch
(i.e., rich prisoner), as opposed to
poor men, or minnows. The Jailer
would have been expected to supplement his salary with fees and bribes
from prisoners who could afford
them.

5 **better lined** wealthier. Cf. 'The lin-
ings of his coffers' (*R2* 1.3.61).

5–6 **than . . . speaker** than I can see any
reason for people to say

7 **Marry** a mild oath, originally from
the name of the Virgin Mary; its occurrence, like the use of prose, fits the
more contemporary and colloquial
tone of the subplot

8 **assure** promise to bestow

11 **estate** settle (financially)

12–13 **the solemnity** the celebrations
surrounding the wedding of Theseus
and Hippolyta

13 **of** from
  *SD Some editors put the Daugh-
  ter's entry later, but see 1.2.83n.

14 **tender** give, hand over

18 **court hurry** See 12–13 above.

22 **strewings** fresh rushes for the floor.
Perhaps an allusion to the proverb
'Rushes for the stranger' (Dent, R213),
which also occurs in Fletcher's *Valentinian* (Bowers, 4: 2.5.93); it means
that strangers get better treatment
than those one sees every day – such
as the Wooer.

---

13 SD *carrying rushes*] *Weber subst.; not in Q*   18 that now;] *1778;* That. Now, *Q*

out. I do think they have patience to make any adversity
ashamed. The prison itself is proud of 'em and   25
they have all the world in their chamber.

JAILER   They are famed to be a pair of absolute men.

DAUGHTER   By my troth, I think Fame but stammers
'em; they stand a grise above the reach of report.

JAILER   I heard them reported in the battle to be the   30
only doers.

DAUGHTER   Nay, most likely, for they are noble suffer-
ers. I marvel how they would have looked had they
been victors, that with such a constant nobility enforce a freedom out of bondage, making misery their   35
mirth and affliction a toy to jest at.

JAILER   Do they so?

DAUGHTER   It seems to me they have no more sense of
their captivity than I of ruling Athens. They eat well,
look merrily, discourse of many things, but nothing   40
of their own restraint and disasters. Yet sometime a
divided sigh, martyred, as 'twere, i'th' deliverance,

24–5 make ... ashamed In Webster,
DM, the imprisoned heroine is said to
show 'a behaviour so noble, / As gives
a majesty to adversity' (4.1.5–6). The
phrase comes from Sidney's *Arcadia*,
1.2, where it refers to the hero
Musidorus.

26 all ... chamber Bawcutt compares
Donne, 'The Good Morrow': 'love, all
love of other sights controls, / And
makes one little room, an every-
where'. Hamlet says that he 'could be
bounded in a nutshell, and count
myself a king of infinite space' (*Ham*
2.2.254–5).

27 absolute perfect, complete

28 troth word of honour: a mild oath
stammers speaks inadequately

29 they ... report They excel even the
high reputation they already have.
grise a small step in a stairway. Also
spelled *grece* (the main heading in
OED); Q's *greise* suggests something
closer to Shakespeare's other uses of

the word in *TN* 3.1.135 and *Oth*
1.3.200, where the F spellings are
grize and *grise* respectively.

30–1 the only doers the only ones
worth mentioning; a way of expressing the superlative. *OED a.* 5 cites
Ham 3.2.125: 'your only jig-maker'.

34–5 enforce either 'strengthen' (*OED
v.* I 2) or 'produce by force' (*OED v.*
III 11)

35–6 their mirth a cause for mirth

36 toy trifle

38 sense consciousness

41 restraint captivity

42 divided broken, incomplete
martyred ... deliverance because
the sigher tried to keep it from getting
out. *Break from* (43), like *deliverance*,
suggests the common comparison between prison and the womb. Cf. Middleton and Rowley's *The Changeling*:
'That sigh would fain have utterance
... / ... how it labours / For liberty
... ' (2.2.104–6).

will break from one of them – when the other presently gives it so sweet a rebuke that I could wish myself a sigh to be so chid, or at least a sigher to be comforted.   45

WOOER   I never saw 'em.

JAILER   The Duke himself came privately in the night and so did they.

Enter PALAMON *and* ARCITE, *above.*

What the reason of it is, I know not. Look, yonder they are; that's Arcite looks out.   50

DAUGHTER   No, sir, no, that's Palamon. Arcite is the lower of the twain; you may perceive a part of him.

JAILER   Go to, leave your pointing; they would not make us their object. Out of their sight.   55

DAUGHTER   It is a holiday to look on them. Lord, the difference of men!   *Exeunt.*

[2.2]   *Enter* PALAMON *and* ARCITE *in prison.*

PALAMON
     How do you, noble cousin?
ARCITE   How do you, sir?

43–4 **presently** at once
49 SD For the staging of this scene, see p. 63 above.
52–3 **the lower** probably the shorter, but perhaps seeming so only in terms of their present positions in the window or windows. The various descriptions of the two men are contradictory. See 4.2.44n.
54 **Go to** an imperative expressing disapproval
     leave leave off
54–5 **they ... object** *Would* is ambiguous: either, 'They don't want to look at *us*', or, 'They would not stare at us as we are doing at them'.
56–7 **Lord ... men** Like Goneril's 'O the difference of man and man!' (*KL*

4.2.26), these words are usually spoken after the exit of the others, as a rueful or contemptuous comparison between the Wooer and the kinsmen.
2.2.0.1 See p. 63 above; Perhaps *prison* is indicated by the fact that the two men are in chains (Palamon is still wearing them in 3.1). But see also 274.
1 In 2.1 the Daughter talks as if Palamon and Arcite had been confined together for a while, yet their opening exchange suggests that they are meeting for the first time since their recovery. As Waith (Oxf[1]) says, the opening dialogue seems intended to show how the two men reached the state of calm resignation described in 2.1.38–46.

49 SD] *after* 48 *Q*   2.2] Scæna 2. *Q*

PALAMON
    Why, strong enough to laugh at misery
    And bear the chance of war; yet we are prisoners,
    I fear, forever, cousin.

ARCITE   I believe it
    And to that destiny have patiently   5
    Laid up my hour to come.

PALAMON   Oh, cousin Arcite,
    Where is Thebes now? Where is our noble country?
    Where are our friends and kindreds? Never more
    Must we behold those comforts, never see
    The hardy youths strive for the games of honour,   10
    Hung with the painted favours of their ladies,
    Like tall ships under sail – then start amongst 'em,
    And as an east wind leave 'em all behind us,
    Like lazy clouds, whilst Palamon and Arcite,
    Even in the wagging of a wanton leg,   15
    Outstripped the people's praises, won the garlands,
    Ere they have time to wish 'em ours. Oh, never

6 **Laid up … to come** resigned my future time

7–8 This brief *ubi sunt* passage (a series of rhetorical questions lamenting a vanished past) evokes a very different Thebes from the one the kinsmen wanted to leave in 1.2. It has no counterpart in *KT* but Boccaccio gives Arcita three stanzas of lament at the ruins of Thebes (4.14–16).

8 **kindreds** *OED* gives no occurrence of the plural use at such an early date and it is possible that the final 's' is an error. Perhaps Palamon's and Arcite's families are meant to be two separate entities.

10 **strive for** make their way towards (in a competition)

11 **painted favours** colourful love-tokens from their ladies (who, by implication, may also be 'painted')

12 **start** burst into activity (*OED v. intrans.* 2a and f)

13 **east wind** proverbially the east wind was 'good for neither man nor beast' (Tilley, 729). The men were not only as fast but (to their competitors) as lethal.

14 **lazy clouds** clouds left behind by the wind rather than driven by it.

15 **in … wanton leg** a variation of 'in the twinkling of an eye', suggesting the element of playfulness that Palamon likes to think their victory involved

16 **Outstripped** The image conflates two ideas: the speed of their victory, probably at running, and the extent to which they excelled even the praise they received (as the Daughter said in 2.1.28–9). Cf. 'she will outstrip all praise, / And make it halt behind her' (*Tem* 4.1.10–11).

17 **have** Dyce suggests *had*, but Palamon has moved from memory into the more immediate historical present.

3 war; yet] *Brooke subst.;* warre yet, *Q*

Shall we two exercise, like twins of honour,
Our arms again and feel our fiery horses
Like proud seas under us; our good swords now   20
(Better the red-eyed god of war ne'er wore),
Ravished our sides, like age must run to rust
And deck the temples of those gods that hate us.
These hands shall never draw 'em out like lightning
To blast whole armies more.

ARCITE   No, Palamon,   25
Those hopes are prisoners with us. Here we are,
And here the graces of our youths must wither
Like a too-timely spring; here age must find us
And, which is heaviest, Palamon, unmarried.
The sweet embraces of a loving wife,   30
Loaden with kisses, armed with thousand Cupids,
Shall never clasp our necks; no issue know us;
No figures of ourselves shall we e'er see,
To glad our age, and like young eagles teach 'em
Boldly to gaze against bright arms and say,   35

18 **twins of honour** one of many references to twins in the sense of equals (see pp. 105–7 above)
19–20 **horses . . . us** a common comparison (Neptune was god of both horses and the sea)
21 **red-eyed . . . war** Mars (the planet got its name because of its red appearance, and the god was often associated with the colour of blood). Coriolanus' eye is 'red as 'twould burn Rome' (*Cor* 5.1.64).
22 ***Ravished** snatched from
  like age . . . rust will be destroyed by lack of use as much as they would have been by age and excessive use. Seward compares 'We shall grow old men and feeble, / Which is the scorn of love and rust of honour' (*The Lover's Progress* Dyce, 11: 2.1).
23 **those gods . . . us** Juno and Athene, traditional enemies of Thebes
25 **blast** destroy; used especially for violent weather conditions
26 **hopes** ours (that we might again enjoy such triumphs) or those that others had built on our youthful promise
28 **too-timely** too early, killed by the return of winter weather, an image probably suggested by *blast* at 25, above
29 **heaviest** most melancholy
31 This personification of love might refer either to the wife or the embraces. Arcite is hardly the martialist that he will later become; rather, he here transforms Palamon's martial imagery into the language of Venus: cf. 1.1.174–6, above.
32 **issue** offspring
33 **figures** copies
34 **glad** gladden
34–5 **like . . . arms** a variation on the proverbial 'Only the Eagle can gaze at the sun' (Dent, E3)

21 wore] *Seward;* ware *Dyce;* were *Q*   22 Ravished] *Seward;* Bravishd *Q*

'Remember what your fathers were, and conquer!'
The fair-eyed maids shall weep our banishments
And in their songs curse ever-blinded Fortune
Till she for shame see what a wrong she has done
To youth and nature. This is all our world.   40
We shall know nothing here but one another,
Hear nothing but the clock that tells our woes.
The vine shall grow but we shall never see it;
Summer shall come and with her all delights,
But dead-cold winter must inhabit here still.   45

PALAMON

'Tis too true, Arcite. To our Theban hounds
That shook the aged forest with their echoes
No more now must we hallow, no more shake
Our pointed javelins whilst the angry swine
Flies like a Parthian quiver from our rages,   50
Struck with our well-steeled darts. All valiant uses,
The food and nourishment of noble minds,
In us two here shall perish; we shall die,

---

37 **fair-eyed maids** Cf. 2.5.29.
38–40 In 1.2.80–1 the two men complained that Justice seemed blind and deaf. Here, paradoxically, Arcite imagines that curses will make Fortune, traditionally blind, see again, and be ashamed.
40 **all our world** Cf. the Daughter's account of them at 2.1.26, which gives a stoic meaning to the same words.
42 **tells** counts, numbers
43 **vine shall grow** poetically suggests both spring and looking forward to the autumn harvest
44–5 **Summer . . . still** perhaps echoing the imaginary epistle from the imprisoned Richard II in *Heroical Epistles* by a friend of both Shakespeare and Fletcher, Michael Drayton (first pub. 1597): 'There pleasant Sommer dwelleth all the yeere, / Frost-starved Winter doth inhabit heere' (Drayton, 2.67–8). Seward suggested that Milton recalled the *TNK* passage in

'Thus with the year, / Seasons return, but not to me returns . . . Or sight of vernal bloom, or summer's rose . . . ' (*Paradise Lost*, 3.40–3).
48 **hallow** call (in a special tone designed to be heard at a distance)
49–51 **whilst . . . darts** The Parthians were said to shoot backwards while retreating. As Seward explains, two ideas are conflated: 'the Bristles and Darts sticking on his back [are compared] to the Arrows on the Archer's Shoulder, and the frequent and furious Turnings of the Boar to the *Parthian*'s turning to shoot as he flies'. Palamon, though elegiac like Arcite, is nostalgic for war rather than love.
51 **well-steeled** overlaid, pointed or edged with steel
   uses exercises (sports and war)
53 **In us . . . perish** They will lose their skill at such activities; perhaps, too, all excellence in such things will die with them.

Which is the curse of honour, lastly,
Children of grief and ignorance.

ARCITE   Yet, cousin,   55
Even from the bottom of these miseries,
From all that Fortune can inflict upon us,
I see two comforts rising, two mere blessings,
If the gods please: to hold here a brave patience
And the enjoying of our griefs together.   60
While Palamon is with me, let me perish
If I think this our prison!

PALAMON   Certainly,
'Tis a main goodness, cousin, that our fortunes
Were twined together; 'tis most true, two souls
Put in two noble bodies, let 'em suffer   65
The gall of hazard, so they grow together,
Will never sink; they must not, say they could.
A willing man dies sleeping and all's done.

ARCITE
Shall we make worthy uses of this place
That all men hate so much?

PALAMON   How, gentle cousin?   70

---

54 **lastly** Seward suggested *lazily*, but
Davenant's adaptation (see t.n.) gives
what must be the intended sense.

55 **Children . . . ignorance** contrasted
with the 'twins of honour', 18, above

58–60 **I see . . . together** The asym-
metrical syntax blurs the rhetorical
climax. Arcite sees two possible comforts (or, if the gods grant them, blessings): the opportunity of exercising
the virtue of patience and the fact that
they are together.

58 **mere** absolute, pure, and hence *rising*
as to the top of a mixture

59 **hold** maintain

60 **enjoying** experiencing (probably
with some sense of pleasure)

63 **main** very great. *OED a*. 6a and b,
cites examples in *H8* and Fletcher's

Mad Lover.

64 **twined** *twyn'd* in Q; cf. *twyning
cherries* at 1.1.179. Both usages are
ambiguous and may refer either to
twinning or twining. But *twinned*
fortunes would have been born at
the same time, whereas Palamon
seems to mean only that their fates are
mutually dependent. (See pp. 105–6
above.)

66 **gall of hazard** bitterness (*OED sb*. 1,
3a) or· suffering (*OED sb*. 2, 3b) inflicted by Fortune

68 **sleeping** as calmly as if he died in his
sleep; similar to the proverbial 'to go
to one's grave like a bed' (Dent,
B192.1)

69 **uses** perhaps referring to Palamon's
complaint in 51–3, above

54 lastly] *Q*; at last *Davenant*; lazily *Seward*   64 twined] (twyn'd) *Q*; twinned *Seward*

ARCITE

    Let's think this prison holy sanctuary,
    To keep us from corruption of worse men.
    We are young and yet desire the ways of honour,
    That liberty and common conversation,
    The poison of pure spirits, might, like women,   75
    Woo us to wander from. What worthy blessing
    Can be but our imaginations
    May make it ours? And here being thus together,
    We are an endless mine to one another;
    We are one another's wife, ever begetting   80
    New births of love; we are father, friends,
      acquaintance,
    We are, in one another, families;
    I am your heir and you are mine. This place
    Is our inheritance; no hard oppressor
    Dare take this from us; here, with a little patience,   85
    We shall live long and loving. No surfeits seek us;
    The hand of war hurts none here, nor the seas
    Swallow their youth. Were we at liberty,
    A wife might part us lawfully, or business;
    Quarrels consume us; envy of ill men   90
    Crave our acquaintance. I might sicken, cousin,
    Where you should never know it, and so perish
    Without your noble hand to close mine eyes,
    Or prayers to the gods. A thousand chances,

---

73 **ways** paths. Cf. 'the perfect ways of honour' (*H8* 5.5.37) and see 1.1.104n.

75 **like women** Though these lines have been taken as evidence of Arcite's misogyny, the comparison probably means 'as if we were women' (RP).

76–9 **What . . . another** If one man can possess any good thing he is capable of imagining, two can imagine still more (cf. *R2* 5.5.6–9).

77 **Can be** can exist

86 **surfeits** See 1.1.190n.

90 **consume** goes (like *part* and *crave*) with *might* in 89. Arcite means that they might be killed in the quarrels of others; it never occurs to him that they might themselves quarrel.

91 **Crave** Though frequently emended (see t.n.), the phrase is clear: Arcite fears, not the envy of others, but his and Palamon's succumbing to (becoming acquainted with) the vice of envying or imitating despicable people, like those described in 1.2.

91 Crave] *Q*; Reave *Seward*; craze *(Theobald)*; carve *(Sympson)*; cleave *(Mason)*; Raze *(Heath)*; Grave *Dyce*

Were we from hence, would sever us.
PALAMON   You have made me –   95
    I thank you, cousin Arcite – almost wanton
    With my captivity: what a misery
    It is to live abroad and everywhere!
    'Tis like a beast, methinks. I find the court here –
    I am sure, a more content; and all those pleasures   100
    That woo the wills of men to vanity,
    I see through now and am sufficient
    To tell the world 'tis but a gaudy shadow
    That old Time as he passes by takes with him.
    What had we been, old in the court of Creon,   105
    Where sin is justice, lust and ignorance
    The virtues of the great ones? Cousin Arcite,
    Had not the loving gods found this place for us,
    We had died as they do, ill old men, unwept,
    And had their epitaphs, the people's curses.   110
    Shall I say more?
ARCITE   I would hear you still.
PALAMON   You shall.
    Is there record of any two that loved
    Better than we do, Arcite?
ARCITE   Sure there cannot.
PALAMON
    I do not think it possible our friendship

---

96 **wanton** sportful, capricious (*OED a* 3a and c). By contrast with Arcite's *contemptus mundi* speech, Palamon offers exaggerated, fanciful praise of prison, recalling the Daughter's description in 2.1.33–6.

98 **abroad** outside
    everywhere at random

99 **like a beast** Palamon redefines 'free' as 'wild', 'homeless'.

100 **a more content** a greater content, perhaps also 'a more content version of the court'. Cf. Davenant: 'I here enjoy a Court: I'm sure I find / A greater satisfaction' (p. 8).

102 **sufficient** qualified, capable (pronounced with four syllables)

103 **gaudy shadow** the reflection of something trivial

104 **That . . . him** As the world has no lasting value, it passes with time.

105 **had we been** would we have been
    old if we had grown old

109 **they** Creon's courtiers

110 **their . . . curses** Cf. 'Give out you lie a-dying, and if you hear the common people curse you, be sure you are taken for one of the prime night-caps' (Webster, *DM*, 2.1.18–20).

111 **I would** I want to (probably pronounced I'd)

112 **record** stressed on second syllable

113 **there cannot** 'Be' is understood.

Should ever leave us.

ARCITE   Till our deaths it cannot.   115

Enter EMILIA *and her* Woman.

And after death our spirits shall be led
To those that love eternally. [*Palamon sees Emilia.*]
                    Speak on, sir.

EMILIA

This garden has a world of pleasures in't.
What flower is this?

WOMAN   'Tis called narcissus, madam.

EMILIA

That was a fair boy, certain, but a fool   120
To love himself. Were there not maids enough?

ARCITE [*to Palamon*]

Pray, forward.

PALAMON   Yes –

EMILIA   Or were they all hard-hearted?

WOMAN

They could not be to one so fair.

---

117 To ... eternally The best-known
paradise of love and friendship was
Spenser's *Faerie Queene*, 4.10.25–7.
*SD Probably this is when Palamon
first sees Emilia (he has certainly done
so by 122). Arcite's 'Speak on, sir' follows a pause in which he waits for Palamon to speak.
118 SP *The last line of Arcite's speech
in Q; all editors since Seward have
agreed in assigning it to Emilia. Q's
reading is not impossible: the two men
have agreed that the prison is their
world and Arcite might gesture towards the garden as he speaks, thus
unintentionally drawing Palamon's attention to the two women. However,
giving the line to Emilia provides her
with a less abrupt opening and re-

inforces the sense that she, like the
young men, lives in a world of her
own.
119 narcissus In the famous myth (see
Ovid, 3.339–510), Narcissus, who had
rejected all the women who loved
him, died of longing for his own reflection in a fountain, finally becoming a flower. Arcite's earlier regret for
the children he and Palamon will
never have shows something of this
narcissistic longing for a mirror of
oneself (compare the urgings of
Shakespeare's first seventeen sonnets). Emilia had described a similar
state in 1.3 (her childhood desire to be
just like her friend), but here feels superior to it.
122 forward go on (speaking)

117 SD] *Leech; not in Q*   118 SP] *Seward; not in Q*   119 SP] *Emil. Q*

EMILIA   Thou wouldst not.

WOMAN
  I think I should not, madam.

EMILIA   That's a good wench.
  But take heed to your kindness, though.

WOMAN   Why, madam?   125

EMILIA
  Men are mad things.

ARCITE   Will ye go forward, cousin?

EMILIA
  Canst not thou work such flowers in silk, wench?

WOMAN   Yes.

EMILIA
  I'll have a gown full o' 'em, and of these.
  This is a pretty colour; will't not do
  Rarely upon a skirt, wench?

WOMAN   Dainty, madam.   130

ARCITE
  Cousin, cousin! how do you, sir? Why, Palamon!

PALAMON
  Never till now was I in prison, Arcite.

ARCITE
  Why, what's the matter, man?

PALAMON [*Indicates Emilia.*]   Behold, and wonder!
  By heaven, she is a goddess.

ARCITE [*Sees Emilia.*]   Ha!

PALAMON   Do reverence.
  She is a goddess, Arcite.

EMILIA   Of all flowers   135
  Methinks a rose is best.

WOMAN   Why, gentle madam?

---

123 **wouldst not** i.e., be hard-hearted.
    Conversations in which a lady both
    encourages and reproves her free-
    speaking lady-in-waiting also occur
    in *MA* 3.4, *Oth* 4.3 and *The Maid's
    Tragedy*, 2.1.
124 **wench** girl (not necessarily a social

inferior)
126 **mad** wild
127 **work** embroider
130 **Dainty** beautifully
134 **Do reverence** bow; kneel; prostrate
    yourself (as Palamon has perhaps
    done?)

132 was I] *Oxf;* I was *Q*

EMILIA

    It is the very emblem of a maid.

    For, when the west wind courts her gently,

    How modestly she blows and paints the sun

    With her chaste blushes! When the north comes near

       her,   140

    Rude and impatient, then, like chastity,

    She locks her beauties in her bud again

    And leaves him to base briars.

WOMAN   Yet, good madam,

    Sometimes her modesty will blow so far

    She falls for't. A maid,   145

    If she have any honour, would be loath

    To take example by her.

EMILIA   Thou art wanton.

ARCITE

    She is wondrous fair.

PALAMON   She is all the beauty extant.

---

137 **emblem** strictly, a combination of motto (usually in a foreign language), picture and verses, all reinforcing a moral or religious adage. Here, as often, the word applies to the picture alone, much like 'symbol' or 'image', except that, as Emilia's subsequent lines indicate, she is also thinking of the kind of fable which emblems illustrated.

138–43 **For . . . briars** For Emilia this is a fable of innocence, like Aesop's fable of the traveller in the wind and the sun: a young girl will respond to gentle courtship but not to rudeness. Her companion points out that the first kind of courtship is as dangerous to a woman's honour as the second.

138 **gently** pronounced with three syllables: 'gentily' (Heath)

139 **blows** blossoms

    paints the sun makes the sunlight more beautiful when it touches her; reverses the usual idea that the sun gilds what it touches

143 **base briars** This allegory, reminiscent of the *Roman de la Rose*, ends either with the lover receiving a harsh rejection or with his abandonment to prostitutes, who are not only 'base' but leave a sting (disease) behind them. 'To leave one in the briars' is proverbial (Dent, B673).

145 **falls** with the usual double meaning: falls from the stem / lets herself be seduced. This line may be completed metrically as the two women laugh at the joke, or the pause may point up the relevance of the image of the rose, used later (5.1) to signify Emilia herself.

147 **wanton** Emilia's unintentional echoing of Palamon (96) indicates the mood of this scene, halfway between two meanings of *wanton*: provocative and merely playful.

148 **extant** in existence

EMILIA

The sun grows high; let's walk in. Keep these
    flowers.
We'll see how near art can come near their colours.   150
I am wondrous merry-hearted; I could laugh now.

WOMAN

I could lie down, I am sure.

EMILIA   And take one with you?

WOMAN

That's as we bargain, madam.

EMILIA   Well, agree then.
                                        Exeunt Emilia and Woman.

PALAMON

What think you of this beauty?

ARCITE   'Tis a rare one.

PALAMON

Is't but a rare one?

ARCITE   Yes, a matchless beauty.   155

PALAMON

Might not a man well lose himself and love her?

ARCITE

I cannot tell what you have done; I have,
Beshrew mine eyes for't; now I feel my shackles.

---

149 **The sun grows high** Women were
reluctant to walk in the sun for fear of
sunburning their pale complexions
(Emilia is no longer the hardy
Amazon of Act 1).

150 The repetition of *near* (see t.n.) may
be a compositor's error, but it is also
the sort of thing that an author might
do. *Oxf* alters the first *near* to 'close';
I agree with Bowers that a less
tautological word might be more
appropriate, but that the evidence
does not justify supplying it.

   art the embroidery mentioned in 127

152 **lie down** alluding to the proverb
'Laugh and lie down' (Dent, L92).
The woman gives a mildly *risqué* dir-
ection to Emilia's phrase, which

Emilia then picks up.

153 The interpretation of this line depends on whether the Woman's *we*
means herself and Emilia or herself
and the person with whom she wants
to lie down. On the first reading,
Emilia's reply acquiesces in a sexual
game; on the second, she coldly dis-
tances herself from her woman's affairs. Should *well* be a misreading of
MS *wele* (or we'll), as RP suggests, the
former interpretation would be more
plausible.

154 **beauty** From the abstract use of this
word at 148, Palamon moves to its
other meaning: a beautiful woman.

158 **Beshrew** curse (in a mild sense)

---

150 ¹near] *Q;* close *Oxf (Taylor)*

PALAMON

You love her then?

ARCITE   Who would not?

PALAMON   And desire her?

ARCITE

Before my liberty.

PALAMON   I saw her first.   160

ARCITE

That's nothing.

PALAMON   But it shall be.

ARCITE

I saw her too.

PALAMON   Yes, but you must not love her.

ARCITE

I will not as you do, to worship her
As she is heavenly and a blessed goddess.
I love her as a woman, to enjoy her: 165
So both may love.

PALAMON

You shall not love at all.

ARCITE   Not love at all!

Who shall deny me?

PALAMON

I that first saw her, I that took possession
First with mine eye of all those beauties in her   170
Revealed to mankind! If thou lovest her,

159–62 Since any relineation of this passage will leave some part-lines on
their own, all emendations (see t.n.)
involve interpretation. (See pp. 120–1
above).

163–5 **I will . . . enjoy her** The text here
is very close to Chaucer: 'For par-
amour I loued her first or [before]
thou, / What wilt thou sain, thou wist
it not or now / Whether she be
woman or goddesse: / Thine is affection of holinesse, / And mine is loue,
as to a creature' (1155–9). Cf. '*Val[en-
tine]*. . . . and is she not a heavenly
saint? *Pro[teus]*. No, but she is an

earthly paragon' (*TGV* 2.4.138–9)
and Longaville's claim that, though
he has sworn not to love a woman, he
is not forsworn since his mistress is a
goddess (*LLL* 4.3.62–3).

171–6 **If . . . her** 'Palamon's anger is reflected in his use of *thou* in place of
the more polite and formal *you*'
(Proudfoot). See pp. 22–3 above for
the use of pronouns as a characterization device. Since Palamon speaks to
very few characters except Arcite in
the course of the play, the distinction
is significant largely for the relationship between them.

159–62] *Leech; Proudfoot lines* desire her? / liberty; / shall be. /

Or entertain'st a hope to blast my wishes,
Thou art a traitor, Arcite, and a fellow
False as thy title to her. Friendship, blood,
And all the ties between us, I disclaim,   175
If thou once think upon her.

ARCITE   Yes, I love her
And, if the lives of all my name lay on it,
I must do so; I love her with my soul:
If that will lose ye, farewell, Palamon.
I say again,   180
I love her and in loving her maintain
I am as worthy and as free a lover,
And have as just a title to her beauty,
As any Palamon, or any living
That is a man's son.

PALAMON   Have I called thee friend?   185

ARCITE

Yes, and have found me so; why are you moved thus?
Let me deal coldly with you: am not I
Part of your blood, part of your soul? you have told
     me
That I was Palamon and you were Arcite.

PALAMON

Yes.

ARCITE Am not I liable to those affections,   190

173 **a traitor** As Seward points out, this
extreme accusation makes more sense
in *KT*, where Palamon reminds
Arcite of the oath each has sworn
'Neither of us in loue to hindre other'
(1135).
fellow companion, ally (sometimes
used in a pejorative sense, but at this
point Palamon is talking of what he
sees as the betrayal of a close
relationship)
174 **False** This word recurs many times
in connection with Arcite, culminat-
ing in 5.4.92. See p. 42 above.
180–1 *In Q this is one line (see t.n.).
Bawcutt's alteration seems justified,

since Arcite said 'I love her' in 176
and 178.
182 **free** noble. A key word in Chaucer,
particularly *The Franklin's Tale*,
which depicts a contest of nobility
among three men and ends with the
question, 'Which was the most free, as
thinketh you?' (1623). This tale was
dramatized by Nathan Field in one of
the *Four Plays in One* on which he collaborated with Fletcher (*c*.1613).
187 **coldly** calmly
187–94 **am . . . alone?** For other examples of this sophistical argument,
see p. 56 above.
190 **affections** emotions

180–1] *Bawcutt; one line Q*   181 love her] *(Walker); love Q*   188 ¹your] *Seward; you Q*

Those joys, griefs, angers, fears, my friend shall
    suffer?

PALAMON
Ye may be.

ARCITE   Why then would you deal so cunningly,
So strangely, so unlike a noble kinsman,
To love alone? Speak truly: do you think me
Unworthy of her sight?

PALAMON   No, but unjust   195
If thou pursue that sight.

ARCITE   Because another
First sees the enemy, shall I stand still
And let mine honour down, and never charge?

PALAMON
Yes, if he be but one.

ARCITE   But say that one
Had rather combat me?

PALAMON   Let that one say so,   200
And use thy freedom. Else, if thou pursuest her,
Be as that cursed man that hates his country,
A branded villain.

ARCITE   You are mad.

PALAMON   I must be,
Till thou art worthy, Arcite; it concerns me.

---

192 **cunningly** craftily
193 **strangely** like a stranger
195 **of her sight** of looking at her. Arcite argues that anyone who sees Emilia must love her; therefore if Palamon forbids him to love he must commit the further absurdity of forbidding his friend even to look at the same woman.
    unjust false to the code of honour
198 **let . . . down** lose my honour
199 **if . . . one** In stage battles one fighter often singles out another and warns others to keep away (see *3H6* 2.4 and *Cor* 1.8.1–2).

201 **use thy freedom** do what you will. Since Palamon assumes that neither of them will ever be in a position to ask Emilia whom she prefers, he must mean that Arcite is obliged to give way to his prior claim so long as they are both in prison.
202–3 **that . . . villain** probably no specific man. But Fletcher may be thinking of Polynices, the son of Oedipus, who attacked his native Thebes (see pp. 40–1 above).
203 **branded** perhaps with the mark of Cain, equally appropriate to the exiled Polynices

203 bc,] *1711;* bc. *Q*

And, in this madness, if I hazard thee 205
And take thy life, I deal but truly.

ARCITE   Fie, sir!
You play the child extremely. I will love her;
I must, I ought, to do so, and I dare,
And all this justly.

PALAMON   Oh that now, that now,
Thy false self and thy friend had but this fortune: 210
To be one hour at liberty and grasp
Our good swords in our hands! I would quickly teach
    thee
What 'twere to filch affection from another;˅
Thou art baser in it than a cutpurse.
Put but thy head out of this window more 215
And, as I have a soul, I'll nail thy life to't.

ARCITE
Thou dar'st not, fool, thou canst not, thou art feeble.
Put my head out? I'll throw my body out
And leap the garden, when I see her next,
And pitch between her arms, to anger thee. 220

Enter Jailer.

PALAMON
No more; the keeper's coming. I shall live

205–6 **And . . . truly** That is, if Palamon is mad, he is also just in his madness, since Arcite deserves death.
207 **play the child** behave childishly
208 **I must, I ought** because he is obliged to be loyal to a declaration of love, once made (see 3.6.41–2)
209 **justly** He replies to Palamon's accusation at 195–6.
214 **cutpurse** thief. A pickpocket took money out of pockets; a cutpurse cut purses off strings or belts.
216 **to't** the window frame
219 **leap** leap into
220 **pitch** aim myself, like a ball

220 SD *Q has *Keeper* throughout the scene, in dialogue, SPs and SDs. Some editors retain it, on the assumption that he is a different character from the *Jailer* of 2.1. However, it seems more likely that the discrepancy is another result of dual authorship (see p. 26 above).
221 **the keeper's coming** If the two prisoners are on an upper level, they might see him approaching below. Alternatively, they might hear him coming. The stage direction for his entrance seems too early if he is to appear at the gallery level.

220 SD] *after 219 Q*   220+ SD Jailer] *1778; Keeper Q*

To knock thy brains out with my shackles.

ARCITE   Do!

JAILER

    By your leave, gentlemen.

PALAMON   Now, honest keeper?

JAILER

    Lord Arcite, you must presently to th' Duke;
    The cause I know not yet.

ARCITE   I am ready, keeper.   225

JAILER

    Prince Palamon, I must awhile bereave you
    Of your fair cousin's company.   *Exeunt Arcite and Jailer.*

PALAMON   And me too,

    Even when you please, of life. – Why is he sent for?
    It may be he shall marry her; he's goodly
    And like enough the Duke hath taken notice   230
    Both of his blood and body. But his falsehood –
    Why should a friend be treacherous? If that
    Get him a wife so noble and so fair,
    Let honest men ne'er love again. Once more
    I would but see this fair one. Blessed garden   235
    And fruit and flowers more blessed that still blossom
    As her bright eyes shine on ye: would I were
    For all the fortune of my life hereafter
    Yon little tree, yon blooming apricock!
    How I would spread and fling my wanton arms   240
    In at her window! I would bring her fruit
    Fit for the gods to feed on; youth and pleasure
    Still as she tasted should be doubled on her

---

222 **Do!** I dare you!
224 **presently** at once
226 **bereave** unintentionally ironic in the circumstances
229 **It . . . marry her** clearly indicates comic paranoia
    goodly handsome
238 as the only luck I would wish for the rest of my life

239 **apricock** The old spelling of the word lent itself to sexual innuendo, and the fruit was thought to produce fruitfulness or to have aphrodisiac qualities. Palamon's language indicates a more sensual attitude towards Emilia than he expressed to Arcite (cf. 244, below).
243 **Still as** whenever

223+ SP JAILER] *1778; Keeper Q*

And, if she be not heavenly, I would make her
So near the gods in nature, they should fear her,   245

Enter Jailer.

And then I am sure she would love me. – How now,
    keeper?
Where's Arcite?
JAILER   Banished. Prince Pirithous
Obtained his liberty, but never more
Upon his oath and life must he set foot
Upon this kingdom.
PALAMON   He's a blessed man.   250
He shall see Thebes again and call to arms
The bold young men that, when he bids 'em charge,
Fall on like fire. Arcite shall have a fortune,
If he dare make himself a worthy lover,
Yet in the field to strike a battle for her   255
And, if he lose her then, he's a cold coward;
How bravely may he bear himself to win her
If he be noble Arcite – thousand ways!
Were I at liberty, I would do things
Of such a virtuous greatness that this lady,   260
This blushing virgin, should take manhood to her
And seek to ravish me.
JAILER   My Lord, for you

---

244 **And . . . heavenly** He is still thinking of his claim that Emilia is a
goddess.
247 **Pirithous** Why Pirithous acts on
Arcite's behalf is never explained.
Chaucer says that they had been
friends for many years in Thebes. In
Davenant's adaptation, the character
corresponding to Pirithous owes his
life to him.
249 **Upon . . . life** Arcite has taken an
oath on pain of death.
253 **a fortune** a chance
255 **strike a battle** make war. In *KT*,

when Palamon escapes from prison,
his intention is to do precisely this.
Here, he assumes that Arcite will
prove his worth as a lover not only by
breaking his oath but by leading an
army against the man who has just released him.
261 **take . . . her** behave like a man. This
joke about women ravishing men
recurs in *The Wild Goose Chase*
(Bowers, 6: 2.1.51–2) and *The Pilgrim*
(Bowers, 6: 4.2.32), both of which
were acted *c.*1621.

I have this charge to –
PALAMON   To discharge my life.
JAILER
No, but from this place to remove your lordship;
The windows are too open.
PALAMON   Devils take 'em   265
That are so envious to me! Prithee, kill me.
JAILER
And hang for't afterward!
PALAMON   By this good light,
Had I a sword I would kill thee.
JAILER   Why, my lord?
PALAMON
Thou bringst such pelting, scurvy news continually,
Thou art not worthy life. I will not go.   270
JAILER
Indeed you must, my lord.
PALAMON   May I see the garden?
JAILER
No.
PALAMON
Then I am resolved; I will not go.
JAILER
I must constrain you then and, for you are dangerous,
I'll clap more irons on you.
PALAMON   Do, good keeper!
I'll shake 'em so, ye shall not sleep;   275
I'll make ye a new morris. – Must I go?

263 **charge** order
     discharge my life execute me
265 **too open** giving too much of a view,
     or too much space for a possible
     escape
266–7 Cf. Posthumus' conversation with
     the Jailer: '*Post[humus]*. I am call'd to
     be made free. *Gaol[er]*. I'll be hang'd
     then' (*Cym* 5.4.193–5).

267 **By . . . light** a common oath. Cf. the
     pun on 'heavenly light' in *Oth* 4.3.63–4.
269 **pelting** worthless
271 **May . . . the garden** i.e., from my
     new cell
273 **for** because
276 **a new morris** a new kind of morris;
     the dance was traditionally performed
     by dancers with bells on their clothes

263 to –] *Oxf*; too. *Q*

JAILER

There is no remedy.

PALAMON   Farewell, kind window.

May rude winds never hurt thee! – Oh, my lady,

If ever thou hast felt what sorrow was,

Dream how I suffer! – Come, now bury me.   280

Exeunt Palamon and Jailer.

[2.3]   *Enter* ARCITE.

ARCITE

Banished the kingdom? 'Tis a benefit,

A mercy I must thank 'em for; but banished

The free enjoying of that face I die for –

Oh, 'twas a studied punishment, a death

Beyond imagination, such a vengeance   5

That, were I old and wicked, all my sins

Could never pluck upon me. Palamon,

Thou hast the start now; thou shalt stay and see

Her bright eyes break each morning 'gainst thy

    window

And let in life into thee; thou shalt feed   10

Upon the sweetness of a noble beauty

That nature ne'er exceeded nor ne'er shall.

Good gods, what happiness has Palamon!

---

280 **bury me** Skeat interprets this to mean that not seeing Emilia again is like death and burial. The line may be more literal if the Jailer leads him downstairs (from an upper level) or through a trap door (from the main stage level), as if into a lower part of the prison.

2.3.0.1 Though Arcite is not yet in the 'poor disguise' which he plans to adopt, he cannot be dressed like a prince, since the countrymen treat him as an equal. He probably wears a plain cloak to cover either his costume from the previous scene or the one for

2.5.

1 **Banished the kingdom?** Webster twice uses a similar entrance line: 'Banished!' (*WD*, 1.1.1) and 'Banished Ancona!' (*DM*, 3.5.1). Arcite, however, is being banished to his own country from an enemy land.

4 **studied** carefully devised

9 **break** (like the day)

13–17 This parallels Palamon's lines at 2.2.250–8; the fact that each man has a soliloquy in which he envies the other man's happiness creates irony at the expense of both. Cf. *KT*, 1234ff. and 1281ff.

2.3] Scæna 3. *Q*

199

Twenty to one, he'll come to speak to her
And, if she be as gentle as she's fair,   15
I know she's his; he has a tongue will tame
Tempests and make the wild rocks wanton.
Come what can come,
The worst is death; I will not leave the kingdom.
I know mine own is but a heap of ruins   20
And no redress there. If I go, he has her.
I am resolved another shape shall make me
Or end my fortunes. Either way I am happy:
I'll see her and be near her, or no more.

Enter four Countrymen, *and one with a garland before them.*
[Arcite stands aside.]

1 COUNTRYMAN
  My masters, I'll be there, that's certain.   25
2 COUNTRYMAN
  And I'll be there.
3 COUNTRYMAN
  And I.

18 **Come . . . come** proverbial (Dent, C529). In Q the last two words are crowded into the line above. The hypermetrical phrase may have been intended as a substitution for 'The worst is death', which, the author perhaps realized, anticipates the end of the speech.
20–1 **a heap . . . there** This is true in Boccaccio, but not in *KT*. See p. 45 above.
22 **shape** disguise, role
  make me bring me success
23 **Or . . . fortunes** perhaps echoes the ambiguous words of Mercury, who, in *KT*, tells Arcite in a dream, 'To Athens shalt thou wend / There is the[e] shapen of thy woe an end' (1391–2)
24 **no more** i.e., dead ('be' is understood)

SD The '*one with a garland*' presumably displays the prize offered for the forthcoming games. Perhaps he is the winner of an earlier competition; cf. 2.5.0.3.
25–62 These lines obviously confused the compositor, who prints them as verse until 39, after which there is no further attempt to make them scan, though they are given initial capitals and unjustified margins, and they are finally printed as prose from 43 to 61. Bowers suggests that the scene may have been written originally in verse and revised as prose. Some editions, most recently Oxf[1], print all the Countrymen's lines as prose. I have indicated a loose blank-verse rhythm where I could perceive it (see pp. 118–23 above).

17–18] *this edn; one line* Q   24.1 Countrymen] *Dyce; Country people* Q   garland] *garlond* Qc; *Garlon* Qu   24.2] *this edn; not in* Q

4 COUNTRYMAN

   Why then, have with ye, boys. 'Tis but a chiding.
   Let the plough play today; I'll tickl't out
   Of the jades' tails tomorrow.

1 COUNTRYMAN   I am sure   30

   To have my wife as jealous as a turkey –
   But that's all one: I'll go through; let her mumble.

2 COUNTRYMAN

   Clap her aboard tomorrow night and stow her,
   And all's made up again.

3 COUNTRYMAN   Ay, do but put

   A fescue in her fist and you shall see her   35
   Take a new lesson out and be a good wench.
   Do we all hold against the Maying?

4 COUNTRYMAN   Hold?

   What should ail us?

3 COUNTRYMAN

   Arcas will be there.

2 COUNTRYMAN   And Sennois

   And Rycas – and three better lads ne'er danced   40

---

28 **have with ye** I'll join you. The first
three countrymen have persuaded the
fourth (a ploughman) to join them in
abandoning work for the day.
a chiding a scolding, from either his
master or his wife

29 **play** remain idle

29–30 **tickl't ... tomorrow** flog the
plough-horses harder to make up for
lost time. Given the numerous sexual
puns that follow, these lines probably
have a double meaning: *jade* is often a
disparaging term for 'woman'.

31 **turkey** turkeycock, proverbially associated with redness and swelling;
see Dent, T612. Waith (Oxf¹) notes
that an emblem book of 1579 depicts
it, with tail spread, defending its
territory.

32 **go through** keep my promise
mumble grumble under her breath

33 **Clap her aboard** in nautical termin-
ology, 'board her like a ship' (*OED v.*

IV 10e)
stow her fill her up, like the hold of a
ship (figuratively, have intercourse
with her and, possibly, get her
pregnant)

34 **made up** both 'reconciled' and 'filled
a gap' (*OED v.* 96d), the latter in a
sexual sense. In other words, 'Give
her a good night's sex, and she'll forgive you.'

35 **fescue** 'A small stick, pin, etc. used
for pointing out the letters to children
learning to read; a pointer' (*OED*,
which gives this as an example).
Here, with the double meaning of
penis.

36 **Take ... out** study a new lesson

37 **hold ... Maying** stick to our intention about taking part in the maying

38 **What should ail us?** What could
stop us?

39–40 **Arcas ... Sennois ... Rycas** See
'Countrymen', List of Roles.

34–5 Ay ... see her] *one line Q*   37–8 Hold? ... us] *one line Q*   39–61] *prose Q*

Under green tree – and ye know what wenches, ha?
But will the dainty dominie, the schoolmaster,
Keep touch, do you think? For he does all, ye know.

3 COUNTRYMAN

He'll eat a hornbook ere he fail. Go to;
The matter's too far driven between him   45
And the tanner's daughter to let slip now;
And she must see the Duke and she must dance too.

4 COUNTRYMAN

Shall we be lusty?

2 COUNTRYMAN   All the boys in Athens
Blow wind i'th' breech on's. And here I'll be,
And there I'll be for our town and here again,   50
And there again – ha, boys, hey for the weavers!

---

42 **dainty** fine; sarcastic, like the other
references to the Schoolmaster
dominie from the vocative form of
dominus – master (Latin); hence, a colloquial term for schoolmaster

43 **Keep touch** keep his promise to be
there
he does all he is the organizer (with
the implication of busybody)

44 **hornbook** flat piece of horn with the
alphabet and other basic information
inscribed on it, for the use of beginning pupils. Possibly with the double
meaning of cuckolding or being
cuckolded.
Go to scoffing expression (here, directed at the idea that the Schoolmaster could resist organizing the
maying)

45 **The matter's ... driven** he is already too committed (sexually); what
he has driven home is obvious

47 **she must see** she insists on seeing

48 **lusty** lively, jolly (a rhetorical
question)

49 **Blow ... on's** will have to run to keep
up with us. (Proudfoot cites *KBP*,
1.62: 'If any of them all blow winde in
the taile on him, Il'e be hang'd'.) 'To

have a breeze in his breech' is proverbial (Dent, B651); here, it is probably used for the sake of a pun on
breaking wind.
breech buttocks

50–1 **And there ... again** Leech suggests that at this point the Second
Countryman gives a demonstration of
the dancing he expects to do in the
May celebrations.

50 **for our town** for the honour of our
town. In drama, morris dancers see
their dance as an expression of local
pride, like 'the *Holloway* Morrice' in
Jack Drum's Entertainment, 1.1. In
KBP Ralph, as May Lord, refers to
these customs: 'With bels on legs, and
napkins cleane unto your shoulders
tide, / With scarfes and Garters as
you please, and Hey for our Town
cri'd: / March out and show your
willing minds by twenty and by
twenty' (4. [Interlude] 51–3).

51 **hey ... weavers** The Second Countryman is a weaver (like the equally
enthusiastic Bottom, Leech points
out) and expects to cheer for his
craft as well as his town. See Fig. 20,
p. 357.

---

41 ye] *Seward;* yet *Q*

1 COUNTRYMAN

This must be done i'th' woods.

4 COUNTRYMAN   ‚   Oh, pardon me.

2 COUNTRYMAN

By any means; our thing of learning says so –
Where he himself will edify the Duke
Most parlously in our behalfs. He's excellent i'th'
    woods;   55
Bring him to th' plains, his learning makes no cry.

3 COUNTRYMAN

We'll see the sports, then every man to's tackle;
And, sweet companions, let's rehearse, by any means,
Before the ladies see us and do sweetly
And God knows what may come on't.   60

4 COUNTRYMAN

Content; the sports once ended, we'll perform.
Away, boys – and hold.   [*Arcite comes forward.*]

ARCITE   By your leaves, honest friends:

52 **This** probably the proposed maying,
including the dance in which the
Second Countryman is trying to get
them to join
Oh, pardon me a mild expression of
doubt, to which the Second Countryman replies by agreeing with the
First: the morris is to interrupt the
hunting in the woods, rather than
forming part of the games at court
53 **our   thing   of   learning** the
Schoolmaster
54 **edify** instruct. He is probably making
fun of the Schoolmaster's vocabulary;
cf. 3.5.94 and 97.
55 **parlously** a contraction of 'peril-
ously', originally meaning 'danger-
ously' but here, as often, 'amazingly',
with a sarcastic inflection (see *OED*)
56 **makes no cry** is unheard, unregarded,
like the cry of hounds, whose sound also
was more musical in the woods. The
countrymen are well aware that their
show could never be performed at court.
57 **every ... tackle** get his equipment
ready for the dance; a conflation of 'every
man as his business lies' (Dent, M104)

and 'stand to one's tackling' (Dent,
T7). There is probably more sexual
innuendo here: the countrymen obviously expect the pairing in the dance
to be followed by pairing in the woods.
59 **do** perform (but see also 43n.)
60 **God ... on't** He may hope for favour
from Theseus but he is probably most
interested in his effect on the women
dancers.
62 **hold** keep your promise to turn up.
The amateur actors' first scene in
MND ends, 'hold, or cut bow-strings'
(1.2.111).
By ... friends a polite apology for in-
trusion, using a common form of address to unknown social inferiors. The
situation here recalls *Per* (2.1), where a
princely hero restores his lost fortunes,
with the help of humble people,
through success in a tournament. RP
points out that in Gower's *Confessio
Amantis*, the source of *Pericles*, it is
success in the 'comun game' (country
sports), not a tournament, that brings
the hero to the attention of the king
and his daughter (Gower, 2.8.678).

53 says] *Seward;* (sees)*; sed Oxf*   61–5] *prose Q*   62 SD] *Leech; not in Q*

Pray you, whither go you?

4 COUNTRYMAN   Whither?

Why, what a question's that?

ARCITE   Yes, 'tis a question,

To me that know not.

3 COUNTRYMAN   To the games, my friend.   65

2 COUNTRYMAN

Where were you bred, you know it not?

ARCITE   Not far, sir;

Are there such games today?

1 COUNTRYMAN   Yes, marry, are there

And such as you never saw; the Duke himself

Will be in person there.

ARCITE   What pastimes are they?

2 COUNTRYMAN

Wrestling and running. – 'Tis a pretty fellow.   70

3 COUNTRYMAN

Thou wilt not go along?

ARCITE   Not yet, sir.

4 COUNTRYMAN   Well, sir,

Take your own time. Come, boys.

1 COUNTRYMAN [*aside to the others*]   My mind misgives me,

This fellow has a vengeance trick o'th' hip;

Mark how his body's made for't.

2 COUNTRYMAN   I'll be hanged, though,

If he dare venture. Hang him, plum porridge!   75

64–5 **Why ... not** Using a common catchphrase (see Dent, Q11.1), Arcite replies literally (but politely) to the scoffing rhetorical question.

65 **games** italicized in Q here and at 66, like a proper name, perhaps because Fletcher thought of them as Olympic games. See Appendix 5, p. 356.

67 **marry** See 2.1.7n.

71 **along** (with us)

72 **My mind ... me** I have an uneasy feeling

73 **vengeance** terrific; a colloquial adjective, like *parlous* (see 55, above).
trick o'th' hip This seems to have been regarded as the key to success in

wrestling; hence, 'to have one on the hip' (Dent, H474) means to have an advantage over someone. 'The reference is not to the hip of the vanquished wrestler, as some think, but to that of the victor. If the wrestler can succeed in hitching his hip in a certain way under his adversary's body, he may often succeed in throwing with almost irresistible violence' (Skeat).

75 **plum porridge** the sort of person who would eat this thick sweet broth 'made of beef, dried fruits, white bread, spices, wine and sugar; eaten at Christmas' (Proudfoot). 'Milksop' derives from the same idea.

He wrestle? He roast eggs! Come, let's be gone, lads.

                                      Exeunt Countrymen.

ARCITE

    This is an offered opportunity
    I durst not wish for. Well I could have wrestled –
    The best men called it excellent – and run
    Swifter than wind upon a field of corn,   80
    Curling the wealthy ears, never flew. I'll venture
    And in some poor disguise be there; who knows
    Whether my brows may not be girt with garlands
    And happiness prefer me to a place,
    Where I may ever dwell in sight of her?   *Exit.*

[2.4]   *Enter Jailer's* Daughter *alone.*

DAUGHTER

    Why should I love this gentleman? 'Tis odds
    He never will affect me: I am base,
    My father the mean keeper of his prison,
    And he a prince. To marry him is hopeless;

---

76 **He ... roast eggs** He'd do the latter better than the former. Skeat notes that turning eggs on a spit before the fire required more patience than intelligence. Herford quotes the proverb, 'Set a fool to roast eggs, and a wise man to eat them.'

78 **Well ... wrestled** 'I once knew how to wrestle well.' The construction also modifies *run* (79).

80–1 **Swifter ... flew** Hickman (144) compares Fletcher's *Bonduca* (*c*.1611–14), where cowards are said to run from battle faster than 'the light shadows, / That in a thought scur ore the fields of Corn' (Bowers, 4: 1.1.93–4). Both passages imitate Virgil's famous description of Camilla: '*Illa vel intactae segetis per summa volaret / gramina nec teneras cursu laesisset*

aristas' [She might have flown o'er the topmost blades of unmown corn, nor in her course bruised the tender ears] (Virgil, 7.808–9), which is often cited (as in Pope's *Essay on Criticism*, 372–3) as an example of verse that mimics the speed it describes.

81 **never** often emended to 'ever' or 'e'er', but the sense is clear and double negatives are not uncommon in this period

83 **girt** circled

84 **happiness prefer me** luck, or success, act in place of a patron to me
    a place an office at court (normally achieved through 'preferment')

2.4.1 **'Tis odds** the odds are enormous that

2 **affect** like or love

---

76 SD] *Exeunt 4 Q* 78 Well] *Seward; Well, Q* 80 Swifter than] *1711;* Swifter, then *Q;* Swifter the *Seward* 2.4] Scæna 4. *Q*

To be his whore is witless. Out upon't,   5
What pushes are we wenches driven to
When fifteen once has found us! – First, I saw him;
I, seeing, thought he was a goodly man;
He has as much to please a woman in him,
If he please to bestow it so, as ever   10
These eyes yet looked on. Next, I pitied him –
And so would any young wench, o' my conscience,
That ever dreamed, or vowed her maidenhead
To a young handsome man. Then, I loved him,
Extremely loved him, infinitely loved him!   15
And yet he had a cousin fair as he too,
But in my heart was Palamon and there,
Lord, what a coil he keeps! To hear him
Sing in an evening, what a heaven it is!
And yet his songs are sad ones. Fairer spoken   20
Was never gentleman. When I come in
To bring him water in a morning, first
He bows his noble body, then salutes me, thus:
'Fair, gentle maid, good morrow; may thy goodness
Get thee a happy husband.' Once, he kissed me.   25
I loved my lips the better ten days after:
Would he would do so every day! He grieves much –
And me as much to see his misery.
What should I do to make him know I love him?
For I would fain enjoy him. Say I ventured   30

5 **To ... whore** to have sex with him
without being married to him
Out upon't a generalized exclamation of disgust, perhaps at the idea
just expressed, perhaps at the situation of women in general
6 **pushes** extremities, expedients
7 **When fifteen ... us** when we are
past the age of puberty. The Wooer
later says (5.2.31) that she is 18. Cf.
'these women, when they are once
thirteene, god speede the plough'
(*The Coxcomb*, Bowers, 1: 1.3.5–6).
First ... him Like Palamon (see
2.2.160, above), she stresses the im-

portance of sight.
13 **maidenhead** virginity
18 **what ... keeps** what noise (or
trouble) he causes (Dent, C505)
20 **his songs** These are mentioned again
at 4.3.81–2; Laertes, similarly, warns
Ophelia against Hamlet's songs
(1.3.30).
23 **salutes** greets
28 **me as much** object of *grieves*
30 **would fain** want to
enjoy love him sexually. The Daughter no longer sees this as *witless* (see 4–
5, above).

To set him free? What says the law then?
Thus much for law or kindred! I will do it!
And this night, or tomorrow, he shall love me.   *Exit.*

[2.5]   *A short flourish of cornets and shouts within. Enter*
THESEUS, HIPPOLYTA, PIRITHOUS, EMILIA; ARCITE *[disguised as
a countryman] with a garland; [attendants and spectators].*

THESEUS
     You have done worthily; I have not seen,
     Since Hercules, a man of tougher sinews.
     Whate'er you are, you run the best and wrestle,
     That these times can allow.

ARCITE   I am proud to please you.

THESEUS
     What country bred you?

ARCITE   This; but far off, Prince.   5

THESEUS
     Are you a gentleman?

ARCITE   My father said so
     And to those gentle uses gave me life.

THESEUS
     Are you his heir?

ARCITE   His youngest, sir.

THESEUS   Your father

---

32 **Thus much** A contemptuous gesture, perhaps snapping her fingers,
supplies the missing beat at the end of
31.
  kindred her father, who will be punished for her action
32–3 **I . . . me** The Q punctuation is
ambiguous: does *this night* refer to setting Palamon free or to his loving her?
Montgomery (see t.n.) emends *or* to
'e're', which he takes to be a variant
spelling, on the grounds that the
Daughter is now too committed to her
own fantasy to think of qualifications

or alternatives to it. The choice here
both depends on and determines
one's reading of her character.
2.5.0.2–3 Arcite may be wearing or carrying the garland; see pp. 103–5 above.
2 **Hercules** Cf. 1.1.66–9 and n.
4 **allow** provide; perhaps Theseus implies that men have degenerated since
the heroic days of Hercules
7 **gave me life** dedicated my life
8 **His youngest** The folktale hero is
always the youngest son – like Orlando, the successful wrestler in *AYL*
1.2.

32] *Dyce;* much / For *Q*   33 or tomorrow,] *Bawcutt;* or tomorrow: *1778;* or (=ere) to-morrow
Oxf   2.5] Scæna 4. *Q*   0.1] This short flo-/ rish of Cor-/ nets and / Showtes with-/ in. *in margin
opp. 0.2–3 Q   A] Oxf;* This *Q*   0.3 *attendants and spectators*] *Proudfoot subst.; &c. Q*

Sure is a happy sire then. What profess you?
ARCITE
A little of all noble qualities.   10
I could have kept a hawk and well have hallowed
To a deep cry of dogs. I dare not praise
My feat in horsemanship, yet they that knew me
Would say it was my best piece; last and greatest,
I would be thought a soldier.
THESEUS   You are perfect.   15
PIRITHOUS [*to Emilia*]
Upon my soul, a proper man.
EMILIA   He is so.
PIRITHOUS [*to Hippolyta*]
How do you like him, lady?
HIPPOLYTA   I admire him.
I have not seen so young a man so noble,
If he say true, of his sort.
EMILIA   Believe,
His mother was a wondrous handsome woman;   20
His face, methinks, goes that way.
HIPPOLYTA   But his body
And fiery mind illustrate a brave father.
PIRITHOUS
Mark how his virtue, like a hidden sun,

9 **a happy sire** because even his youngest son is such a paragon. (The eldest
might be assumed to have more of the
father in him; see *AYL* 1.1.49–51.)
   ***What profess you?** 'What skills
have you?' Q's *prooves* has been accepted by many editors on the assumption that it means, 'What proves
you to be a gentleman?' Ingram's suggestion scans better; cf. Lear's 'What
dost thou profess?' when Kent asks to
be taken into service (*KL* 1.4.11).
10 **noble qualities** qualifications, accomplishments, associated with the
nobility
11 **could have kept** probably 'once knew
how to keep' (cf. 2.3.78, above) rather

than conditional. Arcite means that his
aristocratic accomplishments are above
his present means and poor garments.
   hallowed see 2.2.48n.
13 **feat** achievement
14 **it** horsemanship
   piece accomplishment
15 **perfect** complete
16 **proper** handsome
19 **sort** social class
   Believe believe me (common in
Fletcher; cf. 4.1.47, below)
21 **goes that way** resembles her (cf. the
description at 4.2.105–11)
22 **illustrate** show, give lustre to;
stressed on the second syllable. The
image is developed in the next line.

9 profess] *Littledale (Ingram)*; prooves *Q*

Breaks through his baser garments.

HIPPOLYTA   He's well got, sure.

THESEUS [*to Arcite*]

What made you seek this place, sir?

ARCITE   Noble Theseus,   25

To purchase name and do my ablest service

To such a well-found wonder as thy worth,

For only in thy court, of all the world,

Dwells fair-eyed Honour.

PIRITHOUS   All his words are worthy.

THESEUS [*to Arcite*]

Sir, we are much indebted to your travel,   30

Nor shall you lose your wish. Pirithous,

Dispose of this fair gentleman.

PIRITHOUS   Thanks, Theseus.

[*to Arcite*] Whate'er you are, you're mine, and I shall
     give you

To a most noble service: to this lady, [*Leads him to Emilia.*]

This bright young virgin; pray observe her goodness.   35

You have honoured her fair birthday with your
     virtues

And, as your due, you're hers; kiss her fair hand, sir.

ARCITE

Sir, you're a noble giver. – Dearest beauty,

---

24 **well got** of a noble father, as opposed
to well born (of a noble mother); they
may think that he is the illegitimate
son of some nobleman. Though the
notion of noble birth revealing itself
despite humble dress is generally
taken seriously in the drama (*Cym* and
WT are obvious examples), it is possible that this discussion is *meant* to
seem drawn-out and patronizing.

26 **To purchase name** to win fame (by
desert, not chance). The phrasing,
suggesting that his name at present is
not worth knowing, avoids the need to
give an assumed one. In *KT* Arcite

called himself Philostrate (the recurrence of the name in *MND* is one of
that play's many links with Chaucer);
in *Per* the hero also fights anonymously at a tournament, but the crowd
gives him a name ('the mean knight')
based on his appearance (*Per* 2.2.59
SD).

27 **well-found** established

30 **travel** refers to Arcite's coming from
far off, with a pun on *travail* (his efforts in the sports)

31 **your wish** to be part of the court

35 **observe her goodness** wait on, pay
respect to, this good lady

34 SD] *this edn; not in Q*

Thus let me seal my vowed faith. [*Kisses her hand.*]
                    When your servant,
Your most unworthy creature, but offends you,   40
Command him die: he shall.
EMILIA   That were too cruel.
If you deserve well, sir, I shall soon see't.
You're mine and somewhat better than your rank I'll
   use you.
PIRITHOUS
I'll see you furnished and, because you say
You are a horseman, I must needs entreat you   45
This afternoon to ride, but 'tis a rough one.
ARCITE
I like him better, Prince; I shall not then
Freeze in my saddle.
THESEUS [*to Hippolyta*] Sweet, you must be ready,
And you, Emilia, and [*to Pirithous*] you, friend, and
   all,
Tomorrow by the sun, to do observance   50
To flowery May, in Dian's wood. [*to Arcite*]
                    Wait well, sir,
Upon your mistress. – Emily, I hope
He shall not go afoot.
EMILIA   That were a shame, sir,
While I have horses. [*to Arcite*]
                Take your choice and what
You want at any time, let me but know it;   55
If you serve faithfully, I dare assure you
You'll find a loving mistress.
ARCITE   If I do not,

43 **use** treat
44 **furnished** (with suitable clothes and accoutrements)
46 **one** horse
50 **by the sun** by sunrise
   do observance pay respect; Skeat compares *KT* ('And for to doen his observances to May' (1500)) and *MND* ('To do observance to a morn

of May' (1.1.167))
51 **Dian's wood** Not so-called in *KT* where, however, Theseus' love of hunting is equated with the service of Diana (1682). Given the association of maying with sexual licence, the name seems ironically chosen.
57 **If I do not** (serve faithfully)

39 SD] *Dyce; not in Q*

Let me find that my father ever hated,
Disgrace and blows.

THESEUS   Go lead the way; you have won it.
It shall be so: you shall receive all dues   60
Fit for the honour you have won; 'twere wrong else.
– Sister, beshrew my heart, you have a servant,
That, if I were a woman, would be master.
But you are wise.

EMILIA   I hope, too wise for that, sir.

Flourish. Exeunt.

[2.6]   *Enter Jailer's Daughter alone.*

DAUGHTER
Let all the dukes and all the devils roar,
He is at liberty! I have ventured for him
And out I have brought him; to a little wood
A mile hence I have sent him, where a cedar
Higher than all the rest spreads like a plane   5
Fast by a brook, and there he shall keep close
Till I provide him files and food, for yet
His iron bracelets are not off. Oh, Love,
What a stout-hearted child thou art! My father

---

59 **Disgrace and blows** The comma after *disgrace* in Q clarifies the distinction between what Arcite's fictitious father hated (disgrace) and what an unsatisfactory servant would deserve (blows).

60 **It shall be so** Probably Arcite politely refuses to 'lead the way'. Pericles, offered a place at the head of the table, also demurs (*Per* 2.3.23).

62–4 This exchange, presumably after Arcite's exit, can be played either as sophisticated banter or as a conflict between Theseus' match-making eagerness and Emilia's cool indifference.

62 **beshrew my heart** a mild oath, reinforcing the speaker's commitment

to what follows

64 ²**wise** discreet

2.6.2–4 The Daughter's second sentence, in Q, is lightly punctuated, indicating her excited state of mind, and perhaps it does not matter whether 'to a little wood' is the object of 'I have sent him' or 'I have brought him'. However, it seems from the context, and from *hence*, that the Daughter has brought Palamon out of prison in person, and then directed him to the woods rather than taking him there herself.

5 **a plane** a plane tree

6 **Fast by** close to
close in hiding

8 **Love** personified as the child Cupid

64 SD] *Exeunt omnes. Q*   2.6] Scæna 6. *Q*   3 him;] *Proudfoot subst.*; him *Q*   4 hence] *Seward*; hence, *Q*

Durst better have endured cold iron than done it.　　10
I love him beyond love and beyond reason,
Or wit, or safety; I have made him know it;
I care not, I am desperate. If the law
Find me and then condemn me for't, some wenches,
Some honest-hearted maids, will sing my dirge　　15
And tell to memory my death was noble,
Dying almost a martyr. That way he takes,
I purpose, is my way too. Sure he cannot
Be so unmanly as to leave me here;
If he do, maids will not so easily　　20
Trust men again. And yet he has not thanked me
For what I have done, no, not so much as kissed me,
And that methinks is not so well; nor scarcely
Could I persuade him to become a free man,
He made such scruples of the wrong he did　　25
To me and to my father. Yet I hope,
When he considers more, this love of mine
Will take more root within him. Let him do
What he will with me, so he use me kindly –
For use me so he shall, or I'll proclaim him,　　30
And to his face, no man. I'll presently
Provide him necessaries and pack my clothes up
And where there is a path of ground I'll venture,
So he be with me; by him, like a shadow,

---

10 **endured cold iron** been imprisoned, in fetters
12 **wit** reason, common sense
14 **Find me** detect me
15 **honest-hearted maids** Cf. 'fair-eyed maids' (2.2.37).
23–6 **nor scarcely . . . father** Davenant makes Philander, the counterpart of Palamon, express the scruples described here. Both the RSC and Ashland staged her freeing of Palamon; she brought him up through a trap-door, but he was too dazed to speak to her.

28 **take more root** Cf. Emilia (1.3.58–9) on the love between Theseus and Pirithous.
29 **use me** At 29 she may mean simply 'treat me', but at 30 the meaning is primarily sexual; *kindly* (29) may also mean 'according to nature' (Proudfoot).
31 **no man** impotent. Cf. *unmanly*, 19.
34 **So** provided that
　　he The Q spelling, *hee*, unique in this speech so dominated by *he* and *him*, probably indicates stress on the word.

12 it;] *1711 subst.;* it *Q*　33 path] *Q;* patch *Littledale (Ingleby)*　of] *Q;* on *Proudfoot*

I'll ever dwell. Within this hour the hubbub   35
Will be all o'er the prison: I am then
Kissing the man they look for. Farewell, father!
Get many more such prisoners and such daughters
And shortly you may keep yourself. Now to him.   *Exit.*

[3.1] *Cornets in sundry places. Noise and hallooing as people*
a-Maying. Enter ARCITE *alone.*

ARCITE

The Duke has lost Hippolyta; each took
A several laund. This is a solemn rite
They owe bloomed May and the Athenians pay it
To th' heart of ceremony. Oh, Queen Emilia,
Fresher than May, sweeter   5
Than her gold buttons on the boughs, or all
Th'enamelled knacks o'th' mead, or garden – yea,
We challenge too the bank of any nymph

---

39 **you ... yourself** You will have no
prisoners left to look after, but you
will be in jail yourself.

3.1 Montgomery includes a direction for
placing a bush on stage, and Taylor
suggests that there was a woodland
setting throughout (Taylor & Jowett,
42). There may be an implicit pun on
'wood'; see 3.3.22–3n.

0.1 **hallowing** 'cries of people calling to
each other from a distance or urging
dogs in the chase' (Leech). See 3.2.9.

0.2 **a-Maying** celebrating May (by being
outdoors in pairs or groups, gathering
hawthorn and greenery, and sounding
horns)

2 **laund** a cleared space in a wood,
'probably the same word with *lane*'
(Skeat). In the 1598 edn of Speght's
Chaucer, Theseus rides 'to the land'
(1691) in order to hunt; in the 1602
edn the word is corrected to 'launde'
in the errata list.

rite See t.n.; both meanings are probably intended.

3 **bloomed May** May (either the
month or the hawthorn bush) when it
is in bloom

4 **To ... ceremony** with all possible
ceremony; another example of the
concern first evidenced in 1.1
Queen Emilia perhaps thinking of
her as the Queen of the May

5 **Fresher than May** Cf. *KT*: 'Emelye,
that fairer was to sene / Than is the
lylie upon his stalke grene, / And
fressher than the May (hawthorn) with
floures newe' (1035–7).

6 **buttons** buds

7 **enamelled knacks** trifles of various
colours (Leech)
mead meadow

8 **nymph** i.e., any river made beautiful
by the presence of a nymph. Skeat
compares Spenser's *Prothalamion*,
73–82. See also 4.1.83–8.

---

35 hubbub] *(whoobub)*   3.1] *Actus Tertius.* / *Scæna I. Q*   0.1–2] *Cornets in / sundry places.* /
Noise and / hallowing as / people a May-/ ing. in margin opp. 2.6.39–3.1.0.1 Q   2 laund] *Leech*
(Dyce); land Q; stand (Heath); hand (RP)   rite] *(Right)*

That makes the stream seem flowers: thou, oh jewel
O'th' wood, o'th' world, hast likewise blest a pace   10
With thy sole presence. In thy rumination,
That I, poor man, might eftsoons come between
And chop on some cold thought! Thrice blessed
    chance
To drop on such a mistress, expectation
Most guiltless on't! Tell me, oh Lady Fortune   15
(Next, after Emily, my sovereign), how far
I may be proud. She takes strong note of me,
Hath made me near her and, this beauteous morn,
The prim'st of all the year, presents me with
A brace of horses: two such steeds might well   20
Be by a pair of kings backed, in a field

9 **That ... flowers** because the flowers
  on the bank are reflected in the water
10 **likewise** like the nymph of 8, above
  (Leech)
  pace Q's reading is often amended to
  place, but Proudfoot follows *OED* (*sb.*
  10): 'a passage, a narrow way'.
11 **thy sole presence** in two senses:
  Arcite imagines Emilia somewhere
  in the forest alone and claims that
  her mere presence would bless that
  place
12 **That** if only
  eftsoons quickly
13 **chop ... thought** a complex (or confusing) image. A number of obsolete
  meanings of *chop* denote abrupt and
  unexpected action: to break in upon
  someone or something (*OED v.*[1] 8a
  and b); to make an exchange (*v.*[2] 1–2);
  to snap up and devour one's prey (*v.*[3]).
  Skeat, following *v.*[2], suggests that
  Arcite wants to change Emilia's cold
  thought to a thought of love. Leech
  notes that *v.*[3] can be used as a hunting
  term ('to seize prey before it was away
  from cover'). In a characteristic
  Petrarchan mixture of humility and
  aggression, Arcite seems to want to
  burst upon Emilia (either in person or

in her mind) in the midst of her cold
(chaste) thoughts, perhaps with a pun
on eating (chopping on) leftover
(cold) foods. But it is not only Emilia's
thoughts but Emilia herself that he
hopes to encounter; there may be a
subliminal allusion to the story of the
hunter Actaeon, who came upon the
chaste Diana herself, and was killed
for his presumption.
14 **To ... mistress** to become Emilia's
  servant (as he did in 2.5); perhaps he
  is also still fantasizing about 'acci-
  dentally' meeting her in the woods.
  The rhyme of *chop on* and *drop on*
  seems unintentional.
14–15 **expectation ... on't** without
  hoping for it
15 **Lady Fortune** He had resigned himself to 'the becking of our chance' in
  1.2.116. His worship of Fortune indicates overconfidence and courts
  disaster.
17 **takes ... of** pays a lot of attention
  to
18 **near her** her attendant
19 **prim'st** supreme (cf. 'our prime
  cousin' in 1.2.2)
20 **brace** pair
21 **backed** ridden

10 pace] *Q;* place *Seward*   11 thy rumination] *Q;* thy [... / ...] rumination *Oxf*   13 thought!]
Seward; thought, *Q*

That their crowns' titles tried. Alas, alas,
Poor cousin Palamon, poor prisoner, thou
So little dream'st upon my fortune, that
Thou thinkst thyself the happier thing, to be   25
So near Emilia; me thou deem'st at Thebes,
And therein wretched, although free. But if
Thou knew'st my mistress breathed on me, and that
I eared her language, lived in her eye; oh, coz,
What passion would enclose thee!

Enter PALAMON *as out of a bush, with his shackles; [he] bends his
fist at Arcite.*

PALAMON   Traitor kinsman,   30
Thou shouldst perceive my passion, if these signs
Of prisonment were off me and this hand
But owner of a sword! By all oaths in one,
I and the justice of my love would make thee
A confessed traitor! Oh, thou most perfidious   35
That ever gently looked, the void'st of honour

22 **That ... tried** that decided their
claims to the crown, as in the rivalry
of Eteocles and Polynices

23 **Poor cousin Palamon** At this point
in *KT*, 1542–71, Arcite, far from
gloating, laments that the wrath of
Juno and Mars has led to the extinc-
tion of all the Theban royal family
apart from him and Palamon, and
made him a servant to his mortal
enemy Theseus. Chaucer's Palamon is
nevertheless furious at what he hears,
and it may be that the dramatists decided to provide more motivation for
this anger.

29 **eared** heard (but with a more strongly physical connotation: took it in at
the ear)

30 **What ... thee** i.e., Palamon would be
even more imprisoned (by emotion)
than he is already
passion anger

30.1 *as out of a bush* The bush might be
on stage (see headnote to this scene)

but the *as* might mean that Palamon
enters looking unkempt and ravenous,
like the 'wild man' or 'woodman'
figure of romance. cf. Dessen: '"As
from" is used usually to denote a recently completed offstage action or
event that (1) would have been difficult to stage or (2) can be staged but
has been finessed to speed up the narrative' (p. 134).
shackles perhaps on both wrists and
ankles (see 3.2.14)
bends shakes

34–5 **I ... traitor** I would prove by
combat that you have committed treason (towards love).

36–7 **gently ... token** noble, well-born:
the first contrast is between Arcite's
manner and his behaviour; the
second, between his rank and his lack
of honour. Bawcutt suggests that
gentle token refers to Arcite's coat of
arms or other symbol of rank.

36 void'st] *Seward (Sympson);* voydes *Q*   honour] *Seward;* honour. *Q*

That e'er bore gentle token, falsest cousin
That ever blood made kin: call'st thou her thine?
I'll prove it in my shackles, with these hands,
Void of appointment, that thou liest, and art   40
A very thief in love, a chaffy lord
Not worth the name of villain. Had I a sword
And these house-clogs away –

ARCITE   Dear cousin Palamon –

PALAMON

Cozener Arcite, give me language such
As thou hast showed me feat.

ARCITE   Not finding in   45
The circuit of my breast any gross stuff
To form me like your blazon holds me to
This gentleness of answer. 'Tis your passion
That thus mistakes, the which to you being enemy,
Cannot to me be kind: honour and honesty   50
I cherish and depend on, howsoe'er
You skip them in me, and with them, fair coz,
I'll maintain my proceedings. Pray be pleased
To show in generous terms your griefs, since that
Your question's with your equal, who professes   55

40 **Void of appointment** without weapons and armour (see 1.4.15)
liest one syllable, as indicated by Q's spelling, *ly'st* (Oxf[1])
41 **chaffy** as light and worthless as chaff, the husks of corn
43 **house-clogs** shackles
44 **Cozener** cheater: a common pun (cozeners often won the confidence of their victim by claiming to be a long-lost 'cousin' or relative); see, for instance, *1H4* 1.3.255
44–5 **give ... feat** 'let your language correspond with the vileness of your actions' (Mason)
45–8 **Not ... answer** Arcite retorts that his polite language *is* perfectly consistent with his behaviour, which has been honourable.
47 **blazon** description. 'The original

sense of *blason* in Old French was simply a shield; then it came to mean a coat-of-arms, which is still the sense it has in French; then, in English only, it passed on to the sense of description of arms, and even to description in a general sense' (Skeat).
48–50 **'Tis ... kind** i.e., since passion is a source of suffering for its victim, it is not surprising that it is also cruel to others; *kind* may also mean 'kin' (RA)
51 **depend on** serve (cf. 'I do depend upon the lord', *TC* 3.1.5)
52 **skip** fail to see
53 **maintain** justify
54 **generous** noble, gentlemanly (Latin *generosus* = gentleman)
55 **question** quarrel

42 Not] *Bawcutt (Littledale);* Nor *Q*   43 away –] *Littledale;* away. *Q*

To clear his own way with the mind and sword
Of a true gentleman.

PALAMON   That thou durst, Arcite!

ARCITE

My coz, my coz, you have been well advertised
How much I dare; you've seen me use my sword
Against th'advice of fear. Sure, of another   60
You would not hear me doubted, but your silence
Should break out, though i'th' sanctuary.

PALAMON   Sir,
I have seen you move in such a place, which well
Might justify your manhood; you were called
A good knight and a bold. But the whole week's not
    fair   65
If any day it rain: their valiant temper
Men lose when they incline to treachery
And then they fight like compelled bears, would fly
Were they not tied.

ARCITE   Cousin, you might as well
Speak this and act it in your glass as to   70
His ear which now disdains you.

PALAMON   Come up to me;
Quit me of these cold gyves; give me a sword,
Though it be rusty, and the charity

---

56 **clear** both to clear the way and to
show the innocence of his actions
57 **That thou durst** if only you dared
58 **advertised** made aware (stressed on
second syllable)
60–1 **Sure ... doubted** You would not
let another person accuse me of
cowardice.
61–2 **your ... i'th' sanctuary** You
would break silence to defend me even
in a holy place (or, even if you
were in hiding there).
64 **justify** prove
65–6 **the whole ... rain** i.e., any inconsistency casts doubt over the

whole of a man's reputation. Immediately before Arcite's soliloquy, Chaucer compares the emotional instability
of lovers to the unsettled weather of
Friday, Venus' day: 'Selde is the
Friday all the weeke ilike' (*KT*, 1539).
68 **compelled bears** bears at a bear-
baiting (who are forced to fight).
Skeat compares 'I cannot fly, / But
bear-like I must fight the course' (*Mac*
5.7.1–2).
would which would (Proudfoot)
70 **glass** mirror
72 **Quit** rid
gyves fetters

68 compelled] *Q;* coupel'd *F*

Of one meal lend me. Come before me then,
A good sword in thy hand, and do but say   75
That Emily is thine – I will forgive
The trespass thou hast done me, yea, my life,
If then thou carry't, and brave souls in shades
That have died manly, which will seek of me
Some news from earth, they shall get none but this: 80
That thou art brave and noble.

ARCITE   Be content.
Again betake you to your hawthorn house.
With counsel of the night, I will be here
With wholesome viands. These impediments
Will I file off; you shall have garments and   85
Perfumes to kill the smell o'th' prison. After,
When you shall stretch yourself and say but, 'Arcite,
I am in plight', there shall be at your choice
Both sword and armour.

PALAMON   Oh you heavens, dares any
So nobly bear a guilty business? None   90
But only Arcite; therefore none but Arcite
In this kind is so bold.

ARCITE   Sweet Palamon. [*Offers to embrace him.*]

PALAMON

I do embrace you and your offer; for
Your offer do't I only, sir; your person
Without hypocrisy I may not wish   95

---

77 **yea, my life** and even your killing of me

78 **carry't** win the fight. Skeat compares 'If he scape, / Heaven forgive him too!' (*Mac* 4.3.234–5), which also refers to trial by combat.
in shades in the part of the Elysian fields reserved for military heroes

83 **With ... night** in secrecy, taking only the night into his confidence

88 **in plight** physically fit

90 *****nobly** Q's reading, *noble*, is not im-

possible, but the emendation makes more sense. It gets some confirmation from Davenant's 'Dare any venture so nobly in a cause so guilty?' (Act 3, p. 28).

92–6 Arcite's line is probably accompanied by an offered embrace. Palamon's reply suggests that he accepts it without any softening of his attitude and considers Arcite hypocritical for wishing any contact except in combat.

90 nobly] *Skeat;* noble *Q*   92 SD] *this edn; not in Q*

More than my sword's edge on't.   *Horns.*

ARCITE   You hear the horns;
Enter your musit, lest this match between's
Be crossed ere met. Give me your hand; farewell.
I'll bring you every needful thing. I pray you
Take comfort and be strong.

PALAMON   Pray hold your promise   100
And do the deed with a bent brow. Most certain
You love me not; be rough with me and pour
This oil out of your language. By this air,
I could for each word give a cuff, my stomach
Not reconciled by reason.

ARCITE   Plainly spoken.   105
Yet pardon me hard language. When I spur
My horse I chide him not; content and anger
In me have but one face.   *Horns again.*
                    Hark, sir, they call
The scattered to the banquet. You must guess

---

96 SD Q's SD (see t.n.) presumably
means that the cornets were played to
sound like hunting horns (see Appendix 6, p. 360).
97 *musit Q's *music* is clearly wrong. As
Reed noted in 1778, Davenant
emends to *muise*, of which *muset* and
musit are diminutives: an obsolete
word for the hiding place or small
opening through which a hunted hare
escapes (*OED* quotes *VA* 683–4). The
word is in keeping with Arcite's rather
superior tone in this scene (see also
82, above), making Palamon sound
like one of the small animals involved
in the day's hunting.
98 crossed ere met prevented before we
can meet
101 with . . . brow frowning (not in your
present amiable manner)
103 oil polite words ('court oil' was proverbial for flattery; see Dent, O25)
104–5 my stomach . . . reason Walker

interprets this as conditional: 'If my
anger (which was supposed to make
the stomach flow faster) were not rational', but, given Palamon's contempt for Arcite's reasonableness, the
line may be a statement of fact.
106 pardon . . . language Forgive me
for not using the kind of language you
have asked to hear. The contrast between the calm and the passionate
man, not in *KT*, recalls the already
famous quarrel in *JC*, where Cassius
likewise accuses his opponent of hypocrisy: 'Brutus, this sober form of
yours hides wrongs . . . ' (4.2.40).
Beaumont and Fletcher imitated it to
some extent in 3.2 of *The Maid's Tragedy* (1610). Montgomery (see t.n.)
makes the line a comment on Palamon's manner.
108 one face the same outward appearance
109 scattered as in 1–2, above

96 SD] *this edn; Winde hornes of Cornets / after 95 Q; Wind horns off / Leech (Bertram)*   97 musit]
Knight; Musicke *Q;* muise *Davenant;* muse quick *Seward*   106 Yet . . . language] *Q;* Yet – pardon
me – *Oxf*   107 not] *F;* nor *Q*   108 SD] *Winde hornes / after 106 Q*

I have an office there.

PALAMON   Sir, your attendance   110
Cannot please heaven and I know your office
Unjustly is achieved.

ARCITE   'Tis a good title.
I am persuaded, this question, sick between 's,
By bleeding must be cured. I am a suitor
That to your sword you will bequeath this plea   115
And talk of it no more.

PALAMON   But this one word:
You are going now to gaze upon my mistress –
For, note you, mine she is –

ARCITE   Nay, then –

PALAMON   Nay, pray you!
You talk of feeding me to breed me strength.
You are going now to look upon a sun   120
That strengthens what it looks on; there
You have a vantage on me. But enjoy't till
I may enforce my remedy. Farewell.   *Exeunt.*

[3.2]   *Enter Jailer's* Daughter *alone.*

110 **office** Having overheard his soliloquy, Palamon knows that Arcite will
be there as attendant to Emilia; hence
his anger.
112 ***'Tis ... title** Q's reading (see t.n.)
can make sense as it stands, but is ex-
cessively tortuous for a reply trying to
put an end to Palamon's verbal attacks. *Title*, as in 20–2, means not only
Arcite's court office but his right to
Emilia herself.
113 **this ... between 's** our quarrel
which is ill (because we are both ill
from it)
114 **bleeding** a common medical
remedy, frequently mentioned with a
double meaning (cf. *R2* 1.1.157)
I ... suitor I beseech you

115 **plea** quarrel (usually, in law)
118 **Nay ... Nay** Arcite starts to leave
in disgust and Palamon detains
him.
122 **vantage** advantage. RP notes the
paradox: a combatant normally tried
to gain the advantage by having the
sun in his adversary's eyes, but Palamon (like Arcite in 2.3.9–10) thinks
of Emilia as a source of strength. Cf.
her own view of her influence in
5.3.60–5.
3.2.0.1 The Daughter carries a file (see 8,
below) and perhaps also a bundle containing her clothes and food for Palamon (see 2.6.6–7 and 32), unless she is
assumed to have left these at the
meeting-point.

112 'Tis] *Oxf (Proudfoot')*; If *Q;* I've *Seward*   title.] *Bawcutt;* title, *Q*   3.2] Scæna 2. *Q*

DAUGHTER

He has mistook the brake I meant, is gone
After his fancy. 'Tis now well-nigh morning.
No matter: would it were perpetual night,
And darkness lord o'th' world! – Hark, 'tis a wolf!
In me hath grief slain fear and but for one thing   5
I care for nothing and that's Palamon.
I reck not if the wolves would jaw me, so
He had this file. What if I hallooed for him?
I cannot hallow. If I whooped – what then?
If he not answered, I should call a wolf,   10
And do him but that service. I have heard
Strange howls this livelong night; why may't not be
They have made prey of him? He has no weapons;
He cannot run: the jangling of his gyves
Might call fell things to listen, who have in them   15
A sense to know a man unarmed and can
Smell where resistance is. I'll set it down,

1 **brake** bush. Q's *beak* can mean brook, but, since Palamon enters from a bush, Theobald's suggestion makes sense. Davenant's *beach*, i.e. beech, (perhaps influenced by 3.3.41, below) suggests that he envisaged a woodland setting.
meant directed him to (or, perhaps, intended)

1–2 **gone . . . fancy** wandered off (where his fancy took him). The Daughter first thinks that Palamon went to the wrong meeting-point, then, in the first of many rapid swings to imagining the worst, decides that he deliberately chose not to stay there.

2 **well-nigh** almost

4 **a wolf** Possibly there is an offstage sound at this point, but the Daughter may only be imagining it.

6 **that's** the *one thing* of 5

7 **reck** Q's *wreak* is used, as often in the Renaissance, erroneously for *reck*, care. See *OED* 'wreak' and 'reck' *v.* 3a.

jaw devour; the only *OED* example of this sense

9 **I cannot hallow** Hallowing (or holloaing, or hallooing) is louder than whooping and requires a stronger voice (see *TN* 1.5.272, where Viola talks of making the hills echo with the sound). Montgomery's spelling in 8–9 gives the modern sense.

11 **do . . . service** Instead of 'serving' Palamon in the sexual sense, she might either lead the wolf to where he was or save his life at her own expense, by distracting its attention; either way, the phrase is ironic.

12 **Strange . . . night** Cf. the 'strange screams of death' and the owl that 'Clamor'd the livelong night' during Duncan's murder (*Mac* 2.3.56, 59–60).

15 **fell** deadly

17 **set it down** record it. Waith (Oxf¹) compares *Ham* 1.5.108.

1 mistook] *Seward;* mistook; *Q*   brake] *Weber (Theobald);* Beake *Q;* beach *Davenant;* beck *Seward;* brook *(Sympson)*   7 reck] *(wreake) Q*   8 hallowed] *Q;* hollowed *F;* hallooed *1778;* hollered *Oxf*   14 jangling] *(Iengling) Q*

He's torn to pieces; they howled many together
And then they fed on him. So much for that:
Be bold to ring the bell. How stand I then?   20
All's chared when he is gone – no, no, I lie.
My father's to be hanged for his escape,
Myself to beg, if I prized life so much
As to deny my act – but that I would not,
Should I try death by dozens. I am moped.   25
Food took I none these two days;
Sipped some water. I have not closed mine eyes,
Save when my lids scoured off their brine. Alas,
Dissolve, my life! Let not my sense unsettle,
Lest I should drown, or stab, or hang myself.   30
Oh, state of nature, fail together in me,
Since thy best props are warped! – So, which way
    now?
The best way is the next way to a grave:

18 **they ... together** Wolves were believed to divide their prey among
them: 'if there be many of them ... it
is said, that they howle and call their
fellowes to that feast' (Topsell, 738).

19 ***fed** All editors since 1679 have
emended Q's *feed* but Bowers argues
for retaining it, taking the sentence to
read 'He's torn ... and then they
feed', with 'they howled many together' as a parenthetical interjection.
His suggestion is consistent with the
Daughter's vivid imagining of disaster in the present tense (compare
3.4.5–11), if one can accept the use of
then instead of 'now'.

20 **Be ... bell** Don't hesitate to sound
his death knell.
How ... I What is my situation? Cf.
Ham (Q2) 4.1.55.

21 **All's chared** 'My task is done'
(Weber). See *OED* chare *v.* 4. The
noun is 'chare', still used in the form
of 'chore'.

23–4 **Myself ... act** If she begs her life
and lies about her guilt, she will be left

a penniless beggar when her father
has been hanged in disgrace.

24 **that** i.e., deny what I have done

25 **try ... dozens** experience dozens of
deaths
moped stupefied, bewildered

28 **my ... brine** 'when I closed them to
get rid of their tears' (Leech)

29 **Dissolve** 'Natural' death is envisaged
as an evaporation of the whole being
at once, as opposed to gradual suffering or loss of parts of it: cf. Faustus'
wish to be like beasts whose 'souls are
soone dissolv'd in elements' (Marlowe, *Dr Faustus*, 5.2.1970) and Hamlet's longing for his flesh to 'resolve
itself into a dew' (*Ham* 1.2.130).
Let ... unsettle Skeat compares 'His
wits begin t'unsettle' (*KL* 3.4.162).

31 **state of nature** existence
fail together die all at once, not only
in the *best props* of 32, such as reason

32 **which way now?** She probably starts
to leave, her uncertain movements
showing her loss of direction.

33 **next** nearest

19 fed] *F;* feed *Q*   25 dozens] *Seward; (*dussons)   28 brine] *1711;* bine *Q*

Each errant step beside is torment. Lo,
The moon is down, the crickets chirp, the screech-
   owl   35
Calls in the dawn; all offices are done
Save what I fail in. But the point is this:
An end, and that is all.   *Exit*

[3.3]   *Enter* ARCITE *with meat, wine and files.*

ARCITE
   I should be near the place. Ho! Cousin Palamon?
PALAMON [*from the bush*]
   Arcite?
ARCITE   The same. I have brought you food and files.
   Come forth and fear not; here's no Theseus.

Enter PALAMON.

PALAMON
   Nor none so honest, Arcite.
ARCITE   That's no matter.

---

34 **errant** erring or wandering
   beside away from the path
35–6 **The moon ... dawn** Skeat notes
   the reminiscence of *Mac* 2.2.15: 'I
   heard the owl scream and the crickets
   cry'; cf. also 'The moon is down' (*Mac*
   2.1.2) and see 12n., above. Leech
   points out the Daughter's topsy-turvy
   world, indicated by her substitution
   of the screech-owl for the cock as the
   bird that summons the dawn.
36 **offices** Either a repetition of the idea
   in 21, or a reference to 'offices' like
   Arcite's – official duties at court.
37 **Save ... in** i.e., meeting Palamon and
   filing off his fetters
37–8 **the point ... all** *Point* and *end*
   have the double meaning of 'purpose'
   or 'conclusion'; a point was also a fas-
   tener at the lower end of a doublet,
   used to attach it to the hose (a usage
   which may recur at 3.4.2). The
   Daughter plays on all three meanings,

first attempting to sum up the 'point'
of her speech, then abandoning the
idea of any purpose except to come to
an end.
3.3.0.1 Arcite's entrance with a file parallels the Daughter's. As Taylor notes,
   the presence of a bush, or other
   symbol of the woods, raises 'the tan-
   talizing possibility that the gaoler's
   daughter may be wandering within a
   few feet of the man she is searching
   for' (Taylor & Jowett, 42). Some productions have emphasized this possibility: see p. 87 above but cf. 3.1.30.
1n. This scene, like the previous one,
   must take place late at night (see
   3.1.83), but, unlike the Daughter, the
   men do not comment on the darkness
   and there is no evocation of its
   atmosphere.
2 SD In view of 3, Palamon cannot yet
   be on stage; he may put his head out
   of a bush or speak from off stage.

3.3] Scæna 3. *Q*   2 SD] *this edn; Enter ... as from the bush. Oxf; not in Q*   3 SD] *after 1 Q*

We'll argue that hereafter. Come, take courage! 5
You shall not die thus beastly; here, sir, drink –
I know you are faint – then I'll talk further with you.

PALAMON

Arcite, thou mightst now poison me.

ARCITE   I might,
But I must fear you first. Sit down and, good now,
No more of these vain parleys; let us not, 10
Having our ancient reputation with us,
Make talk for fools and cowards. To your health – [_Drinks_.]

PALAMON

Do!

ARCITE Pray sit down then, and let me entreat you,
By all the honesty and honour in you,
No mention of this woman; 'twill disturb us. 15
We shall have time enough.

PALAMON   Well, sir, I'll pledge you. [_Drinks_.]

ARCITE

Drink a good hearty draught: it breeds good blood,
  man.
Do not you feel it thaw you?

PALAMON   Stay, I'll tell you

6 **beastly** like a beast (as you now are)
9 **must** would have to
  good now please
10 **parleys** hostile exchanges of words
11 **ancient** former
12 **Make talk for** 'behave in such a way
  as to be talked about by' or, possibly,
  'talk in a way fit for'
  To your health Q follows this with
  _&c_. Proudfoot's suggestion, that it
  was a misreading of 'Sir', is a good
  one. Perhaps, however, the phrase indicates some business, such as ceremonial pouring and saluting. Rituals
  of drinking could be very elaborate
  (see William Cartwright's _The Royal
  Slave_ (1636), 3.1.670–716) and much

of the scene is taken up with 'pledg-
ing'. Arcite may drink first in order to
prove that the wine is not poisoned, as
Palamon has suggested. In Berkeley
(1985), Arcite filled out the _&c_. by a
comically melodramatic performance
of death by poison, thus rebuking
what he saw as unworthy suspicions.
13 **Do!** either 'Yes, do drink (and prove
  that there is no poison there)', or an
  expression of mocking toleration for
  whatever else Arcite has been doing
16 **pledge you** drink after you (from the
  same cup)
17 **it ... blood** a common belief (see
  Dent, W461: 'Good wine makes good
  blood')

12 health –] health, &c. _Q_; health, sir! _Proudfoot_   _SD_] Dyce; not in Q   16 SD] Dyce; not in Q   18–
27 Stay ... this?] _prose Q_

After a draught or two more.

ARCITE   Spare it not;
The Duke has more, coz. Eat now.

PALAMON   Yes.

ARCITE   I am glad   20
You have so good a stomach.

PALAMON   I am gladder
I have so good meat to't.

ARCITE   Is't not mad lodging,
Here in the wild woods, cousin?

PALAMON   Yes, for them
That have wild consciences.

ARCITE   How tastes your victuals?
Your hunger needs no sauce, I see.

PALAMON   Not much.   25
But if it did, yours is too tart, sweet cousin.
What is this?

ARCITE   Venison.

PALAMON   'Tis a lusty meat.
Give me more wine. – Here, Arcite, to the wenches
We have known in our days. The Lord Steward's
    daughter –
Do you remember her?

ARCITE   After you, coz.   30

PALAMON
She loved a black-haired man –

ARCITE   She did so; well, sir?

PALAMON
And I have heard some call him Arcite, and –

21 **stomach** appetite; perhaps also anger
(Riv). Arcite is commenting on Palamon's voracious eating.

22-3 **mad . . . woods** a pun: 'wood', or
'wode', as an adjective, could also
mean mad. Cf. 'wode within this
wood' (*MND* 2.1.192). Palamon's
retort (a play on *wild*) sets up a series
of aggressive puns.

25 **sauce** 'Hunger needs no sauce' or

'hunger is the best sauce' (Dent,
H819) is proverbial. Arcite notes the
sharpness of Palamon's reply.

27 **lusty** hearty, but also lust-provoking
– which may explain the direction
the conversation now takes. For an
explicit account of the aphrodisiac
effects of meat and wine, see
Middleton, *The Revenger's Tragedy*
(1607), 1.2.178–90.

23 them] *F*; then *Q*

ARCITE

Out with't, faith.

PALAMON   She met him in an arbour.

What did she there, coz? play o'th' virginals?

ARCITE

Something she did, sir –

PALAMON   Made her groan a month for't.   35

Or two, or three, or ten.

ARCITE   The Marshall's sister

Had her share too, as I remember, cousin;

Else there be tales abroad. You'll pledge her?

PALAMON   Yes.

ARCITE

A pretty brown wench 'tis. There was a time

When young men went a-hunting, and a wood,   40

And a broad beech; and thereby hangs a tale –

Hey ho.

PALAMON   For Emily, upon my life! Fool,

Away with this strained mirth! I say again,

That sigh was breathed for Emily; base cousin,

Dar'st thou break first?

ARCITE   You are wide.

PALAMON   By heaven and earth,   45

There's nothing in thee honest.

ARCITE   Then I'll leave you;

34 **play ... virginals** This small,
plucked keyboard instrument, so called
because 'maids and virgins do most
commonly play on them' (T. Blount,
Glossographia, quoted by Weber),
often inspires puns about losing one's
virginity. Cf. 'Still virginalling /
Upon his palm?' (*WT* 1.2.125–6).

38 **tales** false reports (see Prologue 21n.,
and 41n., below)

39 **brown** brunette

39–41 **There ... beech** Arcite is remembering a seduction in the woods,
like the one the Jailer's Daughter
hoped would follow her rescue of
Palamon.

41 **thereby ... tale** a catch-phrase
(Dent, T48) hinting that the speaker
could say more (probably scandalous)
on the subject, often with a pun on
'tale'/'tail' (as in *Oth* 3.1.8–11)

42 **Hey ho** either a real sigh or an exaggerated, comic one, which Palamon
interprets (rightly or wrongly) as evidence that Arcite is 'treacherously'
thinking of Emilia

45 **break** break your promise not to
mention this woman (though Palamon is in fact the first to speak her
name)
   wide wide of the mark: 'an expression
from archery' (Weber)

45–7 By ... now] *Q lines* honest. / now:

You are a beast now.

PALAMON   As thou mak'st me, traitor.

ARCITE

    There's all things needful – files and shirts, and
        perfumes;
    I'll come again some two hours hence, and bring
    That that shall quiet all –

PALAMON   A sword and armour.   50

ARCITE

    Fear me not. You are now too foul; farewell.
    Get off your trinkets. You shall want nought. ,

PALAMON   Sirrah –

ARCITE

    I'll hear no more.   *Exit.*

PALAMON   If he keep touch, he dies for't.   *Exit.*

[3.4]   *Enter Jailer's Daughter.*

DAUGHTER

    I am very cold and all the stars are out too,
    The little stars and all, that look like aglets;
    The sun has seen my folly. – Palamon! –
    Alas, no, he's in heaven; where am I now?
    Yonder's the sea and there's a ship; how't tumbles!   5

48 **shirts, and** Q has 'shirts, and, perfumes'. The presence of the two commas, even though the compositor was having difficulty squeezing this line into the available space, suggests that the punctuation indicates a deliberate pause to reinforce Arcite's supercilious insistence that Palamon is not only behaving but smelling like a beast.

49 **two hours** Cf. 3.6.1–2, below.

51 **Fear me not** 'Do not doubt me' (Skeat).

52 **trinkets** the fetters, compared to bracelets

53 **keep touch** keeps his promise

3.4.1 **out** extinguished

2 **aglets** originally the metal tag at the end of a lace; then, by extension, gold, silver or metallic ornament (stud, plate or spangle), worn on a dress (*OED*). Davenant reads 'spangles'. Weber notes a comparison between stars and aglets in *Faerie Queene*, 2.3.26. ,

3 **Palamon!** She calls to him, then 'remembers' that he has been killed by wolves.

5 **Yonder's ... ship** For possible sources of this hallucination, see p. 48 above.

52 Sirrah –] *1778;* sir ha: *Q;* Ha? Sir! *Davenant*   3.4] Scæna 4. *Q*

And there's a rock lies watching under water;
Now, now, it beats upon it; now, now, now!
There's a leak sprung, a sound one! How they cry!
Run her before the wind, you'll lose all else.
Up with a course or two and tack about, boys!   10
Good night, good night, you're gone. – I am very
    hungry.
Would I could find a fine frog; he would tell me
News from all parts o'th' world. Then would I make
A carrack of a cockle shell and sail
By east and north-east to the king of pygmies,   15
For he tells fortunes rarely. Now, my father
Twenty to one is trussed up in a trice
Tomorrow morning; I'll say never a word.   *Sings.*

For I'll cut my green coat, a foot above my knee

---

7 **it beats upon it** 'The ship strikes the rock' (Leech).

8 **a leak sprung** Another sexual double meaning: a leaky wench is one who has lost her virginity, and a ship is traditionally female. The Daughter identifies herself with it, and its imaginary sinking coincides with her complete loss of sanity.

9 ***Run her** Q has *Upon her*, possibly influenced by *Up* in 10. *Spoon* and its variant spelling *spoom* (*OED*: to run before the wind or sea) have been suggested as emendations. Weber noted the analogy with *The Double Marriage* (*c.*1620): 'Down with the fore-saile too, we'l spoom before her' (Bowers, 9: 2.1.191). *Run* seems a somewhat more likely source of misreading; the capital letter *R* in the MS seems to have given the compositors trouble, as in the misreading of *Ravishd* as *Bravishd* in 2.2.22. It scans better than *Open*, suggested by Freehafer and adopted by Montgomery and Waith (Oxf¹).

10 **course** small sail attached to lower yards of a ship (Leech)

tack about change direction; cf. Prologue 26, which seems to echo this part of the play

12 **frog** to eat, presumably, in view of her previous line, though she could also be thinking of the animal helpers in fairy-tales. The Daughter still imagines herself by the water – perhaps the lake mentioned later by the Wooer (4.1.53), which may or may not be indicated as the setting for this scene.

14 **carrack** also spelled 'carrick'; a large cargo ship, also used for warfare

17 **trussed up** hanged (by analogy with a fowl made ready for roasting)
in a trice *Trice* originally meant windlass or pulley; *in a trice* means 'at a single pull', that is, instantly.

18 **I'll ... word** Cf. Ophelia's 'Pray let's have no words of this' (*Ham* 4.5.46), which is followed by the song 'Tomorrow is St Valentine's Day'. The Daughter's song, similarly, hints at what she refuses to say.

19–26 For the Daughter's songs, see Appendix 6, pp. 361–3.

---

9 Run] *Skeat;* Vpon *Q;* Up with *1778 (Sympson);* Spoon *(Theobald);* Spoom *Dyce;* Open *Riv (Freehafer)* 10 tack] *F;* (take) 18 SD *Sings*] *Sing / opp. 19 Q* 19 a foot] (afoote)

And I'll clip my yellow locks, an inch below mine eye. 20
  Hey, nonny, nonny, nonny,
He's buy me a white cut, forth for to ride,
And I'll go seek him through the world that is so
  wide,
  Hey, nonny, nonny, nonny.
Oh, for a prick now, like a nightingale,   25
To put my breast against. I shall sleep like a top else.   *Exit.*

[3.5] *Enter* Schoolmaster [GERALD] *and five* Countrymen

SCHOOLMASTER
  Fie, fie,
  What tediosity and disinsanity
  Is here among ye! Have my rudiments
  Been laboured so long with ye, milked unto ye

22 **He's** '*He's* is a common abbreviation of "he shall", still common among the 'vulgar' (Weber); Davenant uses a similar phrase: 'Is'e not stand a step amiss' (Act 3, p. 33).
  cut horse, either with docked tail or gelded
25 **prick** The nightingale supposedly sang with its breast against a thorn in order to stay awake, symbolizing the ravished Philomel who was metamorphosed into the bird; the Daughter is also making a sexual pun on 'penis', which Davenant removed by substituting 'Hawthorn'.
26 **sleep like a top** proverbial for sound sleep (Dent, T440)
3.5.0.1 Perhaps because the author was building his scene around an already existing spectacle (see Appendices 4 and 5) and did not know exactly what it would be like, his opening direction is vague and 'permissive'; the wording in Q (see t.n.) suggests that the last part was added as an afterthought, as it became clear which characters would be needed.

Most editors have taken lines 26–8 as evidence that Q's '*2 or 3 wenches*' ought to be five. The Schoolmaster's questions about the whereabouts of the Wenches, the Taborer and the Bavian may mean that some or all of these characters enter later. If the scene included a 'boscage', or artificial woods (as in Beaumont's masque), they might be on stage but not yet visible to the audience, or visible to them but not to the Schoolmaster. Or his question may be prompted only by self-important fussiness. Or perhaps the mode is presentational: i.e., all the characters enter at once, but come downstage only when called for. Lines 29 and 34 may mean that some of them are not yet completely dressed for the morris.
2 **disinsanity** madness. Either the Schoolmaster is saying the opposite of what he means (Skeat), or he is using *dis* as an intensification (Proudfoot); either way, the word is a unique coinage.

25–6] *Q lines* breast / else. /   3.5] Scæna 6. *Q*   0.1] *Enter a Schoolmaster.* 4. *Countrymen: and Baum* 2. *or* 3. *wenches, with a Taborer. Q*   1–22] *prose Q*

And, by a figure, even the very plum-broth   5
And marrow of my understanding laid upon ye,
And do ye still cry 'Where?' and 'How?' and
   'Wherefore?'
You most coarse-frieze capacities, ye jean judgments,
Have I said, 'Thus let be' and 'There let be'
And 'Then let be', and no man understand me?   10
Proh Deum! Medius Fidius! Ye are all dunces.
For why?
Here stand I. Here the Duke comes; there are you,
Close in the thicket; the Duke appears; I meet him
And unto him I utter learned things   15
And many figures; he hears and nods and hums
And then cries, 'Rare!' and I go forward. At length,
I fling my cap up – mark there! Then do you,

5 **by a figure** 'to put it metaphorically'.
Rhetoric, an important element in
education, involved the study of
tropes and figures – that is, literary
uses of language; Gerald refers to figures again at 16, 22 and 106.

5–6 **plum-broth / And marrow** the
very best. Plum-broth was much like
plum-porridge (see 2.3.75n.). Bone-
marrow was considered the choicest
part of meat.

8 **coarse-frieze** a rough woollen cloth
(*coarse* is tautological). For differentiation of social classes in terms of the
cloth from which their clothes are
made, see 'hempen homespuns'
(*MND* 3.1.77) and (Skeat's example)
'russet yeas and honest kersey noes'
(*LLL* 5.2.413).
   jean a kind of twilled cotton, fustian
cloth (the origin of the modern
'jeans')

9 **'Thus ... let be'** Cf. 'here I'll be /
And there I'll be' (2.3.49–50); perhaps this is how the Schoolmaster
has drilled them in the dance moves,
using the rhetorical divisions 'thus',
'there' and 'then' of a school
exercise.

11 *Proh ... Fidius* Most of Gerald's
Latin consists of common phrases
from school textbooks. Terence's '*Proh
Deum atque hominum fidem*' [by God
and the faith of men] is listed among
the exclamatory interjections in Lily's
famous Latin grammar (first pub.
1540), as is *Medius Fidius*, 'an old
Latin oath, apparently short for *me
dius Fidius adiuuet*, may the divine
Fidius [Jupiter] help me!' (Skeat).
This also occurs in *Wit at Several
Weapons* (*c.*1613), which is attributed
to Middleton, Rowley and possibly
Fletcher (Bowers, 7: 1.2.23–8).

13 **Here stand I** Possibly the Schoolmaster demonstrates the layout of the
entertainment on the ground (like
Launce in *TGV* 2.3.13–32).

16 **hums** makes encouraging non-
committal sounds. There may be
irony at the speaker's expense, if the
audience interprets Theseus' hums
differently from the Schoolmaster (cf.
'I cried "hum", and "well, go to", /
But mark'd him not a word', *1H4*
3.1.156–7).

18 **mark there!** He probably demonstrates the gesture.

8 jean] jave *Q;* sleave *Seward;* jay *or* jaw *(Weber);* jape *Knight;* jane *Dyce*

As once did Meleager and the boar,
Break comely out before him; like true lovers,   20
Cast yourselves in a body decently
And sweetly, by a figure, trace and turn, boys.

1 COUNTRYMAN
And sweetly we will do it, Master Gerald.

2 COUNTRYMAN
Draw up the company. Where's the taborer?

3 COUNTRYMAN
Why, Timothy!

[*Enter* Taborer.]

TABORER   Here, my mad boys, have at ye!   25
SCHOOLMASTER
But, I say, where's these women?

4 COUNTRYMAN   Here's Friz and Maudlin.

[*Enter five* Countrywomen.]

19 **Meleager . . . boar** Theseus was one
of the hunters of the Calydonian boar,
an adventure organized by Meleager
(Ovid, *Met*, 8). Thomas Heywood
dramatized it in *The Brazen Age*.
20 **lovers** of the Duke, in whose honour
they are performing
21 **Cast . . . body** form a group
22 **sweetly** one of the Schoolmaster's favourite words (see 30, below); his
pupils probably parody him at 23
by a figure 'metaphorically speaking'; Gerald is consciously varying a
cliché
trace and turn This expression is
not in *OED*, which does however list
'trace and race' and 'trace and traverse' (IV 12). To 'trace' is to tread a
measure in dancing (*OED* V 2); Pilling takes it to be cognate with the
French *tresse* and the Italian *treccia*,
meaning 'hey', a circular dance forma-

tion in which the dancers weave in
and out (see p. 107 above). Davenant's
'Cast your selves decently into a Body
/ by a Trace, and turn Boyes thus'
(Act 3, p. 33) suggests that Gerald acts
out his instructions.
25 **have at ye** said during a real or mock
attack (see *Ham* 5.2.302); Timothy
probably gives a frenzied burst of
drumming. Davenant's SD is: '*He
strikes up and 1. Country man dances a
Jigg*' (Act 3, p. 33).
26 *****these** Q has *their*, but, as RP points
out, the misreading of *theis* is
common, and the usage would parallel
'Where are these hearts?' (*MND*
4.2.25–6) which also occurs in the
context of a show that is nearly unable
to go on because of someone's
absence.
Friz short for Frances
Maudlin short for Magdalen

25 SD] *this edn; not in Q*   26 these] *Proudfoot;* their *Q*   SD] *this edn; not in Q*

2 COUNTRYMAN

> And little Luce with the white legs and bouncing
> Barbary.

1 COUNTRYMAN

> And freckled Nell that never failed her master.

SCHOOLMASTER

> Where be your ribbons, maids? Swim with your
> bodies
> And carry it sweetly and deliverly   30
> And now and then a favour and a frisk.

NELL

> Let us alone, sir.

SCHOOLMASTER   Where's the rest o'th' music?

3 COUNTRYMAN

> Dispersed, as you commanded.

SCHOOLMASTER   Couple then

> And see what's wanting; where's the Bavian?
> – My friend, carry your tail without offence   35
> Or scandal to the ladies and be sure
> You tumble with audacity and manhood
> And, when you bark, do it with judgment.

BAVIAN   Yes, sir.

27 **bouncing** hefty, strapping. Both Luce and Barbary are described as if they were horses.

28 **Nell ... master** perhaps with a double meaning, if Nell is the tanner's daughter mentioned in 2.3.45–6

29 **Swim** the desired effect in Renaissance dance. The Italian dance-term is *ondeggiare*, translated 'undulation' (Franko, 61).

30 **deliverly** nimbly

31 **favour** possibly like 'honour', the bow or curtsey by partners in a country dance. Participants in Dover's Cotswold Games (see Appendix 5a) received yellow ribbons ('Dover's Favours') for taking part (Whitfield, 130 n.33). Except in the volta, there was no physical contact between male and

female dancers, though kissing might occur at the end. Women sometimes gave their partners a flower or nodded at them.

frisk a lively dance movement, caper or jig

32 **Let us alone** You can count on us.

33 **Dispersed** Musical sounds coming from a variety of locations were popular at masques and concerts; a famous example is Monteverdi's *Vespers*. Davenant included 'a hunt in music', which may have involved 'dispersed' sound effects.

Couple pair off for the dance

34 **wanting** missing

Bavian See List of Roles.

38 **bark** Baboons were thought to be half-dog and half-man (Topsell, 10).

SCHOOLMASTER

   Quo usque tandem! Here's a woman wanting.

4 COUNTRYMAN

   We may go whistle; all the fat's i'th' fire.   40

SCHOOLMASTER

   We have, as learned authors utter, washed a tile.

   We have been *fatuus* and laboured vainly.

2 COUNTRYMAN

   This is that scornful piece, that scurvy hilding

   That gave her promise faithfully, she would be here –

   Cicely, the sempster's daughter.   45

   The next gloves that I give her shall be dogskin!

   Nay, an she fail me once – you can tell, Arcas,

   She swore by wine and bread, she would not break.

SCHOOLMASTER

   An eel and woman,

   A learned poet says, unless by th' tail   50

   And with thy teeth thou hold, will either fail.

---

39 *Quo usque tandem* How long ... ? (Latin). The famous opening of Cicero's first oration against Catiline ('How long, O Catiline, will you abuse our patience?'), often studied in school. Here, an exasperated exclamation (= 'Give me patience!').

40 **go whistle** proverbial (Dent, W313) for doing something in vain
all ... fire proverbial (Dent, F79): everything's ruined. In Sidney's *The Lady of May*, the pedantic schoolmaster Rhombus says, 'all the fat will be ignified' (240).

41 **washed a tile** proverbial (not *learned*, as Gerald claims), meaning to labour in vain (Dent, T289). A *tile* was used to line ovens and fireplaces.

42 *fatuus* foolish (Latin)

43 **piece** creature (contemptuous)
hilding worthless animal, human being or, more specifically, woman. Cf. 'For shame, thou hilding of a devilish spirit' (*TS* 2.1.26).

45 **Cicely** As RP notes, the name seems to have had pejorative connotations; he cites Dekker's *Shoemakers' Holiday* and Rowley's *A Shoemaker a Gentleman*.
sempster male form of seamstress (someone who sews professionally)

46 **Gloves**, often worn in dancing, were a common gift on festive occasions, dogskin being the cheapest kind.

47 **an** if

48 **by ... bread** 'by bread and salt' was a common oath (Dent, *Prov*, B616.11); Chaucer's burlesque knight Sir Thopas swore by ale and bread (Skeat). This seems an allusion to swearing by the sacrament (the most serious of oaths), but may simply be a secular equivalent, suitable to the play's pre-Christian setting.
break break her promise (to take part)

49 **An ... woman** See Dent, W640: 'Who has a woman has an eel by the tail'.

41] *Q lines* have, / Tile, /

In manners this was false position.

1 COUNTRYMAN

A fire ill take her; does she flinch now?

3 COUNTRYMAN   What

Shall we determine, sir?

SCHOOLMASTER   Nothing.

Our business is become a nullity,   55

Yea, and a woeful and a piteous nullity.

4 COUNTRYMAN

Now, when the credit of our town lay on it,

Now to be frampul, now to piss o'th' nettle!

Go thy ways, I'll remember thee, I'll fit thee.

Enter the Jailer's Daughter.

DAUGHTER [*Sings.*]

The George Alow came from the south   60
From the coast of Barbary-a
And there he met with brave gallants of war,
By one, by two, by three-a.

'Well hailed, well hailed, you jolly gallants,
And whither now are you bound-a?   65
O let me have your company

---

52 **In ... position** Gerald applies rules
of arithmetic or grammar to Cicely's
behaviour.
53 **fire ill** Dyce suggested *wildfire* (Greek
fire, highly inflammable), comparing
'A wildfire take you!' (*The Mad Lover*,
Bowers, 5: 5.3.3). Since venereal disease was metaphorically equated with
burning, Leech is probably right in
paraphrasing 'pox take her'.
55 **nullity** a 'non-event'
58 **frampul** *OED* defines as sour-
tempered, disagreeable or (of a horse)
spirited; perhaps also merely capricious, like Lady Frampul in Jonson's

The New Inn (1629).
piss o'th' nettle proverb meaning to
be out of temper (Dent, N132)
59 **Go thy ways** a contemptuous
dismissal
I'll fit thee I'll be revenged in kind
60 **George Alow** name of a ship in a
ballad of 1611. The Daughter's obsession with the sea began in 3.4; she
may also use the 'hail' of the first song
as a way of greeting the others. See
Appendix 6, p. 361.
65–6 The marginal direction in Q (see
t.n.) refers to the seats brought at or
before 97, below.

---

53 fire ill] *Q*; feril *Seward*; wild-fire *Skeat (Dyce)*   60] *South, from / The Q* 65–6] *marginal SD*:
Chaire and / stooles out. *Q*   66–7] *one line Q*

Till we come to the sound-a.'

There was three fools fell out about an howlet:

> The one he said it was an owl,
> The other he said nay, 70
> The third he said it was a hawk,
> And her bells were cut away.

3 COUNTRYMAN
There's a dainty madwoman, Master,
Comes i'th' nick, as mad as a March hare.
If we can get her dance, we are made again; 75
I warrant her, she'll do the rarest gambols.

1 COUNTRYMAN
A madwoman? We are made, boys.

SCHOOLMASTER
And are you mad, good woman?

DAUGHTER   I would be sorry else.
Give me your hand.

SCHOOLMASTER   Why?

DAUGHTER   I can tell your fortune.
You are a fool. Tell ten. – I have posed him. Buzz! 80
– Friend, you must eat no white bread; if you do,

68–72 **There . . . away** See Appendix 6, pp. 361–2.
68 **howlet** alternative spelling for owlet (small owl); can also mean owl
73 **dainty** pretty
74 **i'th' nick** (of time)
    as mad . . . hare a proverb (Dent, H148) based on the fact that hares are at their wildest in March, their breeding season
76 **I warrant her** I'll promise for her
    gambols movements and gestures appropriate to an antic dance
77 **We are made** We can be sure of success. *Made* has the same meaning at 101 and 156, below. A play on 'mad'

and 'made' would have been possible in seventeenth-century pronunciation, as in *TN* 3.4.52–4.
78 **I . . . else** a common catch-phrase (Dent, S665.1)
80 **Tell ten** count to ten. Weber notes that one test of sanity was to make people count their fingers.
    posed baffled
    Buzz! an expression of impatience, perhaps as the Schoolmaster hesitates
81 **eat . . . bread** beget no bastards; compare Fletcher's *The Chances* (*c.*1617), where a baby of unknown parentage is addressed as 'good white bread' (Bowers, 4: 1.5.11).

---

67 Till we] *Weber; till Q;* till I *1711*   69 he] *Bawcutt; not in Q*   71–2] *one line Q*   73 Master] M^r *Q;* Magister *Seward*   73–6] *prose Q*

Your teeth will bleed extremely. – Shall we dance, ho?
– I know you, you're a tinker; sirrah tinker,
Stop no more holes but what you should.

SCHOOLMASTER   *Dii boni,*
A tinker, damsel?

DAUGHTER   Or a conjurer.   85
Raise me a devil now and let him play
Chi passa o'th' bells and bones.

SCHOOLMASTER   Go take her
And fluently persuade her to a peace.
Et opus exegi quod nec Jovis ira, nec ignis –
Strike up and lead her in. [*Taborer plays.*]

2 COUNTRYMAN   Come, lass, let's trip it.   90

DAUGHTER
I'll lead. [*Dances.*]

3 COUNTRYMAN   Do, do!   *Horns.*

SCHOOLMASTER   Persuasively and cunningly.

82 **Your ... extremely** Alludes to the belief that a man's teeth ache when his wife is pregnant (Proudfoot). The Daughter may be addressing more than one countryman, but she seems to be aiming primarily at the Schoolmaster, perhaps confirming what the others have already said about him at 2.3.44–6.

84 **Stop ... should** A tinker mended holes in pots and pans; like the image of leaky ships in 3.4.8, this has a sexual meaning. Cf. the proverb 'A tinker stops one hole and makes two' (Dent, T347). In Fletcher's *The Loyal Subject* (*c.*1618) a street-crier offers to mend 'crackt maiden-heads' (Bowers, 5: 3.5.33).
   Dii boni good gods (Latin)

85 **a conjurer** because to *raise* a devil, or spirit, can also mean to cause an erection. See *RJ* 2.1.23–6.

87 *Chi passa* 'Who's passing down the street?', a popular dance tune
   bells and bones accompaniment to

dancing. (Cf. 'the tongs and the bones', *MND* 4.1.29.) Proudfoot suggests a pun on 'bellibones' (pretty girls or prostitutes).

89 *Et opus ... ignis* From Ovid's conclusion to *Metamorphoses*, 15.871 (actually *Iamque opus*): 'And now my work is done, which neither the wrath of Jove, nor fire, nor sword, nor the gnawing tooth of time shall ever be able to undo.' See p. 110 above. The lines are paraphrased in Fletcher's *Bonduca*, Bowers, 4: 4.3.65–70.

90 **Come, lass** The Second Countryman, apparently the one without a partner (and the one who was demonstrating his dancing skills in 2.3.49–51), tries to follow the Schoolmaster's advice to lead the Daughter in; however, she insists on leading, to the amusement of the Third Countryman. The arrangement probably pairs the two most athletic dancers in the company.

85–6 Or ... play] *one line Q*   87 *Chi passa*] *Weber; Quipassa Q*   90 SD] *this edn; not in Q*   91 SD *Dances*] *this edn; not in Q*   SD *Horns*] *this edn; Winde Hornes: (after* lead) *Q*   91–3 Persuasively ... cue] *Q lines* boyes, / some / Cue; /

Away, boys; I hear the horns. Give me some
    meditation –
And mark your cue.   *Exeunt all but Schoolmaster.*
          Pallas inspire me!

Enter THESEUS, PIRITHOUS, HIPPOLYTA, EMILIA *and train.*

THESEUS
    This way the stag took.
SCHOOLMASTER   Stay and edify!
THESEUS
    What have we here?   95
PIRITHOUS
    Some country sport, upon my life, sir.
THESEUS [*to Schoolmaster*]
    Well, sir, go forward; we will 'edify'.
               [*Chair and stools brought out.*]
    Ladies, sit down; we'll stay it.
            [*Theseus, Hippolyta and Emilia sit.*]
SCHOOLMASTER
    Then, doughty Duke, all hail; all hail, sweet ladies –
THESEUS
    This is a cold beginning.   100

92 **some meditation** a moment to think
93 **Pallas inspire me!** The Schoolmaster's calling on Athene (goddess
of wisdom) suggests that he is going
to improvise the doggerel that
follows.
93 SD Arcite is listed among those entering but has no lines in this scene.
Perhaps the inconsistency results
from the collaborative process (see p.
27 above); perhaps his presence was
found unnecessarily distracting (spectators may wonder whether he and the
Daughter will recognize each other).
At the RSC the Daughter gave him a
dazed look of half-recognition; at
Ashland, he exited at 98, having realized that Emilia was paying no atten-

tion to him. This makes sense, since
the audience will recall that he had
promised to be with Palamon again in
two hours (3.3.49), but omitting him
from the scene is the simplest
solution.
94 **edify** be edified (Theseus' reaction
shows that it is an odd phrase)
96 **country sport** See Beaumont,
Masque, line 70 (Appendix 3).
97 SD This direction is implicit in the
earlier marginal direction (65–6) and
in Theseus' words. Oxf and Oxf[1]
suggest that Theseus gets the chair
and the ladies the stools.
98 **stay** sit through
100 **a cold beginning** This pun on 'hail'
also occurs in *LLL* 5.2.339–40.

93 SD] *after* boyes, 92 *Q*   93.1] *this edn; Enter Thes. Pir. Hip. Emil. Arcite: and traine Q*   97 SP] *F;*
Per. Q SD *Chair . . . out*] *Bawcutt subst.; not in Q* 98 SD] *this edn; not in Q*

SCHOOLMASTER

If you but favour, our country pastime made is.
We are a few of those collected here
That ruder tongues distinguish 'villager'.
And to say verity, and not to fable,
We are a merry rout, or else a *rable*,   105
Or company, or, by a figure, *chorus*,
That 'fore thy dignity will dance a morris.
And I that am the rectifier of all,
By title *pedagogus*, that let fall
The birch upon the breeches of the small ones   110
And humble with a ferula the tall ones,
Do here present this machine, or this frame,
And, dainty Duke, whose doughty dismal fame
From Dis to Daedalus, from post to pillar,
Is blown abroad, help me, thy poor well-willer,   115
And with thy twinkling eyes look right and straight
Upon this mighty 'Moor' of mickle weight.

---

103 **distinguish** describe as
   '**villager**' either an insult from im-
polite tongues or a kind of compliment from those less sophisticated
than the Schoolmaster thinks he and
his pupils are

105 *rable* Dyce restored Q's spelling, arguing that it emphasized the false
rhyme of the speech. Alternatively,
the Schoolmaster might say 'fabble'
and 'rabble'.

106 **by a figure,** *chorus* Q's spelling,
Choris, indicates the forced rhyme. If
the 'figure' (see 22, above) is anything
but a mannerism, the Schoolmaster is
comparing his amateur actors to the
chorus of Greek tragedy (and perhaps
reminding the audience that the play
is supposed to be set in ancient
Greece).

108 **rectifier of all** the one who makes
everything go right

109 **pedagogus** teacher (Latin)

111 **ferula** a stick used for rapping the
hands of pupils

112 **machine** (stressed on first syllable,
like Latin *machina*) and *frame* may
mean the whole show. Skeat takes
them to refer to 'a temporary wooden
stage' for the performance. Something is probably displayed at this
point, perhaps the device described in
117–19. Or Gerald might mean himself: cf. *Ham* 2.2.124 and Appendix 1
line 55n.

113 **dainty Duke** echoes the alliterative
excesses of 'Pyramus and Thisbe' in
MND (esp. 'O dainty duck' (5.1.281))

114 **Dis to Daedalus** Dis is the god of
the underworld; Daedalus the builder
of the Cretan labyrinth. Used mainly
for their alliteration, both names also
belong to the legend of Theseus (see
List of Roles).

117 '**Moor**' Q's spelling, *Morr*, suggests
further distortion of pronunciation for
the sake of the pun on Morris, which
would be unintelligible without some
visual equivalent. The dash following
both *Morr* and *Is* in Q also indicates
some action at this point. For possible
stagings, see Appendix 5c, p. 359.

'Is' now comes in, which, being glued together,
Makes 'Morris' and the cause that we came hither:
The body of our sport, of no small study.   120
I first appear, though rude and raw and muddy,
To speak before thy noble grace this tenor:
At whose great feet I offer up my penner.
The next the Lord of May and Lady bright;
The Chambermaid and Servingman, by night   125
That seek out silent hanging; then mine Host
And his fat Spouse that welcomes to their cost
The galled traveller and with a beck'ning
Informs the tapster to inflame the reck'ning.
Then the beest-eating Clown and next the Fool,   130
The Bavian with long tail and eke long tool,

118 **'Is'** possibly an archaic spelling of 'ice', used for the sake of the pun
120 **body** Most editors suggest 'main part'; in the opening of *Hymenaei* (pub. 1606) Jonson distinguished the soul of a masque (its device and words) from its body (the visual element and the music (Jonson, 7: p. 209)). **of ... study** the result of much thought and research
122 **this tenor** probably, 'to this general effect'. Q's spelling may indicate another forced rhyme, but Waith's suggestion that it means 'ten-syllable line', by analogy with the contemporary use of 'fourteener', is also attractive (see *TxC*, 632).
123 **penner** *OED* gives three possible meanings: a pen-holder; an author; a decorative bodkin. The first is the most likely, either in a figurative sense ('I offer the lines that I have penned') or literally, if the Schoolmaster offers a gift to Theseus, as usually happened at the end of entertainments for a visiting dignitary: see Appendix 4, p. 354.
124 **The next** i.e., after the Schoolmaster, who *first* appeared (121). At this point he takes over the role of the Pedant, presenter of Beaumont's

second antimasque (lines 229–35; see Appendix 4, p. 354), and describes the pairs of dancers in the morris.
the Lord ... Lady King and Queen of the May (sometimes Robin Hood and Maid Marian)
125–6 **The Chambermaid ... hanging** two servants who make love to each other behind the wall hangings (tapestries) at night. Dyce compares 4.3.54–5 ('O, that ever I did it behind the arras!').
127–9 **that ... reck'ning** The hostess welcomes the traveller by inviting him to have a drink on the house, while making signs to the tapster to include it in the (inflated) bill.
128 **galled** blistered from riding horseback
130 **beest** also called 'beestings': 'the first milk drawn from a mammal, especially a cow, after parturition' (*OED*), considered undrinkable – except by a simple country fellow like the clown (see Kökeritz, *MLN*, 532–5)
131 **tool** penis. The Bavian probably provides low comedy, despite the Schoolmaster's warnings at 35–6, above.

122 tenor] *(tenner)*   130 beest-] *(beast)*

Cum multis aliis that make a dance.
Say, 'Ay,' and all shall presently advance.

THESEUS

Ay, ay, by any means, dear *Domine*.

PIRITHOUS

Produce.   135

SCHOOLMASTER

Intrate filii! Come forth and foot it.
    Music. [The villagers, with the Jailer's Daughter, perform a
                                     morris dance.]

SCHOOLMASTER

Ladies, if we have been merry
And have pleased ye with a derry,
And a derry, and a down,
Say the schoolmaster's no clown;   140
Duke, if we have pleased thee too
And have done as good boys should do,
Give us but a tree or twain
For a Maypole and again,
Ere another year run out,   145
We'll make thee laugh and all this rout.

---

132 *Cum multis aliis* with many others
[whom it would take too long to
name] (Latin), a more elaborate form
of *et cetera*
134 **Domine** possibly *dominie*, as at
2.3.43, but Theseus, parodying
Gerald, may be saying it in Latin
135 **Produce** Lead them forth (a literal
translation of the Latin *produce* – or
perhaps Pirithous also says it in
Latin).
136 *Intrate filii* Come in, boys (Latin).
SD See pp. 125–6 above, for a fuller
discussion of this SD. Though, dra-
matically speaking, the Jailer's
Daughter must be among the performers, it is odd that no lines indicate
whether, as one might expect, her

wildness is ironically mistaken for
highly rehearsed skill.
137–46 The Schoolmaster speaks first to
Hippolyta and Emilia on behalf of the
female dancers, then to Theseus on
behalf of the male dancers.
138–9 **derry ... down** refrain of a song
– here, presumably, meaning the song
itself (see Appendix 6, pp. 360–1, for
the possibility that a song was meant
to be performed here) or the dance
144 **Maypole** As Marcus (2–8) has
shown, by 1613 both the desire for
Maygames and Theseus' willingness
to gratify it had political implications;
in Fletcher's *Women Pleased*, 4.1, a
puritanical countryman objects to the
custom. See Appendix 5a, p. 356.

---

136 SP] *1778; not in Q* 136.1–2 *Music ... dance.] Seward subst.; Musicke Dance. Q (after* produce*)* 136 *marginal SD:* Knocke for / Schoole. Enter / The Dance. *opp. 136–8 Q;* SCHOOLMAS-
TER*(knocks for the dance) Oxf* 137 SP] *1778; not in Q* 138 ye] *Seward;* thee *Q* 141 thee] *F;*
three *Q*

THESEUS

    Take twenty, *Domine*. – How does my sweetheart?

HIPPOLYTA

    Never so pleased, sir.

EMILIA   'Twas an excellent dance

    And, for a preface, I never heard a better.

THESEUS

    Schoolmaster, I thank you. One see 'em all rewarded.   150

PIRITHOUS

    And here's something to paint your pole withall.

                       [Gives Schoolmaster money.]

THESEUS

    Now to our sports again.

SCHOOLMASTER

    May the stag thou hunt'st stand long,

    And thy dogs be swift and strong;

    May they kill him without lets   155

    And the ladies eat his dowsets.

             [Theseus and his party depart.] Horns.

    Come, we are all made, *dii deaeque omnes*. Ye have

    danced rarely, wenches.   *Exeunt.*

[3.6]   *Enter* PALAMON *from the bush.*

PALAMON

    About this hour my cousin gave his faith

---

147 **Domine** See 134n., above.
150 **One** someone
151 Pirithous may carry out the order himself, but Theseus would hardly refer to his closest friend so vaguely. More likely, Pirithous adds his own contribution to the official reward handed to the Schoolmaster by some-one else.
153 **stand** give you a good run for your money
155 **lets** hindrance
156 **dowsets** Though the doucets (test-icles) were considered a delicacy, this

is probably meant as another of the Schoolmaster's ineptitudes.
157 **we ... made** probably a reaction to his examination of the contents of the purse
    dii deaeque omnes 'all ye gods and goddesses', an all-purpose classical oath (Latin)
    SD The dramatists do not show what happens to the Jailer's Daughter after the dance. She may be addressed in the Schoolmaster's last line; she may wander off before or after this point.

148–9 *Q lines* Sir. / preface / better.   151 SD] *Dyce subst.; not in Q*   156 SD] *Seward subst.; Winde Hornes. after* made, *157 Q*   3.6] Scæna 7. *Q*

To visit me again and with him bring
Two swords and two good armours. If he fail
He's neither man nor soldier. When he left me
I did not think a week could have restored   5
My lost strength to me, I was grown so low
And crest-fall'n with my wants. I thank thee, Arcite:
Thou art yet a fair foe; and I feel myself,
With this refreshing, able once again
To outdure danger. To delay it longer   10
Would make the world think, when it comes to
      hearing,
That I lay fatting like a swine to fight
And not a soldier. Therefore this blest morning
Shall be the last and that sword he refuses,
If it but hold, I kill him with: 'tis justice.   15
So love and fortune for me!

> *Enter* ARCITE *with armours and swords.*

                              Oh, good morrow.
ARCITE
Good morrow, noble kinsman.
PALAMON   I have put you
To too much pains, sir.
ARCITE   That too much, fair cousin,
Is but a debt to honour, and my duty.
PALAMON
Would you were so in all, sir; I could wish ye   20

3.6.3 **armours** suits of armour (but see
   n. to 16 SD, below)
10 **outdure** outlast; cf. 1.3.5
   it the combat
11 **when ... hearing** when it is generally known
12–13 **like ... soldier** that I was eating
   out of greed, not in order to fit myself
   for a fight
14 **the last** (of their truce)
   that ... refuses Palamon intends to
   give Arcite the choice of weapons (but
   cf. 45–6, below).

15 **If ... hold** as long as it does not
   break
16 **love ... me!** a battle cry, like 'St
   George for England'
   SD *Armours* often amended to 'suits
   of armour', but, as RP points out, it
   would be impractical for Arcite to
   carry so much and for him and Palamon to arm themselves fully on
   stage. The only pieces specifically
   mentioned are breastplates, casques
   and gauntlets.

As kind a kinsman as you force me find
A beneficial foe, that my embraces
Might thank ye, not my blows.

ARCITE   I shall think either,
Well done, a noble recompense.

PALAMON   Then I shall quit you.

ARCITE
Defy me in these fair terms, and you show   25
More than a mistress to me. No more anger,
As you love anything that's honourable!
We were not bred to talk, man; when we are armed
And both upon our guards, then let our fury,
Like meeting of two tides, fly strongly from us;   30
And then to whom the birthright of this beauty
Truly pertains (without upbraidings, scorns,
Despisings of our persons, and such poutings
Fitter for girls and schoolboys) will be seen
And quickly, yours or mine. Will't please you arm,
     sir?   35
Or, if you feel yourself not fitting yet
And furnished with your old strength, I'll stay,
     cousin,
And every day discourse you into health,
As I am spared. Your person I am friends with
And I could wish I had not said I loved her,   40
Though I had died; but, loving such a lady
And justifying my love, I must not fly from't.

PALAMON
Arcite, thou art so brave an enemy
That no man but thy cousin's fit to kill thee.

21 **force me find** 'You' is the understood object.
23 **either** embraces or blows
24 **quit** repay
31–2 **to whom ... pertains** who was
   born to possess this woman

39 **As ... spared** when I am not in attendance on Theseus
40–2 **And ... from't** Perhaps Arcite
   sees himself as trapped in the chivalric code; cf. 266–9, below.
41 **Though ... died** even if suppressed
   feeling had killed me

32 upbraidings] *(obbraidings)*

I am well and lusty; choose your arms.

ARCITE   Choose you, sir.   45

PALAMON

Wilt thou exceed in all, or dost thou do it

To make me spare thee?

ARCITE   If you think so, cousin,

You are deceived, for, as I am a soldier,

I will not spare you.

PALAMON   That's well said.

ARCITE   You'll find it.

PALAMON

Then, as I am an honest man and love,   50

With all the justice of affection

I'll pay thee soundly. [*Chooses armour.*]

                              This I'll take.

ARCITE [*Takes the other.*]   That's mine then.

I'll arm you first.

PALAMON   Do. [*Arcite begins to arm him.*]

                              Pray thee tell me, cousin,

Where got'st thou this good armour?

ARCITE   'Tis the Duke's

And, to say true, I stole it. Do I pinch you?

PALAMON   No.   55

ARCITE

Is't not too heavy?

PALAMON   I have worn a lighter,

But I shall make it serve.

ARCITE   I'll buckl't close.

---

45 **lusty** fit
46 **exceed** surpass me
49 **You'll find it** You will find it
      true.
50 Palamon is topping Arcite's 'as I am a
      soldier'.
51 'with justice and love on my side'; the
      phrase modifies both the preceding
      and following words.

52 **pay thee soundly** pay back the blows
      you have just promised me
55 **Do ... you?** Holmes (166) suggests
      that Arcite's reference to robbing
      Theseus provokes a snort from Pala-
      mon that he misunderstands.
57 **close** tightly – the best way to deal
      with body-armour that is too heavy
      (Holmes, 164)

52 SD *Chooses armour*] *Weber subst.; not in Q   Takes the other*] *Leech; not in Q*   53 SD] *Dyce subst.;
not in Q*

PALAMON

By any means.

ARCITE   You care not for a grand guard?

PALAMON

No, no, we'll use no horses; I perceive
You would fain be at that fight.

ARCITE   I am indifferent.   60

PALAMON

Faith, so am I. Good cousin, thrust the buckle
Through far enough.

ARCITE   I warrant you.

PALAMON   My casque now.

ARCITE

Will you fight bare-armed?

PALAMON   We shall be the nimbler.

ARCITE

But use your gauntlets, though. Those are o'th' least;
Prithee take mine, good cousin.

PALAMON   Thank you, Arcite.   65

How do I look? Am I fall'n much away?

ARCITE

Faith, very little; love has used you kindly.

PALAMON

I'll warrant thee, I'll strike home.

ARCITE   Do and spare not.

---

58 **care not for** don't want
    grand guard a large, heavy piece of armour, 'used only for fights on horseback in the tiltyard' (Holmes, 165). It is unlikely that Arcite could have carried this with the rest of the arms (unless, as Holmes suggests, he used a wheelbarrow), so this question may be hypothetical or jocular.

60 **am indifferent** have no preference

62 **I warrant you** Don't worry, I will.
    casque helmet

63 **Will . . . bare-armed?** One would normally put on the arm-pieces

before the casque, so Arcite now realizes that Palamon is not going to use them. Palamon's decision is obviously designed to shorten an already complicated series of actions. Holmes (166) points out that correct fit matters more with arm- and leg-pieces than with body-armour (adjustable with straps) and that these thus pose greater problems for actors working with all-purpose playhouse gear.

64 **o'th' least** too small. Perhaps another indication that Palamon is the larger of the two (cf. 2.1.52–3 and 5.2.94).

66 **fall'n much away** much thinner

I'll give you cause, sweet cousin.

PALAMON   Now to you, sir.

[Begins to arm Arcite.]

Methinks this armour's very like that, Arcite,   70
Thou wor'st that day the three kings fell, but lighter.

ARCITE

That was a very good one. And that day,
I well remember, you outdid me, cousin;
I never saw such valour. When you charged
Upon the left wing of the enemy,   75
I spurred hard to come up and under me
I had a right good horse.

PALAMON   You had indeed:
A bright bay, I remember.

ARCITE   Yes, but all
Was vainly laboured in me; you outwent me,
Nor could my wishes reach you. Yet a little   80
I did by imitation.

PALAMON   More by virtue.
You are modest, cousin.

ARCITE   When I saw you charge first,
Methought I heard a dreadful clap of thunder
Break from the troop.

PALAMON   But still before that flew
The lightning of your valour. – Stay a little: 85
Is not this piece too strait?

ARCITE   No, no, 'tis well.

PALAMON

I would have nothing hurt thee but my sword:
A bruise would be dishonour.

ARCITE   Now I am perfect.

---

71 **that day ... fell** one of the rare
links between 1.1 and the rest of the
play

78 **bright bay** not poetic; a standard
name for one of the various red–
browns called *bay* (Topsell, 295)

80 **Nor ... you** I longed to reach you
literally and metaphorically (i.e.,
equal you) but could not.

81 **virtue** courage

86 **strait** tight

88 **perfect** complete – fully armed

69 SD] *Dyce subst.; not in Q*   86 strait] *(streight)*

PALAMON

    Stand off then.

ARCITE   Take my sword; I hold it better.

PALAMON

    I thank ye, no; keep it, your life lies on it.   90
    Here's one: if it but hold, I ask no more
    For all my hopes. My cause and honour guard me!

ARCITE

    And me my love!
            They bow several ways, then advance and stand.
            Is there aught else to say?

PALAMON

    This only, and no more. Thou art mine aunt's son
    And that blood we desire to shed is mutual,   95
    In me thine and in thee mine; my sword
    Is in my hand and if thou killest me
    The gods and I forgive thee. If there be
    A place prepared for those that sleep in honour,
    I wish his weary soul that falls may win it.   100
    Fight bravely, cousin; give me thy noble hand.

ARCITE

    Here, Palamon. This hand shall never more
    Come near thee with such friendship.

PALAMON   I commend thee.

---

89 **Stand off** take up your fighting pos-
    ition (see 93 SD)
    hold consider
90 ***I . . . no** Q's punctuation is followed
    by most recent editors, but Seward's
    alteration seems truer to the scene as I
    understand it: both men are deter-
    mined to display equal magnanimity.
    It is possible, however, to envisage an
    interpretation based on the Q punctu-
    ation: Palamon, initially willing to
    take the offered advantage, changes
    his mind in order to avoid giving
    Arcite the moral high-ground.
92–3 **My cause . . . love** The sub-
    junctive verb 'may' is understood in

both speeches. They contrast with
48–50, which associate Palamon and
Arcite with Venus and Mars
respectively.
93 SD An asterisk after 'love' refers to
this direction in the margin, which
seems authorial. The formal bows
suggest that (as Theseus will say in
134, below) the men are behaving precisely as if in a formal trial by combat,
even though no spectators are present.
Is . . . to say? Perhaps Arcite is determined to follow all the formalities;
perhaps (cf. the abrupt 89, above) he
is reluctant to begin the fight.
103 **I commend thee** 'to God' (Oxf[1])

90 I thank ye, no;] *Seward;* I thank ye: No, *Q*   93 SD] *Q lines* se-/ wayes: / advance / stand. *(in
margin opp. 93–6, marked in text by asterisk)*   97 killest] *(killst)*

ARCITE

  If·I fall, curse me, and say I was a coward,

  For none but such dare die in these just trials.   105

  Once more farewell, my cousin.

PALAMON   Farewell, Arcite.

*   They fight. Horns within. They stand.*

ARCITE

  Lo, cousin, lo, our folly has undone us!

PALAMON   Why?

ARCITE

  This is the Duke, a-hunting as I told you;

  If we be found, we are wretched. Oh, retire,

  For honour's sake and safety, presently   110

  Into your bush again. Sir, we shall find

  Too many hours to die in! Gentle cousin,

  If you be seen you perish instantly

  For breaking prison and I, if you reveal me,

  For my contempt. Then all the world will scorn us   115

  And say we had a noble difference,

  But base disposers of it.

PALAMON   No, no, cousin:

  I will no more be hidden, nor put off

  This great adventure to a second trial;

  I know your cunning and I know your cause.   120

  He that faints now, shame take him! Put thyself

104–5 Contradicting Palamon, Arcite replies that he will deserve curses, not commendation, if he dies in a solemn trial by combat.

106 SD Palamon may have the advantage in the fight at the point where it is broken off (see 120 and 123, below, and the taunting 'weak cousin', 125). However, in *KT*, they are equally matched.

108 **as . . . you** Arcite has not told him this before, though he has frequently referred to Theseus.

110 **presently** at once. As Arcite repeats his urging several times, Palamon may

actively resist the attempt to force him back into hiding.

115 **contempt** of his decree of banishment

116–17 **a noble . . . of it** our quarrel was noble, but we handled it basely

119 **adventure** venture

120 'I know why you are making these clever attempts to put off this fight': 'because I am the better fighter'? or, as Bawcutt suggests, 'because you have the weaker side of the quarrel'?

121 **faints** slackens in the fight

121–2 **Put . . . guard** stand on guard at once

110 safety] *Seward;* safely *Q*

Upon thy present guard –

ARCITE   You are not mad?

PALAMON

  Or I will make the advantage of this hour
  Mine own, and what to come shall threaten me
  I fear less than my fortune. Know, weak cousin,   125
  I love Emilia and in that I'll bury
  Thee and all crosses else.

ARCITE   Then come what can come.

  Thou shalt know, Palamon, I dare as well
  Die as discourse or sleep. Only this fears me:
  The law will have the honour of our ends.   130
  Have at thy life!

PALAMON   Look to thine own well, Arcite.

                               They fight again.

Horns. Enter THESEUS, HIPPOLYTA, EMILIA, PIRITHOUS *and
train.*

THESEUS

  What ignorant and mad malicious traitors
  Are you, that 'gainst the tenor of my laws
  Are making battle, thus like knights appointed,

123–5 **Or ... fortune** Palamon
threatens to kill Arcite even if the
latter refuses to fight, because future
punishment (in this life or another)
worries him less than losing a fight on
which so much depends.
126 **bury** lose forever
127 **crosses** obstacles
  come ... come echoes his words at
2.3.18
129 **fears** frightens
130 Neither of us will have the honour of
killing, or being killed by, the other.
131 SD Montgomery inserts a direction
for Theseus to separate the two men,
on the grounds that he later says 'I
sundered you' (5.4.100). Less dramat-

ically, his guards might halt the fight;
they probably watch over Palamon
and Arcite until 304, below.
133 **tenor** purpose, meaning
134 **appointed** armed. What angers
Theseus is not simply that the two
men are fighting but that, by wearing
armour, they show that they are engaging in a trial by combat without
any of the proper formalities (which
would have included an attempt to
reconcile their quarrel). Skeat compares *KT*: 'But telleth me what
myster men ye been, / That been so
hardy for to fighten heere / With-
outen juge or oother officere, / As it
were in a lystes roially' (1710–13).

122 guard –] *Proudfoot*; guard. *Q*

Without my leave and officers of arms?   135
By Castor, both shall die!
PALAMON   Hold thy word, Theseus.
We are certainly both traitors, both despisers
Of thee and of thy goodness. I am Palamon
That cannot love thee, he that broke thy prison –
Think well what that deserves – and this is Arcite: 140
A bolder traitor never trod thy ground;
A falser ne'er seemed friend. This is the man
Was begged and banished; this is he contemns thee
And what thou dar'st do and in this disguise
Against thine own edict follows thy sister,   145
That fortunate bright star, the fair Emilia –
Whose servant, if there be a right in seeing
And first bequeathing of the soul to, justly
I am – and, which is more, dares think her his.
This treachery, like a most trusty lover,   150
I called him now to answer. If thou be'st
As thou art spoken, great and virtuous,
The true decider of all injuries,
Say, 'Fight again' and thou shalt see me, Theseus,
Do such a justice thou thyself wilt envy.   155
Then take my life; I'll woo thee to't.
PIRITHOUS   O heaven,

---

136 **By Castor** In *KT* Theseus swears by
Mars. 'By Castor', in Roman comedy,
is a mild oath, and some commentators (as Proudfoot points out) claim
that only women used it. However, it
is clear from later references in 157
and 228, below, and in 4.1.11, that in
this context it is a serious
commitment.
Hold keep
137–8 **despisers / Of** in (legal) contempt of
142–3 **the man . . . begged** the man for
whom freedom was begged (by
Pirithous)

145 **edict** (of banishment); stressed on
last syllable
follows both pursues and serves (in
his official capacity)
147 **servant** in the courtly love tradition:
Palamon contrasts his *justly* deserved
role of servant with Arcite's usurped
one
147–8 **if . . . soul to** expanding 'I saw her
first' (2.2.160)
151 **to answer** in combat
152 **spoken** said to be
156 **Then** after I have killed Arcite
(emphatic)

145 thine own] *Dyce;* this owne *Q;* this known *1711*

What more than man is this!

THESEUS   I have sworn.

ARCITE   We seek not
    Thy breath of mercy, Theseus; 'tis to me
    A thing as soon to die as thee to say it
    And no more moved. Where this man calls me
        traitor,   160
    Let me say thus much: if in love be treason,
    In service of so excellent a beauty,
    As I love most, and in that faith will perish,
    As I have brought my life here to confirm it,
    As I have served her truest, worthiest,   165
    As I dare kill this cousin that denies it,
    So let me be most traitor and ye please me.
    For scorning thy edict, Duke: ask that lady
    Why she is fair, and why her eyes command me
    Stay here to love her and, if she say 'traitor',   170
    I am a villain fit to lie unburied.

PALAMON
    Thou shalt have pity of us both, O Theseus,
    If unto neither thou show mercy. Stop,
    As thou art just, thy noble ear against us;
    As thou art valiant – for thy cousin's soul,   175
    Whose twelve strong labours crown his memory –
    Let's die together, at one instant, Duke.
    Only a little let him fall before me,
    That I may tell my soul, he shall not have her.

THESEUS
    I grant your wish, for, to say true, your cousin   180

158–60 'tis ... moved The syntax is
  confused, but the meaning is clear:
  Arcite is ready to die as quickly, and
  with as little emotion, as Theseus can
  order his death. Skeat notes that *thee*
  is a dative meaning 'for thee'.
160 Where whereas
168 For scorning 'as for his charge that
  I scorned'; Arcite is dealing with the
  accusations in sequence. See Waith
  (86–98) for the forensic background

to the 'Beaumont and Fletcher'
  plays.
170 she The 1778 reading, 'If *she* say
  traitor', conforms to the sense of the
  passage and the natural stress of the
  line.
175 thy cousin's Hercules'. That Palamon calls him Theseus' *cousin* shows
  his eagerness to make the relationship
  of Theseus and Hercules a parallel to
  that of himself and his cousin.

Has ten times more offended, for I gave him
More mercy than you found, sir, your offences
Being no more than his. None here speak for 'em,
For, ere the sun set, both shall sleep for ever.

HIPPOLYTA

Alas the pity! Now or never, sister,   185
Speak not to be denied. That face of yours
Will bear the curses else of after ages
For these lost cousins.

EMILIA   In my face, dear sister,
I find no anger to 'em, nor no ruin;
The misadventure of their own eyes kill 'em.   190
Yet that I will be woman and have pity,
My knees shall grow to th' ground but I'll get mercy.
Help me, dear sister; in a deed so virtuous,
The powers of all women will be with us.   [*Kneels.*]
Most royal brother –

HIPPOLYTA [*Kneels.*]   Sir, by our tie of marriage –   195

EMILIA

By your own spotless honour –

HIPPOLYTA   By that faith,
That fair hand and that honest heart you gave me –

EMILIA

By that you would have pity in another,

---

183 **None here speak** an imperative
186 **not ... denied** too persuasively to
be withstood
190 **kill 'em** This is a statement, not a
wish, though the verb has been influenced by the plural 'eyes'; Davenant's
adaptation shows that he so understood it: 'My Face is guiltless of their
ruine; but / The Misadventure of
their own Eyes kills e'm' (Act 4, p.
44). To avoid giving the impression
that Emilia was *willing* their deaths
(all her subsequent lines show the
contrary), Seward altered *kill* to
'kills'.
191 **Yet that** to show that (Bawcutt)

192 **but** unless
193–4 **Help me ... with us** Q's punctuation links 'in such a virtuous deed'
both with the previous words and
with those that follow the phrase.
195–211 **Most ... princes** The antiph-
onal pleading (as Waith, Oxf[1], points
out) is characteristic of Fletcher's
style, but also parallels that of the
three queens in the Shakespearean
1.1. Each speaker overlaps with the
previous one; hence the dashes with
which most editors since 1778 have
punctuated the passage.
198 'by whatever that you would invoke
to arouse pity in someone else' (*Riv*)

---

190 kill 'em] *Q;* kills 'em *Seward*   194 SD] *Weber (after* brother*); not in Q*   195 SD] *Weber; not in Q*

By your own virtues infinite –
HIPPOLYTA   By valour,
By all the chaste nights I have ever pleased you –   200
THESEUS
These are strange conjurings.
PIRITHOUS   Nay, then, I'll in too. [*Kneels.*]
By all our friendship, sir, by all our dangers,
By all you love most: wars, and this sweet lady –
EMILIA
By that you would have trembled to deny
A blushing maid –
HIPPOLYTA   By your own eyes, by strength,   205
In which you swore I went beyond all women,
Almost all men, and yet I yielded, Theseus –
PIRITHOUS
To crown all this, by your most noble soul,
Which cannot want due mercy, I beg first –
HIPPOLYTA
Next hear my prayers –
EMILIA   Last, let me entreat, sir –   210
PIRITHOUS
For mercy!
HIPPOLYTA   Mercy!
EMILIA   Mercy on these princes!
THESEUS
Ye make my faith reel. Say I felt
Compassion to 'em both, how would you place it?
                    [*Emilia, Hippolyta and Pirithous rise.*]

200 **chaste nights** nights of chaste (i.e., married) love-making
204–5 **By . . . maid** by your sacred duty as a knight to help maidens in distress. Also, as Proudfoot notes, Theseus has already made a promise to Emilia (230–2, below).
209 **want** be lacking in; Skeat suggests a reminiscence of 'Chaucer's favourite line – "For pite ̧ renneth sone in gentil herte".'
212 **Ye . . . reel** You are shaking my constancy to my oath. RA compares 1.2.65–6 and 5.4.20–1.
213 SD Some editors place this direction (not present in Q) at 269. The decision lies with the director.

201–2 Nay . . . Dangers] *one line Q* 201 SD] *Dyce subst.; not in Q* 213 SD] *Weber; not in Q*

EMILIA
    Upon their lives. But with their banishments.
THESEUS
    You are a right woman, sister: you have pity   215
    But want the understanding where to use it.
    If you desire their lives, invent a way
    Safer than banishment. Can these two live
    And have the agony of love about 'em
    And not kill one another? Every day   220
    They'd fight about you; hourly bring your honour
    In public question with their swords. Be wise then
    And here forget 'em; it concerns your credit
    And my oath equally. I have said they die.
    Better they fall by th' law than one another.   225
    Bow not my honour.
EMILIA   Oh, my noble brother,
    That oath was rashly made and in your anger.
    Your reason will not hold it; if such vows
    Stand for express will, all the world must perish
    Besides, I have another oath 'gainst yours,   230
    Of more authority, I am sure more love,
    Not made in passion neither but good heed.
THESEUS
    What is it, sister?
PIRITHOUS   Urge it home, brave lady.
EMILIA
    That you would ne'er deny me anything

---

215 **right** typical (in a derogatory sense)
222 **question** quarrel. Probably in a double meaning: they would quarrel publicly over her, and thereby bring her honour into question.
223 **credit** reputation
226 **Bow ... honour** Do not make me bend my oath (perhaps by contrast with *stand* in 229 and *stands* in 289) and thereby lose my honour.
227–8 **That ... hold it** 'With clear overtones of the homily "Against Swearing and Perjury"' (Shaheen) – e.g.,

'He that taketh an oath, must doe it with iudgement, not rashly and vnadvisedly'; cf. 4.1.10–11, below.
228 **hold** uphold
229 **Stand ... will** be taken as final decisions
    all ... perish perhaps a necessarily oblique allusion to biblical passages where God is depicted changing his intention of destroying a whole people, as in Genesis, 19.18–21 and Jonah, 3.10
232 **passion** anger
    good heed with full consideration

Fit for my modest suit and your free granting.   235
I tie you to your word now; if ye fail in't,
Think how you maim your honour. Tell me not
(For now I am set a-begging, sir, I am deaf
To all but your compassion) how their lives
Might breed the ruin of my name. Opinion!   240
Shall anything that loves me perish for me?
That were a cruel wisdom. Do men prune
The straight young boughs that blush with thousand
      blossoms,
Because they may be rotten? Oh, Duke Theseus,
The goodly mothers that have groaned for these   245
And all the longing maids that ever loved,
If your vow stand, shall curse me and my beauty
And in their funeral songs for these two cousins
Despise my cruelty and cry woe worth me,
Till I am nothing but the scorn of women.   250
For heaven's sake, save their lives and banish 'em.

THESEUS
On what conditions?

EMILIA   Swear 'em never more

236 **fail** cf. 272 below

237 ***Tell me not** The difficult state of
the text at this point, and the apparent
incompleteness of the line, suggests
that something may have dropped
out. Emilia clearly wants to refute
Theseus' view that the continuing
existence of two men so openly in love
with her might damage her reputation; she also says that she is deaf to
anything else he can say, so some such
interpolation seems justified.

240 ***A** difficult line, as punctuated in Q.
'Opinion' may refer to Emilia's reputation or to the sort of general gossip
that she claims to disregard.

242 **were** would be

242–4 **Do . . . rotten** Emilia stresses *may*
(and perhaps also *might* at 240). Cf.
Brutus in *JC*, deciding to assassinate
Caesar in case he 'might' later become
dangerous (2.1.31). By contrast, she
uses the future tense at 247 when she
envisages the consequences of their
deaths for her reputation.

245 **groaned** in childbirth

246 **the longing maids** Maidens are
frequently imagined, like a chorus, re-
acting to events of the play (cf. 2.2.37
and 2.6.13–17).

249 **woe worth me** woe become of me;
Skeat explains that 'worth' is cognate
with the German *werden* (to become).

252 **Swear 'em** make them swear

236 fail] *Seward;* fall *Q*   237 Tell me not] *this edn; not in Q*   240 name. Opinion!] *this edn;*
name; Opinion, *Q;* name – Opinion; *Seward;* name, opinion! *1778;* name's opinion *(Theo-*
bald)   242 prune] *(proyne)*

To make me their contention, or to know me,
To tread upon thy dukedom, and to be,
Wherever they shall travel, ever strangers　　255
To one another.

PALAMON　　　　　　　　I'll be cut a-pieces
Before I take this oath! Forget I love her?
O, all ye gods, despise me then! Thy banishment
I not mislike, so we may fairly carry
Our swords and cause along; else, never trifle,　　260
But take our lives, Duke; I must love and will
And, for that love, must and dare kill this cousin
On any piece the earth has.

THESEUS　　　　　　　　　　Will you, Arcite,
Take these conditions?

PALAMON　　　　　　　　　He's a villain then.

PIRITHOUS
These are men!　　265

ARCITE
No, never, Duke. 'Tis worse to me than begging
To take my life so basely. Though I think
I never shall enjoy her, yet I'll preserve
The honour of affection and die for her,
Make death a devil.　　270

THESEUS
What may be done? For now I feel compassion.

---

253 **their contention** the reason for
their quarrel
know me show that they know
me
263 **piece** of ground
265 **These are men!** The tone of this
line and its likely effect in performance are uncertain, though admiration
is perhaps more consistent than irony
with Pirithous' behaviour in 3.5 and
4.2. Cf. 'This is a man, a woman'
(Nathan Field, *The Triumph of
Honour*, Bowers, 8: 1.181, from *Four*

Plays in One, a collaboration with
Fletcher).
267–8 **Though . . . her** possibly the same
kind of awareness as in 40–2, above.
Or he may recognize, as Palamon does
not, that Emilia, while begging their
lives, has shown no reluctance to see
them banished forever.
269 **The honour of affection** the
honour of having loved her, or, perhaps, the honour due to love
270 however fearful a death you make for
me

255–6 strangers / To one another] *Seward; one line Q*

PIRITHOUS
    Let it not fall again, sir.
THESEUS   Say, Emilia,
    If one of them were dead, as one must, are you
    Content to take the other as your husband?
    They cannot both enjoy you. They are princes   275
    As goodly as your own eyes and as noble
    As ever fame yet spoke of. Look upon 'em
    And, if you can love, end this difference;
    I give consent. Are you content too, princes?
PALAMON and ARCITE
    With all our hearts.
THESEUS   He that she refuses   280
    Must die then.
PALAMON and ARCITE
                        Any death thou canst invent, Duke.

PALAMON
    If I fall from that mouth, I fall with favour
    And lovers yet unborn shall bless my ashes.
ARCITE
    If she refuse me, yet my grave will wed me
    And soldiers sing my epitaph.
THESEUS [*to Emilia*]   Make choice, then.   285
EMILIA
    I cannot, sir; they are both too excellent;

272 **fall** sometimes emended to 'fail',
    which is what it means (cf. 236,
    above), but the older form is consist-
    ent with the scene's preoccupation
    with falling honourably
273 **must** must be
276 **goodly . . . eyes** Cf. 'to love as one's
    own eye' (Dent, E249.1).
278 **can** The metre seems to require a
    stress on this word, underlining The-
    seus' sarcastic tone towards Emilia in
    this scene.
    difference dispute
282–5 **If . . . epitaph** the first clear indi-
    cation that the two men are followers
    of Venus and Mars respectively

282 **from that mouth** as the result of
    words spoken by her
286–7 *I . . . men* Q's lack of punctu-
    ation at the end of 284 leaves it un-
    certain whether Emilia is saying that
    both men are too good for her (see
    5.3.84–9), or that she will not let
    either of them suffer on her account
    (see 4.2.3–4). In Davenant's adapta-
    tion she states in a soliloquy that her
    refusal to choose results from her un-
    willingness to condemn either man.
    Here, by contrast, the responsibility
    for explaining Emilia's motives rests
    with the performer.

272 fall] *Q;* fail *Skeat*   274 the other] *Seward;* th'other *Q*

257

For me, a hair shall never fall of these men.
HIPPOLYTA
What will become of 'em?
THESEUS   Thus I ordain it
And by mine honour, once again, it stands,
Or both shall die. You shall both to your country   290
And each, within this month, accompanied
With three fair knights, appear again in this place,
In which I'll plant a pyramid; and whether,
Before us that are here, can force his cousin,
By fair and knightly strength, to touch the pillar,   295
He shall enjoy her; th'other lose his head,
And all his friends. Nor shall he grudge to fall,
Nor think he dies with interest in this lady.
Will this content ye?
PALAMON   Yes. There, cousin Arcite,
                         [Offers his hand.]

287 **a hair ... men** Shaheen cites Acts, 27.34: 'There shall not an hair fall from the head of any of you.'

289 **once ... stands** Like his previous oath, just modified, this one is to be immutable (see *stand* in 229).

291–2 **within ... place** The idea that the battle should take place on the same spot as the interrupted duel derives from *KT*, but Chaucer's Theseus proclaims a tournament with a hundred men on each side and allows fifty weeks for its preparation.

293 **plant** fix in the ground
pyramid This word was interchangeable with 'obelisk', and Theseus must mean the latter, since at 294 he refers to it as a pillar. In *KT* the winner is to be the one who either kills his opponent or drives him out of the lists, but Skeat points out that 'Chaucer mentions two stakes, one at each side of the lists.'
whether whichever of the two men (also used in this sense in *KT*, 1856)

297 **And ... friends** i.e., his three

knights will also be beheaded. The awkward syntax lends itself to potentially comic misunderstanding. All commentators note the contrast with *KT*, where Theseus takes precautions that there shall be as few deaths as possible. Seward suggested that 'our authors altered it to render the catastrophe more interesting', comparing Fletcher and Massinger's *The Little French Lawyer* (c. 1621), where the seconds also take part in a duel. Both Sidney's *Arcadia* and Spenser's *Faerie Queene* depict a number of combats with three or four knights on a side, all of whom are expected to risk their lives in the cause. The prototype may be the fight between the two sets of triplets, the Horatii and the Curiatii, described in Livy, 1.24.

297–8 **Nor ... lady** He shall not publicly complain or continue to urge his claim to Emilia. This sounds like the precautions sometimes taken to ensure that speeches from the scaffold did not become inflammatory.

299 SD] *this edn; not in Q*

I am friends again, till that hour.

ARCITE   I embrace ye.   300

THESEUS

Are you content, sister?

EMILIA   Yes, I must, sir,

Else both miscarry.

THESEUS   Come, shake hands again, then,

And take heed, as you are gentlemen, this quarrel

Sleep till the hour prefixed, and hold your course.

                                [Palamon and Arcite shake hands.]

PALAMON

· We dare not fail thee, Theseus.

THESEUS   Come, I'll give ye   305

Now usage like to princes and to friends.

When ye return, who wins, I'll settle here;

Who loses, yet I'll weep upon his bier.   *Exeunt.*

[4.1]   *Enter* Jailer *and* First Friend.

JAILER

Heard you no more? Was nothing said of me

Concerning the escape of Palamon?

Good sir, remember!

1 FRIEND   Nothing that I heard,

---

300 **I embrace ye** Perhaps (despite Theseus' 'shake hands again') Arcite does more than simply take the hand that Palamon offers.

301 **I must** (be content); cf. 273, above

302 **miscarry** die

304 **hold your course** keep your promise (the handclasp is to confirm the oath); perhaps a metaphor from sailing, contrasted with 'tack about' (Abrams, 'Bourgeois', 157).

307 **settle here** enable him to live, as Emilia's husband, in Athens instead of Thebes. Though the play does not raise the question of succession, the winner would presumably be Theseus' heir until Hippolyta had a child. Proudfoot suggests that *here* means 'in my heart'.

4.1 Lawrence (48) notes that the two heroes are absent for the whole of Act 4 – a structural feature which A. C. Bradley (57) finds typical of Shakespeare tragedies.

1 *****Heard** Q's *Heare* is possible, but both characters speak in the past tense throughout. The Jailer has evidently just learned of Palamon's recapture.

304 SD] *this edn; not in Q*   4.1] *Actus Quartus.* / Scæna I. *Q*   0.1 First] *this edn; his Q*   1 Heard] *Bawcutt;* heare *Q*

For I came home before the business
Was fully ended. Yet I might perceive,   5
Ere I departed, a great likelihood
Of both their pardons. For Hippolyta
And fair-eyed Emily, upon their knees,
Begged with such handsome pity that the Duke
Methought stood staggering whether he should
          follow   10
His rash oath or the sweet compassion
Of those two ladies; and, to second them,
That truly noble Prince Pirithous,
Half his own heart, set in too, that I hope
All shall be well. Neither heard I one question   15
Of your name or his 'scape.

Enter Second Friend.

JAILER   Pray heaven it hold so.
2 FRIEND
Be of good comfort, man; I bring you news,
Good news!
JAILER   They are welcome.
2 FRIEND   Palamon has cleared you,
And got your pardon, and discovered how
And by whose means he 'scaped – which was your
          daughter's,·   20

4 **I came home** Thus, this character
(who has no identity in 3.6 except as a
member of Theseus' train) ought
logically to have made his exit somewhere around 3.6.201–13. But the inconsistency is perceived only in retro-
spect. RP compares the successive en-
tries of messengers in *WT* 5.2. See
also p. 14 above.
  business (three syllables)
7 **their** Palamon and Arcite's
10 **staggering** in doubt (cf. 'Ye make my
faith reel' (3.6.212))
14 **Half . . . heart** It may be too literal to

say that the other half of Theseus'
heart is Hippolyta's; the phrase
simply expresses intensity of affection. Cf. 'Half the heart of Caesar,
worthy Maecenas!' (*AC* 2.2.172).
  set in put in his word (Skeat); cf.
Pirithous' 'Nay, then, I'll in too'
(3.6.201)
  that so that
16 **hold** continue
18 **They** the news. The word was plural
as well as singular well into the nineteenth century.
19 **discovered** revealed

19–20 discovered how / And] *Seward;* discoverd / How *Q*   20 'scaped] *F subst.;* escapt *Q*

Whose pardon is procured too; and the prisoner,
Not to be held ungrateful to her goodness,
Has given a sum of money to her marriage:
A large one, I'll assure you.

JAILER   You're a good man
And ever bring good news.

1 FRIEND   How was it ended?   25

2 FRIEND
Why, as it should be. They that never begged
But they prevailed had their suits fairly granted:
The prisoners have their lives.

1 FRIEND   I knew 'twould be so.

2 FRIEND
But there be new conditions, which you'll hear of
At better time.

JAILER   I hope they are good.

2 FRIEND   They are honourable;   30
How good they'll prove, I know not.

Enter Wooer.

1 FRIEND   'Twill be known.

WOOER [*to Jailer*]
Alas, sir, where's your daughter?

JAILER   Why do you ask?

WOOER
Oh, sir, when did you see her?

2 FRIEND   How he looks!

21 **the prisoner** Palamon
23 **a sum of money** Proudfoot com-
    pares Palamon's later gift (5.4.32) and
    the Jailer's remarks at 2.1.1–5.
    to towards, for
24–5 **You're . . . news** probably alluding
    to the proverb, 'From good men
    comes goodness' (Tilley, M518)
27 **But they prevailed** without getting
    what they asked for
    fairly fully

30 **I hope . . . honourable** The Friend's
    distinction between *good* and *honour-
    able* may or may not be a cautious cri-
    tique of the chivalric solution.
31 **'Twill be known** (how good the con-
    ditions are)
33 **How he looks!** a comment on the
    Wooer's haste and agitation (see 51,
    below); *looks* may also refer to the in-
    tensity of his attention to the Jailer's
    reply

24 You're] *this edn.;* (Ye are) *Q*

261

JAILER

    This morning.

WOOER   Was she well? Was she in health? Sir,

    When did she sleep?

1 FRIEND   These are strange questions.   35

JAILER

    I do not think she was very well, for now

    You make me mind her: but this very day

    I asked her questions, and she answered me

    So far from what she was, so childishly,

    So sillily, as if she were a fool,   40

    An innocent, and I was very angry.

    But what of her, sir?

WOOER   Nothing but my pity.

    But you must know it, and as good by me

    As by another that less loves her.

JAILER

    Well, sir?

1 FRIEND   Not right?

2 FRIEND   Not well?

WOOER   No sir, not well: 45

---

35 **questions** (three syllables, as often with words ending in 'ion')

37 **mind her** call her to mind
but only
this very day Unless the Daughter returned home after the morris dance, the Jailer must be talking about her behaviour before she fled in search of Palamon – which would mean that all the events of Act 3 took place in a single day and night. But perhaps there is no point in trying to reconcile the time-scheme of the play (see 4.3.1n.).

39 **what she was** her usual behaviour (Riv)

41 **An innocent** a guileless person, or child. Cyril Tourneur's *The Atheist's Tragedy* (pub. 1611–12) makes a dis-

tinction between fools and 'those fools that we term innocents' (5.1.28).

42 **Nothing . . . pity** 'I want only to express my pity.' Bawcutt suggests that he is disclaiming any intention of mockery (the Jailer may have reacted with suspicion).

43 **by** from

45 **right** in her right mind

45–6 In Q, the Wooer's 'No sir, not well' is placed on the same line as the Second Friend's, and preceded by a long dash, which suggests that it may have been written in the margin and misplaced by the compositor – the more so, as the speech prefix is repeated before his next line (see t.n.) Some editors have suggested realignment (see *TxC*, p. 632).

34–5 ¹Was . . . sleep?] *1778; one line Q*   42–3 Nothing . . . me] *Seward; one line Q*   45–6] *Q (2 Fr.* Not well? – *Wooer,* No Sir not well, / *Woo.* Tis too true,*) Q*

'Tis too true: she is mad.

1 FRIEND   It cannot be!

WOOER

Believe, you'll find it so.

JAILER   I half suspected

What you have told me. The gods comfort her!

Either this was her love to Palamon,

Or fear of my miscarrying on his 'scape,   50

Or both.

WOOER   'Tis likely.

JAILER   But why all this haste, sir?

WOOER

I'll tell you quickly. As I late was angling

In the great lake that lies behind the palace,

From the far shore, thick set with reeds and sedges,

As patiently I was attending sport,   55

I heard a voice, a shrill one, and attentive

I gave my ear, when I might well perceive

'Twas one that sung and, by the smallness of it,

A boy or woman. I then left my angle

To his own skill, came near, but yet perceived not   60

Who made the sound, the rushes and the reeds

---

47 **Believe** See 2.5.19n.
48 ***What ... me** The added *have* seems needed both logically and metrically.
49 **her ... Palamon** We are not told how the Jailer and Wooer have come to know of this love, but even in 2.1 it was becoming obvious and they now know that she had freed Palamon.
50 **miscarrying on** being punished for
52–153 The remainder of the scene is often compared to the scenes of Ophelia's madness (*Ham* 4.5.21–73 and 155–201) and Gertrude's description of her death (4.7.166–83). The unexpected lyricism of the Wooer's narrative associates it with a traditional genre, the complaint of the forsaken lover: it bears some resemblance to *A Lover's Complaint* (probably by Shakespeare), where an unhappy maiden, also sitting by a river, is ob-

served by a sympathetic male listener (see Underwood, passim, and Kerrigan, 394), but in *TNK* it gains unusual poignancy from the fact that the narrator is in love with the woman whose condition he describes.
52 **late** probably in the sense of 'late in the day' or at night (see 37n., above), but the other meaning, 'recently', 'just now', is also possible
   angling fishing
55 **attending sport** waiting for a fish to bite
58 **smallness** high pitch. Skeat quotes *TN*: 'Thy small pipe / Is as the maiden's organ, shrill and sound' (1.4.32–3); both examples, of course, also allude to the boy-actor convention.
59 **angle** rod and line
60 **To ... skill** to fish by itself (tied or stuck into the ground)

48 have told] *Dyce;* told *Q*

Had so encompassed it. I laid me down
And listened to the words she sung, for then,
Through a small glade cut by the fishermen,
I saw it was your daughter.

JAILER   Pray go on, sir.   65

WOOER

She sung much, but no sense; only I heard her
Repeat this often: 'Palamon is gone,
Is gone to th' wood to gather mulberries;
I'll find him out tomorrow.'

1 FRIEND   Pretty soul!

WOOER

'His shackles will betray him, he'll be taken;   70
And what shall I do then? I'll bring a bevy,
A hundred black-eyed maids that love as I do,
With chaplets on their heads of daffadillies,
With cherry-lips and cheeks of damask roses,
And all we'll dance an antic 'fore the Duke   75
And beg his pardon.' Then she talked of you, sir:
That you must lose your head tomorrow morning,
And she must gather flowers to bury you,
And see the house made handsome. Then she sung
Nothing but 'Willow, willow, willow' and, between,   80

---

62 **encompassed it** surrounded the
place where the singer was
64 **glade** an opening in the reeds
67–8 **Palamon . . . mulberries** Gathering berries seems to have been syn-
onymous with truancy. Chaucer's
Pardoner says that he does not care
whether the souls of his parishioners
'goon a–blakeberyed' once they are
dead (*Pardoner's Prologue*, 406). The
Daughter is anxious about Palamon's
safety, but also recalls his apparent
abandonment of her.
71 **bevy** gathering
73 **chaplets** garlands
daffadillies daffodils
74 **damask** red; a variety originally from
Damascus (Oxf[1])
75 **all we'll** For this unusual construc-

tion, cf. 'All we like sheep have gone
astray' (Isaiah 53.6).
an antic an antic/antique dance
75–6 recalling her part in the morris
dance in 3.5
80 **Willow** from the song of 'Willow'
(also sung by Desdemona in *Oth*
4.3.40–57), alluding to the wearing of
a willow garland by a forsaken lover.
Thiselton-Dyer (233) suggests that it
derives from Psalms, 137.1–2, where
the exiled Israelites, weeping beside a
river, hang their harps on the willows.
The appearance of the 'weeping
willow' and the fact that it grows
beside streams might in themselves be
sufficient explanation for the tradition.

63 sung] *F; (song)*

Ever was 'Palamon, fair Palamon'
And 'Palamon was a tall young man'. The place
Was knee-deep where she sat; her careless tresses
A wreath of bullrush rounded; about her stuck
Thousand fresh water-flowers of several colours,   85
That methought she appeared like the fair nymph
That feeds the lake with waters, or as Iris
Newly dropped down from heaven. Rings she made
Of rushes that grew by and to 'em spoke
The prettiest posies: 'Thus our true love's tied',   90
'This you may loose, not me,' and many a one.
And then she wept, and sung again, and sighed,
And with the same breath smiled and kissed her
      hand.

2 FRIEND
      Alas, what pity it is!
WOOER   I made in to her.

82 **Palamon . . . man** a variation on one of the standard openings for ballads about a hero; see Appendix 6, p. 362.
   tall valiant
83 **knee-deep** knee-high with grass and rushes
84 **rounded** encircled
   about her stuck on her were placed (as on a masque costume?)
86 **methought** Taylor suggests transposing this line as 'she appeared me thought', on the grounds that the result, metrically, is 'much more regular' (*TxC*, 632). However, stressing the first syllable of *methought* has the same effect and is consistent with both dramatists' practice.
   nymph spirit that tends the lake
87 **Iris** Juno's messenger and a personification of the rainbow; the Daughter, with her flowers, is also a multi-coloured figure. See Appendix 4, pp. 350–2.
88–9 **Rings . . . rushes** 'a kind of token for plighting of troth among rustic lovers' (Thiselton-Dyer, 229; he cites

the November Eclogue of Spenser's *Shepherd's Calendar*, line 116). There may be an echo of *A Lover's Complaint*: 'Of folded schedules had she many a one, / Which she perus'd, sigh'd, tore, and gave the flood; / Crack'd many a ring of posied gold and bone, / Bidding them find their sepultures in mud' (43–6).
90 **posies** short mottoes, often in rhyme, such as were engraved on the insides of rings
91 **loose** possibly *lose*, for which it is an alternative spelling, but *Riv* points out that *tied* in the first posy goes with *loose* (untie) in the second
93 **smiled . . . hand** Cf. *TN* 3.4.32–3, where this behaviour is taken as evidence of Malvolio's madness. It was apparently a courtly gesture signifying love; Selden's *Titles of Honour* (1614) gives a false etymology of *adoro* from *ad oro* – the gesture of putting the fingers to the lips (41).
94 **made in** pushed my way through

84 wreath] *Seward;* wreake *Q*

She saw me, and straight sought the flood; I saved
   her,   95
And set her safe to land, when presently
She slipped away and to the city made,
With such a cry and swiftness that, believe me,
She left me far behind her. Three or four
I saw from far off cross her – one of 'em   100
I knew to be your brother – where she stayed
And fell, scarce to be got away. I left them with her,

Enter [Jailer's] Brother, [Jailer's] Daughter and others.

And hither came to tell you. Here they are.
DAUGHTER [*Sings.*]
     May you never more enjoy the light (*etc.*).
  Is not this a fine song?
BROTHER   Oh, a very fine one.   105
DAUGHTER
  I can sing twenty more.
BROTHER   I think you can.
DAUGHTER
  Yes, truly, can I. I can sing 'The Broom'
  And 'Bonny Robin'. Are not you a tailor?
BROTHER
  Yes.
DAUGHTER
   Where's my wedding gown?
BROTHER   I'll bring it tomorrow.

95 **straight . . . flood** at once threw herself into the water (or tried to do so)
96 **presently** at once
98 **cry** like a cry of hounds?
100 **cross her** intercept her
101 **stayed** stopped
102 **scarce . . . away** because she was
   exhausted, or because she didn't want
   to accompany them
103 **Here they are** Strangely, the Wooer
   has no further lines in the scene, and
   the Daughter apparently directs none
   to him. See List of Roles and n. on

139 SD, below.
104 No one has yet identified this song,
   though, as Waith (Oxf[1]) points out,
   the & in Q suggests that it was already known to the actor who was to
   sing a stanza or so. Possibly both it
   and the song that ends the scene were
   considered too coarse to print. At this
   point, the Daughter evidently sees no
   one except the Jailer's Brother, who
   may be supporting or carrying her in.
107–8 'The Broom', 'Bonny Robin'
   See Appendix 6, p. 362.

104 *Sings.*] *not in Q*

DAUGHTER

    Do, very early. I must be abroad else   110
    To call the maids and pay the minstrels,
    For I must lose my maidenhead by cocklight;
    'Twill never thrive else.
    [*Sings.*]
               O fair, o sweet (*etc.*).

BROTHER [*to Jailer*]

    You must e'en take it patiently.

JAILER   'Tis true.   115

DAUGHTER

    Good ev'n, good men; pray, did you ever hear
    Of one young Palamon?

JAILER   Yes, wench, we know him.

DAUGHTER

    Is't not a fine young gentleman?

JAILER   'Tis, love.

BROTHER

    By no means cross her, she is then distempered
    Far worse than now she shows.

1 FRIEND [*to Daughter*]   Yes, he's a fine man.   120

DAUGHTER

    Oh, is he so? You have a sister.

1 FRIEND   Yes.

DAUGHTER

    But she shall never have him – tell her so –

---

110 ***early** Q has *rarely* – an obsolete dialect word (sometimes spelled 'rearly') meaning early. Though neither the 1679 nor the 1711 edition alters it, Davenant's adaptation has *early*. There seems a strong case for emendation, unless (as has been argued) the Daughter is meant to speak dialect (Bruster, 291).

    I . . . else 'otherwise I shall be away from home' (Leech)

112 **by cocklight** by dawn, when the cock crows (with the usual sexual pun)

113 **'Twill never thrive** The wedding night will never go well (perhaps, in view of what follows, to *thrive* means to become pregnant).

114 See Appendix 6, p. 362.

119 **cross** contradict. He may be responding to the Daughter's behaviour or to the First Friend's reluctance to answer her.

    distempered ill, deranged

121 **Oh, is he so?** The Daughter jealously takes the Friend's well-meaning agreement as evidence of a plot to marry his sister to Palamon.

110 early] *Davenant;* rarely *Q;* rearly *(Sympson)*   119 means] *1778;* meane *Q*   120 Far] *1711;* For *Q*

For a trick that I know; you'd best look to her,
For if she see him once, she's gone; she's done,
And undone, in an hour. All the young maids   125
Of our town are in love with him, but I laugh at 'em
And let 'em all alone; is't not a wise course?

1 FRIEND   Yes.

DAUGHTER

There is at least two hundred now with child by him –
There must be four – yet I keep close for all this,
Close as a cockle; and all these must be boys   130
(He has the trick on't) and at ten years old
They must be all gelt for musicians
And sing the wars of Theseus.

2 FRIEND   This is strange.

DAUGHTER

As ever you heard, but say nothing.

1 FRIEND   No.

DAUGHTER

They come from all parts of the dukedom to him.   135
I'll warrant ye, he had not so few last night

---

123 For because of
     trick perhaps a (fantasized) prior en-
     gagement to the Daughter which as
     yet is a secret from everyone (cf. 126–
     7, below); perhaps a bed-trick that she
     intends to play on him; perhaps
     meaningless
124 gone pregnant (cf. *LLL* 5.2.672–7)
124–5 done, / And undone seduced
     and ruined
127 let ... alone pay no attention to
     them
130 Close as a cockle proverbial (Dent,
     C499); here meaning both 'I keep
     myself to myself' and 'I keep my legs
     together'
131 the trick on't the technique for be-
     getting only boys. There were many
     theories about how this could be done,
     by diet or will-power.
132 gelt gelded
132–3 gelt ... Theseus Castration was a
     means of preserving the boy's singing
     voice. Cf. the offering to Theseus, in

MND, of 'The battle with the Cen-
taurs, to be sung / By an Athenian
eunuch to the harp' (5.1.44–5).
134 As ... nothing Probably the
     Daughter overhears the friends speak-
     ing aside. Some editors suggest trans-
     ferring her line to the Brother, on the
     grounds that she herself pays no
     attention to the others in the scene,
     but it is characteristic of other 'mad'
     discourse. Ophelia also speaks of
     'tricks i'th' world' (*Ham* 4.5.5) and
     is obsessed with secrecy (see 3.4.18n.,
     above). A similar exchange occurs in
     a Fletcher scene in *The Knight of
     Malta*, a collaboration of 1616–19:
     'Ye are a strange Gentleman' – 'As
     ever thou knew'st' (Bowers, 8: 2.4.14–
     15).
136–7 he ... dispatch Cf. Fletcher and
     Massinger's *The Custom of the Coun-
     try* (1619–20), where Rutilio actually
     does what the Daughter fantasizes
     (Bowers, 8: 3.3.77–82).

As twenty to dispatch – he'll tickle't up
In two hours, if his hand be in.

JAILER   She's lost
Past all cure.

BROTHER   Heaven forbid, man!

DAUGHTER [*to Jailer*]   Come hither!
You are a wise man.

1 FRIEND [*aside*]   Does she know him?

2 FRIEND [*aside*]   No.   140
Would she did!

DAUGHTER   You are master of a ship?

JAILER
Yes.

DAUGHTER
        Where's your compass?

JAILER   Here.

DAUGHTER   Set it to th' north.
And now direct your course to th' wood, where
    Palamon
Lies longing for me. For the tackling,
Let me alone; come, weigh, my hearts, cheerily!   145

---

137 **tickle't up** The *OED* gives no
exact equivalent for the sense implied here, which appears to be a
cross between II 3 ('to give pleasure')
and II 7 c. ('to arouse by tickling,
excite to action'). The Daughter
means both Palamon's sexual potency and his ability to induce
orgasm.

138 **if ... in** metaphorically, if he is
in good form or lucky (see Dent,
H67)

139 SD The Jailer seems the most likely
addressee. Alternatively she might
mean the Wooer, whose silence and
sadness might lead her to think of him

as *wise*. Or *wise* might be used (of
either man) in the ironic sense (cf. Beatrice's 'a wise gentleman' in *MA*
5.1.165–6); she has already enjoyed
telling the Schoolmaster that he is a
fool (3.5.80).

142 **Here** The Jailer either consults an
imaginary compass or pretends to take
some other object for one.

Set ... north 'i.e. find the north by
setting up the compass' (Oxf¹)

145 **Let me alone** rely on me (cf.
3.5.32): presumably the Daughter
mimes the hauling of ropes on an imaginary ship

weigh weigh anchor

139–42] *Q lines* man. / him? / did.   139 SD] *Riv; not in Q*   140 2 FRIEND] *F; 1 Fr. Q*   SD ¹,²*a-
side*] *this edn; not in Q*   145–6 cheerily! / . . . Ugh!] *(Owgh); cheerly all!* O *Leech; cheerily! /* ALL
THE OTHERS. O, O, O! / DAUGHTER. 'Tis up *Bawcutt*

ALL [*severally*]
    Ugh! Ugh! Ugh!
    'Tis up! – The wind's fair! – Top the bowline! –
    Out with the mainsail! – Where's your whistle,
        master?
BROTHER
    Let's get her in.
JAILER
    Up to the top, boy.
BROTHER   Where's the pilot?
1 FRIEND   Here.   150
DAUGHTER
    What kenn'st thou?
2 FRIEND   A fair wood.
DAUGHTER   Bear for it, master;
    Tack about!
    [*Sings.*]
    When Cynthia with her borrowed light (*etc.*).

                                            Exeunt.

146–8 ALL ... master? Bawcutt (see
    t.n.) argues that ALL is not a speech
    prefix but a misreading of part of the
    Daughter's lines. But the collective
    improvisation of a ship under sail is
    both theatrically effective (it may
    parody *Tem* 1.1.5–8) and in keeping
    with the notion of humouring mad-
    ness; it also explains the presence of
    so many otherwise unnecessary char-
    acters in the scene.
.46 Ugh! Q's *Owgh* represents the
    grunts of people lifting an imaginary
    anchor; in a Fletcher scene in *The
    Knight of Malta* (Bowers, 8: 3.1.31–
    62) the same word depicts the sound
    made by a character imitating the
    grunting of a pig.
147 'Tis up! They have finished hoisting
    the imaginary anchor.
    Top the bowline raise or tighten the
    bowline, a rope fastened to the lar-
    board or starboard bow 'for the pur-
    pose of keeping the edge of the sail

steady when sailing on a wind' (*OED*)
149 either an aside to the others about
    the need to get the increasingly dis-
    tracted Daughter indoors, or part of
    the play-acting (with *her* as the ship
    making for land) – or both, if the
    other characters persuade the Daugh-
    ter to go in by steering towards an im-
    aginary offstage wood
150 Up ... top climb up to the top of
    the mast. Perhaps (as Taylor, *TxC*,
    suggests) the Second Friend climbs to
    the upper stage level.
151 What kenn'st thou? 'What can you
    make out?' From the archaic verb
    'ken', which includes the sense of test-
    ing the range of sight or knowledge.
152 Tack about Cf. Prologue 26.
153 unidentified song; Proudfoot points
    out that the line closely resembles one
    in Sackville's Induction to the 'Com-
    plaint of Henry Duke of Buckingham'
    in *A Mirror for Magistrates*
    Cynthia the moon

146 SD] *this edn; not in Q*   152 Tack] *F; (*Take*)*

[4.2]   *Enter* EMILIA *alone, with two pictures.*

EMILIA

Yet I may bind those wounds up, that must open
And bleed to death for my sake else; I'll choose,
And end their strife. Two such young, handsome
     men
Shall never fall for me; their weeping mothers,
Following the dead cold ashes of their sons,   5
Shall never curse my cruelty. [*Looks at one of the pictures.*]
                                        Good heaven,
What a sweet face has Arcite! If wise Nature,
With all her best endowments, all those beauties
She sows into the births of noble bodies,
Were here a mortal woman and had in her   10
The coy denials of young maids, yet, doubtless,
She would run mad for this man. What an eye,
Of what a fiery sparkle and quick sweetness,
Has this young prince! Here Love himself sits
     smiling;
Just such another wanton Ganymede   15
Set Jove afire with, and enforced the god

4.2.0.1 *two pictures* probably miniatures, such as were often exchanged by lovers

1 **bind ... up** literally, prevent those wounds from being given in the forthcoming fight (Leech); metaphorically, keep their wounded friendship from dying

3–6 **Two ... cruelty** Cf. 3.6.245–50. This soliloquy partly anticipates 5.3.41–55.

7–12 **Nature ... man** Nature herself would love Arcite madly, even if she were also as coy as mortal women; that is, it is 'natural' to love him.

14 **Love ... smiling** a common conceit, based on the personification of Love

as Cupid: e.g., 'Love in thine eyes doth build his bower' (Lodge, 2.19), 'Love in the twinkling of your eyelids danceth' (Davies, *Orchestra*, stanza 106)

15 **Just ... another** either *eye* or *smile*. The more usual word order would be: 'With just such another glance (or smile) wanton Ganymede set Jove afire.' Cf. 'This false smile was well exprest, / Just such another caught me' (*Maid's Tragedy*, Bowers, 2: 2.2.51–2).
Ganymede a beautiful boy snatched up from earth by Jove to become cupbearer to the gods (Ovid, 10.155–61)

4.2] Scæna 2. *Q*   6 SD] *this edn; not in Q*   9 sows] *Q; shews F*   12 eye,] *1711; eye? Q*   16 Set ... with] *1778 (Sympson);* Set Love a fire with *Q;* set Jove afire, and *Seward;* he / Set Jove afire with (*Heath*); Set Jove afire once *Oxf*

Snatch up the goodly boy and set him by him,
A shining constellation. What a brow,
Of what a spacious majesty, he carries,
Arched like the great-eyed Juno's, but far sweeter,   20
Smoother than Pelops' shoulder! Fame and Honour,
Methinks, from hence, as from a promontory
Pointed in heaven, should clap their wings and sing,
To all the under-world, the loves and fights
Of gods and such men near 'em. [*Looks at the other picture.*]
                    Palamon   25
Is but his foil; to him, a mere dull shadow;
He's swart and meagre, of an eye as heavy
As if he had lost his mother; a still temper;
No stirring in him, no alacrity;
Of all this sprightly sharpness, not a smile.   30
Yet these that we count errors may become him:
Narcissus was a sad boy, but a heavenly.

18 **constellation** Aquarius (the water-bearer)
What a brow Cf. 'See what a grace was seated on this brow' (*Ham* 3.4.55–62).

20 **great-eyed Juno's** possibly, as Proudfoot suggests, 'grey-eyed' (a common expression in this play – compare 131, below), but Juno is often called 'ox-eyed'

21 **Pelops' shoulder** ivory; see Ovid, 6.403–11. Tantalus served his son Pelops to the gods at a banquet. When they discovered his crime, they reassembled the dismembered body, replacing one shoulder, already eaten, by one of ivory. Leech compares lines in Marlowe, *Hero and Leander*: 'his necke ... surpasst / The white of *Pelops'* shoulder' (64–5).

21–5 **Fame ... 'em** Skeat compares *Philaster*: 'Place me, some god, upon a *Piramis* / Higher than hils of earth, and lend a voyce / Loud as your thunder to me, that from thence / I may discourse to all the under-world / The

worth that dwells in him!' (Bowers, 1: 4.6.90–4).

22 **hence** i.e., from Arcite's brow
promontory a mountainous stretch of land jutting into the sea; also, metaphorically, the highest and farthest point of excellence

23 **Pointed in** of which the peak is in

24 **under-world** the earth below

25 **such ... 'em** such men as this, near to divinity

26 **foil** someone who merely serves to set off the splendour of someone else, as dull metal (foil) sets off a jewel (cf. *Ham* 5.2.255)
to by comparison with

27 **swart** a variation of swarthy: dark
meagre skinny
heavy gloomy

28 **still** lethargic

29 **stirring** liveliness

30 **this** Arcite's
smile trace (perhaps harking back to 14)

32 **Narcissus** Contrast Emilia's earlier attitude to this character, 2.2.120–1.
sad serious

25 SD] *this edn; not in Q*

– 'Oh, who can find the bent of woman's fancy?'
I am a fool, my reason is lost in me,
I have no choice, and I have lied so lewdly   35
That women ought to beat me. On my knees,
I ask thy pardon, Palamon: thou art alone
And only beautiful, and these the eyes,
These the bright lamps of beauty, that command
And threaten love, and what young maid dare cross
     'em?   40
What a bold gravity, and yet inviting,
Has this brown manly face! Oh Love, this only,
From this hour, is complexion! [*Lays Arcite's picture down.*]
                              Lie there, Arcite;
Thou art a changeling to him, a mere gypsy,
And this the noble body. – I am sotted,   45

33 *Bawcutt compares 'O who does know
the bent of women's fantasy?' (*Faerie
Queene*, 1.4.24). Perhaps Emilia is
meant to be (anachronistically) quoting.
   bent direction (which way it bends)
   fancy either love or infatuation, but
   with emphasis on the role of imagination in the emotional experience
35 **choice** capacity to make a choice
   lewdly ignorantly (Skeat compares
   Acts, 17.5)
36 **On my knees** Emilia may kneel to
   the picture at this point, or the phrase
   may be purely metaphorical.
37–8 **alone / And only** uniquely
39–40 **command . . . love** by contrast
   with the smiling love in Arcite's eyes
40 **cross** withstand, or come within
   range of
   cross 'em? No punctuation follows
   these words in Q, where the line ends
   flush with the right margin. It is probably a rhetorical question, meaning
   'What young maid would dare resist
   them?' (or encounter them, in the
   sense of meeting their eyes) but it is
   also possible that *what* means 'what-

ever' and that *command / And threaten*
applies to both *love* and *maid*.
42 **Love** probably addressed to Cupid
   rather than Palamon
43 **complexion** what complexion ought
   to be
44–5 **a changeling . . . body** Fairies and
   gypsies were thought to steal the children of noblemen, leaving their own
   ugly children behind in exchange:
   hence the term 'changeling' for an
   ugly or stupid person.
44 **to him** See 26, above.
   gypsy dark, like an Egyptian; consistent with Palamon's earlier reference
   to Arcite as 'a black-haired man'
   (3.3.31) but odd after 27, above, where
   she calls Palamon 'swart'. It has been
   argued (Underwood, *TNK*, 17) that
   the two men are meant to be indistinguishable. But Emilia's speech is
   probably not evidence of their appearance. Like Lysander, who rejects
   Hermia with 'Away, you Ethiop!'
   (*MND* 3.2.257), she describes each
   man according to the convention that
   makes beauty fair and ugliness dark.
45 **sotted** turned into a sot, a fool

33 'Oh . . . fancy?'] *this edn. (Bawcutt);* Oh . . . fancy? Q   38 these the eyes] Q; these thy eyes F;
they're the eyes *(Mason)*   40 cross 'em?] *Seward;* crosse 'em Q   43 SD] *this edn; not in Q*

Utterly lost. My virgin's faith has fled me.
For if my brother but even now had asked me
Whether I loved, I had run mad for Arcite;
Now, if my sister, more for Palamon.
Stand both together. Now, come ask me, brother.   50
'Alas, I know not!' Ask me now, sweet sister.
'I may go look.' What a mere child is Fancy,
That, having two fair gauds of equal sweetness,
Cannot distinguish, but must cry for both!

Enter Gentleman.

How now, sir?
GENTLEMAN   From the noble Duke your brother,   55
Madam, I bring you news. The knights are come.
EMILIA
To end the quarrel?
GENTLEMAN   Yes.
EMILIA   Would I might end first!
What sins have I committed, chaste Diana,
That my unspotted youth must now be soiled
With blood of princes, and my chastity   60
Be made the altar where the lives of lovers –
Two greater and two better never yet
Made mothers joy – must be the sacrifice

46 **faith** constancy; cf. 'Ye make my faith
   reel' (3.6.212)
48 **Whether** which of the two
   had run would have run
49 **if my sister** (had asked me)
   more for more inclined to
50 **Stand both together** She probably
   places the two pictures side by
   side.
52 **'I . . . look'** 'I cannot answer'
   Fancy See 33, above.
53 **gauds** toys

54 **distinguish** discriminate, decide between them
   *SD Q's SD (see t.n.) may have re-
   sulted from revision – if, for instance,
   Emilia's soliloquy was either added or
   marked for deletion. See pp. 29–30
   above.
60–4 **my chastity . . . beauty** a foreshadowing of her appearance in the
   temple of Diana (5.1)
63 **Made mothers joy** caused mothers
   to rejoice at their birth

46 virgin's] *1711;* Virgins *Q;* Virgin *Seward*   54 SD] *1711; Enter Emil. and Gent: Q*   55 How]
1778; Emil. How *Q*   63 mothers joy] *Q;* mothers' joy *1778*

To my unhappy beauty?

Enter THESEUS, HIPPOLYTA, PIRITHOUS *and attendants.*

THESEUS   Bring 'em in
Quickly, by any means; I long to see 'em.   65
[*to Emilia*] Your two contending lovers are returned,
And with them their fair knights. Now, my fair sister,
You must love one of them.
EMILIA   I had rather both;
So neither for my sake should fall untimely.
THESEUS ˙
Who saw 'em?
PIRITHOUS   I a while.
GENTLEMAN   And I.   70

Enter Messenger.

THESEUS
From whence come you, sir?
MESSENGER   From the knights.
THESEUS   Pray speak,
You that have seen them, what they are.
MESSENGER   I will, sir,

---

64 **unhappy** hapless, bringing
misfortune
Bring 'em in Theseus gives an order
(off stage, or to Pirithous) as he
enters.
68 **You must love** you will have to love
(as a result of the combat); the stress is
on *must*
I . . . both 'I had rather be forced to
love both of them'; cf. her refusal to
make a decision in 3.6.285.
69 **So** thus
70 **a while** briefly
*SD The reference to '*Curtis*' in Q's
SD (see t.n.) is a prompter's annotation, not meant for printing. See p.
123 above. It is hard to see why the
direction calls for *two* messengers,

since Pirithous and the Gentleman are
already available to describe the offstage knights. Some revision may have
taken place at this point; see 54 SD n.,
above.
71 **speak** used transitively here and at 91
72–140 The descriptions follow those in
KT, but with some alterations. Only
two knights (the king of Thrace and
the king of India) are described by
Chaucer: a black-haired knight fighting for Palamon and a yellow-haired
one (with the freckles mentioned in
120) fighting for Arcite. These
speeches are rarely performed, since
neither the messenger convention nor
the homage to Chaucer is meaningful
to a modern audience.

64–5 in / Quickly] *1778;* in quickly, / By Q   70.1] *1711; Enter Messengers. Curtis. after 69 Q*

275

And truly what I think. Six braver spirits
Than these they have brought, if we judge by the
    outside,
I never saw nor read of. He that stands.   75
In the first place with Arcite, by his seeming
Should be a stout man, by his face a prince,
His very looks so say him: his complexion
Nearer a brown than black, stern, and yet noble,
Which shows him hardy, fearless, proud of dangers.   80
The circles of his eyes show fire within him,
And as a heated lion so he looks.
His hair hangs long behind him, black and shining
Like ravens' wings; his shoulders broad and strong;
Armed long and round, and on his thigh a sword,   85
Hung by a curious baldrick, when he frowns,
To seal his will with. Better o' my conscience
Was never soldier's friend.

THESEUS
Thou hast well described him.

PIRITHOUS   Yet a great deal short,
Methinks, of him that's first with Palamon.   90

THESEUS
Pray, speak him, friend.

PIRITHOUS   I guess he is a prince too,

---

77 **stout** valiant
81 **circles ... eyes** probably the rolling
of his eyes (cf. 108, below)
   *fire Dyce's alteration is confirmed
by Skeat's quotation of the equivalent in Chaucer: 'The circles of his
eyen in his heed / They gloweden
bytwixe yelwe and reed ... ' (2131–
2).
82 **heated** angry
   looks refers to his expression, not his
appearance (see 4.1.33n.)
85 **Armed ... round** a pun: the knight
is furnished with arms (in both
senses), which is why the speaker goes
on to mention his sword
86 **a curious baldrick** a finely-made

sword-belt (usually slung from the
shoulder)
87 **To seal ... with** The subject is
'sword'; there may be a pun on sealing
a legal document. Cf. the construction
in 15–16, above.
87–8 **Better ... friend** refers to the
sword; Skeat compares 'A better
[weapon] never did itself sustain /
Upon a soldier's thigh' (*Oth* 5.2.260–
1). For a similar 'epic' phrase see
2.2.20–1.
89–90 **Yet ... Palamon** It is the knight
rather than the description that
Pirithous proposes to surpass; but this
scene is also a competition between
descriptions.

81 fire] *Dyce (Heath);* faire *Q;* far *Seward*

And, if it may be, greater; for his show
Has all the ornament of honour in't.
He's somewhat bigger than the knight he spoke of,
But of a face far sweeter. His complexion   95
Is, as a ripe grape, ruddy; he has felt
Without doubt what he fights for, and so apter
To make this cause his own. In's face appears
All the fair hopes of what he undertakes
And, when he's angry, then a settled valour,   100
Not tainted with extremes, runs through his body
And guides his arm to brave things. Fear he cannot;
He shows no such soft temper. His head's yellow,
Hard-haired, and curled, thick-twined like ivy tods,
Not to undo with thunder. In his face   105
The livery of the warlike maid appears,
Pure red and white, for yet no beard has blessed him;
And in his rolling eyes sits Victory,
As if she ever meant to court his valour.

92 **show** his weapons, trappings, retinue
94 **He's** the Second Knight is
   he the Messenger
97 **what . . . for** i.e., love
   so apter therefore all the more likely
98–9 **In's face . . . hopes** His looks, especially his ruddy complexion, reflect
   his sanguine humour
101 **extremes** violent emotions
104 **Hard-haired** In *KT* the equivalent
   passage is: 'His crispe heer lyk rynges
   was yronne, / And that was yelow,
   and glytered as the sonne' (Chaucer,
   Riv, 2165–6). Turner points out that
   Speght's 1602 edn printed 'of yron'
   for 'yronne' (fashioned); the play's
   striking phrase (presumably meaning
   tightly curled rather than lightly
   waved) results from this misreading.
   *tods bushes
105 **to undo** to be uncurled
   with thunder by the wrath of Jove:
   perhaps referring to the belief that the
   laurel wreath of a conqueror pro-
   tected him against lightning

106 **livery** uniform given to one's
   followers
   the warlike maid either Athene or
   Bellona
107 **red and white** Red on its own is the
   colour of Mars, and thus appropriate
   for a *warlike* goddess; white is associated with maidens (see 5.1.139–42)
   and 'red and white' is the usual shorthand for female beauty. Waith (Oxf[1])
   suggests that this and other details of
   this portrait come, not from Chaucer,
   but from his source in Boccaccio.
108 **rolling eyes** expressing passion (cf.
   'in a fine frenzy rolling' (*MND* 5.1.12)
   and 'you're fatal then / When your
   eyes roll so' (*Oth* 5.2.37–8))
109 *court Q reads *corect*; Dyce's suggestion, *court*, could more plausibly
   have been misread in this way than
   Seward's *crown*. Though the latter
   seems more logical, the idea that a
   female goddess should woo a hero,
   rather than vice versa, is in keeping
   with 2.2.259–62 and 7–12, above.

104 tods] *Littledale*; tops *Q*   109 court] *Littledale*; crown *Seward*; corect *Q*

His nose stands high, a character of honour;   110
His red lips, after fights, are fit for ladies.

EMILIA
Must these men die too?

PIRITHOUS   When he speaks, his tongue
Sounds like a trumpet. All his lineaments
Are as a man would wish 'em, strong and clean;
He wears a well-steeled axe, the staff of gold;   115
His age some five-and-twenty.

MESSENGER   There's another,
A little man, but of a tough soul, seeming
As great as any; fairer promises
In such a body yet I never looked on.

PIRITHOUS
Oh, he that's freckle-faced?

MESSENGER   The same, my lord.   120
Are they not sweet ones?

PIRITHOUS   Yes, they are well.

MESSENGER   Methinks,
Being so few and well disposed, they show
Great and fine art in nature. He's white-haired,
Not wanton white, but such a manly colour,

---

110 **His . . . high** has a high bridge
character sign (from the characters
or letters of the alphabet)
111 **fit for** either fit to kiss ladies or fit to
belong to ladies
112 **'Must . . . too?** This line may be an
aside; no one responds to it. But perhaps that is the point.
113 **lineaments** his shape
114 **clean** well-built (as in 'clean-
limbed')
115 **well-steeled** See 2.2.51.
staff handle
116 **There's another** It is not said which
side this knight (not mentioned in
Chaucer) belongs to. He seems to
combine the qualities of the first and
second knights (i.e., Mars and Venus)
but his distinctive freckles come from
Chaucer's description of Arcite's

knight. Perhaps the audience was
meant to recognize some real person
in the description.
118 **great** in soul
121 **sweet ones** the freckles. Those described in Chaucer, a mixture of
yellow and black (*KT*, 2169–70), are
not said to be sweet.
122 **disposed** arranged
123 **Great . . . nature** Either the freckles
look bigger because there are so few of
them, or they show great as well as
fine art. Paradoxes about nature seeming artificial (and vice versa) abound
in late Shakespeare: see, for instance,
AC 5.2.97–100 and *WT* 4.4.89–92.
white-haired blond
124 **wanton white** the very light blond
of a child (wanton), by contrast with
manly

Next to an auburn; tough and nimble set,   125
Which shows an active soul; his arms are brawny,
Lined with strong sinews. To the shoulder piece,
Gently they swell, like women new-conceived,
Which speaks him prone to labour, never fainting
Under the weight of arms; stout-hearted, still,.   130
But when he stirs, a tiger. He's grey-eyed,
Which yields compassion where he conquers; sharp
To spy advantages and, where he finds 'em,
He's swift to make 'em his. He does no wrongs,
Nor takes none; he's round-faced and when he smiles   135
He shows a lover; when he frowns, a soldier.
About his head he wears the winner's oak
And in it stuck the favour of his lady.
His age, some six-and-thirty. In his hand
He bears a charging-staff, embossed with silver.   140

THESEUS
  Are they all thus?

PIRITHOUS   They are all the sons of honour.

THESEUS
  Now, as I have a soul, I long to see 'em.
  [*to Hippolyta*] Lady, you shall see men fight now.

HIPPOLYTA   I wish it,

---

125 **auburn** yellowish or brownish colour, not, as now, reddish
    nimble set agile
127 **sinews** muscles
128–9 **Gently ... labour** The bulge of his arms next to the constraining shoulder-piece suggests the swelling of early pregnancy and thus a pun on *labour*.
129–30 **never ... arms** possibly a sexual pun
130 **still** in repose (by contrast with 'when he stirs')
131–2 **grey-eyed ... compassion** 'gray eyes, which are a sign of mercy to the vanquished. Probably because gray eyes seem to have been considered as best suited for women, who are gentle

by natural disposition' (Skeat). Waith (Oxf[1]) points out that in this period grey-eyed really meant 'what we should call blue or blue-grey eyes', and cites Elisha Coles, *A Dictionary of English–Latin and Latin–English* (2nd edn, 1679, 'Gray-eyed').
135 **takes none** lets no one wrong him
136 **shows** looks like
137 **the winner's oak** given by the Romans to a victorious soldier (see *Cor* 2.1.125). Skeat notes that *KT* refers to a laurel garland; the alteration was presumably made to balance the image of ivy in the second knight's description (104, above).
140 **charging-staff** a lance for tilting
143 **men** heroes (as in 3.6.264)

But not the cause, my lord. They would show bravely
Fighting about the titles of two kingdoms.   145
'Tis pity love should be so tyrannous.
– O, my soft-hearted sister, what think you?
Weep not, till they weep blood. Wench, it must be.
THESEUS
You have steeled 'em with your beauty. [*to Pirithous*]
                                        Honoured friend,
To you I give the field; pray order it   150
Fitting the persons that must use it.
PIRITHOUS   Yes, sir.
THESEUS
Come, I'll go visit 'em! I cannot stay –
Their fame has fir'd me so; till they appear,
Good friend, be royal.
PIRITHOUS   There shall want no bravery.
                                        Exeunt [all but Emilia].

EMILIA
Poor wench, go weep, for whosoever wins   155
Loses a noble cousin, for thy sins.   *Exit*.

[4.3]   *Enter* Jailer, Wooer *and* Doctor.

144 **bravely** splendidly
145 **titles** rights. The play seems to be
recalling its origin in the legend of
Oedipus' sons fighting over the
throne of Thebes.
147 **what think you?** probably rhetorical
– 'What can you be thinking of?' – in
response to Emilia's weeping
149 **steeled** made them strong: cf. 115,
above
150 **the field** the arranging and decorat-
ing of the tournament. Pirithous is to
act as marshal.
152 **stay** wait
153 **fame** the report he has just heard
appear make a public appearance

154 **be royal** display kingly generosity.
Cf. 'All was royal' (*H8* 1.1.42).
want be lacking
bravery splendour
SD Though Q's SD has all the characters leave at once after 156, it seems
likely that Emilia, who has been sup-
pressing her tears after 148, speaks
her last couplet after the others have
gone.
156 **for thy sins** She feels that the death
of either man will be her fault.
4.3 This is the only all-prose scene in the
play; because Fletcher wrote mainly
in verse, its authorship is disputed;
see p. 30 above.

144–5 bravely / Fighting about] *Seward;* show / Bravely about *Q*   153 so – till] *F subst.;* so; Till
Q   154 SD] *this edn; Exeunt. after 158 Q*   4.3] Scæna 3. *Q*

DOCTOR   Her distraction is more at some time of the
moon than at other some, is it not?

JAILER   She is continually in a harmless distemper:
sleeps little; altogether without appetite, save often
drinking; dreaming of another world and a better;   5
and, what broken piece of matter soe'er she's about,
the name Palamon lards it, that she farces every business withall, fits it to every question.

Enter [Jailer's] Daughter.

Look where she comes; you shall perceive her
behaviour.   10

DAUGHTER   I have forgot it quite. The burden on't was
'Down-a, down-a' and penned by no worse man than
Giraldo, Emilia's Schoolmaster; he's as fantastical too

1–2 The doctor's attempt to attribute the
Daughter's condition either to
'lunacy' or to the menstrual cycle implies that she has been mad for some
time, although only a month or less
has elapsed between 3.6 and 4.2 (see
3.6.290).

2 **other some** some others

3 **continually** that is, not cyclically
harmless unhurtful (to others)
distemper illness

5 **drinking** Cf. 3.2.26–7. Thirst is a
classic symptom of love-sickness,
caused by 'the intense heat and dry-
ness of atrabilious melancholy'
(Beecher, 160).
another . . . better the next world (as
at 21–56, below). Cf. 'Hereafter, in a
better world than this' (*AYL* 1.2.284).

6 **what . . . about** whatever fragmentary conversation she holds

7 **the . . . it** it is permeated with the
name of Palamon (as small pieces of
fat are inserted into a roast to moisten
and flavour it). Skeat compares
'Larded all with sweet flowers' (*Ham*

4.5.38) and 'Larded with many several
sorts of reasons' (*Ham* 5.2.20).
farces stuffs (another metaphor from
cooking)

8 **withall** with it

11 **burden** refrain of a song. The
Daughter's worsening state may be
indicated by the fact that she can no
longer remember the songs she wants
to sing.

12 **Down-a** a common refrain. Skeat
compares *Ham* 4.5.171: 'You must
sing a-down a-down'. Proudfoot cites
Henry Chettle's *Hoffman*, 5.1.56–9
(also a mad scene).

13 **Giraldo** Presumably the 'Master
Gerald' of 3.5.23. The confusion of
name may be the Daughter's, or the
authors', or the Daughter may be
commenting sarcastically on the
Schoolmaster's pretensions (see Appendix 4, pp. 354–5).
fantastical full of absurd ideas.
Holofernes in *LLL* is described as 'ex-
ceeding fantastical, too, too vain'
(5.2.528–9).

1–101] *as verse Q*   8 SD] *after* business *Q*

as ever he may go upon's legs – for in the next world
will Dido see Palamon, and then will ₅she be out of   15
love with Aeneas.

DOCTOR   What stuff's here? Poor soul!

JAILER   Even thus all day long.

DAUGHTER   Now for this charm that I told you of: you
must bring a piece of silver on the tip of your tongue,   20
or no ferry. Then if it be your chance to come where
the blessed spirits are, there's a sight now! We maids
that have our livers perished, cracked to pieces with
love, we shall come there and do nothing all day
long but pick flowers with Proserpine. Then will I   25
make Palamon a nosegay; then let him mark me –
then.

DOCTOR   How prettily she's amiss! Note her a little
further.

DAUGHTER   Faith, I'll tell you, sometime we go to   30

14 **as . . . legs** as he can possibly be
14–16 **for . . . Aeneas** Cf. Antony's
vision of joining Cleopatra in the Elysian fields, where 'Dido and her
Aeneas shall want troops, / And all
the haunt be ours' (*AC* 4.14.53–4).
Leech and Bawcutt suggest that the
Daughter imagines that the Schoolmaster has taught her a song about
Dido and Aeneas, which she rejects as
fantastical because she knows Dido
will love Palamon, not Aeneas. But it
is not necessary to make this connection: *for*, in mad scenes, can be followed by a *non sequitur*.
17 **stuff** rubbish
19–21 **you . . . ferry** It was a classical
burial custom to provide money for
the dead person to pay Charon, who
ferried souls to the other side of the
river Styx.
22 **blessed spirits** Skeat compares '*fe-
lices animae*' (*Aeneid*, 6.39 and 669).
*****are . . . sight** Q's reading (see t.n.)
was accepted by Leech who glossed
sight as colloquial: 'a great number'.

But Mason's suggestion is grammatical and logical, given the play's emphasis on seeing.
23–4 **livers . . . love** The liver was
thought to be the seat of the passions.
25 **Proserpine** the queen of the under-
world, carried off by Pluto while
gathering flowers. Cf. Palamon's first
sight of Emilia in 2.2.
26 **mark me** pay attention; the Q punctuation leaves it unclear whether these
words refer to Palamon or her
listeners.
26–7 – **then** Q's dash may indicate an
omission, an unreadable word in the
MS, or a gap to be filled in by business
or improvisation.
28 **How . . . amiss** Ophelia's madness is
also described as turning everything
to 'prettiness' (*Ham* 4.5.189).
amiss ill
Note observe
30 **Faith . . . you** Perhaps she imagines
that someone has asked her a question
about the other world.

22 spirits are,] *Weber (Mason)*; spirits, as *Q*   26 him mark me –] *Q subst.*; him – mark me –
Seward   27 then.] *Q*; then – *Dyce*

barley-break, we of the blessed. Alas, 'tis a sore life
they have i'th' other place – such burning, frying,
boiling, hissing, howling, chattering, cursing: oh, they
have shrewd measure; take heed! If one be mad, or
hang or drown themselves, there they go – Jupiter   35
bless us! – and there shall we be put in a cauldron of
lead and usurers' grease, amongst a whole million of
cutpurses, and there boil like a gammon of bacon that
will never be enough.

DOCTOR   How her brain coins!   40

DAUGHTER   Lords and courtiers that have got maids
with child, they are in this place. They shall stand in
fire up to the navel and in ice up to the heart, and
there th'offending part burns and the deceiving part
freezes. In troth, a very grievous punishment, as one   45

---

31 **barley-break** a country game generally played by three couples, each of
which had to keep hand in hand while
running; one couple, in the centre of
the field, tried to catch the others as
they ran past. Like other games of this
kind, it was also used metaphorically
for sexual coupling (Proudfoot). Because the central space was called
'hell', it can have a double meaning
(as, e.g., in Middleton and Rowley,
The Changeling, 5.3.162–4). The
Daughter seems to be explaining that
she knows about hell through visiting
it during this game.
we ... blessed Though her version
of the classical afterlife is based on
famous accounts like Book 6 of Virgil's *Aeneid*, the Daughter is also
thinking in Christian terms (compare
2.6.13–17).
32 **other place** Waith (Oxf[1]) notes that
Hamlet also uses this phrase for hell
(*Ham* 4.3.34–5).
34 **shrewd measure** a harsh punishment (not simply 'measure for
measure')

34–6 **one ... they ... we** The shifting
pronouns show the Daughter, who
first describes herself as dead and already 'blessed', realizing instead that
she is in danger of damnation if she
commits suicide for love.
36–9 **there ... enough** The traditional
punishment for usurers, boiling in oil
and lead, is suffered by Barabas in
Marlowe, *The Jew of Malta*, 5.5.
37 **grease** sweat: usurers are fat because
they 'devour' the wealth of others. See
Volpone, Jonson, 5: 1.1.40–3.
38 **cutpurses** See note on 2.2.214.
39 **enough** cooked enough
*Q marks an exit for the Daughter
here but no re-entrance; see p. 33
above. It seems more logical to delete
the first exit than to add an entry; mad
characters do often run in and out,
like Hieronymo, Hamlet and Ophelia,
but in that case one would expect
someone to go after her.
40 **coins** creates fantastic ideas. Cf. 'the
very coinage of your brain' (*Ham*
3.4.137).

---

32 i'th'other] *F*; i'th / Thother *Q*   34 take heed! If] *1778*; take heed: if *Dyce*; take heede, if
Q   37 usurers' grease] *1778*; usurer's grease *1711*; usurers grease *Q*   39 enough.] enough. *Exit. Q*

would think, for such a trifle. Believe me, one would
marry a leprous witch to be rid on't, I'll assure you.

DOCTOR   How she continues this fancy! 'Tis not an engrafted madness but a most thick and profound
melancholy.   50

DAUGHTER   To hear there a proud lady and a proud city
wife, howl together! I were a beast an I'd call it good
sport. One cries, 'Oh, this smoke!', another, 'This
fire!' One cries, 'Oh, that ever I did it behind the
arras!' and then howls; th'other curses a suing fellow   55
and her garden house.
(*Sings.*)

       I will be true, my stars, my fate (*etc.*).   *Exit.*

JAILER   What think you of her, sir?

DOCTOR   I think she has a perturbed mind, which I
cannot minister to.   60

JAILER   Alas, what then?

DOCTOR   Understand you she ever affected any man ere
she beheld Palamon?

JAILER   I was once, sir, in great hope she had fixed her
liking on this gentleman, my friend.   65

---

47 **to ... on't** to avoid it; ironic, since
the men she mentions are presumably
in hell because (like Lucio in *MM*)
they did not marry the women they
seduced
48 **continues** elaborates and sustains her
ideas rather than flitting from one to
the other. Skeat cites 'She is troubled
with thick-coming fancies' (*Mac*
5.3.38).
48–50 **'Tis ... melancholy** The Doctor
distinguishes between psychosis
(*madness*) and the kind of obsessive
neurosis sometimes called *melancholy*. The technical name for the
Daughter's condition was *erotomania*,
or love-melancholy (see pp. 50–1
above).
48–9 **engrafted** fixed, implanted
52 **I were** I would be
an I'd call if I called

53 **sport** joke: that is, the fact that damnation forces the two women into un-
wanted proximity
another Dyce alters to *th'other*, on
the assumption that the Daughter is
still talking about the same women,
but it is equally possible that she is
imagining others.
55 **arras** Tapestry hangings (sometimes
made in Arras) provided a hiding
place for lovers; see 3.5.125–6.
a suing fellow a persistent suitor
56 **garden house** a small house or bower
in a garden, used for 'banquetting'
(see Fumerton, 129) and secret as-
signations such as the one Angelo ar-
ranges in *MM* 5.1.212
57 This song is unidentified.
59–60 an often-noted echo of *Mac* 5.3.40
61 **what then?** What's to be done?
62 **affected** cared for

48–9 engrafted] *1778;* engraffed *Q*   53 another] *Q;* th' other *Dyce*

WOOER   I did think so too, and would account I had a
great penn'orth on't, to give half my state that both
she and I at this present stood unfeignedly on the
same terms.

DOCTOR   That intemperate surfeit of her eye hath distempered the other senses; they may return and settle   70
again to execute their preordained faculties, but they
are now in a most extravagant vagary. This you must
do. Confine her to a place where the light may rather
seem to steal in than be permitted. Take upon you,   75
young sir her friend, the name of Palamon; say you
come to eat with her and to commune of love. This
will catch her attention, for this her mind beats upon;
other objects that are inserted 'tween her mind and
eye become the pranks and friskins of her madness.   80
Sing to her such green songs of love as she says Palamon hath sung in prison. Come to her stuck in as
sweet flowers as the season is mistress of and thereto
make an addition of some other compounded odours
which are grateful to the sense. All this shall become   85

66–7 **a great penn'orth on't** a good
bargain (penny-worth) in it
67 **to give . . . state** if I gave half of what
I am worth
68 **unfeignedly** genuinely
70 **That . . . eye** looking too much at
Palamon; cf. 2.3.8–10. The Doctor
plays on *intemperate* and *distempered*,
both of which mean out of temper, or
balance.
72 **execute . . . faculties** fulfil their
normal functions
73 **in . . . vagary** wandering far and wide
74–5 **Confine . . . permitted** Confine-
ment in a dark room was a common
treatment for madness, because of the
belief that seeing too many different
objects was harmful (see *TN* 4.2).
77 **eat with her** As he explains below
(94–5), the Doctor wants to persuade
the Daughter to eat. Medical books of
the period tell how mental patients are

tricked into eating or sleeping and
thus cured.
commune talk
78 **beats upon** is obsessed by: cf. 'still
'tis beating in my mind' (*Tem* 1.2.176)
80 **pranks . . . madness** means by
which her madness plays tricks and
leaps about. Similarly, the doctor in
Webster, *DM*, asks his patient, 'Can
you fetch a frisk, sir?' (5.2.71).
81–2 **such . . . prison** Cf. 2.3.16–17; the
Doctor has not heard her speak of
this, but the inconsistency would not
be noticed.
81 **green** naive, youthful
82 **stuck in** decked with
84 **compounded odours** perfumes (also
recommended as a cure for melancholy; e.g. in Lemnius, A8–8')
85 **grateful** pleasing
85–6 **become Palamon** fit the role of
Palamon

68 unfeignedly] *1778;* unfainedly *Q*

Palamon, for Palamon can sing, and Palamon is sweet
and every good thing. Desire to eat with her, carve
her, drink to her and, still among, intermingle your
petition of grace and acceptance into her favour.
Learn what maids have been her companions and   90
play-feres and let them repair to her with Palamon in
their mouths, and appear with tokens, as if they suggested for him. It is a falsehood she is in, which is
with falsehoods to be combated. This may bring her
to eat, to sleep, and reduce what's now out of square   95
in her into their former law and regiment. I have seen
it approved, how many times I know not, but to make
the number more I have great hope in this. I will,
between the passages of this project, come in with my
appliance. Let us put it in execution and hasten the   100
success, which, doubt not, will bring forth comfort.

                                                    Exeunt.

[5.1]   *Flourish. Enter* THESEUS, PIRITHOUS, HIPPOLYTA,
                        attendants.

86–7 **for ... thing** This sounds like a
quotation from a song, but I have not
traced it.

87–8 **carve her** Q's reading has been
emended to *crave* and *carve for her*.
But *carve* can be used intransitively
with a dative pronoun. Webster's *WD*
shows that to carve to someone was a
sign of respect: 'I carved to him at
supper-time.' 'You need not have
carved him in faith' (1.2.126–9).

88 **still among** from time to time

91 **play-feres** companions, playfellows
(already archaic)
repair go

92 **tokens** love-tokens, small gifts

92–3 **suggested for him** were wooing
on his behalf

94 **bring** persuade

95 **reduce** restore
out of square disordered

96 **regiment** rule, regimen

97 **it** this treatment
approved tried with success

how ... not innumerable times

97–8 **to make ... this** I hope to make
the number more, thanks to this case.

99 **passages** stages, events

100 **appliance** treatment (drugs, diet,
etc.)

100–1 **hasten the success** get results as
soon as possible; *success* means result,
whether good or bad

101 SD The flourish in Q's SD obviously
belongs with the entrance of Theseus
at the beginning of the next scene.

5.1 In *KT* the lists are held in an amphitheatre with an altar to each of the three
gods. It is not clear whether the play
requires one onstage altar or three.
Seward treats the three invocations as
separate scenes; Montgomery (Oxf),
suggests that they may be thought of
as occurring simultaneously in three
different locations. But the atmosphere
of each temple could be created by the
colours and trappings of its group of
worshippers. See p. 63 above.

87–8 carve her] *F;* crave her *Q;* carve for her *Seward*   5.1] *Actus Quintus.* / Scæna I. *Q*   0.1 *Flour-*
ish.] *Dyce; after 4.3.101 Q*

THESEUS
    Now let 'em enter and before the gods
    Tender their holy prayers. Let the temples
    Burn bright with sacred fires and the altars
    In hallowed clouds commend their swelling incense
    To those above us. Let no due be wanting.   5
    They have a noble work in hand, will honour
    The very powers that love 'em.

    Flourish of cornets. Enter PALAMON *and* ARCITE *and their*
                knights.

PIRITHOUS   Sir, they enter.
THESEUS
    You valiant and strong-hearted enemies,
    You royal german foes, that this day come
    To blow that nearness out that flames between ye: 10
    Lay by your anger for an hour and, dove-like,
    Before the holy altars of your helpers,
    The all-feared gods, bow down your stubborn bodies.
    Your ire is more than mortal; so your help be;
    And, as the gods regard ye, fight with justice.   15
    I'll leave you to your prayers and betwixt ye

---

2 **Tender** offer
3 **fires** (two syllables)
4 **swelling** billowing into clouds
6 **will honour** that will honour
7 SD This bare direction probably indicates a spectacular processional entrance to music, with each side, as Montgomery (Oxf) suggests, emerging from one of the two stage doors; the knights, elaborately costumed and armed, must live up to their descriptions in 4.2.
9 **german** closely related
10 'to destroy your closeness of relationship and affection'. The image may derive from one of the strangest episodes of Statius' *Thebaid* (12.420–46),

when the wife and sister of Polynices, wandering over the Theban battlefield, attempt to burn his body on the funeral pyre of his brother and mortal enemy Eteocles. They find that even the flames on the pyre are in conflict, symbolizing the undying hatred of the two men. Cf. 'Like the two slaughtered sons of Oedipus, / The very flames of our affection / Shall turn two ways' (Webster, *WD*, 5.1.197–200).
11 **dove-like** in peace
15 **as . . . ye** as you are acting in the sight of the gods
16 **prayers** (two syllables)

I part my wishes.

PIRITHOUS   Honour crown the worthiest.

Exeunt Theseus and his train.

PALAMON

The glass is running now that cannot finish
Till one of us expire. Think you but thus:
That were there aught in me which strove to show   20
Mine enemy in this business, were't one eye
Against another, arm oppressed by arm,
I would destroy th'offender, coz, I would,
Though parcel of myself. Then from this gather
How I should tender you.

ARCITE   I am in labour   25
To push your name, your ancient love, our kindred
Out of my memory and i'th' selfsame place
To seat something I would confound. So hoist we
The sails that must these vessels port, even where
The heavenly limiter pleases.

PALAMON   You speak well.   30
Before I turn, let me embrace thee, cousin.

17 **part my wishes** divide my good
   wishes equally
18 **The glass** the sands of the hour glass
   once it has been turned upside down,
   an image of the irreversibility of the
   process that has been set in motion
   and perhaps also a metatheatrical reference to the end of the play.
20 **aught** anything
   show show itself
22 **arm . . . arm** one arm dominating
   the other
24 **parcel** part (cf. 'part and parcel').
   Bawcutt suggests an allusion to the
   biblical 'If thy right eye offend thee,
   pluck it out . . . ' (Matthew, 5.29–30).
25 **tender** behave towards
28 **To seat . . . confound** 'to place there
   another person, whom I should wish
   to destroy' (Skeat); *something* (the
   stress falls on *thing*) shows the de-
   personalizing effect of the process

Arcite describes.
29 **port** bring to port
30 **limiter** God or Jove; also, perhaps,
   Terminus, the classical god of limits
   and boundaries. In Peacham's *Min-
   erva Britanna* (1612) his image is accompanied by the verse: 'I am the
   bound of things, which God aboue /
   Hath fixt, and none is able to remoue'
   (193). See p. 109 above.
31–3 It is not clear when the men embrace or whether they do so once or
   twice. Palamon's request may be re-
   inforced at 32, to which Arcite's reply
   gives consent. If Palamon's line comments on their action, 'One farewell'
   is Arcite's request for a second embrace, presumably just before the exit
   of Palamon and his knights.
31 **turn** turn away and depart. They will
   not meet again until the (offstage)
   combat.

17 SD *Exeunt*] *1711 subst.; Exit Q*

This I shall never do again.

ARCITE   One farewell.

PALAMON

Why, let it be so. Farewell, coz.

ARCITE   Farewell, sir.

Exeunt Palamon and his knights.

[*Arcite addresses his three knights.*]

Knights, kinsmen, lovers – yea, my sacrifices –
True worshippers of Mars, whose spirit in you   35
Expels the seeds of fear and th'apprehension
Which still is father of it: go with me
Before the god of our profession; there
Require of him the hearts of lions and
The breath of tigers, yea the fierceness too,   40
Yea, the speed also – to go on, I mean:
Else wish we to be snails. You know my prize
Must be dragged out of blood; force and great feat
Must put my garland on, where she sticks
The queen of flowers. Our intercession then   4
Must be to him that makes the camp a cistern

34 **my sacrifices** 'alluding to the fact that, if defeated, they were to be put to death' (Skeat). Arcite sees them as sacrifices on the altar of Mars.

36–7 **the seeds . . . of it** anything that could give rise to fear, such as *apprehension* (awareness) of a reason for it

37 **still** always

38 **profession** what we profess (soldiership)

39 **Require** ask

39–40 **hearts . . . tigers** courage and endurance. (*Breath* means the ability not to get 'out of breath'.)

41 **go on** go forward

42 **Else** otherwise (they are to be quick to advance and slow to retreat)

43 **feat** warlike deeds. Q's *feate* may be a misreading of *feats*.

44 **garland** the victor's wreath, but also

Emilia, the prize
where (possibly two syllables)

44–5 **she sticks . . . flowers** Various emendations (see t.n.) have attempted to regularize the metre and grammar of these lines. Both Emilia (whom Arcite called a queen in 3.1.4) and the rose (which, as Skeat thinks, he heard her praise in 2.1.136) are the *queen of flowers* – the most beautiful flower in the garland with which she will crown him if he wins. If *where* is taken as 'whereas', the lines could also point a contrast between the 'force and great feat' of Mars and the softer rewards of Venus; her statue, if it is visible, might be the *she* of 44.

45 **intercession** prayer

46–7 **that makes . . . of men** Cf. the 'blood-sized field' (1.1.99).

33 SD *Exeunt . . . knights*] *Seward; after* coz *Q*   SD *Arcite . . . knights*] *this edn; not in Q*   34 sacrifices –] *1711 subst.;* Sacrifices *Q*   37 father of] *Weber (Theobald);* farther off *Q;* farther of *1711*   44 on] *Q;* on me *Littledale*   she sticks] *Q;* she will stick *Seward;* she sticks, *Bawcutt*   46 cistern] *(cestron)*

Brimmed with the blood of men. Give me your aid
And bend your spirits towards him.
          They [prostrate themselves before the altar, then] kneel.
Thou mighty one, that with thy power hast turned
Green Neptune into purple; whose approach   50
Comets prewarn; whose havoc in vast field
Unearthed skulls proclaim; whose breath blows down
The teeming Ceres' foison; who dost pluck
With hand armipotent from forth blue clouds
The masoned turrets; that both mak'st and break'st   55
The stony girths of cities: me thy pupil,
Youngest follower of thy drum, instruct this day
With military skill, that to thy laud

47 **Brimmed with** brimming over with
48 *SD Q has only '*they kneele*'; but
   Theseus' commands at 13, 61 SD and
   129 SD indicate a more elaborate
   ritual.
49–61 This long, sustained, carefully
   controlled sentence (like the one that
   follows the sound effects at 61 SD)
   requires a delivery quite unlike Arcite's previous style. The intention may
   be to transform him into an embodi-
   ment of the qualities associated with
   Mars.
49–50 an obvious reminiscence of 'The
   multitudinous seas incarnadine, /
   Making the green one red' (*Mac*
   2.2.59–60)
50 **Neptune** the sea
   *whose approach Seward's addition
   (see t.n.), filling an obvious gap in
   sense and metre, has been generally
   accepted.
51 **prewarn** forecast. (Comets were
   omens of war, among other disasters.)
52 **Unearthed** unearthèd; excavated (as
   Waith (Oxf[1]) notes, the earliest use in
   this sense recorded by *OED*). If it also
   means unburied, as Bawcutt suggests,
   it may be another echo of 1.1.
53 **teeming Ceres** the fertile goddess of
   fruits and grain

foison harvest
53–5 **who . . . turrets** Arcite may visualize the kind of emblematic picture
   where divine action is shown by a
   hand coming from a cloud (as on the
   title-page of Beaumont and Fletcher's
   King and No King, pub. 1619).
54 *armipotent mighty in arms: see
   KT, 1982. Leigh Hunt (1855) noted
   that Chaucer took the adjective from
   Boccaccio's *la casa del suo Dio Armipo-
   tente* ('the house of the battle-strong
   god' (*Teseida*, 7.32)), which in turn
   derives, as Skeat points out, from Statius' *Armipotens* (*Thebaid*, 7.78). The
   phrase 'armipotent Mars' is used in
   LLL 5.2.651.
   blue clouds clouds of smoke
   (Proudfoot)
55 **masoned** built by masons; cf. 'And
   broils root out the work of masonry'
   (*Son* 55) and Saturn's lines in *KT*,
   2463–5: 'Mine is the ruin of the high
   hals, / The falling of the toures and of
   the wals / Upon the minor, or on the
   carpenters.'
   mak'st because walls were built for
   war, to keep enemies out
56 **stony girths** walls
58 **laud** praise

47 Brimmed] (Brymd)   48 SD] Dyce; subst.; They kneele. Q   50 whose approach] Seward; not in
Q   54 armipotent] Seward; armenypotent Q

I may advance my streamer and by thee
Be styled the lord o'th' day. Give me, great Mars,   60
Some token of thy pleasure.

> *Here they fall on their faces, as formerly, and there is heard*
> *clanging of armour, with a short thunder, as the burst of a*
> *battle, whereupon they all rise and bow to the altar.*

Oh great corrector of enormous times;
Shaker of o'er-rank states; thou grand decider
Of dusty and old titles, that heal'st with blood
The earth when it is sick and cur'st the world   65
O'th' pleurisy of people: I do take
Thy signs auspiciously and in thy name
To my design march boldly. Let us go.

> *Exeunt [Arcite and his knights].*

Enter PALAMON *and his knights, with the former observance.*

PALAMON
   Our stars must glister with new fire or be
   Today extinct. Our argument is love,   70

---

59 **streamer** banner
60 **styled** called
61.1–3 The sound-effects need to be recognizable as those of a battle (compare the offstage '*noise of a sea-fight*' in *AC* 3.10.0.3–4). They may be combined with some visual effect corresponding to the signs offered to Palamon and Emilia later in the scene. Perhaps the statue of Mars extends a garland to Arcite, signifying his triumph (the garland is referred to at 44, above, and later at 5.3.130–1 and 5.4.79–80). Chaucer describes a voice saying, 'Victory!'; this will become the offstage shouting at 5.3.91 SD.
61.1 *as formerly* See above, 48 SD.
62–6 See headnote on 1.2 for this view of war as a cure for decadent societies and compare 1.2.23–4.

62 **enormous times** ages full of enormities (crimes)
63 **o'er-rank** overripe – that is, rotten
64–5 **heal'st ... sick** bleeding was recommended as a treatment for illnesses caused by excess. Waith (Oxf¹) compares 3.1.114.
66 **pleurisy** excess; a metaphorical reference to the lung condition pleurisy, sometimes spelled 'plurisy', which was mistakenly derived from Latin *plus, pluris* (more) and thought to result from a harmful excess of humours
68.2 *with ... observance* i.e., with whatever rituals have already been performed by Arcite and his knights
69 **Our stars** fates; also, perhaps, a reference to their costumes (see Appendix 4, p. 352). Cf. 5.3.19–20.
70 **argument** subject of contention

---

65 cur'st] *Seward;* curst *Q*   66 pleurisy] *Seward;* pluresie *Q;* plurisy *Weber*   68 design march boldly.] *1711;* designe; march boldly, *Q*

Which, if the goddess of it grant, she gives
Victory too; then blend your spirits with mine,
You whose free nobleness do make my cause
Your personal hazard. To the goddess Venus
Commend we our proceeding and implore   75
Her power unto our party.   *Here they kneel as formerly.*
Hail, sovereign queen of secrets, who hast power
To call the fiercest tyrant from his rage
And weep unto a girl; that hast the might,
Even with an eye-glance, to choke Mars's drum   80
And turn th'alarm to whispers; that canst make
A cripple flourish with his crutch and cure him
Before Apollo; that mayst force the king
To be his subject's vassal and induce
Stale gravity to dance! The polled bachelor –   85
Whose youth, like wanton boys through bonfires,

72 **blend** Oxf[1]'s *bend* makes sense, as a parallel to 48, above, and in view of the stress both Arcite and Palamon give to proper obeisance, but so does the Q reading. The dramatists may have intended to make the two invocations exemplify, respectively, Strife and Love, the two principles that, according to Empedocles, cause the separation or blending of elements. At Ashland Palamon and his knights blended their voices, speaking the first lines of the invocation in unison.

73 **free** generous. See 2.2.182n.
   do Though the subject is *nobleness*, the verb agrees with *you* (the three knights).

77 **secrets** because love, especially court-ly love, depended on secrecy

78–9 **To . . . a girl** to make him weep in front of a girl (presumably because she has rejected his love). Theobald suggested *into* for Q's *unto* (i.e., until he became as weak as a girl).

80 **choke** silence

81 **alarm** a call to arms, often with a roll of drums – perhaps similar to the

sound-effects heard from Mars' altar at the end of Arcite's invocation
   whispers perhaps of *secrets* (77) or the talk of lovers in bed?

82 **flourish . . . crutch** wave his crutch in the air. RP compares *AWW* 2.3.39–43; see also 83–5 below

83 **Before Apollo** sooner even than Apollo, the god of healing

85 **Stale gravity** the grave, elderly man
   polled bald

86–7 **Whose . . . flame** who in his youth leaped over (avoided) the flames of love as boys do the flames of bonfires. The verb agrees with *boys* rather than its actual subject, *youth*.

86 **bonfires** (Pronounced with three syllables: bon-fi-ers; see 3n., above.) The word still had its etymological meaning of 'bone fires': fires to burn bones and other rubbish, lighted at a time of peace-making (to bury the bone of discord) or of celebration (from which resulted a false etymology from the French *bon* (good)). Proudfoot cites Frazer, *The Golden Bough* (abridged edn, London, 1957, ch. 62) for the practice of jumping over them.

79 And] *Q; To Seward*   unto] *Q; into (Theobald).*   85 polled] *(pould)*

Have skipped thy flame – at seventy, thou canst catch
And make him, to the scorn of his hoarse throat,
Abuse young lays of love. What godlike power
Hast thou not power upon? To Phoebus thou   90
Add'st flames hotter than his: the heavenly fires
Did scorch his mortal son, thine him; the huntress
All moist and cold, some say, began to throw
Her bow away and sigh. Take to thy grace
Me thy vowed soldier, who do bear thy yoke   95
As 'twere a wreath of roses, yet is heavier
Than lead itself, stings more than nettles.
I have never been foul-mouthed against thy law;

87 **seventy** T. Spencer comments on the
fact that Palamon's three examples of
the power of Venus refer to a man of
seventy, a man of eighty (108), and a
man of ninety (130): 'The result is
that what impresses us . . . is not the
power of love, but a series of images of
decay' (p. 273).

88–9 **make . . . love** make a fool of himself by murdering youthful love songs
with his hoarse voice (Skeat). This description (and 107–15, below) recalls
Chaucer's account of the elderly hero
of *The Merchant's Tale*, who croaks
out a song to his young wife on his
wedding night (1844–54).

89–90 **What godlike . . . upon?** The list
of gods vanquished by Cupid recalls
the procession in *The Faerie Queene*,
3.11.

90 **Phoebus** Apollo, in his role as sun
god

92 **his mortal son** Phaeton (see 1.2.85–
7n.) was scorched by Jupiter's thunderbolt; Apollo burned with love for
many mortal women, such as Daphne.
the huntress Diana. Palamon's tentative reference to the well-known
story of her love for the shepherd
Endymion may be motivated by respect for the goddess whom Emilia
serves.

93 **moist** The moon is called 'the moist
star' in *Ham* 1.1.118 because of its relation to the tides.
cold chaste

96 **a wreath of roses** In *VA*, Venus says
that she led Mars 'captive in a red rose
chain' (110).
is ('it', the yoke, is . . .)

98 **thy law** in particular, secrecy, according to the rules of courtly love. Most
of Palamon's speech is about the importance of not talking about one's
sexual experiences. Many editors have
pointed out the contrast with 3.3,
where Palamon and Arcite remin-
isce about conquests that appear to
have been common knowledge ('I
have heard'; 'Else there be tales
abroad'). At least, Palamon's insistence in 100–1 may be true: the women
mentioned by the two cousins in 3.3
do not appear to have been married.
Littledale points out a close parallel to
Fletcher's *Women Pleased*, where the
hero tells his best friend, 'I never lov'd
him, / Durst know his name, that
sought a Virgin's ruin, / Nor ever
tooke I pleasure in acquaintance /
With men, that give as loose raynes
to their fancies / As the wilde
Ocean . . . ' (Bowers, 5: 1.1.137–41).

91 his:] *Seward subst.;* his *Q*

Ne'er revealed secret, for I knew none – would not,
Had I kenned all there were. I never practised   100
Upon man's wife nor would the libels read
Of liberal wits. I never at great feasts
Sought to betray a beauty, but have blushed
At simpering sirs that did. I have been harsh
To large confessors and have hotly asked them   105
If they had mothers – I had one, a woman,
And women 'twere they wronged. I knew a man
Of eighty winters, this I told them, who
A lass of fourteen brided. 'Twas thy power
To put life into dust: the aged cramp   110
Had screwed his square foot round;
The gout had knit his fingers into knots,
Torturing convulsions from his globy eyes
Had almost drawn their spheres, that what was life
In him seemed torture. This anatomy   115
Had by his young fair fere a boy, and I
Believed it was his, for she swore it was –

---

100 **kenned ... were** known 'all secrets
  in existence' (Leech)
100–1 **practised / Upon** tried to seduce
101 **libels** attacks on women in general
  or particular
102 **liberal** licentious
103 **betray a beauty** (by talking about
  her in public)
105 **large confessors** men who boast –
  both much and grossly (*Riv*, paraphrase) – of their sexual triumphs
  hotly angrily
106–7 **If ... wronged** Palamon is quoting his own words.
106 **If ... mothers** a proverbial rebuke,
  used only by men, to remarks that, by
  degrading all women, ultimately reflect even on the legitimacy of the
  speaker's birth (Dent, M1201.1). Cf.
  Troilus' refusal to believe that he has
  just heard Cressida betraying him:
  'Think we had mothers' (*TC* 5.2.130).

109 **brided** married
  thy Venus'
110 **To put ... dust** not only to breathe
  life into the half-dead old man (as
  God created Adam from dust: Genesis, 2.7), but to create new life from
  him by making his bride pregnant
  aged cramp the rheumatism inci-
  dent to old age
111 **screwed ... round** twisted his
  straight (or sturdy) foot; perhaps alludes to squaring the circle
113–14 **Torturing ... spheres** His eyes
  rolled in his head until they seemed
  ready to come out of their sockets. Cf.
  Ham 1.5.17.
114–15 **what ... torture** In so far as he
  moved, it was with the jerks and
  twitches of someone being tortured.
115 **anatomy** skeleton
116 **fere** wife

104 simpering] *(simpring)*

And who would not believe her? Brief, I am,
To those that prate and have done, no companion;
To those that boast and have not, a defier;   120
To those that would and cannot, a rejoicer.
Yea, him I do not love that tells close offices
The foulest way nor names concealments in
The boldest language. Such a one I am
And vow that lover never yet made sigh   125
Truer than I. Oh, then, most soft sweet goddess,
Give me the victory of this question, which
Is true love's merit, and bless me with a sign
Of thy great pleasure.
       Here music is heard; doves are seen to flutter. They fall
            again upon their faces, then [rise to] their knees.
Oh thou that from eleven to ninety reign'st   130
In mortal bosoms, whose chase is this world

118 **And . . . her?** Many commentators take this to be sarcastic and it is often cut in performance. But RSC's Gerald Murphy spoke with excited intensity, as if describing a miracle. **Brief** in short

118–21 ***I am . . . rejoicer** Q's punctuation (see t.n.) makes sense until the last two words, which are left dangling. Seward's emendation seems to restore the intended parallelisms: Palamon claims to avoid the rake, who actually has done what he boasts of; to defy the slanderer, who gratuitously harms women's reputations; and to sympathize with the unsuccessful (perhaps impotent?) lover, even the old man of 107–18. The implied verb with the auxiliaries *have not*, *would* and *cannot* is 'do' in the sense of 'have sex with'.

121 **rejoicer** *OED* defines this as 'one who causes rejoicing', but cites no other example from the period. The context suggests 'encourager'.

122 **Yea** an intensifier, as if Palamon thought this behaviour even more

meritorious than what he had previously described
close offices secret functions. Both *close* and *office* have the double meaning of 'privy'; hence, perhaps, the occurrence of *foulest* in the next line, with the added double meaning of 'muddiest road' (RP).

123 **concealments** things that should be concealed

127 **question** quarrel

128 **true love's merit** the reward of the true lover

129 **thy great pleasure** thy greatness's, or thy grace's, will

129.1 *doves* birds sacred to Venus. They may have been held by someone behind the altar (or by an actor representing a statue of Venus) so that they would flutter but not fly away.

131–2 RP notes a parallel with Chaucer's *Troilus and Criseyde*: 'But O Fortune . . . Soth is, that under God ye bene oure hierdes, / Though to us bestes ben the causes wrie' (3.617–20).

131 **chase** hunting-ground

118 am,] *Seward;* am *Q*   119 companion;] *Seward;* Companion *Q*   120 defier;] *Seward;* defyer *Q*   121 rejoicer.] *Seward;* Rejoycer, *Q*   129.2 *rise to] this edn;* on *Q*

And we in herds thy game: I give thee thanks
For this fair token, which, being laid unto
Mine innocent true heart, arms in assurance
My body to this business. Let us rise   135
And bow before the goddess.   *They [rise and] bow.*
                    Time comes on.
                    Exeunt [Palamon and his knights].

Still music of recorders. Enter EMILIA *in white, her hair about her shoulders, wearing a wheaten wreath. One [maid] in white holding up her train, her hair stuck with flowers. One [maid] before her carrying a silver hind, in which is conveyed incense and sweet odours, which being set upon the altar, her maids standing aloof, she sets fire to it. Then they curtsey and kneel.*

EMILIA

O sacred, shadowy, cold and constant queen,
Abandoner of revels, mute contemplative,
Sweet, solitary, white as chaste, and pure

133 **laid unto** added to: Palamon is armed both with the consciousness of the purity of his love and the confidence of Venus' favour, as shown by the music and the doves. The *token* might also be some small object to wear near his heart (as Emilia wears the men's pictures).

136 **Time comes on** Our time is up, or, the hour of the combat is at hand.

136.1–5 The procession recalls the opening of the play (1.1.0.1–7), with Emilia, in her bridal dress, taking the place of Hippolyta.

136.1 *Still* soft
recorders a contrast with the martial music for Arcite and his knights and the soft music (perhaps of a lute) accompanying the signs from Venus

136.3 *stuck* adorned

136.4 *silver* because appropriate to Diana, the moon goddess: the moon's metal, according to astrology and medical theory, was silver (Proudfoot). See below, 146.
hind a female deer; sometimes a symbol of virginity, and thus doubly appropriate to a procession to Diana's altar. As the hind is being symbolically sacrificed to Diana, there is also the suggestion that Emilia, like Arcite's three friends, is herself to be a sacrifice. See pp. 103–5 above.

136.5 *aloof* at a slight distance

139–40 **pure … snow** Cf. 'the fann'd snow that's bolted / By th' northern blasts twice o'er' (*WT* 4.4.363–5). Most descriptions of the goddess Diana are equally applicable to the moon.

136 SD] *Oxf; They bow. after 134 Q*   136.1 *recorders*] *Littledale subst.; records Q*   136.2 *wearing*] *Dyce; not in Q   maid*] *this edn; not in Q*   136.3 *maid*] *this edn; not in Q*

As wind-fanned snow, who to thy female knights   140
Allow'st no more blood than will make a blush,
Which is their order's robe: I here, thy priest,
Am humbled 'fore thine altar. Oh, vouchsafe
With that thy rare green eye, which never yet
Beheld thing maculate, look on thy virgin;   145
And, sacred silver mistress, lend thine ear,
Which ne'er heard scurrile term, into whose port
Ne'er entered wanton sound, to my petition
Seasoned with holy fear. This is my last
Of vestal office. I am bride-habited,   150
But maiden-hearted; a husband I have 'pointed,
But do not know him. Out of two, I should
Choose one and pray for his success, but I
Am guiltless of election. Of mine eyes,
Were I to lose one, they are equal precious;   155

140 **female knights** Skeat compares 'virgin knight' in *MA* 5.3.13. The most famous female knight of the period was Spenser's Britomart, the defender of chastity and married love, who appears in Books 3–5 of *The Faerie Queene*; she literally fights for chastity, but Diana's knights normally are only metaphorical warriors.

140–2 **to thy ... robe** 'Fullness of the blood' was associated with an excess of the sanguine (sensual) humour; hence the association of whiteness with virginity, and the fascination with blushing as a symbol both of modesty and of the potential for sensuality.

144 **green eye** This term puzzled Seward, who suggested 'sheen [extremely shining]'. Weber argues, with examples, that '*Green eyes* were considered as peculiarly beautiful.' One reason might be the association of green with youth, immaturity and innocence (RP notes the phrase 'green-sickness' for the illness of adolescent virgins). In *Oth*, green eyes are associated with jealousy (3.3.166). Emilia appears anxious that Diana not be jealous of her decision to marry.

145 **maculate** spotted, impure

146 **silver mistress** Diana, in her role as moon goddess

147 **scurrile** scurrilous
port short for portal: entrance

148 **wanton** lewd

149–50 **my last ... office** my last duty as a virgin (though not strictly a vestal, or worshipper of Vesta)

150 **bride-habited** dressed as a bride

151 **maiden-hearted** Proudfoot ('New', 257–8) notes the contradiction with 4.2.46 ('My virgin's faith has fled me'). But the flight may have been temporary.
a ... 'pointed I have a husband who is fated (appointed) to me (cf. 1.1.29–30).

154 **guiltless of election** 'I have made no choice.' To choose would make her guilty, both in betraying her service to the virgin goddess and, as she goes on to say, in condemning one of the men to death.

152 him.] *Seward subst.;* him, Q   154 election. Of] *Dyce subst.;* election of Q

I could doom neither: that which perished should
Go to't unsentenced. Therefore, most modest Queen,
He of the two pretenders that best loves me
And has the truest title in't, let him
Take off my wheaten garland, or else grant   160
The file and quality I hold I may
Continue in thy band.

Here the hind vanishes under the altar and in the place
ascends a rose tree, having one rose upon it.

See what our general of ebbs and flows,
Out from the bowels of her holy altar,
With sacred art advances: but one rose!   165
If well inspired, this battle shall confound
Both these brave knights and I, a virgin flower,
Must grow alone, unplucked.

Here is heard a sudden twang of instruments, and the rose
falls from the tree, [which then descends].

The flower is fall'n; the tree descends. Oh, mistress,
Thou here dischargest me; I shall be gathered –   170
I think so – but I know not thine own will;

158 **pretenders** claimants
160 **wheaten garland** symbol of virginity, already mentioned in 1.1. Also of peace, as Skeat points out, comparing *Ham* 5.2.41: 'peace should still her wheaten garland wear'.
161 **file and quality** rank and status (as a virgin)
162.1–2 The disappearance of the hind and its replacement by the rose tree was probably accomplished by the same means as the disappearing banquet in *Tem* 3.3.51 SD: perhaps a stagehand under a trapdoor, as Waith (Oxf[1]) suggests; perhaps a reversible table.
163 **our . . . flows** Diana as the moon, who rules the tides
164 **the bowels** the depths. The image may have been suggested by the fact that classical augury involved interpreting the entrails of sacrificial animals.

166 **If well inspired** if this interpretation is divinely inspired (that is, correct)
confound destroy
167–8 **I . . . unplucked** perhaps recalling Theseus' warning to Hermia in *MND* 1.1.77 that the unmarried virgin is like the rose 'withering on the virgin thorn'. But the comparison is common.
168.1 *a sudden twang* May be similar to the 'strange, hollow, and confused noise' that ends the masque at *Tem* 4.1.138. Not necessarily made by strings (RP).
168.2 *which then descends* Some such direction is implied by Emilia's next lines.
170 **dischargest me** release me from your service (i.e., give me permission to marry)

165 art] *this edn;* act *Q*   168.2 *which then descends*] Dyce *subst; not in Q*

Unclasp thy mystery! – I hope she's pleased;
Her signs were gracious.   *They curtsey and exeunt.*

[5.2]   *Enter* Doctor, Jailer *and* Wooer *in the habit of
                    Palamon.*

DOCTOR
Has this advice I told you done any good upon her?
WOOER
Oh, very much. The maids that kept her company
Have half persuaded her that I am Palamon.
Within this half hour she came smiling to me
And asked me what I would eat and when I would
    kiss her.   5
I told her, 'Presently!' and kissed her twice.
DOCTOR
'Twas well done. Twenty times had been far better,
For there the cure lies mainly.
WOOER   Then she told me
She would watch with me tonight, for well she knew
What hour my fit would take me.
DOCTOR   Let her do so.   10

172–3 **Unclasp ... gracious** There seems to be a pause after Emilia's plea; she asks to know, not only what will happen, but what the goddess wishes (which means, which of the two men she has chosen). As no stage business is indicated, it may be that there is no reply and that Emilia in these lines (addressed more to herself than to her maids) tries to talk herself into an optimistic interpretation. Or the signs to which she refers in 173 may be, not those already seen, but new omens occurring at this point.

5.2.0.1 **the habit of** He probably wears Palamon's old costume, which Palamon would not have needed after Act 3.

1–6 Printed as verse in Q, but with irregular lineation (see t.n.). Lines 1–2, though unscannable as blank verse,

work fairly well as alexandrines. Line 5 scans as blank verse if *I would* is pronounced 'I'd'. See pp. 122–3 above.

2 **maids** See n. to 39 SD, below.

6 **'Presently!'** at once (as also 11 below)

9 **watch** stay awake to watch over

10–11 **fit ... fit her** The Daughter imagines that Palamon, suffering from a malarial type of fever such as was caught in prison, will have regular intervals of fever and shivering. The Doctor's pun on *fit* involves two other meanings: 1. attack of sexual desire and 2. 'enter her' (compare 'stow her' in 2.3.33). In Fletcher's *Wit Without Money* (*c.*1614), the rakish hero sings the heroine a song beginning 'The fit's upon me now' (Bowers, 6: 5.4.53).

5.2] Scæna 2. *Q*   2–6] *Q lines* company / this / what I / told her / twice.

And, when your fit comes, fit her home, and
   presently.

WOOER
   She would have me sing.

DOCTOR
   You did so?

WOOER   No.

DOCTOR   'Twas very ill-done then;
   You should observe her every way.

WOOER   Alas,
   I have no voice, sir, to confirm her that way.   15

DOCTOR
   That's all one, if ye make a noise.
   If she entreat again, do anything.
   Lie with her if she ask you.

JAILER   Whoa there, Doctor!

DOCTOR
   Yes, in the way of cure.

JAILER   But first, by your leave,
   I'th' way of honesty.

DOCTOR   That's but a niceness.   20
   Ne'er cast your child away for honesty.
   Cure her first this way; then if she will be honest,
   She has the path before her.

JAILER   Thank ye, Doctor.

---

11 **home** thoroughly
12 **would have me** wanted me to
14 **observe** humour, gratify
16 Skeat compares *AYL*: ''Tis no matter how it be in tune, so it make noise enough' (4.2.9).
18 **Whoa** Q's *Hoa* clearly means stop.
19 **in the way of** The phrase as used by the Doctor means 'as part of the cure'; the Jailer means 'as far as honour allows' (see *OED sb*. 35f), which is also how the Daughter uses the phrase (71, below). That *way* may also mean

path or direction is indicated by 22–3.
20 **honesty** chastity (and the reputation for it)
   niceness excessive delicacy
21 **cast** . . . **away** lose your child (to madness)
22 **will be** wants to be
23 **the path** i.e., marriage
   Thank ye It is tempting to assign this speech to the Wooer, who has more reason to be grateful for the advice. If the Jailer says it, he must be either puzzled or sarcastic.

11] *Q lines* home, / presently. /   18 Whoa] *(Hoa)*

DOCTOR
　　Pray bring her in and let's see how she is.
JAILER
　　I will, and tell her   25
　　Her Palamon stays for her. But, Doctor,
　　Methinks you are i'th' wrong still.   *Exit Jailer.*
DOCTOR   Go, go,
　　You fathers are fine fools. Her honesty?
　　An we should give her physic till we find *that*!
WOOER
　　Why, do you think she is not honest, sir?   30
DOCTOR
　　How old is she?
WOOER   She's eighteen.
DOCTOR   She may be,
　　But that's all one, 'tis nothing to our purpose.
　　Whate'er her father says, if you perceive
　　Her mood inclining that way that I spoke of,
　　Videlicet, the 'way of flesh' – you have me?   35
WOOER
　　Yes, very well, sir.
DOCTOR   Please her appetite
　　And do it home, it cures her, *ipso facto*,
　　The melancholy humour that infects her.
WOOER
　　I am of your mind, Doctor.

26 **stays** is waiting
29 'If we had to treat her medically until
we discovered whether or not she was
a virgin ... (we would go on forever).'
A supposedly scientific test of virginity is depicted (and ridiculed) in Middleton and Rowley's *The Changeling*,
4.1.
32 **that's all one** that makes no
difference
nothing ... purpose irrelevant

35 *Videlicet* that is to say (Latin)
the 'way of flesh' towards sexual
desire (proverbial: Dent, W166)
you have me? 'You see what I mean?'
Both this exchange and *videlicet* occur
in the Polonius–Reynaldo scene (*Ham*
2.1.59, 65–6), of which this speech
seems a curious reminiscence.
37 **home** See 11, above.
ipso facto by that very act (Latin)

24] *Q lines* in / is. /   27–8 Go ... honesty?] *one line Q*   35 *Videlicet*] *roman Q*   'way of flesh']
italic Q   36 Yes] *F;* Yet *Q*

Enter Jailer, Daughter *and Maid.*

DOCTOR

You'll find it so. She comes; pray, humour her.   40

JAILER

Come, your love Palamon stays for you, child,
And has done this long hour, to visit you.

DAUGHTER

I thank him for his gentle patience;
He's a kind gentleman and I am much bound to him.
Did you ne'er see the horse he gave me?

JAILER   Yes.   45

DAUGHTER

How do you like him?

JAILER   He's a very fair one.

DAUGHTER

You never saw him dance?

JAILER   No.

DAUGHTER   I have, often.

39 SD *Enter . . . Maid* The maid has no
lines; her function is presumably to
keep an eye on the Daughter (RP) or
to assist the Doctor in his deception.
Most directors simply remove her.
Wells (*TxC*) and Waith (Oxf¹), arguing that the Daughter would not have
had a personal servant, suggest that
Maide is a misreading of 'madde',
which means that the Daughter
should enter looking dishevelled. But
'mad' is not used at any of her earlier
entrance SDs, where it would be still
more appropriate. Bowers is surely
right: *Maid* in this context means one
of the friends (or *play-feres*) to whom
the Doctor and Wooer have already
referred (4.3.90–1; 5.2.2). The dramatists may have wished to recreate the
visual effect of 2.2, where Palamon
and Arcite (here corresponding to the
Wooer and the Doctor) observe
Emilia and her woman (corresponding to the Daughter and her maid or

friend). In *Pericles* another 'maid',
equally silent, enters with Marina and
is referred to in the text as her companion (5.1.79).

40 *humour her* Q's *honour her* might
work as it stands: *honour* could mean
to bow, as partners did at the start and
end of a dance, and as the Wooer finally does at 69. The interim of nearly
30 lines is curious: perhaps the Doctor
continues to coach the Wooer in the
background; perhaps either the
Wooer or the Daughter is too nervous
to begin the impersonation. At Ashland, the Daughter at first refused to
look at the Wooer, using her ramblings
about the horse to postpone the confrontation of her fantasy with the
reality before her.

41 *stays* See 26, above.

44 *bound* obliged

45 *the horse . . . me* parallels the horses
given by Emilia to Arcite (see 3.1.18–
20 and 5.4.49–50)

40 humour] *Seward;* honour *Q*

He dances very finely, very comely,
And for a jig, come cut and long tail to him,
He turns ye like a top.

JAILER   That's fine indeed.   50

DAUGHTER

He'll dance the morris twenty mile an hour –
And that will founder the best hobby-horse,
If I have any skill, in all the parish –
And gallops to the tune of 'Light o' love'.
What think you of this horse?

JAILER   Having these virtues.   55
I think he might be brought to play at tennis.

DAUGHTER

Alas, that's nothing.

JAILER   Can he read and write too?

DAUGHTER

A very fair hand, and casts himself th'accounts
Of all his hay and provender. That ostler

---

49 **jig** comic dance
   come ... tail proverbial (Dent C938): whatever happens. Literally, whether a horse has a docked tail or one that has been allowed to grow. Holdsworth gives examples of bawdy contemporary meanings for both *cut* and *tail* as well as for *horse*, *jig* and *dance*.
50 **ye** (= for you), a redundant survival of the old dative case
51 **dance the morris** an echo of her earlier activities in 3.5. Proudfoot suggests a reminiscence of 'Will Kemp's famous morris dance from London to Norwich in 1600'.
52 **founder** make lame
   hobby-horse A man dressed as a horse normally featured in morris dances (as in Fletcher's *Women Pleased*, 4.1). The word also meant prostitute.
53 **have any skill** know anything about it
54 **'Light o' love'** a popular tune refer-

ring to a faithless lover; also a term for a prostitute. Dancing to this tune meant being fickle. See Appendix 6, pp. 362–3.
56 **brought** brought up, trained. Skeat and Littledale suggested that this passage alludes to a celebrated performing horse of the 1590s, Marocco, or 'Banks's horse' (after the name of his owner).
57 **that's nothing** he does that already
58 **fair hand** good handwriting (like that of a professional scribe)
   casts himself 'reckons up for himself' (Bawcutt)
59 **provender** feed
59–60 **That ... him** proverbial: see Dent, R133.1. Ostlers were often accused of stealing the feed that they were paid to give the horses of lodgers. Littledale cites an ostler's complaint about a too-clever horse, which occurs in both Jonson's *New Inn* (3.1) and the Fletcher collaboration *Love's Pilgrimage* (1.1).

54 tune] *Seward;* turne *Q*   'Light o' love'] *Seward; Light a'love Q*

Must rise betimes that cozens him. You know   60
The chestnut mare the Duke has?

JAILER   Very well.

DAUGHTER

She is horribly in love with him, poor beast!
But he is like his master, coy and scornful.

JAILER

What dowry has she?

DAUGHTER   Some two hundred bottles
And twenty strike of oats – but he'll ne'er have her.   65
He lisps in's neighing, able to entice
A miller's mare. He'll be the death of her.

DOCTOR

What stuff she utters!

JAILER

Make curtsey, here your love comes.

                                    [*Wooer comes forward and bows.*]
WOOER   Pretty soul,

How do ye? [*She curtseys.*]
                            That's a fine maid! There's a curtsey!   70

DAUGHTER

Yours to command i'th' way of honesty.
How far is't now to th'end o'th' world, my masters?

---

60 **betimes** early
63 **his master** Palamon
   coy standoffish
64 **What ... she?** The Jailer shows the
   same concerns as in 2.1.
   bottles bundles (of hay)
65 **strike** a (variable) number of bushels
67 **A miller's mare** proverbial, apparently as a symbol of sobriety (see
   Tilley, M960)
   He'll ... her The Daughter identifies
   herself with the lovelorn mare, rejected by Palamon's horse.
69 **Make curtsey** Presumably the Wooer
   approaches and bows, in keeping with

his aristocratic impersonation. The
Daughter may attempt an equally
courtly response.
71 See 19–20, above.
72 **to ... world** a proverbial expression
   (Dent, *Prov* W906.11) for absolute
   devotion. The question may not be
   complete nonsense: she imagined herself seeking Palamon throughout the
   world (3.4.23), and now wonders how
   long it will be before her journey's
   end. RA compares 'an endless thing'
   (Prologue 27) and 'an end, and that is
   all' (3.2.38).

67] *Q lines* Mare, / her. /   69 SD *Wooer ... forward*] *Oxf subst.; not in* Q   *and bows*] *this edn; not in*
Q   70 SD] *Oxf; not in* Q

DOCTOR

Why, a day's journey, wench.

DAUGHTER [*to Wooer*]   Will you go with me?

WOOER

What shall we do there, wench?

DAUGHTER   Why, play at stool-ball;

What is there else to do?

WOOER   I am content,   75

If we shall keep our wedding there.

DAUGHTER   'Tis true,

For there, I will assure you, we shall find

Some blind priest for the purpose, that will venture

To marry us, for here they are nice and foolish.

Besides, my father must be hanged tomorrow   80

And that would be a blot i'th' business.

Are not you Palamon?

WOOER   Do not you know me?

DAUGHTER

Yes, but you care not for me. I have nothing

But this poor petticoat and two coarse smocks.

WOOER

That's all one; I will have you.

DAUGHTER   Will you surely?   85

WOOER

Yes, by this fair hand, will I. [*Takes her hand.*]

---

74 **play at stool-ball** probably, make love. Stool-ball was an indoor country game similar to cricket or baseball, played by young people, especially women: a stool was used in place of the wicket or home plate. Women apparently caught the ball in their laps, a fact which encouraged sexual double meanings. In Middleton's *Women Beware Women*, Isabella is asked, 'Can you catch a ball well?' and replies, 'I have catch'd two in my lap at one game' (3.3.81–2).

75 **am content** agree

76 **keep** celebrate

78 **blind priest** meant either literally (so that he would not recognize the disparity in their rank) or figuratively (referring to an incompetent priest like Sir Oliver Martext in *AYL* 3.3)

79 **nice** over-scrupulous

80 The Daughter's casualness about the prospect of her father's death has been compared with that of Mopsa in Sidney's *Arcadia* (Thompson, 'Jailers').

84 **petticoat** long overskirt
smocks undergarments, like the modern nightshirt or nightgown

85 **That's all one** See 32n., above.

86 SD] *Leech; not in Q*

DAUGHTER   We'll to bed then.
WOOER

E'en when you will. [*Kisses her.*]
DAUGHTER [*Rubs off the kiss.*]
                    Oh, sir, you would fain be nibbling.
WOOER

Why do you rub my kiss off?
DAUGHTER   'Tis a sweet one
And will perfume me finely against the wedding.
Is not this your cousin Arcite? [*Indicates the Doctor.*]
DOCTOR   Yes, sweetheart,   90
And I am glad my cousin Palamon
Has made so fair a choice.
DAUGHTER [*to Doctor*]   Do you think he'll have me?
DOCTOR

Yes, without doubt.
DAUGHTER [*to Jailer*]   Do you think so too?
JAILER   Yes.
DAUGHTER

We shall have many children. [*to Doctor*]
                    Lord, how you're grown!

86 **then** That is, 'after we are married'. *Then* could mean 'Now, therefore', but the Jailer would be unlikely to keep silent in that case. See also 87 SP n.

87 SD Probably the Wooer kisses the Daughter on the mouth, in keeping with the Doctor's earlier advice; the English custom that allowed women to kiss men on meeting and parting is often commented on in the period. It would however be possible for him to kiss only her hand, in which case her rubbing it would be reminiscent of Lady Macbeth's sleepwalking scene.
SP Seward gave this line to the Jailer, on the ground that the Daughter has no objections to being kissed. Her response (88–9) is self-explanatory.

88–9 **'Tis ... wedding** Perhaps the Daughter sniffs her fingers or rubs them elsewhere to spread the perfume and prolong the experience of the kiss. Cf. her reaction to the real Palamon's kiss, 2.4.25–7.

89 **against** in preparation for

90–2 **Is ... choice** Cf. her enlisting other characters in her fantasies in 4.1.141–52. Line 90 scans if *Is not* is elided like 'isn't'.

94 **Lord ... grown** Either Arcite is meant to be rather short (cf. 2.1.52–3), or the Doctor was played by an unusually tall – or fat – actor. How completely the Daughter is shown to be deceived at this point is a matter for actors and director.

87 SD *Kisses her*] Dyce; *not in Q*   SP DAUGHTER] *Q*; JAILER *Seward*   SD *Rubs ... kiss*] Oxf *subst.*; *not in Q*   90 SD] Oxf *subst.*; *not in Q*

My Palamon, I hope, will grow too, finely,   95
Now he's at liberty. Alas, poor chicken,
He was kept down with hard meat and ill lodging!
But I'll kiss him up again.

Enter Messenger.

MESSENGER
What do you here? You'll lose the noblest sight
That e'er was seen.

JAILER   Are they i'th' field?

MESSENGER   They are.   100
You bear a charge there too.

JAILER   I'll away straight.
I must e'en leave you here.

DOCTOR   Nay, we'll go with you;
I will not lose the sight.

JAILER [*to Doctor*]   How did you like her?

DOCTOR
I'll warrant you, within these three or four days
I'll make her right again.   [*Exit Jailer with Messenger.*]
[*to Wooer*]   You must not from her,   105
But still preserve her in this way.

WOOER   I will.

96 **chicken** child (cf. *Mac* 4.3.218)
97 **kept down** kept from growing; but, with *up* in the next line, also sexual. The contrast with the Daughter's fantasies about Palamon's incredible potency in 4.3 may indicate her gradual return to reality.
   hard meat coarse food
101 **bear a charge** have an official role
   straight immediately
102 **we'll ... you** Bowers argues that this means the Jailer must remain to the end of the scene and leave with the Doctor. No director, to my knowledge, has staged the scene this way.

Perhaps the Doctor merely pretends that the Wooer will also accompany them and then, having got rid of the other characters, holds the Wooer back to finish the final stages of his 'cure'. Only performance can show how far the Jailer knows what is going on and how he feels about it.
103 **How ... her?** What is your diagnosis?
105 **right** in her right wits (cf. 4.1.45)
   from her leave her
106 **still ... way** keep up this pretence towards her

95 too, finely,] *Weber;* too finely *Q*   103 sight] *Dyce;* Fight *Q*   105 SD *Exit . . . Messenger.*] *Oxf; not in Q*

DOCTOR
    Let's get her in.
WOOER [*to Daughter*]
                          Come, sweet, we'll go to dinner
    And then we'll play at cards.
DAUGHTER   And shall we kiss too?
WOOER
    An hundred times.
DAUGHTER   And twenty?
WOOER   Ay, and twenty.
DAUGHTER
    And then we'll sleep together.
DOCTOR   Take her offer.   110
WOOER [*to Daughter*]
    Yes, marry, will we.
DAUGHTER   But you shall not hurt me.
WOOER
    I will not, sweet.
DAUGHTER   If you do, love, I'll cry.   *Exeunt.*

[5.3]   *Flourish. Enter* THESEUS, HIPPOLYTA, EMILIA,
                  PIRITHOUS *and attendants.*

EMILIA
    I'll no step further.
PIRITHOUS   Will you lose this sight?
EMILIA
    I had rather see a wren hawk at a fly

107 **Let's ... in** in the same excuse that
    gets the characters off stage in 4.1.149
108 **play at cards** often a cover for
    flirting
109 **And twenty?** a phrase used in bal-
    lads to mean an indefinite, or infinite,
    number (cf. 'a year and a day')
110 **Take her offer** This perhaps follows
    hesitation on the Wooer's part.
5.3.0.1–2 Q also mentions the names of
    two actors who were to play attend-

ants, T. Tucke and Curtis. See p. 70
above.
1 **Will ... sight?** closely echoes the
    previous scene (5.2.102)
2 **a wren ... a fly** a struggle in which a
    weak creature will destroy a still
    weaker one, as opposed to the forth-
    coming combat, in which both parties
    are strong
    hawk at pursue

109 twenty?] *(RP); twenty. Q*   112 SD] *Flourish Exeunt. Q*   5.3] Scæna 3. *Q*   0.1 *Flourish] after*
5.2.112 Q   0.2 *attendants.] some Attendants, T. Tucke: Curtis. Q*

Than this decision. Every blow that falls
Threats a brave life; each stroke laments
The place whereon it falls and sounds more like   5
A bell than blade. I will stay here.
It is enough my hearing shall be punished
With what shall happen, 'gainst the which there is
No deafing, but to hear, not taint mine eye
With dread sights it may shun.

PIRITHOUS [*to Theseus*]   Sir, my good lord,   10
Your sister will no further.

THESEUS   Oh, she must.
She shall see deeds of honour in their kind,
Which sometime show well, pencilled. Nature now
Shall make and act the story, the belief
Both sealed with eye and ear. [*to Emilia*]
                         You must be present: 15
You are the victor's meed, the prize and garland

---

3 **decision** trial by combat

4–5 **each . . . falls** The sword of each man will grieve to hurt the other; compare 'When this [log] burns, / 'Twill weep for having wearied you' (*Tem* 3.1.18–19).

6 **bell** death knell
stay stop

9 **No deafing. . .hear** no way not to hear

9–10 **to hear . . . shun** a difficult construction; Emilia means that she cannot avoid hearing the fight, but refuses to see it. 'I will stay here' might also be taken as the subject of both *hear* and *taint* in the following sentence – she will stop there in order only to hear, not see.

10 SD The characters presumably cross the stage in the order given in the opening SD. Thus Theseus and Hippolyta are on their way off stage, unaware of Emilia's decision, when Pirithous interrupts the procession by calling to them.

12 **in their kind** in nature, reality, as opposed to art (cf. 1.1.121–9)

13 **sometime** possibly interchangeable with 'sometimes', but may also have the sense of 'at some time'
show appear
pencilled painted; 'The old meaning of *pencil* was a *paint-brush*' (Skeat).

15 **Both . . . ear** The deeds about to be performed will be believed only by those who have the evidence of both senses ('sealed' suggests a formal legal document). Theseus appears to be replying directly to Emilia's earlier speech, but it is possible that he has not heard it.

16 **meed** reward
*prize Q's *price* is generally accepted, perhaps because the financial language recurs in 32 and 112–14, below. But although Emilia *has* a price she does not seem to *be* one; *prize* is consistent with 135, below.

---

9 hear,] *Leech*; hear; *Q*   13 well, pencilled] *Weber (Mason)*; well pencild *Q*; well-pencil'd *1778*   16 prize] *this edn.*; price *Q*

To crown the question's title.

EMILIA   Pardon me;
If I were there, I'd wink.

THESEUS   '   You must be there:
This trial is as 'twere i'th' night, and you
The only star to shine.

EMILIA   I am extinct.   20
There is but envy in that light which shows
The one the other. Darkness, which ever was
The dam of horror, who does stand accursed
Of many mortal millions, may even now,
By casting her black mantle over both   25
That neither could find other, get herself
Some part of a good name and many a murder
Set off whereto she's guilty.

HIPPOLYTA   You must go.

EMILIA
In faith, I will not.

THESEUS   Why, the knights must kindle
Their valour at your eye. Know, of this war   30
You are the treasure and must needs be by
To give the service pay.

EMILIA   Sir, pardon me;

---

17 **the question's title** the right to the
object (Emilia) over which the question (trial by combat) is taking place
Pardon me a polite refusal
18 **wink** shut my eyes
19–20 **This trial . . . shine** As in 29–30
below, Theseus plays with the idea
that Emilia's eyes will give both light
and heat to the combatants (cf.
3.1.120–1 and Sidney, *Astrophil and
Stella*, Sonnet 41).
20 **extinct** dead (no longer giving light)
21 **envy** malice (Mason)
22–8 **Darkness . . . guilty** Darkness,
normally a cover for murder, could
make up for its crimes by preventing

the combatants from seeing each
other – as in the *Iliad*, when Poseidon
spreads a mist over Achilles' eyes in
order to save Aeneas from death
(20.291–5), or *MND*, when Puck pre-
vents the duel between Lysander and
Demetrius by leading them astray in
the dark (3.2.401–30).
23 **dam** mother
28 **Set off** compensate for; the object of
the sentence is 'murder'
whereto of which (*to* which she has
to plead guilty)
29 **In faith** a mild oath; Emilia's strong-
est refusal yet

23 dam] *Q*; dame *F*

310

The title of a kingdom may be tried
Out of itself.

THESEUS   Well, well, then, at your pleasure.
Those that remain with you could wish their office   35
To any of their enemies.

HIPPOLYTA   Farewell, sister.
I am like to know your husband 'fore yourself
By some small start of time; he whom the gods
Do of the two know best, I pray them he
Be made your lot.   *Exeunt all but Emilia.*

EMILIA
Arcite is gently visaged, yet his eye   41
Is like an engine bent, or a sharp weapon
In a soft sheath; mercy and manly courage
Are bedfellows in his visage. Palamon
Has a most menacing aspect; his brow   45
Is graved and seems to bury what it frowns on,
Yet sometime 'tis not so, but alters to
The quality of his thoughts. Long time his eye
Will dwell upon his object. Melancholy

33–4 **The . . . itself** Emilia has on several occasions been compared to a kingdom (cf. 4.2.145–6). Echoing Theseus' use of *title* in 17, she points out that a decisive battle need not take place in the disputed territory.

39 **know best** know to be the better (for you). The distinction between 'better' and 'best' was less fixed grammatically than at present.

40 SD Theseus' last speech implies that Emilia is left with at least two attendants; perhaps one (the Woman of 2.2?) remains with her while the other rushes in and out with news of the fight. Lines 60–6 could be addressed to the servant if Emilia were trying to justify a decision which keeps the latter from seeing the fight (as Theseus indicated at 35–6). Most directors give Emilia only one attendant, who remains off stage while she so-

liloquizes and enters only when there is something to report at 66. The absence of an exit direction at 72 in Q need not mean that further information is conveyed by another servant, though it would be in keeping with the 'multiple messengers' device already used in 4.1.1–103. See p. 125 above for indications of exits in playtexts.

42 **engine bent** a weapon (like a bow) ready to be discharged

44 **bedfellows** are seen close together, despite their apparent contradiction; cf. 'strange bedfellows' (*Tem* 2.2.40)

45 **aspect** expression (stressed on second syllable)

46 **graved** engraved, furrowed; also a play on *bury*

47 **to** according to

48 **quality** nature

40 SD] *Dyce subst.; Exeunt Theseus, Hipolita, Perithous, &c. Q*

Becomes him nobly. So does Arcite's mirth.   50
But Palamon's sadness is a kind of mirth,
So mingled as if mirth did make him sad
And sadness merry. Those darker humours that
Stick misbecomingly on others, on them
Live in fair dwelling.   55

Cornets. Trumpets sound as to a charge.

Hark how yon spurs to spirit do incite
The princes to their proof! Arcite may win me
And yet may Palamon wound Arcite to
The spoiling of his figure. Oh, what pity
Enough for such a chance? If I were by   60
I might do hurt, for they would glance their eyes
Toward my seat and in that motion might
Omit a ward or forfeit an offence
Which craved that very time. It is much better
I am not there.

Cornets; a great cry and noise within, crying, 'A Palamon!'

                    Oh, better never born   65

51–3 Cf. Cleopatra's praise of Antony's 'heavenly mingle' of 'sad' and 'merry' (*AC* 1.5.53–61).

53–5 **Those ... dwelling** Emilia uses two different antitheses: *darker* versus *fair* and *stick* versus *live*. The darker sides of Arcite and Palamon – anger and melancholy – are set against their amiable appearance and also contrasted with the less natural, and thus less attractive, combination of humours in other men.

56 **spurs to spirit** the trumpets (which supposedly inspire courage). They are first specified at this point – to indicate the beginning of the combat, by contrast with the horns and cornets of earlier scenes. Since the fight is meant to be taking place at a distance, they may have been blown from outside the auditorium.

57 **proof** trial

58–9 **to ... figure** so that he is left mutilated. *Figure* is more likely to mean face than body.

59–60 **what pity / Enough** 'Would be' is understood; cf. the use of 'enough' in 4.3.39.

60–5 **If ... not there** Thompson (203) points out that Sidney, *Astrophil and Stella*, Sonnet 53, depicts this situation from the man's point of view.

63 **fail** to take defensive action or miss the chance of a successful attack

64 SD **'A Palamon!'** shouts of support and praise for Palamon. Since Emilia expects to hear the fight (see 7–10 above), Shirley (63) suggests that the offstage sounds include not only shouts but the clash of swords on armour, such as Arcite hears at 5.1.61 SD.

---

54 them] *Q;* him *Seward*   65 SD] *after 64 Q*

Than minister to such harm!

Enter Servant.

What is the chance?

SERVANT
The cry's 'A Palamon!'

EMILIA   Then he has won.
'Twas ever likely.
He looked all grace and success and he is
Doubtless the prim'st of men. I prithee, run   70
And tell me how it goes.

Shout, and cornets; cries of 'A Palamon!'

SERVANT   Still 'Palamon'!

EMILIA
Run and enquire.   [*Exit Servant.*]
Poor servant, thou hast lost.
Upon my right side still I wore thy picture,
Palamon's on the left. Why so, I know not;
I had no end in't else; chance would have it so.   75
On the sinister side the heart lies. Palamon
Had the best-boding chance.

Another cry and shout within, and cornets.

This burst of clamour
Is sure th'end o'th' combat.

Enter Servant.

66 **What . . . chance?** 'What has happened?' The Servant has not gone far
enough to get a view of the fight, and
can only report what the crowd is
shouting.
69 **success** (stressed on the first syllable); cf. 1.1.209
70 **prim'st** best (cf. 1.2.2)
72 **Poor servant** Emilia apparently addresses the portrait of Arcite, who
became her 'servant' in 2.5.33–4.
73 **still** always

75 **end** purpose
   else Though *else* usually means
   'otherwise', in this passage it is redundant. Some editors suggest
   emending, for instance by placing it
   with the next word, but this does not
   really help.
76 **sinister** left (from the Latin; stressed
   on second syllable)
77 **best-boding chance** the best luck, as
   indicated by the omens

66 SD] *after* chance Q   67–8 Then . . . likely.] *one line* Q   72 SD] *Dyce subst.; not in* Q   75 in't
else;] *Dyce;* in't; else *Q;* in't; chance *Seward*   77 SD] *after* 75 Q

SERVANT

    They said that Palamon had Arcite's body
    Within an inch o'th' pyramid, that the cry   80
    Was general, 'A Palamon!' But anon
    Th'assistants made a brave redemption and
    The two bold titlers at this instant are
    Hand to hand at it.

EMILIA   Were they metamorphosed
    Both into one! – Oh, why? There were no woman   85
    Worth so composed a man: their single share,
    Their nobleness peculiar to them, gives
    The prejudice of disparity, value's shortness,
    To any lady breathing.

Cornets. Cry within, 'Arcite! Arcite!'
    More exulting?

    'Palamon' still?

SERVANT   Nay, now the sound is 'Arcite!'   90

EMILIA

    I prithee, lay attention to the cry.
       Cornets; a great shout and cry, 'Arcite! Victory!'
    Set both thine ears to th' business.

SERVANT   The cry is
    'Arcite and victory!' Hark! 'Arcite! Victory!'
    The combat's consummation is proclaim'd

---

82 **Th'assistants ... redemption** Arcite's three knights rescued him.

83 **titlers** Palamon and Arcite (fighting over their title to Emilia)

84 **Hand to hand** in single combat
Were they if only they were

84–6 **Were ... man** Emilia wishes the two men could be one, so that she would not have to choose between them, then, with characteristic self-abasement, retracts this wish on the grounds that each on his own is already worth more than any woman. Cf. the description of the meeting of the French and English rulers at the Field of the Cloth of Gold: 'they clung / In their embracement, as they grew together, / Which had they, what four thron'd ones could have weigh'd / Such a compounded one?' (*H8* 1.1.9–12).

87–9 **gives ... breathing** 'injures any lady living with an unequal comparison and shows her lack of value' (Proudfoot)

88 **value's shortness** coming short in value

94–5 **The ... instruments** The cornets announce the end of the fight. Oddly phrased: perhaps (since Emilia has already been deceived once as to whether the combat is over) the Servant is explaining the musical code to her.

94 **consummation** conclusion

88 value's] *1778;* values *Q*   89 SD] *after 88 Q*

By the wind instruments.

EMILIA   Half-sights saw   95

That Arcite was no babe. God's lid, his richness
And costliness of spirit looked through him; it could
No more be hid in him than fire in flax,
Than humble banks can go to law with waters
That drift winds force to raging. I did think   100
Good Palamon would miscarry, yet I knew not
Why I did think so. Our reasons are not prophets
When oft our fancies are. (*Cornets.*)
                                        They are coming off.
Alas, poor Palamon!

Enter THESEUS, HIPPOLYTA, PIRITHOUS, ARCITE *(as victor) and*
                        attendants.

THESEUS

Lo, where our sister is in expectation,   105
Yet quaking and unsettled. – Fairest Emily,
The gods by their divine arbitrament
Have given you this knight; he is a good one
As ever struck at head. Give me your hands:

95 **Half-sights saw** even someone half-
blind could see
96 **God's lid** a rather strong oath for
Emilia, based originally on 'God's
eyelid' and usually abbreviated to
''slid'
96–7 **his richness . . . him** By contrast
with Theseus and Pirithous in 4.2,
Emilia sees the battle as one of spirit
against spirit. Having spoken earlier
of Arcite's apparent gentleness, she
now stresses the energy beneath that
surface. *Richness* may mean that she
recalls his humble appearance when
she first saw him in 2.5.
97 **costliness** rarity
looked through Cf. 'your spirits
shine through you' (*Mac* 3.1.127).
98 **fire in flax** conflates two proverbs:
'Fire that's close kept burns most of

all' (Dent, F265) and 'Put not fire to
flax' (Dent, F278), based on the fact
that flax is quick to catch fire
99–100 The ironic idea of river banks
trying to sue the water that floods
them adds another, undeveloped,
image of lawlessness and tyranny.
100 **drift winds** driving winds (Skeat)
103 **coming off** leaving the tournament
field
104.1–2 This is the third victory procession in the play. Arcite may be wearing a garland, or it may be borne in
front of him.
106 **unsettled** unfixed, both metaphorically and more literally – she has
not yet been attached to the winner
107 **arbitrament** decision
109 **As . . . head** Cf. the similar reference
to Palamon in 115–16.

103 SD] *after 104 Q*   104 SD *attendants.*] *attendants, &c. Q*

Receive you her, you him, be plighted with   110
A love that grows as you decay.

ARCITE   Emilia,
To buy you, I have lost what's dearest to me,
Save what is bought; and yet I purchase cheaply,
As I do rate your value.

THESEUS   Oh, loved sister,
He speaks now of as brave a knight as e'er   115
Did spur a noble steed. Surely the gods
Would have him die a bachelor, lest his race
Should show i'th world too godlike. His behaviour
So charmed me that methought Alcides was
To him a sow of lead. If I could praise   120
Each part of him to th'all I have spoke, your Arcite
Did not lose by't. For he that was thus good
Encountered yet his better. I have heard
Two emulous Philomels beat the ear o'th' night
With their contentious throats, now one the higher,   125
Anon the other, then again the first,
And by and by out-breasted, that the sense
Could not be judge between 'em. So it fared
Good space between these kinsmen, till heavens did

---

110 **plighted** betrothed. Perhaps Theseus joins their hands at this point,
but the action may be delayed (see
138n.).
111 **Emilia* the 1778 editors' substitution; it scans better and is perhaps
more appropriate at this point
112 **what's . . . me** Palamon
117 **his race** his descendants – like those
of the Titans who warred on the Olympian gods and were almost totally
destroyed by Jupiter (see Ovid, 6)
119 **Alcides** Hercules ('so named because Amphitryon, his step-father,
was the son of Alcaeus' (Skeat))
120 **To** by comparison with

a sow of lead literally, an ingot; figuratively, dull and heavy. 'Lead, when
first cast, is run into large masses,
called *sows* or *pigs*, according to the
size of them' (Skeat). Cf. 'A sow of
Lead is swifter' (Fletcher, *The
Woman's Prize* (*c.*1611), Bowers, 4:
4.1.19).
120–1 **If . . . spoke** if I could say as much
about each part of him as I have said
about him as a whole
122 **Did** would
127 **out-breasted** out-sung. 'Breast'
could mean voice, as in *TN* 2.3.20.
the sense (of hearing)
129 **Good space** a good while

---

111 Emilia] *1778; Emily Q*   121 to th'all] to' thall *Q*

Make hardly one the winner. [*to Arcite*]
                    Wear the garland   130
With joy that you have won. – For the subdued,
Give them our present justice, since I know
Their lives but pinch 'em. Let it here be done.
The scene's not for our seeing; go we hence,
Right joyful, with some sorrow. [*to Arcite*]
                     Arm your prize;   135
I know you will not loose her. – Hippolyta,
I see one eye of yours conceives a tear,
The which it will deliver.   *Flourish.*

EMILIA   Is this winning?
Oh, all you heavenly powers, where is your mercy?
But that your wills have said it must be so,   140
And charge me live to comfort this unfriended,
This miserable prince, that cuts away
A life more worthy from him than all women,
I should and would die too.

HIPPOLYTA   Infinite pity
That four such eyes should be so fixed on one   145

130 **hardly** with difficulty, after a hard fight (Skeat)

130–1 **Wear . . . won** Theseus may emphasize *wear* (perhaps Arcite has taken off the garland) or *with joy*. Bawcutt glosses *With joy . . . won* as 'rejoice in your victory'.

132 **our present justice** immediate death

133 **Their . . . 'em** To live in dishonour would be torture to them. 'This doom of Palamon and his three knights would be revolting, if it were not that the spectators might be expected to know enough of Chaucer's story to make them suspect that the sentence would not really be executed' (Skeat).

134 **for our seeing** for us to see

135 **Arm** 'offer your arm' (Knight). Skeat suggests 'embrace, like the German *umarmen*'.

136 **will not loose** are unwilling to part with

137 **conceives** With *deliver*, this compares her tear to the birth of a child (cf. *Tim* 1.2.110–11). Perhaps Theseus consoles Hippolyta in silence while Emilia is speaking her next lines.

138 SD The flourish, presumably at a signal from Theseus, might be expected to come at the end of the scene to signal the departure of the royal party. If it is not an error, it may mark the moment at which Arcite and Emilia finally take hands in sign of betrothal, or, as Bawcutt suggests, Arcite's taking Emilia's arm. In any case, the triumphant music contrasts ironically with Emilia's words at 138.

141 **unfriended** bereaved of his friend

144 **should and would** ought to and would want to

145 **one** one person (Emilia)

That two must needs be blind for't.

THESEUS   So it is.   *Exeunt.*

[5.4]   *Enter* PALAMON *and his* Knights, *pinioned*; Jailer,
        Executioner, Guard [*and others, carrying a block and axe*].

PALAMON

There's many a man alive that has outlived
The love o'th' people; yea, i'th' selfsame state
Stands many a father with his child. Some comfort
We have by so considering. We expire
And not without men's pity; to live still,   5
Have their good wishes. We prevent
The loathsome misery of age, beguile
The gout and rheum that in lag hours attend
For grey approachers; we come towards the gods
Young and unwappered, not halting under crimes   10

---

146 **two** two of those four eyes
   blind closed forever (in death)
   So it is Theseus either agrees with
   Hippolyta or states that Palamon's
   death is the will of fate (and therefore
   not a cause for pity).
5.4.0.1–2 In some productions, 5.3 and
   5.4 are continuous: Palamon and his
   knights enter at 5.3.104, remaining on
   stage as the bridal party leaves and the
   execution party enters. Though Palamon's presence can give extra point to
   the betrothal of Arcite and Emilia, the
   pause created by the processional
   entry and the setting up of a scaffold
   may be designed to allow a more plausible period of time for all the events
   described in 48–85. Possibly Palamon
   addresses his friends downstage while
   the scaffold is being erected or '*put out*'
   behind him (as in Fletcher and Massinger's *Sir John Van Olden Barnavelt*
   (1619), 5.3.55)). Proudfoot suggests
   that this 'stage of death' may be 'the
   same structure as the altar in 5.1', thus
   sustaining the imagery of sacrifice (see
   5.1.34). For a possible change of inten-

tion about this scene, see p. 31 above.
   pinioned Probably only their hands
   are bound, either before or behind
   them; the actions implied at 21 and
   32–5 would be posssible, if awkward.
   They may be released at a later stage.
5–6 **to live … wishes** 'We have their
   good wishes, that our lives might be
   prolonged' (Skeat).
6 **prevent** anticipate (and thus avoid)
7 **beguile** outwit
8 **rheum** catarrh, resulting in coughing
   and spitting
   lag late-coming. Skeat compares 'I
   could be well content / To entertain
   the lag end of my life / With quiet
   hours' (*1H4* 5.1.24–6).
   attend lie in wait
9 **grey approachers** people who approach death in old age
10 **unwappered** unexhausted. *OED*
   gives this as the only example of the
   negative, but 'wappered' occurs as an
   earlier variant of the later colloquial
   'woppered' or wearied.
   halting limping (under the weight of
   their sins)

5.4] Scæna 4. Q   0.2 *and … axe*] Oxf subst.; *not in* Q   1 SP] *1711; not in* Q   outlived] (out liv'd)
10 unwappered] Q; unwarp'd *Seward*; unwappen'd *Knight*

Many and stale. That sure shall please the gods,
Sooner than such, to give us nectar with 'em,
For we are more clear spirits. [*to Knights*]
                              My dear kinsmen,
Whose lives for this poor comfort are laid down,
You have sold 'em too, too cheap.

1 KNIGHT   What ending could be 15
Of more content? O'er us the victors have
Fortune, whose title is as momentary
As to us death is certain. A grain of honour
They not o'erweigh us.

2 KNIGHT   Let us bid farewell
And with our patience anger tottering Fortune,   20
Who at her certain'st reels. [*They embrace.*]

3 KNIGHT   Come, who begins?

PALAMON

E'en he that led you to this banquet shall
Taste to you all. [*to Jailer*] Aha, my friend, my friend,

---

11 **stale** old (and unrepentant: hence,
not purified)
  That refers to *we* in 9
12 **such** the *grey approachers*. Cf. his
earlier words at 2.2.105–10.
  nectar the drink served at the table of
the Olympian gods, to which heroes
were invited
13 **for** because
  clear refined, uncorrupted; there may
be a submerged pun on *spirits* and
nectar. Cf. 'Clear-spirited cousin'
(1.2.74), 'pure spirits' (2.2.75 and
1.2.97n.)
  kinsmen Arcite's knights were also
called his 'kinsmen' in 5.1.34, and
Palamon is his 'prime cousin' (1.2.2),
so the tournament has been a fight
within a single family.
16–19 **O'er us ... o'erweigh us** The
victors have the advantage over us
only in fortune, not honour.
17–18 **whose ... certain** This parallelism with too many variables is particu-

larly characteristic of late Shakespeare
(e.g., *Cym* 1.1.1–3). The short duration of the victor's good luck is compared with the certainty of death for
the vanquished. Ironically, the first
part of the statement will prove true
before the second.
17 **title** possession
  momentary short-lived
19 **bid farewell** (to each other)
20–1 **tottering ... reels** Fortune is
often pictured standing on a wheel or
a turning ball, as Fluellen describes
her in *H5* 3.6.32–6.
22 **banquet** perhaps the feast with the
gods that Palamon has already envisaged (12), or else the feast with Death,
described in, for instance, *RJ* 5.3.86
and *Ham* 5.2.365
23 **Taste** act as taster before the others
eat, to ensure that the food is wholesome. Cf. Webster, *WD*: 'let you or I /
Be her sad taster, teach her how to die'
(5.6.92–3).

---

11 stale.] *this edn;* stale: Q   21 SD] *this edn; not in* Q

Your gentle daughter gave me freedom once;
You'll see't done now forever. Pray, how does she?   25
I heard she was not well; her kind of ill
Gave me some sorrow.
JAILER   Sir, she's well restored
And to be married shortly.
PALAMON   By my short life,
I am most glad on't. 'Tis the latest thing
I shall be glad of; prithee, tell her so.   30
Commend me to her and, to piece her portion,
Tender her this. [*Gives him his purse.*]
1 KNIGHT   Nay, let's be offerers all.
2 KNIGHT
Is it a maid?
PALAMON   Verily I think so.
A right good creature, more to me deserving
Than I can 'quite or speak of.
THE KNIGHTS [*to Jailer*]   Commend us to her.   35
                                   They give their purses.

24–34 the only point at which Palamon
shows any awareness of the Daughter's existence (but cf. 4.1.18–24)
25 **You'll see't done** you'll give me freedom (in death); cf. Posthumus telling
his Jailer, 'I am call'd to be made free'
(*Cym* 5.4.193–4)
26 **her . . . ill** the fact that her illness was
insanity
28 **By . . . life** adapting the common
oath 'By my life'
29 **latest** last
31 **piece** improve, repair (an image
drawn from sewing, meaning to
patch). According to 4.1.21–4, Palamon has already made such a gift.
This is not necessarily inconsistent
(see 32n., below), but Spalding suggested, and some have agreed (see
Proudfoot), that the dialogue from
23–36 is an interpolation intended to
tie the two plots together.
portion dowry

32 **Tender** offer
Nay . . . all Since it was customary
for the condemned person to give
gifts to those officiating at an execution (see, e.g., the end of Chapman's
Tragedy of the Duke of Byron (1607–
8)), the knights offer money ear-
marked for a special purpose. 'Nay'
may mean that the knight stops Palamon and adds something to the purse
he was about to hand over.
33 **Is . . . maid?** 'Is this her first marriage?' but with a double meaning. Cf.
The London Prodigal, where someone
who has received a ribald reply to this
question corrects himself with 'Is she
married, I meane, syr?' (Brooke,
1.2.82–6). Palamon's answer does not
necessarily mean that he knew of her
love for him (as he does in Davenant's
version), but an actor might take this
opportunity to show it.
35 **'quite** requite, recompense

32 SD] *Dyce; not in Q*   35 SP] *this edn; All K. Q*

JAILER

   The gods requite you all and make her thankful.

PALAMON

   Adieu; and let my life be now as short

   As my leave-taking.   *He lays his head on the block.*

1 KNIGHT   Lead, courageous cousin.

2 AND 3 KNIGHT

   We'll follow cheerfully.

         A great noise within, crying, 'Run, save, hold!'

        Enter in haste a Messenger.

MESSENGER

   Hold, hold! Oh, hold, hold, hold!   40

        Enter PIRITHOUS *in haste.*

PIRITHOUS

   Hold, ho! It is a cursed haste you made

   If you have done so quickly! – Noble Palamon,

   The gods will show their glory in a life

   That thou art yet to lead.

PALAMON   Can that be,

   When Venus, I have said, is false? How do things

     fare?   45

---

38 SD Q's *Lies on the block* probably indicates that he was meant to lie prostrate with his head on the block. Dyce moved the direction to follow 39 – but see note to 41–2, below.

40 Most directors eliminate this apparently unnecessary character, making Pirithous himself the one to stop the execution. The reason for the duplication may be that it was found impossible for an actor to enter breathless with haste and then give a convincing rendition of the very difficult speech that follows.

41–2 Hold . . . quickly It looks as if the execution is meant to be stopped at the last possible moment, as the executioner is raising his axe. Pirithous' words (the verbs are in the indicative, not the conditional) suggest that he does not yet know whether Palamon is still alive; perhaps the audience is meant to be in equal suspense. Decapitations could be convincingly staged, as in *The Tragedy of the Duke of Byron* and *Sir John Van Olden Barnavelt*, where Fletcher even included the gruesome detail of the executioner, in his haste, striking off the victim's fingers along with his head. For the last-minute rescue in Edwards's *Damon and Pithias*, see p. 47 above.

43 will show are determined to show

45 When . . . false He has not said this, unless to himself; see pp. 46–7 above.

38 SD] *this edn; Lies on the Blocke. Q*   39 SP] *Littledale, subst.; 1.2.K. Q*

PIRITHOUS

    Arise, great sir, and give the tidings ear
    That are most rarely sweet and bitter.

PALAMON   What

    Hath waked us from our dream?

PIRITHOUS   List, then. Your cousin,

    Mounted upon a steed that Emily
    Did first bestow on him, a black one, owing   50
    Not a hair-worth of white, which some will say
    Weakens his price and many will not buy
    His goodness with this note – which superstition
    Here finds allowance – on this horse is Arcite
    Trotting the stones of Athens, which the calkins   55
    Did rather tell than trample; for the horse
    Would make his length a mile, if 't pleased his rider
    To put pride in him. As he thus went counting

47 ***rarely** Q reads *early*. Seward substituted *dearly*, pointing out the parallel with 129; his colleague Sympson suggested *rarely* (compare 4.1.110). *Early* has been defended by Bawcutt and Bowers, but the concept of strangely bittersweet news is easier to convey than that of news that is first sweet (Palamon is safe) and then bitter (Arcite is dying).

47–8 **What ... dream?** He may mean either that he was half-way to the sleep of death or simply that life is a dream, a common theme of the late romances. For another possible explanation, see pp. 57–8 above.

48–85 **List ... appears** For the language of this 'messenger speech', which stands out even in this linguistically remarkable play, see pp. 108–9 above.

50 **owing** owning

51 **Not a hair-worth** The common phrase 'not worth a hair' (Dent H19) is here literally true. Not all writers shared this belief about all-black horses (Topsell does not), but Weber quotes Cotgrave's definition of the French *zain* 'A horse that's al of one dark colour, without any starry spot or mark about him, and thereby commonly vicious.' In some allegories the good and bad horses of Plato's *Phaedrus* are also white and black, and in Boiardo's *Orlando Innamorato* a black horse faster than the wind is the gift of an evil ruler.

53 **note** characteristic

54 **allowance** confirmation

55 **calkins** the parts of a horse-shoe which are turned up and pointed to prevent the horse from slipping

56 **tell** count (see 58, below)

56–8 **for ... him** The horse is so light on his feet that he barely touches the stones and seems capable of taking 'mile-long paces' (Leech). Renaissance romances feature a number of horses who actually had this power, notably Brigliadoro, who appears both in Boiardo's *Orlando Innamorato* and in Ariosto's sequel, *Orlando Furioso*.

58 **put ... him** encourage his mettle. (*Pride* here has the sense of *OED sb.* B II 10.)

47 rarely] *1778 (Sympson)*; early *Q*; dearly *Seward*

The flinty pavement, dancing as 'twere to th' music
His own hoofs made (for, as they say, from iron   60
Came music's origin), what envious flint,
Cold as old Saturn and, like him, possessed
With fire malevolent, darted a spark,
Or what fierce sulphur else, to this end made,
I comment not. The hot horse, hot as fire,   65
Took toy at this and fell to what disorder
His power could give his will; bounds, comes on end,
Forgets school-doing, being therein trained
And of kind manage; pig-like he whines
At the sharp rowell, which he frets at rather   70
Than any jot obeys; seeks all foul means
Of boist'rous and rough jad'ry to disseat
His lord, that kept it bravely. When nought served –
When neither curb would crack, girth break, nor
    diff'ring plunges

60–1 **from iron . . . origin** a belief found in the story of Jubal (Genesis, 4.21–2)

62 **Cold . . . Saturn** In *KT*, the monster which frightens Arcite's horse is actually sent by Saturn; here 'Shakespeare reduces Saturn to a simile' (Thompson, 207) and the cause of the accident remains mysterious.

65 **comment not** will not speculate about (*what*, in 61 and 64, is the object of this verb). Pirithous reserves judgement as to whether the horse took fright naturally, at a spark from the flint, or whether some supernatural agency drove him mad.
hot as fire Thompson (207) compares a reference earlier in *KT* to Arcite's 'corser, starkinge as the fire' (1502).

66 **Took toy** was seized by a sudden mad impulse. Skeat quotes *Philaster* (Bowers, 1: 5.3.135–6): 'What if a toy take um 'ith heeles now, and they runne all away?'
this whatever it was, the spark or sulphur
fell to abandoned himself to
what whatever

67· **comes on end** bucks and rears

68 **school-doing** the techniques he had been taught in the riding school. In fact, the ability to rear up 'on his hind hoofs' (5.4.76), and to hold that position, was said to be the quality most admired in a horse, especially on occasions of 'pompe or Triomphe' (Topsell, 324–5). Like Arcite, whose superb horsemanship is about to be described, the horse is doing, with fatal results, exactly what he has been trained to do.

69 **of kind manage** well-trained, as in the French *manège*. See *OED sb.* 1a.

70 **rowell** spur

72 **jad'ry** a pun on the pejorative use of 'jade' (horse) to mean ignoble and treacherous behaviour, as in 'You always end with a jade's trick' (*MA* 1.1.144)

73 **it** his seat on horseback. *Disseat* (72), also used in *Mac* (5.3.21), is here used both as a verb and also (implicitly) to indicate the noun to which *it* refers.
bravely splendidly

74 **diff'ring plunges** different violent movements

Disroot his rider whence he grew, but that   75
He kept him 'tween his legs – on his hind hoofs
On end he stands,
That Arcite's legs, being higher than his head,
Seemed with strange art to hang. His victor's wreath
Even then fell off his head and presently   80
Backward the jade comes o'er and his full poise
Becomes the rider's load. Yet is he living,
But such a vessel 'tis, that floats but for
The surge that next approaches. He much desires
To have some speech with you. Lo, he appears.   85

Enter THESEUS, HIPPOLYTA, EMILIA, ARCITE [*carried*] *in a chair.*

PALAMON

Oh miserable end of our alliance!
The gods are mighty. Arcite, if thy heart,
Thy worthy, manly heart, be yet unbroken,
Give me thy last words. I am Palamon,
One that yet loves thee dying.

ARCITE   Take Emilia   90

75 **Disroot** Waith (Oxf¹) notes that this is *OED*'s first example of the word.
whence he grew i.e., from the saddle in which, because of his good horsemanship, he seemed to grow. The confusion between *he* and *him* in the next passage may reflect this centaur-like union of horse and rider.

77 **On . . . stands** In Q this line appears in isolation, as the last half of a line, as if the compositors had been unable to read the first half. It is possible that the scribe or compositor failed to realize that the phrase was meant to replace 'on his hind hooves', which appears immediately above it in the previous line. (See Waller, 'Printer's', 69). Bowers points out, however, that this assumption requires a further, unproven one: that the play was set up

from an authorial manuscript in which this revision was made in the process of writing (as it would have to be, to connect with the following phrase). In fact, as Skeat says, 'the half-line is rather effective'. See J. C. Maxwell (100) for the suggestion that short lines in 'heroic narrative' are imitations of the Virgilian half-line.

79 **His victor's wreath** the garland (see 5.3.130)

81–2 **his . . . load** The full weight of the horse fell on his rider.

83–4 **such . . . approaches** Cf. 'Even as men wrack'd upon a sand, that look to be wash'd off the next tide' (*H5* 4.1.97–8).

86 **alliance** both friendship and blood relationship

79 victor's] *1711;* victors *Qc;* victoros *Qu* 85 SD *cărried*] *Dyce; not in Q*

And, with her, all the world's joy. Reach thy hand;
Farewell. I have told my last hour. I was false
Yet never treacherous. Forgive me, cousin.
One kiss from fair Emilia. [*Emilia kisses Arcite.*]
                'Tis done.
Take her. I die.

PALAMON   Thy brave soul seek Elysium!   [*Arcite dies.*]

EMILIA

I'll close thine eyes, Prince; blessed souls be with thee.   96
Thou art a right good man and, while I live,
This day I give to tears.

PALAMON   And I to honour.

THESEUS

In this place first you fought: e'en very here
I sundered you. Acknowledge to the gods   100
Our thanks that you are living.
His part is played and, though it were too short,
He did it well; your day is lengthened and
The blissful dew of heaven does arrose you.
The powerful Venus well hath graced her altar   105
And given you your love. Our master Mars

---

91 **world's joy** In *KT*, Arcite has a
longer *contemptus mundi* speech, in
which he asks despairingly, 'What is
this world? What asketh man to have?'
(2777).

92 **told** counted, measured (perhaps
with a pun on 'tolled')

92–3 **false ... treacherous** Lines 115–
20 explain why Arcite sees himself as
false but continues to deny Palamon's
accusations of treason (3.6.140–51).

94 SD Weber's suggestion (see t.n.) may
be right, despite the wording here,
but Arcite's earlier 'reach thy hand'
suggests that he is incapable of
movement.
   'Tis done i.e., the kiss, his life, and
perhaps also their contention.

95 **seek** (may it) seek

98 **This day** the anniversary of this day
   to honour to honouring Arcite's
memory (Skeat)

99 **very here** in this very place (cf. 'now,
very now', *Oth* 1.1.88)

101 **Our thanks** Dyce suggests *your
thanks*. Perhaps this incomplete line
was followed by some action corresponding to the command.

104 **arrose** sprinkle, with a suggestion of
holy water; the word still exists in the
modern French *aroser*

105 **graced her altar** granted her grace
to the worshippers at her altar

106 **Our master Mars** Perhaps he uses
the royal we, or he may stress the pronoun, since, as Proudfoot points out,
Mars, the patron of soldiers, is worshipped by most of the others on stage.

---

94 SD] *Bawcutt; not in Q; kisses her. / Weber*   95 SD] *1711; not in Q*   101 Our] *Q; Your Dyce*
104 arrose] (arowze*)*

Hath vouched his oracle and to Arcite gave
The grace of the contention. So the deities
Have showed due justice. Bear this hence.

PALAMON   Oh, cousin!
That we should things desire, which do cost us   110
The loss of our desire! That nought could buy
Dear love, but loss of dear love! [*Arcite's body is carried out.*]

THESEUS   Never Fortune
Did play a subtler game. The conquered triumphs;
The victor has the loss; yet in the passage
The gods have been most equal. – Palamon,   115
Your kinsman hath confessed the right o'th' lady
Did lie in you, for you first saw her and
Even then proclaimed your fancy. He restored her
As your stol'n jewel and desired your spirit
To send him hence forgiven. The gods my justice   120
Take from my hand and they themselves become
The executioners. Lead your lady off

---

107 **vouched** made good. Theseus seems to have learned what Palamon and Arcite were promised in 5.1.
108 **grace** the success. Grace (by definition, something that cannot be earned or worked for) is thus associated with both Venus and Mars.
109 **this** Arcite's body
111 **loss ... desire** the loss of what we (also) desire (in this case, his friendship with Arcite)
112 **SD** Some editors place this direction even earlier. Palamon's lines will of course have a different effect if they are spoken as he stands by the woman he has won and calls after the friend he has lost. It would also be possible and effective to place Arcite's funeral procession at the end of the play. It is likely, however, that Theseus would be obeyed at once,

and the abruptness with which he dismisses Arcite parallels the haste with which he had earlier consigned Palamon and his knights to instant execution.
112–13 **Never ... game** Both Palamon and Arcite are presumably Fortune's antagonists. In Chaucer's *Book of the Duchess*, Fortune, 'ful of gyle', plays chess with a knight and checkmates him by taking away his lady (618–82).
114 **the passage** '(of arms), combat' (Oxf[1])
115 **equal** impartial, in the sense of giving exactly the same to each
116 **Your ... confessed** Cf. the report of Iago's and Roderigo's offstage confessions in *Oth* 5.2.321–9.
118 **fancy** love, possibly in the sense of something 'engend'red in the eyes' (*MV* 3.2.67)

112 SD] *Oxf; not in Q*

And call your lovers from the stage of death,
Whom I adopt my friends. A day or two
Let us look sadly and give grace unto   125
The funeral of Arcite, in whose end
The visages of bridegrooms we'll put on
And smile with Palamon – for whom an hour,
But one hour since, I was as dearly sorry
As glad of Arcite, and am now as glad   130
As for him sorry. Oh, you heavenly charmers,
What things you make of us! For what we lack
We laugh, for what we have are sorry, still
Are children in some kind. Let us be thankful
For that which is, and with you leave dispute   135
That are above our question. Let's go off
And bear us like the time.   *Flourish. Exeunt.*

123 **your lovers** the other knights: friends, but with the additional sense of 'fellow-lovers'; one at least has been described as having 'felt / Without doubt what he fights for' (4.2.96–7)
  the stage of death Presumably the three other knights are still waiting on or beside the scaffold. As with 102–3, above, the phrase also encourages the metatheatrical awareness that often accompanies a play's ending.
124–8 **A day ... Palamon** Cf. 'With mirth in funeral, and with dirge in marriage' (*Ham* 1.2.12) and see pp. 35–7 above.
124 **A day or two** Shaheen points out the echo of the apocryphal Ecclesiasticus, 38.17 (printed in all English Bibles from 1535 to 1826), which advises mourning, weeping and lamentation for 'a day or two', after which it is right to let oneself be comforted.
126 **in whose end** at the conclusion of which

131 **charmers** the gods, who work through 'charms' or supernatural powers
135–6 **leave ... question** refrain from disputing with beings too high to argue with. Cf. Jupiter's warning (*Cym* 5.4.93–113) that mortals have no business questioning the gods.
137 **bear ... time** i.e., 'sadly for the funeral, then happily for the wedding' (*Riv*). Cf. 'The weight of this sad time we must obey' (*KL* 5.3.324). In Boccaccio and Chaucer the funeral of Arcite is described at length and the casting of valuable objects on his funeral pyre created something of a sensation in the 1566 performance of *Palamon and Arcite* (Elliott, 223). No such spectacle is called for here and, as Berggren notes, the ending seems deliberately abrupt and frustrating (14). Most recent productions have rounded it off in some way: a procession, a tableau, a repeat of the opening song, the reappearance of the Jailer's Daughter.

133 sorry, still] *Weber (Mason);* sorry still, *Q*

[EPILOGUE]

[*Enter* Speaker of the Epilogue.]

I would now ask ye how ye like the play,
But, as it is with schoolboys, cannot say.
I am cruel fearful! Pray yet, stay a while,
And let me look upon ye. No man smile?
Then it goes hard, I see. He that has   5
Loved a young handsome wench, then, show his face –
'Tis strange if none be here – and, if he will,
Against his conscience let him hiss, and kill
Our market. 'Tis in vain, I see, to stay ye:
Have at the worst can come then! Now, what say ye?   10
And yet mistake me not: I am not bold;
We have no such cause. If the tale we have told
(For 'tis no other) any way content ye –
For to that honest purpose it was meant ye –

EPILOGUE The most likely speaker is a
boy actor dressed as a woman (see
List of Roles), since the childish
phrase *cruel fearful* would give point
to the comparison of the character
with the boy (if not schoolboy) that
he really is. His speech is constructed
as a dialogue with the spectators. The
original punctuation indicates (with
colons) a number of long pauses
where they are invited to react: after
look upon ye in 4, the boy holds a
pause while he looks at them; after
show his face in 6, he pretends to be
disappointed at the lack of response
to his challenge; at 9, he dares anyone
to hiss; at the end of 10 he invites a
response, then cuts it off with an
afterthought. As in the play itself, the
act of choosing is deliberately
deferred as long as possible, perhaps
so that, when the audience is finally
allowed to express its feelings, the
applause will be all the greater. Such
an epilogue would of course be

unthinkable unless the authors had
confidence both in the play and in the
speaker. It is possible, as RP suggests,
that the play's unexpectedly sombre
ending left its audience in stunned
silence and that the function of the
Epilogue was to restore a lighter
mood.

2 **cannot say** cannot speak for shyness
3 **cruel** terribly
   stay a while wait (before you applaud
   or hiss) (*Riv*)
5 **it goes hard** things are going badly
8–9 **hiss . . . market** start a negative reaction which will ruin our chance of
   making a profit
10 **Have at** let's face
12 **cause** cause to be bold (that is, confidence about our play). Cf. Rosalind's
   equally apologetic epilogue to *AYL*.
   the tale 'alluding to the title of the
   source' (Leech), and also suggesting
   that 'the play is not to be taken too
   seriously' (Proudfoot)
14 **meant ye** intended for you

EPILOGUE 0.1] *Oxf subst.; not in Q*

We have our end; and ye shall have ere long,   15
I dare say, many a better, to prolong
Your old loves to us. We, and all our might,
Rest at your service. Gentlemen, goodnight!

Flourish. [*Exit.*]

FINIS

---

15 **end** purpose
17 **Your old loves** The actor, while thanking his audience, acknowledges his company's many years of success.
18 **Gentlemen** Though the audience would have included women, the actor implies that the loyal and understanding playgoers will be men. Blackfriars, as Gurr (165) points out, was 'the playhouse situated closest to the Inns of Court' and its repertory was traditionally 'aimed precisely at law students and gallants'.

18 SD *Exit.*] *Oxf subst.; not in Q*

APPENDICES

Source material for *The Two Noble Kinsmen* can be found in G. Harold Metz's *Sources of Four Plays Attributed to Shakespeare*, which reprints Chaucer's *The Knight's Tale* and brief extracts from Beaumont's *The Masque of the Inner Temple and Gray's Inn*, Sidney's *The Arcadia*, Plutarch's *The Life of Theseus* and Sidney's *The Lady of May*. These appendices do not attempt to duplicate his valuable and easily accessible collection. Instead, the first two provide supplementary material on John Fletcher, still a little-known figure, while the others focus on problems of production. The verses in Appendix 1 may be part of the context in which *The Two Noble Kinsmen* was written (see pp. 9–10 above). The frontispiece to the 1647 Beaumont and Fletcher Folio (Appendix 2) is an important factor in the creation of Fletcher's posthumous reputation as Beaumont's other self. The Beaumont masque (Appendix 3) is printed in full because, as will be clear from my Introduction and from Appendix 4, I do not think its influence is confined to the morris dance episode. The remaining appendices provide information and conjecture which, although perhaps more detailed than most readers will want, might be of interest to anyone thinking of staging the play.

APPENDIX 1
JOHN FLETCHER, 'UPON AN HONEST MAN'S FORTUNE'

This is a modernized text of the verses printed in the 1647 Folio of Beaumont and Fletcher's *Comedies and Tragedies*, immediately after *The Honest Man's Fortune*. They do not directly comment on the play or performance, and the use of the indefinite article in the title may be significant. However, the unusual placement of the poem suggests that the Folio editors must have known some tradition linking it with the play. The manuscripts give a variety of titles, the most appropriate of which is 'Against Astrologers'; a commonplace book belonging to the Skipwith family (members of the Huntingdon circle) describes them simply as 'Verses by Jack: Fletcher' (Beal, 1: 1.80–1).

<blockquote>

You that can look through heaven and tell the stars,
Observe their kind conjunctions and their wars,
Find out new lights and give them where you please –
To those men honours, pleasures; to those ease;
You that are God's surveyors and can show   5
How far and when and why the wind doth blow,
Know all the charges of the dreadful thunder,
And when it will shoot over or fall under:
Tell me, by all your art I conjure ye –
Yes, and by truth – what shall become of me?   10
Find out my star, if each one, as you say,
Have his peculiar angel and his way;
Observe my fate; next fall into your dreams,
Sweep clean your houses, and new line your schemes,
Then say your worst: or have I none at all?   15
Or is it burnt out lately? Or did fall?
Or am I poor, not able, no full flame?
My star, like me, unworthy of a name?
Is it, your art can only work on those
That deal with dangers, dignities, and clothes,   20

</blockquote>

1 **You** The poem is addressed to astrologers.
3 **lights** possibly in the sense of *OED sb.* 6b: 'Illumination or enlightenment'. But it may have a special astrological sense.
14 **houses** the location of each star
schemes (*sceames* in F) astrological charts

With love or new opinions? You all lie:
A fishwife hath a fate, and so have I,
But far above your finding. He that gives
Out of his providence to all that lives,
And no man knows his treasure, no, not you;   25
He that made Egypt blind, from whence you grew
Scabby and lousy, that the world might see
Your calculations are as blind as ye;
He that made all the stars you daily read,
And from thence filch a knowledge how to feed,   30
Hath hid this from you; your conjectures all
Are drunken things, not how but when they fall.
Man is his own star, and the soul that can
Render an honest and a perfect man
Commands all light, all influence, all fate;   35
Nothing to him falls early or too late.
Our acts our angels are, or good or ill,
Our fatal shadows that walk by us still,
And when the stars are labouring, we believe
It is not that they govern, but they grieve   40
For stubborn ignorance; all things that are
Made for our general uses are at war,
Even we among our selves, and from the strife
Your first unlike opinions got a life.
O man, thou image of thy maker's good,   45
What canst thou fear, when breathed into thy blood
His spirit is, that built thee? What dull sense
Makes thee suspect, in need, that providence?
Who made the morning, and who placed the light
Guide to thy labours? Who called up the night   50
And bid her fall upon thee like sweet showers
In hollow murmurs, to lock up thy powers?
Who gave thee knowledge? Who so trusted thee,

26 **Egypt** associates astrologers first with the plagues that God inflicted on Egypt
  (Exodus, 7–12), then with Pharaoh's magicians, also mentioned in the biblical passage, and the gypsy fortune-tellers, their descendants
32 **fall** pun: prophecies that come true are said to *fall* right, but F argues that they are
  like drunks, constantly falling by accident
35 **Commands** (*command* in F)
  light refers back to 3, above
  influence an astrological term for the effect of the heavens on human beings (see
  also 60 and 64, below)
37 **angels** by contrast with the *angel* of 12, above
49–54 Dyce prints this as a series of statements, with 'who' in apposition to 'providence'
  in 48, but the passage seems to be a series of rhetorical questions similar to those
  God asks in Job, 38–41.

To let thee grow so near himself, the tree?
Must he then be distrusted? Shall his frame   55
Discourse with him, why thus and thus I am?
He made the angels thine, thy fellows all,
Nay, even thy servants, when devotions call.
Oh, canst thou be so stupid then, so dim,
To seek a saving influence, and lose him?   60
Can stars protect thee? Or can poverty,
Which is the light to Heaven, put out his eye?
He is my star, in him all truth I find,
All influence, all fate, and when my mind
Is furnished with his fullness, my poor story   65
Shall outlive all their age, and all their glory.
The hand of danger cannot fall amiss
When I know what, and in whose power, it is.
Nor want, the curse of man, shall make me groan;
A holy hermit is a mind alone.   70
Doth not experience teach us all we can
To work ourselves into a glorious man?
Love's but an exhalation, to best eyes,
The matter spent; and then the fool's fire dies.
Were I in love, and could that bright star bring   75
Increase to wealth, honour, and every thing,
Were she as perfect good as we can aim –
The first was so, and yet she lost the game.
My mistress then be knowledge and fair truth:
So I enjoy all beauty and all youth,   80
And though to time her lights and laws she lends,
She knows no age that to corruption bends.
Friends' promises may lead me to believe,
But he that is his own friend knows to live.
Affliction, when I know it, is but this: 85
A deep allay whereby man tougher is
To bear the hammer, and, the deeper still,

54 **the tree** That is, God himself is the tree of knowledge.
55 **his frame** the thing that he framed (man)
62 **light** to the guide showing the way to
67 **hand** (*band* in F)
69 **curse** (Seward: *cause* in F)
74 **fool's fire** will-o'-the-wisp (cf. the French *feu follet*)
78 **The first** Eve, the first wife
81–2 Knowledge and Truth submit to Time (whose daughter Truth proverbially is),
but not to Age, which is personified, in *bends*, as a stooping figure. Cf. the attitude to
age in *TNK*, esp. 1.2 and 2.2.
86 **allay** alloy
87–8 **the deeper … will** The more deeply God stamps us with suffering, the more we
resemble his image.

We still arise more image of his will;
Sickness, an humorous cloud 'twixt us and light,
And death, at longest, but another night.　　　　　90
Man is his own star, and that soul that can
Be honest is the only perfect man.

89 **humorous** An improper balance in the body of its moist humours, like choler and phlegm, was thought to be a source of illness; hence, sickness resembles a cloud full of rain.

APPENDIX 2
THE PORTRAIT-FRONTISPIECE OF JOHN FLETCHER, 1647

For the 1647 Folio of Beaumont and Fletcher's *Comedies and Tragedies*, the publisher Humphrey Moseley commissioned William Marshall, a well-known engraver of emblematic portraits, to provide an image of Fletcher that would make up for the lack of any available portrait of his collaborator Francis Beaumont. Marshall's engraving is based on an anonymous portrait of Fletcher, now in the National Portrait Gallery, London, but the emblematic trappings are his own. The idea of making Fletcher's bust arise from the twin peaks of Parnassus, thus implying that his own talent was infused with that of his deceased friend (see pp. 55–8 above for the idea of one soul in two bodies) may have been suggested by Sir John Berkenhead, whose verses appear under the portrait. The banner above it, supported by Comedy and Tragedy, identifies Fletcher as *Poetarum ingeniosissimus Joannes Fletcherus, Anglus, Episcopi Lond[iniensis] Fili[us]*.

> Felicis aevi ac Praesulis Natus; comes
> Beaumontio; sic, quippe Parnassus, biceps;
> Fletcherus unam in Pyramida furcas agens.
> Struxit chorum plus simplicem vates duplex;
> Plus duplicem solus: nec ullum transtulit;   5
> Nec transferendus: Dramatum aeterni sales,
> Anglo Theatro, Orbi, Sibi, superstites.
> Fletchere, facies absq$_3$ vultu pingitur:
> Quantus! vel umbram circuit nemo tuam.

Berkenhead was a well-known propagandist who edited the official royalist journal, *Mercurius Aulicus*, until the defeat of Charles I in 1645. His verses (made extremely difficult by their forced metaphysical wit) seem never to have been translated: this version is slightly adapted from that of Richard Proudfoot, and Roland Mayer of the classics department of King's College, London.

The Most Ingenious of Poets, John Fletcher, Englishman, Son of the Bishop of London

Son of a happy age and father, friend to Beaumont and thus a two-headed Parnassus, Fletcher forces the two to join in a single monu-

17 John Fletcher, by William Marshall: frontispiece to *Comedies and Tragedies Written by Francis Beaumont and John Fletcher*, Humphrey Moseley, 1647 .

ment. As the double author wrought a chorus that seemed of one piece, the single author doubled it. He imitated no one, nor is he to be imitated. Eternal wit of the plays, surviving the English stage, the Globe, Wit itself. Fletcher, your features are depicted here, but not your spirit – so great, that no one can compass even your shadow.

The notes which follow are mostly by Roland Mayer, with additions by Richard Proudfoot and me. They are keyed to the line numbers of the Latin original. Berkenhead also contributed, in English, one of the large number of commendatory poems prefixed to the 1647 folio. 'JB' refers to this poem, which, as Mayer points out, is the best gloss on the Latin.

1 *Praesulis* Renaissance classicizing Latin for 'bishop'. Cf. JB's reference to 'thy father's crosier'.

2 *biceps* 'double-headed', a term often used by poets, deriving ultimately from Ovid (*Met.* 2.221)

3 Cf. a different but possibly related conceit in JB: 'a twin-horned crescent then, now one full moon'. *Pyramida* has the general sense of 'monument', but its shape is important to the conceit of the two peaks, like the two authors, fusing into one.

4 *chorum* 'Chorus' is figurative for 'play'; i.e., the parts of the dramas composed jointly cannot be distinguished. Cf. JB: 'Each piece is wholly two yet never splits.'

5 I.e., when Fletcher wrote on his own he doubled their joint output. Cf. JB: 'that other strives to double which survives'. Possibly also a reference to Fletcher's skill at complex plots, which is praised in other commendatory verses.

7 *Orbi* the world – but, as Proudfoot notes, this is a punning reference to the Globe and the closing of the theatres
Sibi The reflexive pronoun could refer to *sales* (wit; literally 'salt') or to Fletcher 'himself'; Fletcher's wit might be said to survive itself in the sense that the victory of Parliament was generally depicted in royalist propaganda as a triumph of dullness. The line may also refer to the closing of the theatres by Parliament in 1642.

8 The point lies in the difference between *facies* (features) and *vultus*, which was taken to mean *animi ingenium*, perhaps 'characteristics'. Art's inability to capture this quality is also lamented in Ben Jonson's verses on the engraving of Shakespeare in the 1623 Folio: 'O, could he but haue drawne his wit / As well in brasse, as he hath hit / His face'.

9 *umbram* Like 'shadow' in English, *umbra* could mean the picture itself, or Fletcher's ghost, or the outline which the artist has been unable to trace.

APPENDIX 3

FRANCIS BEAUMONT, *THE MASQUE OF THE INNER TEMPLE AND GRAY'S INN*

Reproduced from the edition of Philip Edwards, in *A Book of Masques*, ed. S. Wells and T. J. B. Spencer, Cambridge University Press, 1967, pp. 131–42. The masque was first printed in an undated quarto (c. 1613); a shorter, possibly earlier, manuscript seems the basis for the version in the 1647 Beaumont and Fletcher Folio. Edwards, like other modern editors, prints the Q text. His notes and collations are not reproduced here; however, two points should be noted. First, 'country sports' (line 227) is 'clownish sports' in F. Second, lines 229–37 may suggest that the She-Fool presents the dance, but Bowers argues that '*ushering them in*' should appear on a line by itself after the list of performers, making it clear that the Pedant, like Gerald in *The Kinsmen*, is the presenter.

[DRAMATIS PERSONAE

Mercury
Iris
Four Naiads ⎫
Five Hyades ⎪ The first anti-masque
Four Cupids ⎬
Statues ⎭
A Pedant ⎫
A May Lord ⎪
A May Lady ⎪
A Servingman ⎪
A Chambermaid ⎪
A Country Clown or Shepherd ⎬ The second
A Country Wench ⎪ anti-masque
An Host ⎪
An Hostess ⎪
A He-Baboon ⎪
A She-Baboon ⎪
A He-Fool ⎪
A She-Fool ⎭

Fifteen Olympian Knights; the masquers
Chorus of Twelve Priests of Jupiter]

THE MASQUE

presented before his Majesty, the Queen's Majesty,
the Prince, Count Palatine and the Lady Elizabeth their
Highnesses, in the Banqueting House at Whitehall
on Saturday the twentieth day of February, 1613

* * *

*To the worthy Sir Francis Bacon, his Majesty's Solicitor-General, and the
grave and learned Bench of the anciently allied houses of Gray's Inn and
the Inner Temple, the Inner Temple and Gray's Inn.*

Ye that spared no time nor travail in the setting forth, ordering, and
furnishing of this masque, being the first fruits of honour in this kind   5
which these two societies have offered to his Majesty, will not think
much now to look back upon the effects of your own care and work; for
that whereof the success was then doubtful, is now happily performed
and graciously accepted. And that which you were then to think of in
straits of time, you may now peruse at leisure. And you Sir Francis
Bacon especially, as you did then by your countenance and loving af-   10
fection advance it, so let your good word grace it and defend it, which is
able to add value to the greatest and least matters.

This Masque was appointed to have been presented the Shrove Tues-
day before, at which time the masquers, with their attendants and   15
divers others, gallant young gentlemen of both houses, as their convoy,
set forth from Winchester House, which was the rendezvous, towards
the Court, about seven of the clock at night.

This voyage by water was performed in great triumph. The gentlemen masquers being placed by themselves in the King's royal barge   20
with the rich furniture of state, and adorned with a great number of
lights placed in such order as might make best show.

They were attended with a multitude of barges and galleys, with all
variety of loud music, and several peals of ordnance. And led by two
admirals.   25

Of this show his Majesty was graciously pleased to take view, with the
Prince, the Count Palatine and the Lady Elizabeth their Highnesses, at
the windows of his privy gallery upon the water, till their landing,
which was at the privy stairs; where they were most honourably received by the Lord Chamberlain, and so conducted to the vestry.   30

The hall was by that time filled with company of very good fashion,
but yet so as a very great number of principal ladies and other noble
persons were not yet come in, whereby it was foreseen that the room
would be so scanted as might have been inconvenient. And thereupon
his Majesty was most graciously pleased, with the consent of the   35

341

gentlemen masquers, to put off the night until Saturday following, with this special favour and privilege, that there should be no let as to the outward ceremony of magnificence until that time.

At the day that it was presented, there was a choice room reserved for the gentlemen of both their houses, who coming in troop about seven of 40 the clock, received that special honour and noble favour, as to be brought to their places by the Right Honourable the Earl of Northampton, Lord Privy Seal.

The Device or Argument of the Masque

Jupiter and Juno, willing to do honour to the marriage of the two 45 famous rivers Thamesis and Rhene, employ their messengers severally, Mercury and Iris, for that purpose. They meet and contend: then Mercury for his part brings forth an anti-masque all of spirits or divine natures: but yet not of one kind or livery (because that had been so much in use heretofore) but as it were in consort like to broken music. And preserving the propriety of the device (for that rivers in nature are 50 maintained either by springs from beneath, or showers from above), he raiseth four of the Naiads out of the fountains, and bringeth down five of the Hyades out of the clouds to dance. Hereupon Iris scoffs at Mercury for that he had devised a dance but of one sex, which could have no life: but Mercury, who was provided for that exception, and in 55 token that the match should be blessed both with love and riches, calleth forth out of the groves four Cupids, and brings down from Jupiter's altar four Statues of gold and silver, to dance with the Nymphs and Stars: in which dance, the Cupids being blind, and the Statues having but half life put into them, and retaining still somewhat of their 60 old nature, giveth fit occasion to new and strange varieties both in the music and paces. This was the first anti-masque.

Then Iris for her part, in scorn of this high-flying device, and in token that the match shall likewise be blessed with the love of the 65 common people, calls to Flora her confederate (for that the months of flowers are likewise the months of sweet showers and rainbows) to bring in a May-dance, or rural dance, consisting likewise not of any suited persons, but of a confusion or commixture of all such persons as are natural and proper for country sports. This is the second anti-masque. 70

Then Mercury and Iris, after this vying one upon the other, seem to leave their contention: and Mercury, by the consent of Iris, brings down the Olympian Knights, intimating that Jupiter, having after a long discontinuance revived the Olympian games, and summoned thereunto from all parts the liveliest and activest persons that were, had enjoined 75 them, before they fell to their games, to do honour to these nuptials. The Olympian games portend to the match celebrity, victory, and felicity. This was the main masque.

The fabric was a mountain with two descents, and severed with two traverses. 80

At the entrance of the King

The first traverse was drawn, and the lower descent of the mountain discovered; which was the pendant of a hill to life, with divers boscages and grovets upon the steep or hanging grounds thereof, and at the foot of the hill, four delicate fountains running with water and bordered with sedges and 85
water-flowers.

Iris first appeared, and, presently after, Mercury, striving to overtake her.

Iris apparelled in a robe of discoloured taffeta figured in variable colours, like the rainbow, a cloudy wreath on her head, and tresses. 90

Mercury in doublet and hose of white taffeta, a white hat, wings on his shoulders and feet, his caduceus in his hand, speaking to Iris as followeth.

Mercury. Stay, stay!
    Stay light-foot Iris, for thou strivest in vain,
    My wings are nimbler than thy feet. 95
Iris.   Away,
    Dissembling Mercury; my messages
    Ask honest haste, not like those wanton ones
    Your thund'ring father sends.
Mercury.   Stay foolish maid, 100
    Or I will take my rise upon a hill,
    When I perceive thee seated in a cloud
    In all the painted glory that thou hast,
    And never cease to clap my willing wings
    Till I catch hold of thy discolour'd bow, 105
    And shiver it beyond the angry power
    Of your curst mistress to make up again.
Iris. Hermes forbear, Juno will chide and strike;
    Is great Jove jealous that I am employ'd
    On her love-errands? she did never yet 110
    Clasp weak mortality in her white arms,
    As he hath often done: I only come
    To celebrate the long-wish'd nuptials,
    Here in Olympia, which are now perform'd
    Betwixt two goodly rivers, which have mix'd 115
    Their gentle-rising waves, and are to grow
    Into a thousand streams, great as themselves;
    I need not name them, for the sound is loud
    In heaven and earth; and I am sent from her,
    The queen of marriage, that was present here, 120
    And smil'd to see them join, and hath not chid
    Since it was done: good Hermes let me go.

Mercury. Nay you must stay; Jove's message is the same,
  Whose eyes are lightning, and whose voice is thunder,
  Whose breath is any wind he will, who knows   125
  How to be first on earth as well as heaven.
Iris. But what hath he to do with nuptial rites?
  Let him keep state upon his starry throne,
  And fright poor mortals with his thunderbolts,
  Leaving to us the mutual darts of eyes.   130
Mercury. Alas, when ever offer'd he t'abridge
  Your lady's power, but only now in these,
  Whose match concerns his general government?
  Hath not each god a part in these high joys?
  And shall not he, the king of gods, presume   135
  Without proud Juno's licence? Let her know
  That when enamour'd Jove first gave her power
  To link soft hearts in undissolved bonds,
  He then foresaw, and to himself reserv'd
  The honour of this marriage: thou shalt stand   140
  Still as a rock, while I, to bless this feast,
  Will summon up with my all-charming rod
  The Nymphs of fountains, from whose wat'ry locks,
  Hung with the dew of blessing and increase,
  The greedy rivers take their nourishment.   145
  You Nymphs, who bathing in your loved springs,
  Beheld these rivers in their infancy,
  And joy'd to see them, when their circled heads
  Refresh'd the air, and spread the ground with flowers:
  Rise from your wells, and with your nimble feet   150
  Perform that office to this happy pair,
  Which in these plains you to Alpheus did,
  When passing hence through many seas unmix'd,
  He gain'd the favour of his Arethuse.

Immediately upon which speech, four Naiads arise gently out of their sev-   155
eral fountains, and present themselves upon the stage, attired in long habits
of sea-green taffeta, with bubbles of crystal intermixed with powdering of
silver, resembling drops of water, bluish tresses, on their heads garlands of
water-lilies. They fall into a measure, dance a little, then make a stand.

Iris. Is Hermes grown a lover? by what power,   160
  Unknown to us, calls he the Naiades?
Mercury. Presumptuous Iris, I could make thee dance
  Till thou forgott'st thy lady's messages,
  And rann'st back crying to her; thou shalt know
  My power is more: only my breath, and this,   165
  Shall move fix'd stars, and force the firmament

> To yield the Hyades, who govern showers
> And dewy clouds, in whose dispersed drops
> Thou form'st the shape of thy deceitful bow.
> You maids, who yearly at appointed times   170
> Advance with kindly tears the gentle floods,
> Descend, and pour your blessing on these stream
> Which rolling down from heaven-aspiring hills,
> And now united in the fruitful vales,
> Bear all before them, ravish'd with their joy,   175
> And swell in glory till they know no bounds.

Five Hyades descend softly in a cloud from the firmament to the middle part
of the hill, apparelled in sky-coloured taffeta robes, spangled like the
heavens, golden tresses, and each a fair star on their head; from thence des-
cend to the stage, at whose sight the Naiads seeming to rejoice, meet and join   180
in a dance.

> *Iris.* Great wit and power hath Hermes, to contrive
>   A lifeless dance, which of one sex consists.
> *Mercury.* Alas poor Iris, Venus hath in store
>   A secret ambush of her winged boys,   185
>   Who lurking long within these pleasant groves,
>   First struck these lovers with their equal darts;
>   Those Cupids shall come forth, and join with these,
>   To honour that which they themselves begun.

Enter four Cupids from each side of the boscage, attired in flame-coloured   190
taffeta close to their body like naked boys, with bows, arrows, and wings of
gold, chaplets of flowers on their heads, hoodwinked with tiffany scarfs;
who join with the Nymphs and the Hyades in another dance. That ended,
Mercury speaks.

> *Mercury.* Behold, the Statues which wise Vulcan plac'd   195
>   Under the altar of Olympian Jove,
>   And gave to them an artificial life,
>   Shall dance for joy of these great nuptials:
>   See how they move, drawn by this heavenly joy,
>   Like the wild trees which follow'd Orpheus' harp.   200

The Statues enter, supposed to be before descended from Jove's altar, and to
have been prepared in the covert with the Cupids, attending their call.
  These Statues were attired in cases of gold and silver close to their body,
faces, hands and feet, nothing seen but gold and silver, as if they had been
solid images of metal, tresses of hair as they had been of metal embossed,   205
girdles and small aprons of oaken leaves, as if they likewise had been carved
or moulded out of the metal: at their coming, the music changed from violins
to hoboys, cornets, etc. And the air of the music was utterly turned into a
soft time, with drawing notes, excellently expressing their natures, and the

measure likewise was fitted unto the same, and the Statues placed in such 210
several postures, sometimes all together in the centre of the dance, and some-
times in the four utmost angles, as was very graceful besides the novelty.
And so concluded the first anti-masque.

Mercury. And what will Juno's Iris do for her?
Iris. Just match this show, or my invention fails; 215
    Had it been worthier, I would have invok'd
    The blazing comets, clouds, and falling stars,
    And all my kindred meteors of the air,
    To have excell'd it, but I now must strive
    To imitate confusion: therefore thou, 220
    Delightful Flora, if thou ever felt'st
    Increase of sweetness in those blooming plants
    On which the horns of my fair bow decline,
    Send hither all the rural company,
    Which deck the May-games with their country sports, 225
    Juno will have it so.

The second anti-masque rush in, dance their measure, and as rudely depart:
consisting of

A Pedant,

May Lord,	*May Lady,*
Servingman,	*Chambermaid,*
A Country Clown, or Shepherd,	*Country Wench,*
An Host,	*Hostess,*
A He-Baboon,	*She-Baboon,*
A He-Fool,	*She-Fool, ushering them in.*

230

235

All these persons apparelled to the life, the men issuing out of one side of the
boscage, and the women from the other; the music was extremely well fitted,
having such a spirit of country jollity as can hardly be imagined, but the
perpetual laughter and applause was above the music.

The dance likewise was of the same strain, and the dancers, or rather 240
actors, expressed every one their part so naturally and aptly, as when a
man's eye was caught with the one, and then passed on to the other, he could
not satisfy himself which did best. It pleased his Majesty to call for it again
at the end, as he did likewise for the first anti-masque, but one of the Statues
by that time was undressed. 245

Mercury.   Iris, we strive
    Like winds at liberty, who should do worst
    Ere we return. If Juno be the queen
    Of marriage, let her give happy way
    To what is done, in honour of the state 250
    She governs.
Iris.   Hermes, so it may be done

Merely in honour of the state, and these
That now have prov'd it, not to satisfy
The lust of Jupiter in having thanks   255
More than his Juno, if thy snaky rod
Have power to search the heavens, or sound the sea,
Or call together all the ends of earth,
To bring in anything that may do grace
To us, and these; do it, we shall be pleas'd.   260
Mercury. Then know that from the mouth of Jove himself,
Whose words have wings, and need not to be borne,
I took a message, and I bare it through
A thousand yielding clouds, and never stay'd
Till his high will was done: the Olympian games   265
Which long have slept, at these wish'd nuptials
He pleas'd to have renew'd, and all his knights
Are gather'd hither, who within their tents
Rest on this hill, upon whose rising head
Behold Jove's altar, and his blessed priests   270
Moving about it: come you holy men,
And with your voices draw these youths along,
That till Jove's music call them to their games,
Their active sports may give a blest content
To those, for whom they are again begun.   275

The Main Masque

*The second traverse is drawn, and the higher ascent of the mountain is dis-
covered, wherein, upon a level after a great rise of the hill, were placed two
pavilions, open in the front of them; the pavilions were to sight as of cloth
of gold, and they were trimmed on the inside with rich armour and military*   280
*furniture hanged up as upon the walls, and behind the tents there were rep-
resented in perspective the tops of divers other tents, as if it had been a
camp. In these pavilions were placed fifteen Olympian Knights, upon seats
a little embowed near the form of a croisant; and the Knights appeared first
as consecrated persons, all in veils, like to copes, of silver tiffany, gathered,* 285
*and falling a large compass about them, and over their heads high mitres
with long pendants behind falling from them: the mitres were so high that
they received their hats and feathers, that nothing was seen but veil. In the
midst, between both the tents upon the very top of the hill, being a higher
level than that of the tents, was placed Jupiter's altar, gilt, with three great* 290
*tapers upon golden candle-sticks burning upon it: and the four Statues, two
of gold and two of silver, as supporters, and Jupiter's Priests in white robes
about it.*

*Upon the sight of the King, the veils of the Knights did fall easily from
them, and they appeared in their own habit.*   295

The Knights' Attire

*Arming doublets of carnation satin, embroidered with blazing stars of silver
plate, with powderings of smaller stars betwixt; gorgets of silver mail; long
hose of the same with the doublets, laid with silver lace spangled, and
enriched with embroidery between the lace; carnation silk stockings
embroidered all over, garters and roses suitable; pumps of carnation satin,* 300
*embroidered as the doublets; hats of the same stuff and embroidery, cut like
a helmet before, the hinder part cut into scallops, answering the skirts of
their doublets; the bands of the hats were wreaths of silver in form
of garlands of wild olives; white feathers with one fall of carnation; belts of
the same stuff and embroidered with the doublet; silver swords; little Italian* 305
bands and cuffs embroidered with silver; fair long tresses of hair.

The Priests' Habits

*Long robes of white taffeta, long white heads of hair; the High Priest a cap
of white silk shag close to his head, with two labels at the ears, the midst
rising in form of a pyramis, in the top thereof a branch of silver; every* 310
Priest playing upon a lute: twelve in number.

*The Priests descend and sing this song following, after whom the Knights
likewise descend, first laying aside their veils, belts, and swords.*

The First Song

Shake off your heavy trance, 315
And leap into a dance
Such as no mortals use to tread,
Fit only for Apollo
To play to, for the moon to lead,
And all the stars to follow. 320

*The Knights by this time are all descended and fallen into their place, and
then dance their first measure.*

The Second Song

On blessed youths, for Jove doth pause,
Laying aside his graver laws 325
For this device;
And at the wedding such a pair,
Each dance is taken for a prayer,
Each song a sacrifice.

The Knights dance their second measure. 330

The Third Song

Single. More pleasing were these sweet delights,
　　If ladies mov'd as well as knights;
　　Run ev'ry one of you and catch
　　A nymph, in honour of this match,　　　　　　　335
　　And whisper boldly in her ear.
　　Jove will but laugh, if you forswear.
All. And this day's sins he doth resolve
　　That we his priests should all absolve.

The Knights take their ladies to dance with them galliards, durets, corantoes,　340
etc., and lead them to their places. Then loud music sounds, supposed to call
them to their Olympian games.

The Fourth Song

　　Ye should stay longer if we durst:
　　Away! Alas that he that first　　　　　　　　345
　　Gave Time wild wings to fly away,
　　Hath now no power to make him stay.
　　But though these games must needs be play'd,
　　I would this pair, when they are laid,
　　　And not a creature nigh them,　　　　　　350
　　Could catch his scythe, as he doth pass,
　　And cut his wings, and break his glass,
　　　And keep him ever by them.

The Knights dance their parting measure and ascend, put on their swords
and belts, during which time the Priests sing the fifth and last song.　　355

　　Peace and silence be the guide
　　To the man, and to the bride!
　　If there be a joy yet new
　　In marriage, let it fall on you,
　　　That all the world may wonder!　　　　　360
　　If we should stay, we should do worse,
　　And turn our blessing to a curse,
　　　By keeping you asunder.

FINIS

APPENDIX 4
BEAUMONT'S 1613 MASQUE AND
THE TWO NOBLE KINSMEN

The masque form was very hierarchical. Participants in the main masque normally played only idealized abstractions, historical characters or figures from classical myths, and represented them through silent dancing; the serious singing and acting roles were taken by professionals, as were the comic or grotesque roles in the antimasques that normally preceded the entrance of the main masque. The flexibility of Beaumont's plot was probably made necessary because of the constantly changing plans for the wedding that it was meant to celebrate (see Introduction, p. 36). At short notice, it may have been difficult to integrate the professional antimasquers (the King's Men and perhaps others) with the amateurs from the two Inns of Court who were financing and performing in the main masque.

Beaumont's solution was to have Iris and Mercury, representing Juno and Jupiter respectively, compete to present the most appropriate wedding entertainment. The first antimasque is Mercury's: a dance of Naiads (nymphs of the springs which water the rivers), who are joined by the Hyades (nymphs of clouds and showers). To Iris's scornful comment that a dance of one sex only is lifeless, he brings on four Cupids and then transforms four statues who take part in the final dance of the sequence. Iris, by way of a reply to what she calls the 'confusion' of Mercury's offering, invites country dancers to celebrate with their May games (Beaumont perhaps devised this antimasque while the wedding celebrations were still expected to take place in May). Finally Iris and Mercury reconcile their difference, and Iris allows Mercury to present, on behalf of Jupiter, the main masque of Olympian knights. Just as Jonson had made Chivalry awake from her long sleep for *Prince Henry's Barriers* in 1610, so 'the Olympian games / Which long have slept' are described here as 'renew'd' for the benefit of the wedding (265–7). The knight-masquers appear '*as consecrated persons*' (285), and musicians dressed as priests invite them to perform their dances, first on their own and then with partners from the audience.

From the point of view of *The Two Noble Kinsmen*, it would be interesting to know whether the King's Men were allowed to keep the costumes worn in the antimasques. Costumes for nymphs, for Iris, for a 'pedant', and for various country people, would already have been needed for *The Winter's Tale* and *The Tempest* and may have been in the company's wardrobe, but it is not known how

18 Costume design by Inigo Jones for a Naiad in *Tethys' Festival* by Samuel
   Daniel, 1610

much was lost in the Globe fire. No costume designs from Beaumont's masque
survive, but Jones's drawing of a Naiad for Daniel's *Tethys' Festival* in 1610
(Fig. 18) gives some idea of how these figures might have looked – and hence,
what inspired the Wooer's description of the Jailer's Daughter at the edge
of the lake:

> methought she appeared like the fair nymph
> That feeds the lake with waters, or as Iris
> Newly dropped down from heaven.
>
> (4.1.86–8)

The company may also have acquired at least some of the clothes from the main masque. The expenses borne by the Inner Temple and Gray's Inn took months to recover (see Edwards' introduction to Beaumont, 128) and Gray's Inn ordered the masquers to bring back their costumes 'whereby some profitt might be made' (Orbison, 8). If the Inn hoped to sell them elsewhere, the players were the most obvious buyers. Some details of the play suggest that the authors may have written in the knowledge that specific costumes were available. In 5.1, Palamon tells his knights, 'Our stars must glister with new fire or be / Today extinct' (5.1.69–70). At the beginning of 5.3, when Emilia refuses to be present at the tournament, Theseus tries to change her mind:

> THESEUS.   You must be there:
> This trial is as 'twere i'th' night, and you
> The only star to shine.
> EMILIA   I am extinct.
>
> (5.3.18–20)

The references to stars burning brighter or going out are obviously appropriate to the situations of the characters and bind Palamon and Emilia together through their language long before they are bound together by the plot. But there may be another reason for the image. The stage direction for the entry of the masquers in Beaumont's masque describes their costumes as

> *Arming doublets of carnation satin, embroidered with blazing stars of silver plate, with powderings of smaller stars betwixt . . .*
>
> (296–7)

The Olympian knights of the masque are in some ways counterparts of the knights in the play. If Palamon and his knights wore the same costumes, Palamon's line becomes a witty allusion to the stars on their doublets. Inigo Jones's design for a knight with an *impresa* shield (Fig. 19), undated but ascribed by Orgel & Strong to this period, shows the kind of work in which Burbage and Shakespeare had been involved both in *Pericles* and in their commission for the Earl of Rutland (see p. 12 above). It may give some idea of the decorative function the knights were intended to have in the play (see p. 68 above). The prospect of being able to use the masque costumes might have encouraged the authors to include characters who, otherwise, are not really necessary. Fletcher and Shakespeare might even, at some point, have considered the possibility of dramatizing the final tournament (as the fight at the barriers, a similar courtly event, was dramatized in Act 5 of Webster's *White Devil*). It seems odd to reduce Chaucer's two hundred knights to six if the fight was always expected to take place off stage in any case.

19 Costume design by Inigo Jones for a knight with an *impresa* shield,
  *c.*1613

The masque settings are less likely to have been re-used in the theatre, since
they depended on complex and expensive machinery for scene changes, and
The Two Noble Kinsmen can be performed equally effectively with or without
elaborate scenery. However, it may be significant that the masque's two main
settings, the temple and the woods, are also those required by the play. Taylor

suggests that the whole of Act 3 was meant to have a woodland setting (Taylor & Jowett, 42), and the 'boscage', as it is called in the Beaumont masque, might have reappeared in the two final scenes of Act 5. Bawcutt (12) suggests that a temple may have been visible both at the beginning of the play and in 5.1, though the quarto stage direction *'Exeunt towards the Temple'* (1.1.218) is not conclusive evidence of the fact. The temple scene may have resembled the final tableau of Beaumont's masque: *'Jupiter's altar, gilt, with three great tapers upon golden candle-sticks burning upon it: and the four Statues, two of gold and two of silver, as supporters, and Jupiter's Priests in white robes about it'* (290–3). 5.1 would thus be the play's equivalent to Beaumont's main masque, with the morris dance, as Waith says (Oxf[1], 32–3) serving as the equivalent of its antimasque.

A curious feature of the morris dance in *The Two Noble Kinsmen* is the role of the Schoolmaster, Gerald, the general factotum who 'does all, ye know' (2.3.43). This character belongs to a subcategory of the comic type known as the pedant. He is usually compared with Rhombus in Sidney's *The Lady of May* (1578–9) and Holofernes in *Love's Labour's Lost*, but the organizer of country-house entertainments is often depicted as a minor comic hanger-on who enjoys the sound of his own voice. Campion's Entertainment for Queen Anne at Caversham House in April 1613 includes among its presenters a gardener who, in 'antic fashion', makes a doggerel speech offering gifts to the guest of honour, and Jonson's Entertainment for Charles I's visit to Welbeck, performed in May 1633, features a 'Schoolemaster of Mansfield' who introduces country sports and re-uses the phrase about the fat in the fire (cf. *TNK* 3.5.40) already used by Sidney (Jonson, 7.193–6). When the Jailer's Daughter first encounters Gerald, she reads his palm and announces that he is a tinker. Later, in her madness, she refers to a 'fantastical' character that she calls 'Giraldo, Emilia's Schoolmaster' (4.3.13), who is supposed to have written a song. Is this the same person as Gerald? If the latter is supposed to be known personally to the court (Theseus calls him 'dear *Domine*' at 3.5.134 (RP)), this fact makes the morris-dance episode, and particularly Emilia's kind words for it, more intelligible. A remote possibility, given that the morris dance in 3.5 would be recognized as belonging to a court entertainment, is that the King's Men were making fun of the pretensions of some court figure with an Italian name. As it happens, there were several possible targets. Two are musicians – Alfonso Ferrabosco, who composed songs for all of Jonson's masques before 1611, and Giovanni Coperario, who, as everyone must have known, was in fact the Englishman John Cooper. Ferrabosco seems to have quarrelled with Jonson following their collaboration on the masque *Love Freed from Ignorance and Folly* in February 1611 (Chan, 272n.), which might have provided a motive for Fletcher to satirize him. But Gerald, with his mysterious 'machine' (3.5.112), might also be a satire on Constantino de' Servi, a visiting architect who had worked for the Medici. Campion, whose masque for the Somerset wedding in December 1613 de' Servi designed, described him as being 'too much of himself' – i.e., too full of himself – and the Italian was blamed for its failure: in particular, his cloud machine creaked as it came down and its ropes were inartistically visible (Strong, 96). Court performances generally managed to generate ill will among all parties involved, as is clear from Jonson's satires on his collaborator Inigo Jones. The morris-dance episode may give us a dim echo of some other real-life quarrel.

APPENDIX 5
THE MORRIS

(a) *Country sports*

The success of Beaumont's country-dance antimasque probably had something to do with the phenomenon that Leah Marcus has called 'the politics of mirth': the encouragement of traditional pastimes by the Jacobean court. While this encouragement was no doubt a way of defusing popular unrest and counteracting puritanism, the events themselves were genuinely well-liked. In May–June 1613 Queen Anne made a progress to Bath and Bristol, and it was reported that she had been particularly delighted not only with the aristocratic entertainments offered her but also with the 'country sports' (Chamberlain, 1.147).

The most famous sports were the Cotswold Games. Michael Drayton described them in *Polyolbion*, and in the year of its publication (1612) they took on a new lustre when Captain Robert Dover, a member of Gray's Inn, began to preside over them (Whitfield, 13–14). Since Beaumont's masque was partly sponsored by Gray's Inn, his linking of a main masque of Olympic games with an antimasque of rural May games would have been highly topical. Support for Dover's games, and insistence on their antiquarian value, became commonplace among both courtiers and literary men. An anniversary volume, *Annalia Dubrensia* (1636), contained verses from Jonson, Drayton, Heywood and many others. Many of them compared Dover to Hercules and Theseus, supposedly the respective originators of the Olympian and Pithian games (see Whitfield, 115–16, 150).

(b) *The dance*

The illustrated map to the section of Drayton's poem dealing with the Cotswolds (Fig. 20) shows a group of country dancers whose banner reads 'Heigh for Cotswold', the standard cry of dancers loyal to their local team (compare the Second Countryman's 'hey for the weavers' (2.3.51)). The nature of the dance in the play can only be glimpsed from Beaumont's statement (240–3) that much of the delight of the antimasque came from the variety of individual performances within the dance structure. The participants include figures associated with the traditional morris, as well as others who appear to have been fashionable in seventeenth-century shows: the Bavian, or baboon, is a variation on the ape or monkey; the comic Host reappears, and sings, in *The Lover's Progress* (1623); and a comic Chamberlain dances with a pair of

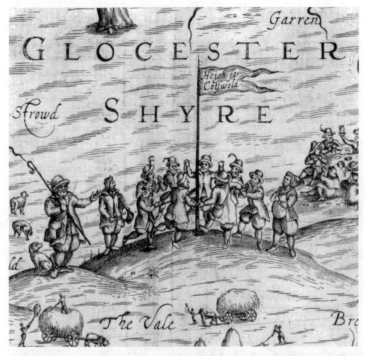

20 Morris dancers: detail from Drayton, *Polyolbion*, between pp. 226 and 227

apes in Shirley's *Cupid and Death* (1652). It is surprising that no hobby-horse is mentioned either in Beaumont's masque or in the play, since it was normally regarded as indispensable to the morris (see especially 4.1 of Fletcher's *Women Pleased* (1618)). Probably the Bavian was his replacement: both roles involve animal impersonation and wild, indecent gestures (Fig. 21).

Julian Pilling, who has examined the scene from the point of view of a dance historian, notes several possible types of morris dance. In one with six dancers, a Maid Marian and a fool, the dancers, all dressed differently, compete for the favour of a lady in the centre of a ring (Pilling, 26). In another type they are in pairs, with both men and women taking part and perhaps dancing round a maypole (28). As noted above (pp. 107–8) either kind of dance could be made thematically relevant to the play. Pilling thinks that the Schoolmaster and Pirithous' lines (3.5.142–3, 150) imply the presence of a painted maypole on stage. The maypole, of course, had a phallic significance, and the morris itself was seen by its opponents – for instance, Philip Stubbes, in his *Anatomy of Abuses* (1583) – as an occasion for licentious behaviour. The recent productions that have had the resources to perform the dance fully have made

21 Morris dancers, including the Jailer's Daughter and 'Bavian': RSC at the Mermaid Theatre, London, 1987

the most of its sexual implications (see pp. 81–2, 87, above).

Stubbes gives a smug account of how dancers were once taken for madmen, 'for who seing them leap, skip & trip like Goates & hindes, if hee never saw them before, would not think them either mad, or els possest with some furie?' (O1ʳ–O2). A fashion for 'mad' dancing developed; in France at the same period, the mad dance 'cultivated an "official" grotesque style' (Franko, *Dance,* 95). In England, the apparently absurd idea of involving the mad Daughter in an aristocratic entertainment would recall Jonson's *Love Freed from Ignorance and Folly* (1611), where the performers were 'she-fools', and Campion's masque, where Mania (personifying madness) introduces a dance of 'franticks'.

(c) *The rebus*

There is no indication of how the performers created the rebus on 'morris'. Gerald asks Theseus to look first at a 'mighty "Moor" of mickle weight' (*Morr* in the quarto spelling) and then at 'Is', which, 'being glued together, / Makes "Morris"' (3.5.117–19) – aptly enough, since *morris* was often derived (wrongly) from *moorish*. Bawcutt, annotating this passage, suggests that 'possibly the Schoolmaster held up two emblematic pictures, or there may even have been two characters on stage, one dressed as a Moor and one as Winter' – that is, 'ice'. Perhaps a Moor actually appears: a real actor in costume, an artificial figure (even a doll), or, as Leech's note suggests, the word *Morr* on a board. The phrase 'of mickle weight' might mean that Gerald is lifting a heavy object – perhaps something like the shield carried in *Pericles* which represents 'a black Ethiop reaching at the sun' (2.2.20). How the two parts of this rebus were 'joined together' is not explained. In some modern productions (Berkeley, RSC) the villagers march on, each carrying one of the letters that spell out 'morris'. But the Schoolmaster has already told the dancers to 'Break comely out' before Theseus (3.5.20), which seems to mean that he wants their entrance, in costume, to have a surprise effect.

I think it most likely that the mighty Moor was one of the artificial giants, stuffed with brown paper and tow, who used to head the procession at the annual Midsummer Watch, while his bearers let off fireworks to clear the way (Robertson & Gordon, xvii). The Midsummer Watch, in the early sixteenth century, often included morris dancers. Most of its pageantry was later transferred to the Lord Mayor's Show, where the Moors were usually replaced by wild men, but the giants, brought out and re-used year after year, were well remembered. Fletcher could have read of midsummer customs in Stow's *Survey of London* of 1603 (1.101–3; quoted in Robertson & Gordon, xvi–xvii), which mentions both giants and morris dancers. Since the pageants often had labels attached to them to make their meaning clearer, perhaps the Schoolmaster simply attached a label saying 'Is' to the giant Moor. Or perhaps it made some sort of hissing sound, or perhaps *is*, an alternative spelling for *ice*, indicates some other kind of pageant. Rebuses are quite common in the period; Jonson's *Alchemist* contains a particularly absurd one (Jonson 5: 2.6.19–24) and Lord Mayor's Shows liked to play on the name of the incoming mayor.

APPENDIX 6
THE MUSIC

The songs that open and close Act 1 were probably written especially for the play. 'Roses, their sharp spines being gone' is similar to others used in wedding masques: for example, Campion's song for the marriage of Lord Hay in 1607, which also accompanies the strewing of flowers: 'Earth hath no princelier flowers / Than roses white and roses red (Campion, p. 215). The song has been popular outside its original context; it was used in a 1901 *Twelfth Night* at Her Majesty's Theatre and in two later productions of *A Midsummer Night's Dream* (Gooch & Thatcher, 5.1963–4). The absence of songs for the fifth act is surprising in a play concerned so much with balance, but elaborate musical effects are specified for the temple scene (5.1) and solemn music probably accompanied the final exit of all the characters in 5.4. The cornets mentioned in many stage directions were the most frequently used stage instruments (Austern, 172–3), capable of both brass and wind sounds. The sixteenth-century cornet had finger-holes instead of valves (Sider, 401); it could mimic hunting horns, but also play chamber music and dances (403). It seems generally thought that trumpets distinguish royalty from the minor dignitaries announced by cornets (404). In *The Two Noble Kinsmen* trumpets are specified only in 5.3, where Emilia hears them from off stage. The intention must have been to make this scene, in decibels at least, the play's climax.

Given the apparent connection between *The Two Noble Kinsmen* and Beaumont's masque, it would be interesting to know whether the company used any music from the latter in the play. Unfortunately, the masque description does not identify a composer. Some surviving music of the period, attributed in manuscript to Giovanni Coperario and given the general title of 'Gray's Inn', has subtitles which might associate it with Beaumont's masque: 'the Maypole', 'the two merry maids', 'the morris'. It would be attractive to think that these tunes were actually used in the morris-dance scene, but, although Andrew Sabol (573, 577–8, 583) accepts this attribution, most other music historians have been sceptical about it. Philip Edwards draws attention to an anonymous piece in the same manuscript, called 'Sir Francis Bacon's Masque I', which seems a still more plausible attribution; Bacon was the prime mover of this particular masque, which is why Beaumont dedicated his descriptive pamphlet to him.

The morris was usually accompanied with singing (Olson, 425), and Beaumont's masque description seems to distinguish between 'the music' (237) and 'the dance' (240). A wedding song and dance in a similar scene of

Massinger's *Guardian* (*c*.1633) are clearly separate events. So it is possible that the direction at 3.5.135 of *The Two Noble Kinsmen* once included a song as well as a dance; this might explain why the compositor has set Gerald's final doggerel (3.5.136–45) as if it were a song.

In the text of the play as it survives, however, all the songs after Act 1 belong to the Jailer's Daughter. Only fragments are quoted in the text, sometimes followed by '&.', which probably means that she was meant to sing more than one verse. They are popular songs and belong to an English rather than a classical setting. The first (3.4.19), is based on 'Childe Waters', where the heroine offers to follow her lover as a page and he tells her,

> Then you must cutt your gowne of greer
> An inche above your knee,
> Soe must you doe your yellow loekes
> Another inch above your eye.
>> (Sargent & Kittredge, 122)

Thematically, it resembles the ballads of 'Young Beichan' and the 'Fair Flower of Northumberland', in which a young woman sets a prisoner free out of love for him: in the first (as in 'Child Waters') he eventually marries her, while in the second he betrays and abandons her.

At 3.5.60 the Daughter's choice of 'The George Alow' seems vaguely relevant to her obsession with ships at sea in 3.4. A ballad called 'The second parte of the Sailor's onely Delight: Shewing the brave fight between *George-Aloe*, the *Sweepe-stakes* and certain *French-men* at Sea' was registered with the Stationers' Company in 1611 (Rollins, 955). As the surviving words do not coincide exactly with the Daughter's, Rollins thinks she may have sung the (lost) first part, but in fact some of the surviving ballad is similar to the lines quoted in the play:

> 'O hail, O hail, you lusty gallants,
> With hey, with ho, for and a nony no,
> From whence is your good ship, and whether is she bound'
>> And along the course of Barbary.
>> (Sargent & Kittredge, 610–11)

'There was three fools' (3.5.68) has no obvious relation to the scene except in so far as the Daughter enjoys calling everyone else a fool. It is a variation on 'There were three jolly Welshmen' or 'There were three men of Gotham'. A broadside (*Choice of Inuentions, Or Seuerall sorts of the figure of three*) published in 1632, and said to go to the tune of 'Rock the Cradle, Sweet John', has survived as a nursery rhyme (Opie & Opie, 421–3). In the broadside, the words corresponding to the Daughter's are:

> Though all the day they hunting were,
> .Yet no sport could they see,
> Untill they spide an Owle
> as she sate in a tree:

> The first man said it twas a Goose,
> the second man said nay,
> The third man said it was a Hawke,
> but his Bels were falne away.
> (Opie & Opie, 422)

At 4.1.80 the Wooer describes her as singing the famous willow song of forsaken lovers, often referred to in drama. 'Palamon, fair Palamon' and 'Palamon was a tall young man' (4.1.81–2) are probably adaptations of traditional songs; for instance, 'When Samson was a tall young man' (Chappell, 1.241); 'Robin Hood's Progress to Nottingham' begins, 'Robin Hood was a tall young man' (Sargent & Kittredge, 330). 'O fair, o sweet' (4.1.114) is perhaps (as Dyce suggests) the beginning of the seventh song from Sidney's *Certaine Sonnets*, published with the *Arcadia* in all editions since 1598: 'O faire, O sweet, when I do look on thee, / In whom all joys so well agree ... '. Fletcher's song for his own comedy, *Women Pleased*, begins 'O fair sweet face, O eyes celestial bright' (3.4.49). The other snatches in this scene, 'May you never more enjoy the light' (4.1.104) and 'When Cynthia with her borrowed light' (4.1.152), have not been identified. The Daughter's songs usually bear some relation to what she wants to talk about, so it is possible that this last one, which follows the collective fantasy about sailing to the woods, was a song of the sea.

The Jailer's Daughter refers to still more songs than she sings. '*Chi passa*' (Who is passing?), which she requests (3.5.87), was a very popular dance tune, and 'The Broom' (4.1.107), if it is the same as 'The Bonny Broom', was also well known – Weber traced it to William Wager's *The Longer Thou Livest* (1559–68), where it is quoted, and the tune is given in Chappell (2.458–61). Fletcher parodied it in *The Loyal Subject*, where a disbanded ensign and his men draw attention to the plight of the army by becoming street-sellers and crying their wares; the song begins,

> Broom, Broom, the bonnie Broom,
> Come buy my Birchen Broom,
> Ith' warres we have no more room,
> Buy all my bonnie Broom.
> (Bowers, 5: 3.5.1–4)

It is usually assumed that 'Bonny Robin', which is mentioned at the same time (4.1.108), is the same as the song from which Ophelia sings the refrain, 'For bonnie sweet Robin is all my joy' (Chappell, 1.234). Waith quotes evidence (Morris, 601–3) that 'Robin was probably "one of the cant words for penis"', whether by derivation from the French *robinet* (spiggot) or from a version of the Robin Hood legend linked to the wilder side of May games. In 4.3 the Daughter no longer remembers her songs, and in 5.2 she has stopped singing altogether, though she talks about an imaginary horse dancing to 'Light o' love' (5.2.54), a tune named in other plays, as here, for the sake of its title (see Chappell 1.221–5). Margaret recommends it to Beatrice in a scene of *risqué* conversation among women (*MA* 3.4) rather like the one between Emilia and her Woman in 2.2. Her reference to the ferry and the Elysian fields (4.3.19–25) may once have accompanied one of the 'Charon songs' of which there are many in the seventeenth century. Robert Johnson, the chief composer for the King's Men, wrote what may have been the first of them and set a number of Fletcher's other songs, including laments for forsaken women (see Cutts, 120–1).

Gooch & Thatcher list nine original musical scores for the play, to which can be added the one by Todd Barton for Nagle Jackson's production at Ashland, Oregon, in 1994.

ABBREVIATIONS AND REFERENCES

Quotations and references relating to *The Two Noble Kinsmen* are keyed to the present edition. Those relating to Shakespeare's other works are keyed to *Riv* in the following list. Translations of Boccaccio's *Teseida* are taken from McCoy; those of classical texts from the Loeb editions cited below. Chaucer quotations are cited from Speght, but line numbers are keyed to Chaucer, *Riv*, in the list below; this edition is occasionally quoted for comparison where Speght's text is very inaccurate. Plays in the 'Beaumont and Fletcher canon' are quoted, whenever possible, from the Bowers edition, cited as Bowers + volume number. Those not at present available in this edition are cited from Dyce, by act and scene numbers only, as Dyce gives no line numbers. Titles of collected editions of Shakespeare other than the Folios are simplified as *Works* if they include the poems and as *Plays* if they do not; titles of editions of the play alone, including the Quartos, are given as *The Two Noble Kinsmen*; and variations in the spelling of the name Shakespeare are not recorded.

In all references, place of publication is London unless otherwise stated.

ABBREVIATIONS

ABBREVIATIONS USED IN NOTES

*	precedes commentary notes involving readings altered from the early edition on which this edition is based
Qc	corrected state of Q
Qu	uncorrected state of Q
repr.	reprint
SD	stage direction
SP	speech prefix
subst.	substantively
t.n.	the textual notes at the foot of each page
this edn	a reading adopted for the first time in this edition

SHAKESPEARE'S WORKS AND WORKS PARTLY BY SHAKESPEARE

AC	*Antony and Cleopatra*
AW	*All's Well That Ends Well*
AYL	*As You Like It*
CE	*The Comedy of Errors*
Cor	*Coriolanus*
Cym	*Cymbeline*
E3	*Edward III*
Ham	*Hamlet*
1H4	*King Henry IV, Part 1*
2H4	*King Henry IV, Part 2*
H5	*King Henry V*
1H6	*King Henry VI, Part 1*
2H6	*King Henry VI, Part 2*
3H6	*King Henry VI, Part 3*
H8	*King Henry VIII*
JC	*Julius Caesar*
KJ	*King John*
KL	*King Lear*
LC	*A Lover's Complaint*
LLL	*Love's Labour's Lost*
Luc	*The Rape of Lucrece*
MA	*Much Ado About Nothing*
Mac	*Macbeth*
MM	*Measure for Measure*
MND	*A Midsummer Night's Dream*
MV	*The Merchant of Venice*
MW	*The Merry Wives of Windsor*
Oth	*Othello*
Per	*Pericles*
PP	*The Passionate Pilgrim*
PT	*The Phoenix and the Turtle*
R2	*King Richard II*
R3	*King Richard III*
RJ	*Romeo and Juliet*
Son	*Sonnets*
TC	*Troilus and Cressida*
Tem	*The Tempest*
TGV	*The Two Gentlemen of Verona*
Tim	*Timon of Athens*
Tit	*Titus Andronicus*
TN	*Twelfth Night*
TNK	*The Two Noble Kinsmen*
TS	*The Taming of the Shrew*

VA	*Venus and Adonis*
WT	*The Winter's Tale*

MODERN PRODUCTIONS CITED

Ashland	Ashland, Oregon, directed by Nagle Jackson, 1994
Berkeley	Berkeley, California, directed by Julian Lopez-Morillas, 1985
New York	New York, directed by Beth F. Milles, 1993
Philadelphia	Philadelphia, directed by Eleanor Holdridge, 1993
RSC	Swan Theatre, Stratford-upon-Avon, directed by Barry Kyle for the RSC, 1986

REFERENCES

EDITIONS OF *THE TWO NOBLE KINSMEN* COLLATED

1711	*The Works of Mr. Francis Beaumont, and Mr. John Fletcher*, vol. 7 (1711)
1778	*The Dramatick Works of Beaumont and Fletcher*, ed. George Colman, vol. 10 (1778)
Bawcutt	*The Two Noble Kinsmen*, ed. N. W. Bawcutt, New Penguin Shakespeare (Harmondsworth, 1977)
Bowers	*The Two Noble Kinsmen*, ed. F. Bowers, in *The Dramatic Works in the Beaumont and Fletcher Canon*, gen. ed. F. Bowers, vol. 7 (Cambridge, 1989)
Brooke	*The Shakespeare Apocrypha*, ed. C. F. Tucker Brooke (Oxford, 1918)
Dyce	*The Two Noble Kinsmen*, ed. A. Dyce, in *The Works of Beaumont and Fletcher*, vol. 11 (1846)
Dyce[1]	*The Two Noble Kinsmen*, ed. A. Dyce, in *The Works of William Shakespeare*, 2nd edn, vol. 8 (1866)
F	*Fifty Comedies and Tragedies. Written by Francis Beaumont and John Fletcher, Gentlemen* (1679)
Kittredge	*The Two Noble Kinsmen*, ed. G. L. Kittredge, in *Works* (Boston, 1935), revised by Irving Ribner in the Kittredge Shakespeare (Waltham, Mass., Toronto and London, 1969)
Knight	*The Pictorial Edition of the Works of Shakespeare*, ed. C. Knight, vol. 8 (2nd edn, revised 1867)
Leech	*The Two Noble Kinsmen*, ed. Clifford Leech, Signet (1966)
Littledale	*The Two Noble Kinsmen*, ed. H. Littledale, The New Shakspere Society (1876; repr. 1885)
Oxf	*The Two Noble Kinsmen*, ed. W. Montgomery, in *Works*,

ed. S. Wells and G. Taylor, with J. Jowett and W. Montgomery (Oxford, 1986); notes to this edn in *TxC* (see Other Works, below)

Oxf[1]   *The Two Noble Kinsmen*, ed. E. M. Waith, The Oxford Shakespeare (Oxford, 1989)

Proudfoot   *The Two Noble Kinsmen*, ed. G. R. Proudfoot, Regent's Renaissance Drama Series (Lincoln, Nebr., 1970)

Proudfoot[1]   G. R. Proudfoot, materials for projected edition of Shakespeare apocrypha

Q   *The Two Noble Kinsmen*, the First Quarto (1634)

Riv   *Works*, gen. ed. G. Blakemore Evans, Riverside Shakespeare (Boston, Mass., 1974)

Seward   *The Works of Mr. Francis Beaumont, and Mr. John Fletcher*, ed. L. Theobald, completed by T. Seward, vol. 10 (1750)

Skeat   *The Two Noble Kinsmen*, ed. W. W. Skeat, Pitt Press Series (Cambridge, 1875)

Sympson   *see* Seward ⎱ refers to readings proposed by them
Theobald   *see* Seward ⎰ which Seward adopted in his edn

Waller   F. O. Waller, 'A critical, oldspelling edition of *The Two Noble Kinsmen*', unpubl. Ph.D. thesis, University of Chicago (1957)

Weber   *The Works of Beaumont and Fletcher*, ed. H. Weber, vol. 13 (Edinburgh, 1812)

OTHER WORKS

Abrams   R. Abrams, 'Gender confusion and sexual politics in *The Two Noble Kinsmen*', *Themes in Drama: Drama, Sex and Politics*, 7 (Cambridge, 1985)

Abrams, 'Bourgeois'   R. Abrams, '*The Two Noble Kinsmen* as bourgeois drama', in Frey

Abrams, 'W.S.'   R. Abrams, 'W[illiam] S[hakespeare's] "Funeral Elegy" and the turn from the theatrical', *SEL* 36 (1996), 435–60

Akrigg   G. P. V. Akrigg, *Shakespeare and the Earl of Southampton* (Cambridge, Mass., 1968)

Akrigg, *Letters*   *Letters of King James VI and I* (Berkeley, Los Angeles, London, 1984)

Anderson   D. Anderson, *Before the Knight's Tale: Imitation of Classical Epic in Boccaccio's 'Teseida'* (Philadelphia, 1988)

Armstrong   E. A. Armstrong, *Shakespeare's Imagination: A Study of the Psychology of Association and Inspiration* (Lincoln, Nebr., and London, 1963)

AT   Ann Thompson, personal communication

Aubrey J. Aubrey, *Brief Lives*, ed. A. Clark, 2 vols (Oxford, 1898)

Austern L. P. Austern, 'Music in children's drama, 1597–1613', unpubl. Ph.D. thesis, University of Chicago (1984)

Bachinger K. Bachinger, 'Maidenheads and mayhem: a morris-dance reading of William Shakespeare's and John Fletcher's *The Two Noble Kinsmen*', *Salzburger Studien zur Anglistik und Amerikanistik*, 16 (1990), 23–38

Bacon F. Bacon, *The Essays*, ed. J. Pitcher (Harmondsworth and New York, 1985)

Bald R. C. Bald, *Bibliographical Studies in the Beaumont and Fletcher Folio of 1647* (Oxford, 1938)

Baldwin T. W. Baldwin, *The Organization and Personnel of the Shakespearean Company* (Princeton, 1927)

Baskervill C. R. Baskervill, *The Elizabethan Jig and Related Song Drama* (Chicago, 1929; repr. New York, n.d.)

Bate J. Bate, *Shakespeare and Ovid* (Oxford, 1993)

Beal P. Beal, *Index of English Literary Manuscripts*, vol. 1 (London and New York, 1980)

Beaumont F. Beaumont, *The Masque of the Inner Temple and Gray's Inn*, ed. P. Edwards, in S. Wells and T. J. B. Spencer, *A Book of Masques* (Cambridge, 1967)

Beecher D. A. Beecher, 'Lovesickness, diagnosis and destiny in the Renaissance theaters of England and Spain: the parallel development of a medico-literary motif', in Louise and Peter Fothergill-Payne (eds), *Parallel Lives: Spanish and English National Drama 1580–1680* (Lewisburg, Pa., London and Toronto, 1991)

Belsey C. Belsey, 'Love in Venice', *SS*, 44 (1992), 41–58

Bentley G. E. Bentley, *Shakespeare and Jonson* (Chicago, 1945)

Berggren P. S. Berggren, '"For what we lack, / We laugh": incompletion and *The Two Noble Kinsmen*', *Modern Language Studies*, 14 (1984), 3–17

Berry R. Berry, 'Metamorphoses of the stage', *SQ*, 33 (1982), 5–16

Bertram P. Bertram, *Shakespeare and 'The Two Noble Kinsmen'* (New Brunswick, NJ, 1965)

Bevington D. Bevington (ed.), *Antony and Cleopatra*, New Cambridge Shakespeare (Cambridge, 1990)

Birrell F. Birrell, review of *The Two Noble Kinsmen* in *Nation & Athenaeum*, 31 March 1928

Black J. Black, 'The latter end of Prospero's commonwealth', *SS*, 43 (1991), 29–39

Blincoe N. Blincoe, '"Fury-Innocent" as used in *The Two Noble Kinsmen*', *N&Q*, 240 (1995), 337–8

Blincoe, 'Sex' N. Blincoe, '"Sex individual" as used in *The Two Noble Kinsmen*', *N&Q*, 233 (1988), 484–5

Boas F. S. Boas, *Giles and Phineas Fletcher, Poetical Works*, 2 vols (Cambridge, 1909; repr. 1970)

Boccaccio G. Boccaccio, *Teseida, delle Nozze d'Emilia*, ed. A. Roncaglia (Bari, 1941)

Bowers F. Bowers (ed.), *The Dramatic Works in the Beaumont
(+vol. no.) and Fletcher Canon*, 8 vols (Cambridge, 1966–   )

Bowers, 'Readability and regularization in old-spelling texts of
'Readability' Shakespeare', *Huntington Library Quarterly*, 50 (1987), 199–227

Bradbrook M. C. Bradbrook, 'Shakespeare as collaborator', in C. Leech and J. M. R. Margeson (eds), *Shakespeare 1971* (Toronto, 1971)

Bradbrook, *Webster* M. C. Bradbrook, *John Webster, Citizen and Dramatist* (1980)

Bradley A. C. Bradley, *Shakespearean Tragedy* (1922)

Bray A. Bray, *Homosexuality in Renaissance England* (1982)

Brockbank P. Brockbank (ed.), *Coriolanus*, Arden Shakespeare (1976)

Brookes S. Brookes [C. W. Brookes], 'The black horse: tales from the old dramatists, no. III, showing how a lady may be married by chance, yet happily', *Gentleman's Magazine*, NS 2 (1869), 726–37

Brown K. Brown, 'More light, more light!', *Essays in Criticism*, 34 (1984), 1–13

Browne W. Browne, *Poems*, ed. G. Goodwin, vol. 1 (London and New York; repr. 1971)

Brownlow F. W. Brownlow, *Two Shakespearean Sequences* (London and Pittsburgh, Pa., 1977)

Bruster D. Bruster, 'The Jailer's Daughter and the politics of madwomen's language', *SQ*, 46 (1995), 277–300

Burrow J. A. Burrow, entry on Chaucer in A. C. Hamilton (ed.), *Spenser Encyclopedia* (Toronto, London and Buffalo, 1990)

Burrow, '*KT*' J. A. Burrow, 'Chaucer's *Knight's Tale* and the three ages of man', in J. A. Burrow, *Essays on Medieval Literature* (Oxford, 1984), 27–48

Calasso R. Calasso, *The Marriage of Cadmus and Harmony*, trans. T. Parks (1990; first publ. in Italy, 1988)

Campion T. Campion, *Works*, ed. W. R. Davis (New York, 1967)

Carney J. E. Carney, 'The ambiguities of love and war in *The Two Noble Kinsmen*', in C. Levin and K. Robertson (eds), *Sexuality and Politics in Renaissance Drama* (Lewiston, Pa., 1991)

Cartwright W. Cartwright, *Plays and Poems*, ed. G. Blakemore Evans (Madison, 1951)

Catullus   *Catullus*, trans. F. W. Cornish (1913); rev. edn G. P.
                      Goold, Loeb Classics (Cambridge, Mass. and London,
                      1988)

Chamberlain   J. Chamberlain, *Letters*, ed. N. E. McLure, 2 vols (Phil-
                      adelphia, 1939)

Chambers   E. K. Chambers, *The Elizabethan Stage*, 4 vols (Oxford,
                      1923)

Chambers, *WS*   E. K. Chambers, William Shakespeare: *A Study of Facts
                      and Problems*, 2 vols (Oxford, 1930)

Chan   M. Chan, *Music in the Theatre of Ben Jonson* (Oxford,
                      1980)

Chappell   W. Chappell, *Popular Music of the Olden Time*, 2 vols
                      (London, 1859; repr. New York, 1965)

Charney   M. Charney and H. Charney, 'The language of mad-
                      women in Shakespeare and his fellow dramatists', *Signs:
                      Journal of Women in Culture and Society*, 3 (1977), 21,
                      451–60

Chaucer, *Riv*   *The Riverside Chaucer*, ed. F. N. Robinson, rev. L. D.
                      Benson (Oxford, 1987)

Cicero   Cicero, *De Amicitia*, trans. W. A. Falconer, Loeb Classics
                      (London and Cambridge, Mass., 1971)

Clare   J. Clare, *'Art made tongue-tied by authority': Elizabethan
                      and Jacobean Dramatic Censorship* (Manchester and New
                      York, 1990)

Clark   S. Clark, *The Plays of Beaumont and Fletcher: Sexual
                      Themes and Dramatic Representation* (New York,
                      London, Toronto, 1994)

Clements   R. M. Clements, 'A new look at *The Two Noble Kins-
                      men*', unpubl. Ph.D. thesis, University of California,
                      Berkeley (1974)

Constant   P. Constant, report on a production of the translation by
                      Réaud at Courneuve, in M. T. Jones-Davies (ed.),
                      Société Française Shakespeare: Actes du Congrès 1979
                      (1980)

Cotgrave   R. Cotgrave, *A French–English Dictionary* (1650)

Cottis   N. Cottis, '*The Two Noble Kinsmen* at Plymouth',
                      Guardian, 5 August 1968

Craik   T. W. Craik, personal communication

CSPV   *Calendar of State Papers Venetian*, ed. H. F. Brown, vol.
                      12 (1905)

Cumberland   R. Cumberland, *Palamon and Arcite, or The Noble Kins-
                      men. alter'd from Beaumont & Fletcher*, British Library
                      Add MS 25,990 (n.d.)

Curtis   A. Curtis, review of *The Two Noble Kinsmen*, *Financial
                      Times*, 4 February 1970

Cutts   J. P. Cutts, 'Robert Johnson: King's musician in His

	Majesty's public entertainment', *Music and Letters*, 36 (1955), 110–25
Davenant	[W. Davenant], *The Rivals* (1668)
Davies	J. Davies, *The Poems of Sir John Davies*, ed. R. Krueger (Oxford, 1975)
Dawson	A. B. Dawson, '*Tempest* in a teapot', in M. Charney (ed.), *Bad Shakespeare* (Rutherford, NJ and London, 1988)
Deighton	K. Deighton, *The Old Dramatists: Conjectural Readings* (Westminster, 1896)
Dekker	T. Dekker, *The Dramatic Works of Thomas Dekker*, ed. F. Bowers, vol. 2 (Cambridge, 1955)
Dent	R. W. Dent, *Shakespeare's Proverbial Language: An Index* (Berkeley, Toronto, London, 1981)
Dent, *Prov*	R. W. Dent, *Proverbial Language in English Drama Exclusive of Shakespeare, 1495–1616* (Berkeley, Toronto, London, 1984)
De Quincey	T. De Quincey, *Works*, vol. 10: *Style and Rhetoric and Other Papers* (Edinburgh, 1863)
Desens	M. C. Desens, *The Bed-Trick in English Renaissance Drama* (Newark, Del., London and Toronto, 1994)
Dessen	A. Dessen, *Recovering Shakespeare's Theatrical Vocabulary* (Cambridge, 1995)
Digby Day	Richard Digby Day, programme note for his production of *The Two Noble Kinsmen*, 1973
Dircks	R. J. Dircks (ed.), *The Unpublished Plays of Richard Cumberland*, 2 vols (New York, 1991)
Donaldson	E. T. Donaldson, *The Swan at the Well: Shakespeare Reading Chaucer* (New Haven and London, 1985)
Donne	J. Donne, *The Complete English Poems*, ed. A. J. Smith (Harmondsworth and New York, 1971)
Downes	J. Downes, *Roscius Anglicanus*, ed. M. Summers (1929; repr. New York, 1968)
Drayton	M. Drayton, *Works*, ed. J. W. Hebel *et al.*, 5 vols (Oxford, 1961)
Dryden	J. Dryden, *Of Dramatic Poesy and Other Critical Essays*, ed. George Watson, 2 vols (London and New York, 1962)
Durand	W. Y. Durand, '*Palamon and Arcite, Progne, Marcus Geminus*, and the theater in which they were acted, as described by John Bereblock', *PMLA*, 20 (1905), 508–17
Dyce (+vol. no.)	A. Dyce (ed.), *The Works of Beaumont and Fletcher*, 11 vols (1843–46)
Edwards	P. Edwards, 'On the design of *The Two Noble Kinsmen*', *Review of English Literature*, 5 (1964), 89–105; repr. in Leech (Signet edn)
Edwards, *Damon*	R. Edwards, *Damon and Pythias*, ed. A. Brown and F. P. Wilson, Malone Society Reprints (Oxford, 1957)

EETS	Early English Texts Society
Elliott	J. R. Elliott, Jr, 'Queen Elizabeth at Oxford: new light on the royal plays of 1566', *ELR*, 18 (1988), 218–29
ELN	*English Language Notes*
ELR	*English Literary Renaissance*
ES	*English Studies*
Euripides	*Euripides*, trans. A. S. Way, 4 vols, Loeb Classics. (Cambridge, Mass. and London, 1912)
Everett	B. Everett (ed.), *All's Well That Ends Well* (Harmondsworth and New York, 1970)
Farnham	W. E. Farnham, 'Colloquial contractions in Beaumont, Fletcher, Massinger and Shakespeare as a test of authorship', *PMLA*, 31 (1916), 326–58
Ferrand	J. Ferrand, *A Treatise on Lovesickness*, trans. and ed. D. A. Beecher and M. Ciavolella (Syracuse, NY, 1990)
Fineman	J. Fineman, 'Fratricide and cuckoldry: Shakespeare's doubles', in M. M. Schwartz and C. Kahn (eds), *Representing Shakespeare: New Psychoanalytic Essays* (Baltimore and London, 1980)
Finkelpearl	P. J. Finkelpearl, *Court and Country Politics in the Plays of Beaumont and Fletcher* (Princeton, 1990)
Florio	*Essays of Montaigne*, trans. J. Florio, ed. G. Saintsbury, 3 vols (1892)
Foakes	R. A. Foakes, 'Tragicomedy and comic form', in A. R. Braunmuller and J. C. Bulman (eds), *Comedy from Shakespeare to Sheridan* (Newark, Del., London and Toronto, 1986)
Foakes, 'Playhouses'	R. A. Foakes, 'Playhouses and players', in A. R. Braunmuller and M. Hattaway (eds), *The Cambridge Companion to English Renaissance Drama* (Cambridge, 1990)
Ford	P. Ford, review of *The Two Noble Kinsmen* by Bristol drama department, *Manchester Guardian*, 17 July 1964
Forker	C. R. Forker, *Fancy's Images: Contexts, Settings, and Perspectives in Shakespeare and His Contemporaries* (Carbondale and Edwardsville, Ill., 1990)
Foster	D. W. Foster, *Elegy by W. S.: A Study in Attribution* (Newark, Del., London and Toronto, 1989)
Foxe	J. Foxe, *Acts and Monuments*, 2 vols (1583)
Franko	M. Franko, *The Dancing Body in Renaissance Choreography, c.1416–1589* (Birmingham, Ala., 1986)
Franko, *Dance*	M. Franko, *Dance as Text: Ideologies of the Baroque Body* (Cambridge, 1993)
Freehafer	J. Freehafer, 'A textual crux in *The Two Noble Kinsmen*', *ELN*, 7 (1969–70), 254–7
Freehafer, 'Cardenio'	J. Freehafer, '*Cardenio*, by Shakespeare and Fletcher', *PMLA*, 84 (1969), 501–13

Frey	C. H. Frey (ed.), *Shakespeare, Fletcher and 'The Two Noble Kinsmen'* (Columbia, Mo., 1989)
Frye	N. Frye, 'Romance as masque', in C. McGinnis Kay and H. E. Jacobs (eds), *Shakespeare's Romances Reconsidered* (Lincoln, Nebr., 1978)
Fuller	T. Fuller, *The Worthies of England*, abr. and ed. J. Freeman (1952)
Fumerton	P. Fumerton, *Cultural Aesthetics: Renaissance Literature and the Practice of Social Ornament* (Chicago and London, 1991)
Furness	H. H. Furness, Jr., *'The Gloss of Youth': An Imaginary Episode in the Lives of William Shakespeare and John Fletcher* (Philadelphia and London, 1920)
Galen	Galen, *Galen on the Usefulness of the Parts of the Body* (Ithaca, NY, 1968)
Gayley	C. M. Gayley, *Francis Beaumont. Dramatist* (1914)
Gerard	J. Gerard, *The Herbal, or General History of Plants* (1597)
Gibbs	P. Gibbs, review of *The Two Noble Kinsmen* (Reading University), *Daily Telegraph*, 15 July 1959.
Gillam	D. Gillam, 'Lovers and riders in Chaucer's "Anelida and Arcite"', *ES*, 63 (1982), 394–401
Gillies	J. Gillies, *Shakespeare and the Geography of Difference* (Cambridge, 1994)
Gooch & Thatcher	B. N. S. Gooch and D. Thatcher (eds), *A Shakespeare Music Catalogue*, 6 vols (Oxford, 1991)
Gossett	S. Gossett, *The Influence of the Jacobean Masque on the Plays of Beaumont and Fletcher* (New York and London, 1988)
Gower	J. Gower, *Confessio Amantis*, in *The English Works of John Gower*, ed. G. C. Macaulay, 2 vols (EETS), vol. 2 (London, New York, Toronto, 1901; repr. 1957)
Graville	A. Graville, *Le Beau Romant des deux amans Palamon & Arcita et de la belle et saige Emilia*, ed. Yves le Hir (Paris, 1965)
Greg	W. W. Greg, *A Bibliography of the English Printed Drama to the Restoration*, 4 vols (1939–59)
Guarini	G. Guarini, *Il Pastor Fido e Il Compendio della Poesia Tragicomica*, ed. G. Brognoligo (Bari, 1914)
Gurr	A. Gurr, *Playgoing in Shakespeare's London* (Cambridge and New York, 1987)
Hadorn	P. Hadorn, *'The Two Noble Kinsmen* and the problem of chivalry', *Studies in Medievalism*, 4 (1992), 45–57
Hamilton	A. C. Hamilton (ed.), *The Spenser Encyclopedia* (Toronto, London and Buffalo, 1990)

Hamlin	W. Hamlin, 'A select bibliographical guide to *The Two Noble Kinsmen*', in Frey
Hardy	J. Hardy, review of *The Two Noble Kinsmen* (Cherub Theatre Co.), *The Stage and Television Today*, 6 December 1979
Harington	J. Harington (trans.), Lodovico Ariosto, *Orlando Furioso in English Heroical Verse* (1591)
Harrier	R. Harrier, 'Another note on "Why the Sweets Melted"', *SQ*, 18 (1967), 67
Harrison	A. W. Harrison, *The Beginnings of Arminianism to the Synod of Dort* (1926)
Hart	A. Hart, 'The vocabulary of *The Two Noble Kinsmen*', *RES*, 10 (1934), 274–87
Hart, *Act One*	M. Hart, *Act One: An Autobiography* (New York, 1959)
Harting	J. E. Harting, *The Birds of Shakespeare* (Chicago, 1965). First publ. as *The Ornithology of Shakespeare* (1871)
Hartwig	J. Hartwig, *Shakespeare's Tragicomic Vision* (Baton Rouge, 1972)
Haydocke	R. Haydocke (trans.), P. Lomazzo, *A Tracte Containing the Artes of Curious Paintinge, Carvinge and Building* (1598)
Heath	B. Heath, MS notes on 1750 edn of Beaumont and Fletcher, British Library Add MS 31,910 (n.d.)
Hedrick	D. K. Hedrick, '"Be rough with me": the collaborative arenas of *The Two Noble Kinsmen*', in Frey
Henslowe	P. Henslowe, *Henslowe's Diary*, ed. R. A. Foakes and R. T. Rickert (Cambridge, 1961)
Herford	C. H. Herford (ed.), *The Two Noble Kinsmen*, Temple Dramatists (1897)
Heywood	T. Heywood, *A Marriage Triumphe Solemnized, in an Epithalamium* (1613)
Hickman	A. Hickman, 'Bonduca's two ignoble armies and *The Two Noble Kinsmen*', *Medieval and Renaissance Drama in England*, 4 (1989), 143–71
Hillman	R. Hillman, *Intertextuality and Romance in Renaissance Drama* (New York, 1992)
Hobday	C. H. Hobday, 'Why the sweets melted: a study in Shakespeare's imagery', *SQ*, 16 (1965), 3–17
Hogan	C. B. Hogan, *The London Stage, 1660–1800, Pt 5: 1776–1800* (Carbondale, Ill., 1968)
Holdsworth	R. V. Holdsworth, 'Sexual allusions in *Love's Labour's Lost*, *The Merry Wives of Windsor*, *Othello*, *The Winter's Tale*, and *The Two Noble Kinsmen*', *N&Q*, 231 (1986), 351–3
Holmes	M. Holmes, *Shakespeare and His Players* (New York, 1972)

Homer	Homer, *The Iliad*, trans. A. T. Murray, Loeb Classics (London and New York, 1924)
Hope	J. Hope, *The Authorship of Shakespeare's Plays: A Socio-linguistic Study* (Cambridge, 1994)
Hopkinson	A. F. Hopkinson, *Shakespeare's Doubtful Plays*, 3 vols (1894)
Hopkinson MS	MS notes and other items pasted into his edn of *Shakespeare's Doubtful Plays*, Folger Shakespeare Library (n.d.)
Horsnell	H. Horsnell, review of *The Two Noble Kinsmen* (Old Vic), *The Drama*, 24 March 1928
Horton	T. B. Horton, 'Distinguishing Shakespeare from Fletcher through function words', *SSt*, 22 (1994), 314–35
Hosley	R. Hosley, 'The playhouses', in C. Leech and T. W. Craik (eds), *The Revels History of Drama in English, Vol. III: 1576–1613* (1975)
Houston	J. P. Houston, *Shakespearean Sentences: A Study in Style and Syntax* (Baton Rouge and London, 1988)
Hoy	C. Hoy, 'The shares of Fletcher and his collaborators in the Beaumont and Fletcher canon', *SB*, 13 (1960), 77–108
Hoy, 'Language'	C. Hoy, 'The language of Fletcherian tragicomedy', in J. C. Gray (ed.), *Mirror up to Shakespeare: Essays in Honour of George Hibbard* (Toronto, 1984)
Hudson	H. N. Hudson (ed.), *The Complete Works of William Shakespeare*, vol. 19 (Cambridge, Mass., 1881)
Hugo	F.-V. Hugo (trans.), *Oeuvres Complètes de William Shakespeare: Les Apocryphes*, vol. 1 (Paris, 1866)
Hunt	L. Hunt (ed.), *Beaumont and Fletcher; or, the Finest Scenes, Lyrics, and Other Beauties of Those Two Poets* (1855)
Ingram	R. W. Ingram, 'Patterns of music and action in Fletcherian drama', in J. H. Long (ed.), *Music in English Renaissance Drama* (Lexington, Ky., 1968)
JCS	G. E. Bentley, *The Jacobean and Caroline Stage*, 7 vols (Oxford, 1958–68)
J.E.H.	J.E.H., review of *The Two Noble Kinsmen* (Cherub Theatre Company), *Kentish Gazette*, 23 November 1979
Jocquet	D. Jocquet, *Les Triomphes, Entrées, Cartels, Tournois, Cérémonies, et Aultres Magnificences, faites en Angleterre, & au Palatinat, pour le Mariage etc.* (Heidelberg, 1613)
Jones	E. Jones, *Scenic Form in Shakespeare* (Oxford, 1971)
Jones, *Origins*	E. Jones, *The Origins of Shakespeare* (Oxford, 1977)

Jones, *Knight*	T. Jones, *Chaucer's Knight: The Portrait of a Medieval Mercenary* (New York, 1980, 1985)
Jones, *Ring*	W. Jones, *Finger-Ring Lore* (1877)
Jonson	*Ben Jonson*, ed. C. H. Herford and P. and E. Simpson, 11 vols (Oxford, 1925–63)
Jorgensen	P. Jorgensen, *Shakespeare's Military World* (Berkeley, 1956)
KBP	F. Beaumont, *The Knight of the Burning Pestle*, ed. C. Hoy, in Bowers, vol. 1
Kerrigan	J. Kerrigan (ed.), *Shakespeare: The Sonnets and A Lover's Complaint* (Harmondsworth and New York, 1986)
King	T. J. King, *Casting Shakespeare's Plays: London Actors and their Roles, 1590–1642* (Cambridge, 1992)
Kinsley	J. Kinsley (ed.), *Poems of John Dryden*, vol. 4 (Oxford, 1958)
Kökeritz	H. Kökeritz, *Shakespeare's Pronunciation* (New Haven and London, 1953)
Kökeritz, *MLN*	H. Kökeritz, 'The beest-eating clown: *The Two Noble Kinsmen*, 3.5.151', *MLN*, 61 (1964), 532–5
KT	Geoffrey Chaucer, *The Knight's Tale*; *see* Speght
Lamb	C. and M. Lamb, *Dramatic Specimens and the Garrick Plays*, ed. E. V. Lucas (1903)
Langbaine	G. Langbaine, *An Account of the English Dramatic Poets* (1691; repr. Menston, Yorks., 1971)
Laroque	F. Laroque, *Shakespeare's Festive World*, trans. J. Lloyd (Cambridge, 1993)
Laurentius	A. Laurentius [André du Laurens], *A Discourse of the Preservation of the Sight: of Melancholike Diseases; of Rheumes, and of Old Age*, trans. R. Surphlet (1599)
Lavin	J. A. Lavin, 'Elizabethan theatre and the inductive method', in *Elizabethan Theatre II*, ed. D. Galloway (1970)
Lawrence	W. J. Lawrence, 'New light on *The Two Noble Kinsmen*', *TLS*, 14 July 1921, 450
Lee	B. Lee, review of *The Two Noble Kinsmen* (Cherub Theatre Company) in *The Scotsman*, September 1979
Leech, *Plays*	C. Leech, *The John Fletcher Plays* (1962)
Lemnius	L. Lemnius, *The Touchstone of Complexions*, trans. T. Newton (1581)
Lester	S. L. Lester, *Shakespeare around the Globe: A Guide to Notable Postwar Revivals* (New York, Westport, Conn. and London, 1986)
Leyris	P. Leyris, 'Le chant de cygne de Shakespeare', *Nouvelle Revue Française*, 215 (1970), 45–57
Lief & Radel	M. Lief and N. F. Radel, 'Linguistic subversion: the

artifice of rhetoric in *The Two Noble Kinsmen'*, *SQ*, 38 (1987), 405–25

Limon   J. Limon, *The Masque of Stuart Culture* (Newark, Del., London and Toronto, 1990)

Lindley   D. Lindley, *The Trials of Frances Howard: Fact and Fiction at the Court of King James* (London and New York, 1993)

Lodge   *Complete Works of Thomas Lodge*, 4 vols (facsimile), Hunterian Club (Glasgow, 1893; repr. New York, 1963)

Loughrey & Taylor   B. Loughrey and N. Taylor (eds), *Thomas Middleton, Five Plays* (Penguin, 1988)

Lucian   Lucian, *Toxaris*, in *Lucian*, trans. A. M. Harmon, 8 vols; vol. 5, Loeb Classics (Cambridge, Mass. and London, 1972)

MacCary   W. T. MacCary, *Friends and Lovers: The Phenomenology of Desire in Shakespearean Comedy* (New York, 1985)

McCoy   B. M. McCoy (trans.), *The Book of Theseus, Teseida delle Nozze d'Emilia* (New York, 1974)

MacDonald   M. MacDonald, 'Women and madness in Tudor and Stuart England', *Social Research*, 53 (1986), 261–81

McDonald   R. McDonald, 'Reading *The Tempest'*, *SS*, 43 (1991), 15–28

McKeithan   D. M. McKeithan, *The Debt to Shakespeare in the Beaumont and Fletcher Plays* (Austin, Tex., 1938; repr. New York, 1970)

McMillan   S. McMillan, *The Elizabethan Theatre and 'The Book of Sir Thomas More'* (Ithaca, NY and London, 1987)

McMullan   G. McMullan, *The Politics of Unease in the Plays of John Fletcher* (Amherst, Mass., 1994)

McMullan & Hope   G. McMullan and J. Hope (eds), *The Politics of Tragicomedy: Shakespeare and After* (London and New York, 1992)

Magnusson   L. Magnusson, 'The collapse of Shakespeare's high style in *The Two Noble Kinsmen'*, *English Studies in Canada*, 13 (1987), 375–90

Marcus   L. S. Marcus, *The Politics of Mirth: Jonson, Herrick, Milton, Marvell, and the Defense of Old Holiday Pastimes* (Chicago and London, 1986)

Marlowe   C. Marlowe, *The Complete Works of Christopher Marlowe*, ed. F. Bowers, 2 vols (Cambridge, 1973)

Masefield   J. Masefield, 'On playing *The Two Noble Kinsmen'*, in *Thanks before Going, with Other Gratitude for Old Delight, including a 'Macbeth' Production and Various Papers not before Printed* (London and Toronto, 1947)

Mason   J. Monck Mason, *Comments on the Plays of Beaumont and Fletcher, with an Appendix Containing some Further*

	Observations on Shakespeare, Extended to the Late Editions of Malone and Steevens (1798)
Massinger	P. Massinger, *The Poems and Plays of Philip Massinger*, ed. P. Edwards and C. Gibson, 5 vols (Oxford, 1976)
Masten	J. A. Masten, 'Beaumont and/or Fletcher: collaboration and the interpretation of Renaissance drama', *ELH*, 59 (1992), 337–56
Maxwell	B. Maxwell, *Studies in Beaumont, Fletcher, and Massinger* (Chapel Hill, NC, 1939)
Maxwell, 'Virgilian	J. C. Maxwell, 'Virgilian half-lines in Shakespeare's "heroic narrative"', *N&Q*, 198 (1953), 100
Melchiori	G. Melchiori and M. Melchiori (trans.), *I Drammi Romanzeschi*, vol. 6, in G. Melchiori (ed.), *Teatro Completo di William Shakespeare* (Milan, 1981)
Metz	G. H. Metz, *Four Plays Ascribed to Shakespeare: An Annotated Bibliography* (New York and London, 1982)
Metz, *Sources*	G. H. Metz (ed.), *Sources of Four Plays Ascribed to Shakespeare* (Columbia, Mo., 1989)
Metz, '*TNK*	G. H. Metz, '*The Two Noble Kinsmen* on the twentieth-century stage', *Theatre History Studies*, 4 (1984), 63–9
Middleton	T. Middleton, *Women Beware Women*, in Loughrey and Taylor
Middleton *Rev*	T. Middleton, *The Revenger's Tragedy*, in Loughrey and Taylor
Middleton & Rowley	T. Middleton and W. Rowley, *The Changeling*, in Loughrey and Taylor
Mills	L. J. Mills, *One Soul in Bodies Twain: Friendship in Tudor Literature and Stuart Drama* (Bloomington, Ind., 1937)
Mincoff	M. Mincoff, 'The authorship of *The Two Noble Kinsmen*', *ES*, 33 (1952), 97–115
Mincoff, *SQ*	M. Mincoff, '*Henry VIII* and Fletcher', *SQ*, 12 (1961), 239–60
Mitford	J. Mitford, *Cursory Notes on Various Passages in the Text of Beaumont and Fletcher as Edited by the Rev. Alexander Dyce: and on His 'Few Notes on Shakespeare'* (1856)
MLN	*Modern Language Notes*
MLR	*Modern Language Review*
Morris	H. Morris, 'Ophelia's "Bonny Sweet Robin"', *PMLA*, 73 (1958), 601–3
Mowat	B. Mowat, '"A local habitation and a name": Shakespeare's text as construct', *Style*, 23 (1989), 335–51
MSC	Malone Society Collections
Muir	K. Muir, *Shakespeare as Collaborator* (1960)
Mulryne	J. R. Mulryne, 'Shakespeare's *Knight's Tale: Two Noble*

	Kinsmen and the tradition of chivalry', in M. T. Jones-Davies (ed.), *Le Roman de Chevalerie au Temps de la Renaissance* (Paris, 1987)
N&Q	*Notes and Queries*
Nashe	T. Nashe, *Works*, ed. R. B. McKerrow (1910), rev. F. P. Wilson (1958), 5 vols (repr. New York, 1966)
Neely	C. T. Neely, '"Documents in madness": reading madness and gender in Shakespeare's tragedies and early modern culture', *SQ*, 42 (1991), 315–38
Nichols	J. Nichols, *The Progresses, Processions, and Magnificent Festivities of King James the First*, 4 vols (1828; repr. New York, n.d.)
OED	*Oxford English Dictionary*, 2nd edn, prepared by J. A. Simpson and E. S. C. Weiner (Oxford, 1989)
Olson	B. Olson, 'The morris dance in drama before 1640', *Quarterly Journal of the University of North Dakota*, 10 (1920), 422–35
Opie & Opie	I. Opie and P. Opie (eds), *The Oxford Dictionary of Nursery Rhymes* (Oxford, 1951)
Orbison	T. Orbison, 'The Middle Temple documents relating to George Chapman's *The Memorable Masque*', in MSC 12 (Oxford, 1983)
Orgel	S. Orgel, 'The poetics of incomprehensibility', *SQ*, 42 (1991), 431–7
Orgel & Strong	S. Orgel and R. Strong, *Inigo Jones: The Theatre of the Stuart Court*, 2 vols (Berkeley, 1973)
Ovid	*Shakespeare's Ovid, being Arthur Golding's Translation of the Metamorphoses*, ed. W. H. Rouse (Carbondale, Ill., 961)
Ovid, *Heroides*	Ovid, *Heroides*, trans. Grant Showerman (1914); rev. edn G. P. Goold, Loeb Classics (Cambridge, Mass. and London, 1977)
Ovid, *Met.*	Ovid, *Metamorphoses*, trans. F. J. Miller, Loeb Classics (London and New York, 1916)
Paradin	C. Paradin, *Heroical Devises* (1591; repr. Delmar, NY, 1984)
Parrot	H. Parrot, *Laquei Ridiculosi: or Springes for Woodcocks* (1613)
Partridge	A. C. Partridge, *The Problem of 'Henry VIII' Reopened: Some Linguistic Criteria for the Two Styles Apparent in the Play* (Cambridge, 1949)
Paster	G. K. Paster, *The Body Embarrassed: Drama and the Disciplines of Shame in Early Modern England* (Ithaca, NY, 1993)
Peacham	H. Peacham, *Minerva Britanna* (1612)
Peacham, *Period*	H. Peacham, *The Period of Mourning* (1613)

Pearson   D. Pearson, '"Unkinde" Theseus: a study in Renais-
                 sance mythography', *ELR*, 4 (1974), 276–98
Pilling   J. Pilling, 'The wild morisco or the historical morris',
                 English Dance and Song, 44 (1984), 26–9
Plutarch   Plutarch, *Plutarch's Lives of the Noble Grecians and
                 Romans, Englished by Sir Thomas North*, intro. George
                 Wyndham (1895)
PMLA   *Publications of the Modern Language Association of
                 America*
Potter   L. Potter, 'Two "Noble Kinsmen"', in *En torno a Shake-
                 speare* (Valencia, 1987)
Potter, 'Spectacle'   L. Potter, '*The Two Noble Kinsmen*: spectacle and narra-
                 tive', in F. Laroque (ed.), *The Show Within*, 2 vols
                 (Montpellier, 1992)
Potter, 'Topicality' L. Potter, 'Topicality or politics? The 1634 *Two Noble
                 Kinsmen*', in McMullan & Hope
Pratt   R. A. Pratt, 'Chaucer's use of the *Teseida*', *PMLA*, 62
                 (1947), 598–621
Proudfoot, 'New' G. R. Proudfoot, 'Shakespeare and the new dramatists
                 of the King's Men, 1606–1613', in J. R. Brown and B.
                 Harris (eds), *Later Shakespeare*, Stratford-upon-Avon
                 Studies 8 (1966)
RA   R. Abrams, personal communication
Réaud   [V. Réaud] (trans. and adapt.), *Les Deux Nobles Cousins*
                 (Chatillon-sous-Bagneux, 1978)
Regan   R. Regan, *Review of The Two Noble Kinsmen* (Reading
                 University), *Stratford-upon-Avon Herald*, 17 July 1959
RES   *Review of English Studies*
Reynolds   F. Reynolds, *Edward the Black Prince, or, She Never Told
                 Her Love*, BL Add MS 42,889 [*c*.1828]
Richmond   H. Richmond, 'Performance as criticism: *The Two
                 Noble Kinsmen*', in Frey
Richmond,   H. Richmond, 'The persistent afterlife of Shakespeare
    'Afterlife'   and Fletcher', *N&Q*, 238 (1993), 232–4
Riggs   D. Riggs, *Ben Jonson: A Life* (Cambridge, Mass., 1989)
Ritz   J.-G. Ritz (trans. and ed.), *Les Deux Nobles Cousins*
                 (Paris, 1982)
Roberts   J. A. Roberts, 'Crises of male self-definition in *The Two
                 Noble Kinsmen*', in Frey
Robertson &   J. Robertson and D. J. Gordon (eds), *A Calendar of
    Gordon   Dramatic Records in the Books of the Livery Companies of
                 London, 1485–1640*, MSC 3 (Oxford, 1954)
Rolfe   W. J. Rolfe (ed.), *The Two Noble Kinsmen* (New York,
                 1883)
Rollins   H. E. Rollins (ed.), *An Analytical Index to the Ballad-
                 Entries (1557–1709) in the Registers of the Company of*

	Stationers in London (Chapel Hill, NC, 1924; repr. Hatsboro, Pa., 1967)
Rollins, 'Note'	H. E. Rollins, 'A note on Richard Edwards', *RES*, 4 (1928), 204–6
Rose	M. B. Rose, *The Expense of Spirit: Love and Sexuality in English Renaissance Drama* (Ithaca, NY and London, 1988)
RP	G. R. Proudfoot, personal communication
RSC, Promptbook	Promptbook of *The Two Noble Kinsmen* (Swan Theatre, 1986) at Shakespeare Centre, Stratford-upon-Avon
Sabol	A. J. Sabol (ed.), *Four Hundred Songs and Dances from the Stuart Masque* (1978; repr. Hanover, NH and London, 1982)
Sargent & Kittredge	H. C. Sargent and G. L. Kittredge, *English and Scottish Popular Ballads, Edited from the Collection of Francis James Child* (Boston and New York, 1904)
SB	*Studies in Bibliography*
Schoenbaum	S. Schoenbaum, *Internal Evidence and Elizabethan Dramatic Authorship* (1966)
Scott	W. Scott (ed.), *Modern British Drama in Five Volumes*, vol. 1 (1811)
Scragg	L. Scragg, *The Metamorphosis of Gallathea* (Washington, DC, 1982)
SEL	*Studies in English Literature*
Selden	J. Selden, *Titles of Honour* (London, 1614)
Seneca	Seneca, *Seneca's Tragedies*, trans. F. J. Miller, 2 vols, Loeb Classics (London and New York, 1917)
Seward, *B and F*	*The Works of Mr. Francis Beaumont and Mr. John Fletcher*, ed. L. Theobald, completed by T. Seward, 10 vols. (1750)
Shaheen	N. Shaheen, *Biblical References in Shakespeare's Late Romances* (Newark, Del., forthcoming)
Shepherd	S. Shepherd, *Amazons and Warrior Women: Varieties of Feminism in Seventeenth-Century Drama* (Brighton, 1981)
Shewring	M. Shewring, '*The Two Noble Kinsmen* revived: chivalric romance and modern performance images', in M. T. Jones-Davies (ed.), *Le Roman de Chevalerie au Temps de la Renaissance* (Paris, 1987)
Shirley	F. A. Shirley, *Shakespeare's Use of Off-stage Sounds* (Lincoln, Nebr., 1963)
Sider	J. W. Sider, 'Shakespeare's cornets', *SQ*, 22 (1971), 401–4
Sidney	P. Sidney, *Sir Philip Sidney*, ed. K. Duncan-Jones (Oxford and New York, 1989)
Sidney, *Arcadia*	P. Sidney, *The Countess of Pembroke's Arcadia*, ed. Victor Skretkowicz (Oxford, 1987)

Simonds	P. M. Simonds, *Myth, Emblem, and Music in Shakespeare's 'Cymbeline': An Iconographic Reconstruction* (Newark, Del., London and Toronto, 1992)
Smidt	K. Smidt, *Unconformities in Shakespeare's Tragedies* (Basingstoke and London, 1989)
Smith	B. R. Smith, *Homosexual Desire in Shakespeare's England* (Chicago and London, 1991)
Smith, *Blackfriars*	I. Smith, *Shakespeare's Blackfriars Playhouse* (New York, 1964)
Smith, 'Statistical'	M. W. A. Smith, 'Statistical inference in *A Textual Companion* to the Oxford Shakespeare', *N&Q*, 236 (1991), 73–8
Snyder	S. Snyder (ed.), *All's Well That Ends Well* (Oxford, 1993)
Spalding	W. Spalding, *A Letter on Shakspere's Authorship of 'The Two Noble Kinsmen'*, ed. J. H. Burton, New Shakspere Society (1876)
Speght	T. Speght (ed.), *The Workes of our Ancient and Learned English Poet, Geffrey Chaucer* (2nd edn, 1602)
Spencer, 'Shakespeare	T. J. B. Spencer, 'Shakespeare v. the rest: the old controversy', *SS*, 14 (1961), 76–89
Spencer, *SQ*	C. Spencer, '*Macbeth* and Davenant's *The Rivals*', *SQ*, 20 (1969), 225–9
Spencer, '*TNK*'	T. Spencer, '*The Two Noble Kinsmen*', *Modern Philology*, 36 (1939), 255–76 (repr. in Leech, Signet edn)
Spenser, *Yale*	E. Spenser, *The Yale Edition of the Shorter Poems of Edmund Spenser*, ed. William A. Oram *et al.* (New Haven, 1989)
Spevack	M. Spevack, *A Complete and Systematic Concordance to the Works of Shakespeare*, vol. 3 (Hildesheim, 1968)
Spurgeon	C. F. E. Spurgeon, *Shakespeare's Imagery and What It Tells Us* (Cambridge, 1935)
SQ	*Shakespeare Quarterly*
S.R.L.	S.R.L., review of *The Two Noble Kinsmen* (Old Vic), *Morning Post*, 13 March 1928
SS	*Shakespeare Survey*
SSt	*Shakespeare Studies*
Statius	*Statius*, trans. J. H. Mozley, 2 vols, Loeb Classics (Cambridge, Mass. and London, 1967)
Steevens	G. Steevens, *Supplement to the Edition of Shakespeare's Plays published in 1778 by Samuel Johnson and George Steevens*, 2 vols (London, 1780)
Strong	R. Strong, *Henry, Prince of Wales and England's Lost Renaissance* (1986)
Stow	J. Stow, *A Survey of London* (1603), ed. C. L. Kingsford, 2 vols (Oxford, 1908)

Stubbes	P. Stubbes, *The Anatomy of Abuses* (1583; repr. Amsterdam and New York, 1972)
Swinburne	A. C. Swinburne, *A Channel Passage* (1927)
Tanis & Horst	J. Tanis and D. Horst, *Images of Discord: A Graphic Interpretation of the Opening Decades of the Eighty Years' War* (Bryn Mawr, Pa. and Grand Rapids, Mich., 1993)
Tarlinskaja	M. Tarlinskaja, *Shakespeare's Verse: Iambic Pentameter and the Poet's Idiosyncrasies* (New York, Bern, Frankfurt am Main and Paris, 1987)
Taylor	G. Taylor, 'Introduction', 'Canon and chronology', in S. Wells and G. Taylor (eds), *William Shakespeare: A Textual Companion* (Oxford, 1987)
Taylor & Jowett	G. Taylor and J. Jowett, *Shakespeare Reshaped, 1606–1623* (Oxford, 1993)
Theseyde	*Le Theseyde du Sieur Jean Bocace Gentilhomme Florentin*, trans. D.C.C. (Paris, 1597)
Thiselton-Dyer	T. F. Thiselton-Dyer, *Folk-Lore of Shakespeare* (New York, 1884, repr. 1966)
Thompson	A. Thompson, *Shakespeare's Chaucer: A Study in Literary Origins* (Liverpool, 1978)
Thompson, 'Jailers''	A. Thompson, 'Jailers' Daughters in *The Arcadia* and *The Two Noble Kinsmen*', *N&Q*, 224 (1979), 140–1
Thompson & Thompson	A. and J. O. Thompson, *Shakespeare: Meaning and Metaphor* (Brighton and Iowa City, Ia., 1987)
Thomson	L. Thomson, 'A quarto "marked for performance": evidence of what?', *Medieval and Renaissance Drama in England* 8 (1996), 176–210
Thorn-Drury	G. Thorn-Drury (ed.), *Covent Garden Drollery* (1928)
Tilley	M. P. Tilley, *A Dictionary of the Proverbs in England in the Sixteenth and Seventeenth Centuries* (Ann Arbor, 1950)
Times	Anon. review of *The Two Noble Kinsmen* (Reading University), *Times*, 15 July 1959
TLS	*Times Literary Supplement*
Tonson	*The Works of Mr. Francis Beaumont, and Mr. John Fletcher*. Printed for J. Tonson, 7 vols (1911)
Topsell	E. Topsell, *The Historie of Foure-Footed Beastes* (1607)
Tourneur	C. Tourneur, *The Atheist's Tragedy*, ed. Irving Ribner, The Revels Plays (1964)
Trollope	A. Trollope, MS notes in Folger Shakespeare Library copy of Dyce (ed.), *The Works of Beaumont and Fletcher*, vol. 11 (1866)
Turner	R. K. Turner, Jr., '*The Two Noble Kinsmen* and Speght's Chaucer', *N&Q*, 225 (1980), 175–6
TxC	S. Wells and G. Taylor, with J. Jowett and W. Mont-

gomery, *William Shakespeare: a Textual Companion* (Oxford, 1987)

Tyacke · N. Tyacke, *Anti-Calvinism* (Oxford, 1987)

Tynan · K. Tynan, *He that Plays the King: A View of the Theatre* (London, New York and Toronto, 1950)

Underwood · R. A. Underwood, *Shakespeare on Love: the Poems and the Plays. Prolegomena to a Variorum Edition of 'A Lover's Complaint'*, Salzburg Studies in English Literature (Salzburg, 1985)

Underwood, *TNK* · R. A. Underwood, *The Two Noble Kinsmen and its Beginnings*, Salzburg Studies in English: Elizabethan and Renaissance Studies, no. 117 (Salzburg, 1993)

Virgil · Virgil, *The Aeneid*, trans. H. R. Fairclough, rev. edn, Loeb Classics (Cambridge, Mass. and London, 1978)

Wack · M. F. Wack, *Lovesickness in the Middle Ages: The 'Viaticum' and its Commentaries* (Philadelphia, 1990)

Waith · E. M. Waith, *The Pattern of Tragicomedy in Beaumont and Fletcher* (New Haven and London, 1952)

Waith, 'Sh and F' · E. M. Waith, 'Shakespeare and Fletcher on love and marriage', *SSt*, 18 (1986), 235–50

Waldron · F. G. Waldron, *Love and Madness; or, The Two Noble Kinsmen*, Larpent MS no. 1094, Huntington Library (1795)

Walker · S. Walker, *A Critical Examination of the Text of Shakespeare*, 3 vols (1860)

Wallace · C. W. Wallace, 'New Shakespeare discoveries: Shakespeare as a man among men', *Harper's Monthly Magazine*, cxx (1910), 489–510

Waller, 'Printer's' · F. O. Waller, 'Printer's copy for *The Two Noble Kinsmen*', *SB*, 11 (1958), 61–84

Warren · R. Warren, 'Shakespeare at Stratford-upon-Avon, 1986', *SQ*, 38 (1987), 82–9

Webster, *DM* · J. Webster, *The Duchess of Malfi*, ed. J. R. Brown, The Revels Plays (1964)

Webster, *WD* · J. Webster, *The White Devil*, ed. J. R. Brown, The Revels Plays (1960)

Wells · S. Wells (ed.), *The Oxford Anthology of Shakespeare* (Oxford, 1987)

Werstine · P. Werstine, 'On the compositors of *The Two Noble Kinsmen*', in Frey

Whiter · W. Whiter, *A Specimen of a Commentary on Shakespeare* [1794], ed. Alan Over and Mary Bell (1967)

Whitfield · C. Whitfield (ed.), *Robert Dover and the Cotswold Games: Annalia Dubrensia* (London and Ossining, NY, 1962)

Wickham · G. Wickham, '*The Two Noble Kinsmen*, or, *A Midsummer*

	Night's Dream, Part II?', in G. R. Hibbard (ed.), *Elizabethan Theatre* VII (1980)
Williamson	H. Williamson, *The Myth of the Conqueror* (New York, 1978)
Wiltenburg	J. Wiltenburg, 'Madness and society in the street ballads of early modern England', *Journal of Popular Culture*, 21 (1988), 101–27
Wright	G. T. Wright, *Shakespeare's Metrical Art* (Berkeley, Los Angeles and London, 1988)
Wyatt	T. Wyatt, *The Complete Poems*, ed. R. A. Rebholz (New Haven and London, 1978)
York	Promptbook of York Theatre Royal production of *The Two Noble Kinsmen* (1970), in Shakespeare Collection, Birmingham Public Library

INDEX

This index covers the Introduction, Commentary and Appendices. Names of characters in the play refer only to their historical or mythical existence. *OED* references are only to words given as 'first-time' usage.